LONGMAN LINGUISTICS LIBRARY

GENERATIVE GRAMMAR

Generative Grammar

Geoffrey Horrocks

LONGMAN
LONDON AND NEW YORK

Longman Group UK Limited,
Longman House, Burnt Mill, Harlow,
Essex CM20 2JE, England
and Associated Companies throughout the world.

Published in the United States of America
by Longman Inc., New York

First published 1987

British Library Cataloguing ... Publication Data

Horrocks, Geoffrey
Generative grammar. – (Longman linguistics
library)
1. Generative grammar
I. Title
415   P158

ISBN 0-582-01473-5   CSD
ISBN 0-582-29131-3   PPR

Library of Congress Cataloging in Publication Data

Horrocks, Geoffrey C.
Generative grammar.

(Longman linguistics library)
Bibliography: p.
Includes index.
1. Generative grammar. 2. Government-binding
theory. 3. Generalised phrase structure grammar.
4. Lexical-functional grammar. I. Title. II. Series.
P158.H65 1987   415   86-24758
ISBN 0-582-01473-5
ISBN 0-582-29131-3 (pbk.)

Set in Linotron 202 10/11pt Times
Produced by Longman Singapore Publishers (Pte) Ltd.
Printed in Singapore

Contents

Preface

The purpose of this book is to provide a critical review of the
development of generative grammar (transformational and non-
transformational) over the last twenty years, and to draw some
conclusions about the general direction of research in the field.
I hope that it will help to bring the reader up to date by bridging
the gap between the frameworks presented in many currently
available textbooks and those assumed in much of the recent
scholarly literature. And since the majority of the new generation
of textbooks now emerging deal with one theoretical approach
to the exclusion of others, I hope too that the broader scope of
this book will prove to be useful. A comparative approach allows
one to concentrate as much on the evaluation of competing
theories in terms of the issues that unite and divide them as on
the presentation of the current, and almost certainly ephemeral,
technical apparatus they employ. I have not, however, felt
obliged to try to achieve comprehensive coverage from either a
diachronic or a synchronic point of view. I have taken Chomsky's
work as the central consideration and tried to present as
complete a picture as I can of current (or near-current) thinking.
But from previous stages of the development of the theory I have
selected for discussion only those aspects that seem to me to have
been most important in their influence on contemporary
research. I could see little point in expounding the controversies
of the 1970s except in so far as conclusions of contemporary
relevance emerged from them. I have also deliberately excluded
from discussion a number of theories of generative grammar that
have their roots in different approaches to language from that
which informs the Chomskyan programme. This should not be
interpreted as a value judgement. I simply felt that there were

real advantages in selecting for inclusion theories which could more readily be compared with Chomsky's because they belong in large part to the same tradition and operate within a common framework of discussion. Those, then, who are hoping to find a systematic treatment of theories such as Montague Grammar, Dik's Functional Grammar or Hudson's Word Grammar will be disappointed. What they will find is a treatment of Generalised Phrase Structure Grammar and Lexical-Functional Grammar. These theories are deliberate reactions to Chomsky's approach and their advocates generally define their positions in terms of the issues and principles on which they disagree with Chomsky. Many background assumptions are shared and simply taken for granted, and even where substantive differences exist it is usually possible to make illuminating comparisons. By restricting the scope of the book in this way it has been possible to achieve a reasonable degree of conceptual coherence, and I hope that, by presenting these three theories in a broadly comparative way, readers will be given some insight into the problems involved in establishing a theory of grammatical representation and also some encouragement to think discriminatively and independently about the goals of generative grammar and the development of the means of achieving them.

It remains to thank the friends, colleagues and students who, over the years, have taught me in many different ways most of what I know about linguistics in general and generative grammar in particular. It would take up a great deal of space to name them all but I feel that particular thanks are due to Sidney Allen, Bob Borsley, Ruth Kempson, Terry Moore, Bobby Robins, Neil Smith, Geoff Pullum and Gerald Gazdar. Martin Harris and Bobby Robins both read through the final draft of this book and made a number of very valuable observations and criticisms which have resulted in the elimination of several errors and infelicities of presentation. Any remaining misinterpretations or misrepresentations of the work of authors I have chosen for discussion are, of course, my responsibility.

In an attempt to make a sometimes rather forbidding subject at least appear to be palatable I have deliberately avoided the use of footnotes and I have also tried to keep references to specific works in the main body of the text to a minimum. For those who want to know where I get the evidence from to support what I say there are fairly comprehensive lists of scholarly works at the end of each chapter which can be regarded simultaneously as providing suggestions for further reading.

Finally, I should like to thank my wife, Gill, for her patience and encouragement during the writing of this book. Our transition from London to Cambridge was not as smooth as it might have been and her support, as always, has been invaluable.

Cambridge
June 1986   G.C.H.

For Cliff, Anne and Sophie

For Gill, Amy and Sophie

Chapter 1

Aims and assumptions

1.1 Introduction

In the period from the mid-1950s to the mid-1960s Chomsky established a set of objectives for theoretical linguistics which subsequently he himself has consistently sought to attain, and which have continued to direct the course of research for many linguists to the present day. Naturally, during the course of the last thirty years, there have been many modifications, some of them quite radical, to the concrete proposals first put forward in an attempt to achieve these stated goals, and there have also been shifts of focus from one objective to another as work has progressed and previously unanswerable questions have become tractable in the light of new discoveries. But the ultimate goals themselves have changed very little, and it is an essential prerequisite to an understanding of the development of generative grammar to have a clear picture of the aims and philosophical underpinnings of the Chomskyan programme; it is only with these in mind that the full force of the arguments for or against some technical innovation can be appreciated. This is true equally of Chomsky's own revisions and of those advanced by linguists who regard themselves as rivals and critics. It is testimony to Chomsky's prestige in the field, and to the central role that his work has played in its development, that even those generative grammarians who disagree with him tend nevertheless to justify their proposals on the grounds that these achieve the more or less agreed objectives more successfully than his. It is the purpose of this chapter to provide an informal introduction to some of the more important leading ideas of the generative enterprise. Many of the points and issues raised here will be dealt with in more detail and with greater precision in later chapters, where the merits and demerits of various proposals aimed at executing these ideas will be considered.

1.2 Competence and performance

Central to Chomsky's approach to the study of language is a distinction drawn between a native speaker's **competence** and his **performance**. The former is defined as the speaker's internalised grammar of his language, his tacit or unconscious knowledge of the system of rules and principles which underlies his capacity to speak and understand the language of his speech community. The latter is the speaker's actual use of language on particular occasions, and includes not only directly observable utterances, spoken and written, but also the speaker's use of language to clarify his thoughts, and other phenomena 'observable' only by introspection, such as his ability to pass judgements on the acceptability of utterances in terms of their sound, form and meaning. and his awareness, perhaps partly subconscious, of the existence of various systematic structural and semantic correspondences between certain utterance types, as reflected in his ability to form questions corresponding to statements, passive analogues to active sentences, and so on. The assumption is, then, that the speaker's linguistic capabilities are grounded in, and ultimately explained by, his competence. It is important to note that competence is viewed not as a skill but as a system of knowledge which underlies various skills; it is what the speaker must know in order to be able to perform.

It is evident that performance will only ever be a direct and accurate reflection of competence in ideal circumstances. The utterances produced by speakers tend to have not only properties which are determined by the rules of their internalised grammars, but also properties which derive from factors such as memory limitation, lack of concentration, division of attention, nervousness, inebriation and a whole host of factors which are not, it may be assumed with some plausibility, linguistic in character. It is also often the case that judgements of acceptability are made not instinctively (*ie* by reference to one's competence alone), but rather self-consciously, say by reference to some rule of good usage taught at school ('avoid split infinitives', 'do not end a sentence with a preposition', and so on). Equally, an utterance may be rejected not so much on the basis of its linguistic properties as because the hearer cannot readily imagine a context in which the utterance in question could be used appropriately. For example, someone lacking the imagination to construct the sort of context that is typically elaborated in stories for young children might have difficulty in accepting a decontextualised utterance of [1].

[1] *The furious carrot slammed the door.*

The problem, then, is one of determining just which aspects of performance *are* linguistic in character and so constitute a reflection of the properties of competence. The solution to this problem is not self-evident, and it is obviously possible in principle to draw the line between linguistically relevant and linguistically irrelevant performance phenomena in many different places. As we shall see (3.1, 3.8, 4.1 and 4.9), this question of demarcation is one of the issues which divides different schools of generative grammarians. It should be stressed, however, that this indeterminacy in no way undermines the theoretical value of the distinction itself, to which we now turn.

Despite the indirectness of the relationship between competence and performance, Chomsky believes that the best hope for progress in linguistics is for researchers to concentrate on the elucidation of competence, to concentrate on giving an explicit account of what native speakers know that enables them to perform in the way they do.

A number of important questions arise at this point. The first we have already touched on, namely that of deciding which performance data the theory of competence is to account for. Chomsky's answer to this is unequivocal. The central data which linguistic theory must account for are the introspective intuitions and judgements of native speakers in matters such as grammatical structure, well-formedness, paraphrase relations, ambiguity and so on. But even after we have decided which aspects of performance are to be discounted we must still decide on the basis of what is left just what the unobservable system that underlies this set of capabilities must be like. Can this system be extracted from a sample of the language by mechanical procedure, or must it incorporate principles which are not extractable by any such process? The answer to this question is, not surprisingly, controversial, and Chomsky's view of the matter will be discussed in some detail below (see especially 2.3.11).

The main issue here, however, is the justification of the decision to concentrate on competence when it is clear that there are going to be great difficulties in assessing its character on the basis of the available evidence. Indeed, some linguists, for example those advocating the rival theory of Generalised Phrase Structure Grammar (*cf* Ch. 3), argue that this available evidence, including not only introspective judgements but also other aspects of performance such as parsing abilities, is *not* sufficient to justify Chomsky's view that the grammars which linguists construct may plausibly be regarded as models of native speakers' internalised grammars (*cf* 3.1). For them, linguists' grammars have no real-world interpretation and are to be judged by criteria such as formal precision, generality and elegance of formulation and the extent to which they advance co-operative research ventures with neighbouring disciplines. This is important, because it brings to light the fact that what is controversial about Chomsky's position is not that he has decided to restrict and idealise the domain of enquiry but that, having done so, he is still prepared to adopt a realist interpretation of the grammars he constructs. The long and, many would argue, successful Western tradition of grammatical research and theorising gives one grounds for believing that grammar can be studied in isolation in a worthwhile way, and it is, of course, traditional that linguists abstract away from the full range of observable phenomena and concentrate on those aspects which they believe can be satisfactorily handled in a systematic fashion. But it is one thing to do this when no claims are being made about the 'reality' of the grammars so constructed (and these artefacts are judged by their utility in some domain such as foreign language teaching) and quite another to do this when claims of psychological reality are involved. Who is to say whether or not in these circumstances the chosen domain of evidence is indeed sufficient to support such a hypothesis? This question is taken up below (1.3).

If for the moment we interpret Chomsky's decision to concentrate on competence simply as a decision to concentrate on grammar, the justification is straightforward. The domain of grammar can be given a reasonably clear preliminary definition that offers the linguist a limited and coherent object of enquiry. That is to say, the factors which influence actual performance in its totality are so varied, and their nature and the manner of their interaction so little understood, that the ordinary creative use of language by native speakers is of necessity going to resist illuminating investigation if it is approached in a monolithic way. It is good methodological sense to adopt a modular approach to the study of language and to deal first with those aspects that seem to lend themselves to systematic treatment. This position only becomes controversial in the context of Chomsky's realism, to which we now turn.

1.3 The interpretation of grammars

Assuming that it is reasonable for any linguist to delimit the domain of fact that his theory seeks to account for, we might nevertheless find fault with Chomsky for asserting that the grammars which his theory sanctions are models of the native speaker's competence. Surely there can never be positive evidence that this or that formulation corresponds to the way in which linguistic knowledge is in fact represented in the native speaker's internalised grammar?

Chomsky's reply to this objection is that it is the condition of research in any subject that is regarded as an empirical discipline that the theories set up to account for the facts that fall within its domain are always in some degree underdetermined by those facts. If this were not so, and if theories could somehow be extracted from samples of data by analysis and generalisation, the theories in question would be nothing more than reduced versions of the facts that the investigator began with and could in no sense be said to explain those facts. In practice, however, most scientific theories are not simply sets of inductive generalisations extracted from a corpus of data; they are rather hypotheses from whose constructs predictions about the behaviour of some set of objects can be deduced and whose reliability can be tested in terms of whether the predicted behaviour matches the observed behaviour. Theories can, of course, be compared in terms of how well the facts follow from the assumptions made. Efficient accounts of the observable phenomena are those which not merely make correct predictions but which do so by employing principles of some generality and predictive power, and furthermore, principles characterised by formal simplicity and compatibility with other theories in related domains. If it is accepted that a science such as physics has been able to progress because scientists have been willing to speculate and advance hypotheses as underlying explanations for observable phenomena, and if one is prepared to accept that such a methodology means that no scientific theory will ever be demonstrably correct, it follows that there can be no concept of 'physically real' independent of whatever is normal scientific practice at the time in the field of physics. Obviously it may be the case that the world is constituted in ways which are quite different from those which contemporary physicists propose, but as the principles of modern physics are highly abstract principles of great explanatory power it is reasonable to ask whether this is at all likely.

Relating this to linguistics, it is Chomsky's view that the question of whether his, or anyone else's, theory of competence is the correct one is meaningless. What is psychologically real is whatever the best available theory of competence comprises. Again, it may be the case that the theory in question is fundamentally misconceived, but assuming that linguistics has matured as a discipline to the point there the principles it employs are not merely statements of the superficially obvious but have some degree of generality and predictive power, as Chomsky would argue that it has now begun to do, it is again reasonable to ask whether a theory which provides a penetrating account of the data in its domain could somehow have achieved this degree of success by accident, the system under investigation being 'in reality' completely different in its essential properties. Adopting the procedures that are routine in the other sciences, what is needed in linguistics according to Chomsky is a proper set of criteria for evaluating the success of theories of competence.

It is sometimes objected that Chomsky's proposals are essentially formal in character and that the drawing of psychological conclusions is unwarranted. But given that the data of linguistics as conceived by Chomsky (cf 1.4) are psychological in character, it is in his view as ridiculous for a linguist to devise an efficient theory of the linguistic facts but to refuse to regard his theory as having implications for the study of mental faculties as it would be for a physicist, having made careful observations of the behaviour of falling objects, to set up a theory of gravity but to regard this as no more than a convenient fiction that allowed him to talk intelligibly about the behaviour of those objects.

Those who wish to call into question the validity of Chomsky's analogy with the practice of the natural sciences might try to show that the actual practice of linguists revealed a problem of indeterminacy more serious than, and fundamentally different in character from, that faced by, say, physicists. For example, while it is probably true that no one would require independent (ie non-physical) evidence in favour of ascribing physical reality to the formal constructs of theoretical physics, it is not generally regarded as unreasonable to ask for independent evidence (for example from experimental psychology, neurophysiology or whatever) for the psychological reality of the constructs of Chomskyan linguistics. This contrast would perhaps be a telling one if one took the view that Chomsky's characterisation of competence, designed to account for native speakers' introspective judgements over a certain domain, should also be required to account for data in other domains, such as the results of psychological experiments on language processing. If, contrary to Chomsky's view, such an extension of the domain is thought desirable, as indeed it is by proponents of Lexical-Functional Grammar (*cf* Ch. 4), then the theoretical apparatus proposed would have to be compatible with current theories about the nature of the parsing mechanisms employed by human beings. But it is perfectly legitimate, in the absence of compelling evidence to the effect that the speaker's internalised representation of grammatical knowledge is utilised in a direct way in language processing, simply to deny that observations about language processing have any relevance to the central tasks of theoretical linguistics. The desirability of such a move is discussed in some detail in 4.9. It is, however, worth pointing out here that such a restriction is justified to the extent that it permits the execution of a fruitful research strategy. One is not, after all, very surprised to discover that the physicists' laws of motion do not actually predict with any accuracy the movements of one's pet dog at any given moment; indeed, if physicists had set themselves the task of accounting for the movements of all animate beings in the universe over and above the tasks normally regarded as falling within the domain of their science, there is good reason to think that physics would be a much less successful science today than in fact it is. The point being made is simply that the inclusion of 'independent' evidence within the domain of theoretical linguistics as conceived by Chomsky is not necessarily going to be very helpful. The only way to judge the value of such a move ultimately is to construct theories that seek to account for this broader range of data and which presuppose direct use of the grammatical knowledge-store in language processing, and to see if this proves to be a fruitful line of enquiry. To the extent that lexical-functional grammars have succeeded in unifying research in linguistics and experimental psychology they constitute a serious challenge to Chomsky's stance. They do not, however, show that Chomsky's position is 'wrong' in any absolute sense, since it is undeniable that many very valuable insights have come out of research conducted within the more restricted domain that he advocates (see in particular 2.3).

All this said, it is still true that in linguistics there is considerably more room for disagreement about what constitutes a reasonable analysis or interpretation of a given range of data than would ordinarily be the case in physics; this is reflected in the proliferation of theoretical frameworks which has characterised the field in the last twenty years, and indeed in the rapid turnover of proposals within any given framework. For many linguists, and adherents of Generalised Phrase Structure Grammar would for the most part be numbered among them (*cf* 3.1), this state of affairs suggests very strongly that linguistics should remain an autonomous discipline with a 'liberal' methodology that examines linguistic phenomena from its own point of view, judges proposals by its own criteria, and makes no claims about the physical or psychological reality of its constructs. On this view linguistic theories have no real-world interpretation at all. Notice that on the question of the autonomy of linguistics this position is exactly the same as Chomsky's. The major difference lies in the belief that currently available evidence and techniques of analysis are not sufficient to guarantee that the abstract characterisations of the knowledge-domain that Chomsky calls competence are in any sense models of what native speakers have actually internalised. It should be made clear, however, that the position taken by different linguists on the matter of the interpretation of formal grammars is ultimately a reflection of personal taste. If one accepts Chomsky's analogy with the natural sciences one will incline to 'realism'; if one feels linguistics cannot yet be regarded as a 'hard' science because of the relative indeterminacy of its subject matter and framework of analysis one will incline to an 'instrumentalist' position, treating formal grammars as convenient fictions meeting certain criteria of adequacy and designed to fulfil some practical purpose. This practical purpose may, of course, be the characterisation of a system of rules to explain certain aspects of the verbal behaviour of human beings, but one stops short of equating the rule system with the speaker's internalised representation of grammatical knowledge.

Assuming for the moment that a realist interpretation of grammars is not unreasonable, Chomsky has to defend himself against those critics who argue that treating knowledge of grammar as an independent faculty of mind in isolation from the study of other systems of knowledge and belief prevents the serious investigation of the links between grammar, language use and the rest of cognition. Chomsky's reply, as we have seen, rests in part on the traditional linguistic argument that all grammarians have seen fit to abstract away from non-grammatical phenomena. One would not, for example, expect to find an appendix in an authoritative reference grammar of German giving a description of the effects of drunkenness, nervousness or a bad cold on the speech of native speakers. It is equally routine for the authors of such grammars to abstract away from the very real heterogeneity of actual speech communities and to present some sort of community norm. But Chomsky has to go further than this, given that he is adopting a realist position; just because it is convenient for the linguist to idealise the data and restrict the domain of enquiry in a certain way does not mean that native speakers have compartmentalised their knowledge in the same way. Chomsky's defence rests essentially upon an analogy. He suggests that a monolithic approach to the study of the human body would be self-evidently ridiculous; it has never been normal scientific practice to assume, without knowledge or investigation, that all bodily organs are constituted in exactly the same way. Furthermore, the conventional isolation for the purposes of special study of various body parts has done nothing to inhibit investigation of the body as an integrated system; it has in fact done a great deal to promote understanding. Simply to assume that the mind must be an undifferentiated mass and to argue that any approach which supposes otherwise will have serious consequences for the progress of understanding is quite irrational. For Chomsky, the issue of modularity is an empirical one, and his approach stands or falls according to whether or not it brings to light organisational principles that explain grammatical facts in an illuminating way but which have no relevance outside the domain of grammar.

Clearly a number of areas of investigation can be distinguished in a pre-theoretical way as independent constructs; for example, conceptualisation, reasoning, the psychology of visual perception, grammar, and so on. Obviously at the outset of investigation we simply do not know whether the mental organs involved share identical, or similar, internal structure, and so we cannot determine whether or not they can be described successfully by means of the same formal apparatus. If we make an initial assumption for the purpose of investigation that these independently characterisable systems really do constitute independent faculties of mind, we can try to develop a theory of each that is sufficiently explicit to test for empirical adequacy and to compare with the others in terms of internal organisation. It may, of course, turn out that a class of phenomena which had led one to think in terms of some independent faculty appear to be far better characterised in terms of the constructs set up to account for some apparently different range of facts. In this case the initial assumption of two independent systems would be shown to be false, and progress would have been made.

It is, of course, possible for those who feel inclined to adopt a less modular approach to argue that it is methodologically superior to assume that the store of language-knowledge (comprising say grammar, a conceptual system and a system of pragmatic competence that forms the basis of our ability to use language effectively and appropriately) is a network of mutually constraining systems that is employed directly as a producer-parser by native speakers; this would constitute a 'stronger' hypothesis which its proponents would argue should not be abandoned in favour of a weaker position such as Chomsky's, allowing for much more complex networks of unrelated systems, until there is compelling evidence to falsify it. Once again the only rational approach is to proceed in line with one's convictions, to try to develop formal models in a sufficiently explicit and detailed way to ensure a degree of testability in the face of available evidence, and to decide on the basis of the results whether or not one's initial assumptions turn out in the end to constitute a fruitful research strategy. What this means in effect is that virtually all linguists, when they set themselves the task of constructing the grammar of some language, construct a model not of actual examples of speech behaviour but of the regular patterns that are discernible in whatever part of that behaviour they have decided for reasons of methodology or philosophical commitment should fall within the scope of their theories. And if the linguists in question happen to be realists, they will adopt a position concerning the organisation of the mind that follows from their chosen delimitation of the linguistic domain. Now according to the influential view advocated by Popper no science is in a position to establish procedures for discovering the correct theory to account for a given range of data; the characteristic property of empirical theories is that they can be *falsified*, but never confirmed in any absolute sense, by the evidence available, and it is the responsibility of scientists to frame their theories in such a way that they are not rendered immune from falsification. From this point of view, there is perhaps a somewhat greater chance of falsification if one sets out to investigate the possibility that several independently characterisable systems are in fact based upon the same organisational principles than if one system is investigated in isolation. To this extent it is arguable that the position adopted by Lexical-Functional Grammar in its efforts to make the theory of competence the centrepiece of an *overall* theory of verbal behaviour is indeed a 'stronger' position than that adopted by Chomsky (*cf* 4.9). But once again, this does not show that Chomsky is wrong in any absolute way, because Chomsky can point to substantial achievements that have resulted directly from the pursuit of a research programme within the more restricted domain that he has advocated (see Ch. 2, especially 2.3).

1.4 The data of linguistic theory

In the period prior to the development of Chomsky's theory of grammar in the 1950's many linguists argued that linguistics should concern itself with the description of regularities observable in corpora of utterances produced spontaneously by native speakers of the language under investigation. Such utterances were felt to constitute 'hard facts' in sharp distinction to information volunteered by a native speaker about his language, which was dismissed as unreliable and subjective. One of Chomsky's great achievements is that by extending the scope of the subject to include native speakers' judgements of structure, relatedness, ambiguity, acceptability and so on, he effectively liberated the discipline from the straightjacket of physicalism. Almost all linguists today are prepared to accept that the data of linguistics should include the introspective judgements of native speakers, and, as we have seen, there are many who would argue for a still wider extension to include further aspects of performance.

There are a number of reasons why this kind of extension of the data to be accounted for has become generally accepted. From a commonsense point of view it is simply absurd to wait for native speakers to produce utterances which would allow linguists to infer whether some language has a particular grammatical characteristic when it is perfectly possible for the linguist as a native speaker to ask all the important questions and answer them himself. More importantly there are many phenomena which all native speakers are aware of but which would never become known to the linguist no matter how many utterances he collected. For example, how would we ever know that [2] below is ungrammatical or that [3] is ambiguous?

[2] *They say Horrocks to have fallen behind schedule.*
[Ungrammatical sentences are prefixed with an asterisk throughout this book in accordance with the now well-established practice.]
[3] *My daughter loves ballet more than her friends.*

At what point could we ever be sure that the failure of utterances of the form of [2] to appear in a sample of speech was not accidental? There are, after all, perfectly well-formed sentences of exactly parallel structure such as [4].

[4] *They believe Horrocks to have fallen behind schedule.*

Similarly, we all know that [5], in contrast with [3], is not ambiguous.

[5] *My daughter loves ballet more than her friends do.*

But it is hard to imagine what kind of observation of the physical form of [3] and [5] (or of the behaviour of the utterer) is going to give us this information. It is, of course, possible to argue that linguistics should have nothing to do with facts of this sort but there are many who feel, in my view rightly, that such a posture leads to a wholly unacceptable trivialisation of the domain of enquiry. Although it is undeniable that speakers' judgements begin to falter as utterances increase in length and complexity, it nevertheless remains true that there are indefinitely large numbers of utterances that speakers can pass various kinds of judgement about with confidence and near-total agreement. In such circumstances it seems perverse to deny that there are facts here to be dealt with.

We must now consider just what it means to commit linguistic theory to giving an account of the introspective judgements of native speakers. Knowing a language is not simply a matter of having learned by heart a list of expressions; standard formulas are a very small part of our linguistic knowledge. To see the force of this, one might take a (written) utterance at random from the pages of this book and try to find it repeated somewhere in the collection of books in the British Library. Unless the utterance happened to be a quotation or a conventional formula, such a search would almost certainly be fruitless. Clearly a language cannot be equated with a set of actual utterances, however large.

Nor would the definition be successful if it were extended to include all the utterances that might be produced. Many utterances exhibit false starts, hesitations, slips of the tongue and so on. We can dismiss such phenomena as linguistically irrelevant because all speakers of English can make a clear distinction between utterances such as [6] and utterances such as [7].

[6] *I . . . . (cough) . . . er . . . was . . . er . . . wondering . . . (throat-clearing noise) . . . look! . . . um . . . will you tell her I shan't, I mean won't, be coming.*

[7] *I was wondering if you would tell her that I won't be coming.*

Both are potential utterances, but since speakers have no difficulty drawing a distinction in status between them, it seems reasonable to conclude that knowledge of language cannot be defined simply in terms of potentiality of occurrence.

Chomsky interprets our sense of what is or is not well-formed as an aspect of our performance that reflects an essential property of our internalised grammatical knowledge, or competence. This underlying system is said to define the set of well-formed **sentences** of a language. The term sentence is used here to describe abstract objects that belong to the theory of competence (in non-realist terms theoretical constructs that belong to the study of grammar rather than of language use) in terms of which the notion of well-formedness can be given a precise character-isation. Actual utterances, spoken or written by individuals at particular times and in particular places, may or may not be utterances of well-formed sentences, depending on whether or not grammatically irrelevant factors distort the product in ways not determined by competence. From this point of view the primary task of the linguist in his efforts to characterise competence is to characterise the set of well-formed sentences of the language under investigataion.

But there are, of course, other aspects of performance which are plausibly regarded as relevant to the determination of the nature of competence. We can, for example, make judgements about structure, structural relations, meaning, and so on. The extent to which grammatical knowledge is accessible to intro-spection naturally varies. All speakers potentially have conscious knowledge of the fact that an utterance such as *my daughter has grown another foot* is ambiguous, while relatively few speakers in all probability have conscious knowledge of the nature of the systematic relationship between sentences with active transitive verbs and corresponding sentences with passive verb forms. They must, nevertheless, have *tacit* knowledge of this relationship to be able to perform in the way that they do, and in principle this knowledge could be raised to the level of consciousness, at least in an informal way. Other aspects of the grammatical system, for example the status of *Chomsky* as subject or object (assuming these to be categories of mental representation) in an utterance such as *they believe Chomsky to be wrong*, cannot be determined by reference to introspection, and their investigation has to proceed by indirect means. If, for example, it was argued that *Chomsky* is a subject because the object of belief from a logical point of view is the proposition that 'Chomsky is wrong', there might be consequences elsewhere in the grammar that were directly testable and which allowed this proposal to be distinguished empirically from the proposal that *Chomsky* is an object because pronouns in this position have accusative case marking (*they believe him to be wrong*). As always, performance is an imperfect guide to competence, but it is the only direct evidence available to the linguist, and the only empirical criterion that theories of competence can be judged by is whether they make predictions that accord with the intuitions of native speakers.

It was argued above that our intuitions of well-formedness were a reflection of one aspect of our competence, namely our knowledge of the set of well-formed sentences of the language(s) we speak, but that many other linguistic capabilities could also be regarded as reflections of aspects of competence. We might, then, argue that to know the grammar of a language is not only to know what constitutes a well-formed sentence in that language, but also to know what the structural properties of well-formed sentences are, to know what kinds of structural permutation of well-formed sentences are permitted in the formation of other well-formed sentences, to know how each well-formed sentence is to be pronounced, to know what each well-formed sentence means, to know whether it is ambiguous, whether it means the same as, or implies the truth of the proposition expressed by, some other well-formed sentence, and so on. These are the kinds of knowledge, reflected in various performance skills, which any theory of competence must surely seek to explain. In this connection sentences are to be thought of as the theoretical units in terms of which a satisfactory explanation might be constructed, the units in terms of which all other grammatical units can be accounted for and by reference to which all grammatical processes and principles can be explained. It is important to note that apart from the characteristically realist interpretation, which makes sentences objects of knowledge rather than simply units of grammar, the sentence–utterance distinction is entirely traditional. Without some notion of formal constructs independent of physical realisation it would be hard to explain how two phonetically very different objects, say the utterances of a given string of words by a middle-aged male Glaswegian and by a teenage female Cockney, can be judged in some sense to be utterances of the 'same' sentence.

1.5 Generative grammars and levels of adequacy

Let us assume, then, that a minimal task for a linguist's grammar is that it should define the notion 'well-formed sentence'. A grammar that achieves this objective is said to be **observationally adequate**. For this objective to be met the grammar in question must be capable of specifying for any random string of words drawn from the dictionary of a language (assuming that the dictionary in question lists all the different forms of words as possible choices) whether or not that string is a well-formed sentence of that language. Traditionally, grammars have not been characterised with sufficient precision and the rules they embody have not been framed in a sufficiently explicit way for observational adequacy to be achieved. Typically a few examples of each construction type are offered and the reader is left to work out for himself whether some new sentence constructed along the same lines is also grammatical (well-formed). Such analogical reasoning may, of course, be dangerous, as examples [2] and [4] discussed above show. To be observationally adequate a grammar must be fully explicit, so that a *yes* or *no* answer is given to the question, asked of *any* string of words from a given language, 'is this string a sentence?' Such fully explicit grammars are called **generative grammars**, and an observationally adequate generative grammar **generates** the set of well-formed sentences of the language under investigation.

The attainment of observational adequacy is no mean feat, since it is clear that there is no finite bound on the number of well formed sentences in any (natural) language. The vast majority of utterances in any language are novel in the sense that they have not been uttered in precisely that form before. The point was made earlier, when it was suggested that the search for repetitions of any of the written utterances in this book in any corpus of English utterances would be futile because the proportion of a speaker's performance that consists of memorised formulas is very small indeed. To the extent that utterances have a direct relationship with sentences, it seems, therefore, that there will be an indefinitely large set of sentences just as there is an indefinitely large set of utterances. Chomsky, however, has argued that many of the constraints on the form and complexity of utterances are not to be regarded as reflecting properties of the underlying system of competence. For example, there are constraints on the physical length of utterances imposed by the energy and enthusiasm of the speaker, the willingness and ability of the listener to pay attention, and ultimately by the fact of human mortality. Since it is clear that none of these limiting factors is grammatical in character, it is reasonable to abstract away from them in any investigation of grammar/competence. It follows that there is no such thing as 'the longest sentence of English'. Take, for example, the sentences begun in [8].

[8i] *I like linguistics and Chomsky and chocolate cake and model railways and beautiful girls and French food and travelling abroad and working in Cambridge and* . . . . . .

[8ii] *This is the politician who attacked the journalist who wrote the article that criticised the policy that upset the voters who . . . . . .*

[8iii] *?The terrorist that the police that the press . . . . . . criticised arrested escaped.* (*Cf* the simpler *the terrorist that the police arrested escaped.*)

On purely grammatical grounds there is no non-arbitrary cut-off point for sentences of these types. Of course utterances of lengthy sentences of the first two types rapidly become insufferably tedious. And utterances of sentences of the third kind that have more than one or two so-called **centre-embeddings** rapidly become incomprehensible without pencil and paper and a great deal of concentration. But it is at least arguable that the incomprehensibility follows from limitations on short-term memory and computational ability and not from any deficiencies of form. [8iii] after all is formally parallel to the perfectly acceptable utterance in parentheses which follows it; the only difference is that the embedding process has been repeated. It is, therefore, perfectly possible for an utterance to be unacceptable to native speakers (for non-grammatical reasons) but nevertheless to be grammatically well-formed. The important point about the sentences begun in [8], though, is that, if there are no grammatically imposed limits on sentence length, there can be no grammatically imposed limits on the number of well-formed sentences. Any of [8i], [8ii] or [8iii] could stop at any of an infinite number of points.

The significance of this is that an observationally adequate grammar cannot simply list the set of well-formed sentences of some language. A grammar must consist of a *set of rules* which define infinite classes of well-formed structures. (From a realist point of view this is a necessary assumption anyway, since it cannot be the case that our minds have infinite storage capacity. Competence (knowledge of grammar) must be a finite system with the capacity to define the membership of an infinite set.) It is perhaps also worth pointing out that the infiniteness of natural languages constitutes another argument in favour of extending the domain of linguistics to include native speaker intuitions. Since no set of sentences, however large, can be equated with a language, it follows that grammatical rules arrived at by analysis and generalisation from a corpus will have to be interpreted as having predictive power with respect to strings not in the corpus if they are to constitute a definition of the sentences of the language. But we would have no basis for testing the validity of extrapolations from the attested examples constructed in conformity with the rules if we could not appeal to the intuition of native speakers.

In view of what was said in the preceding section about the data of linguistic theory, it is clear that the attainment of observational adequacy is not in itself a sufficient criterion of adequacy for a proposed grammar. It is not enough for a grammar simply to define the set of well-formed sentences of a language, it must also assign a structural description to each well-formed sentence that provides a basis for explaining native speakers' judgements about pronunciation, meaning, structure and structural relations. A grammar that achieves this objective is said to be **descriptively adequate**. Realists will, of course, attribute knowledge of descriptively adequate grammars to native speakers, instrumentalists will not. But from either point of view some overall theory of grammar is required as a basis for choosing between different proposals for characterising the grammar of a given language. It is important for linguists to operate within the constraints of a general theory that excludes certain logical possibilities. If there were no such general theory, linguists could invent new descriptive apparatus without any constraints on its form or function, in order to provide a description of some novel grammatical phenomenon in a hitherto unanalysed language, or even to describe some very familiar phenomenon in a novel way. The problem with such an approach is that it excludes nothing as impossible. Any conceivable construction is predicted to be a possible construction of some natural language, and every conceivable grammatical rule or principle is predicted to be a possible rule or principle of the grammar of some language. If it is true that the vast majority of linguists would be surprised to learn that there was a language spoken by a group of South American Indians in the Amazon rain forest in which passive sentences were exactly the same as their active counterparts except that the order of words was completely reversed, so that the last word of an active sentence was the first word of the corresponding passive and the first word of the active the last of the passive, it follows that the vast majority of linguists have some preconceived idea of what the grammars of natural languages can be like. Ideally such ideas should be formalised sufficiently to constitute a general theory of grammar which could be put to the test in a confrontation with (more or less) descriptively adequate grammars of various natural languages. Obviously, the relationship between individual grammars and the general theory will be a complex one. The discovery that the grammar of a language has a rule-type that is not compatible with the theory of grammar as currently conceived may entail that the theory has to be modified in the relevant respects. On the other hand it may turn out that a more careful analysis of the data from the language in question yields a solution involving the interaction of two familiar rule-types so that no adjustment of the overall theory is necessary. In general the ultimate objective should be an overall theory which is as restrictive as possible in terms of the descriptive apparatus it sanctions while remaining compatible with the diversity of the data it purports to account for.

Such a restrictive theory, unlike the 'anything goes' approach discussed above, is an empirical theory because it makes testable predictions about what is a possible natural-language grammar. Only those descriptively adequate grammars that are compatible with its requirements will be genuinely adequate, and if its requirements are sufficiently restrictive, it may turn out that only one descriptively adequate grammar for each language has the necessary properties. Failing that, some evaluation of the small set of compatible descriptively adequate grammars will be necessary in terms of overall simplicity and generality of formulation. A theory of this general sort constitutes an explanation of why it is that the grammars of natural languages are constituted in the way(s) that they are; why it is that from the indefinitely large range of logically conceivable types of rule and principle only a handful are ever exploited in the grammars of human languages. By contrast, a theory that excludes nothing as impossible can in turn explain nothing. In Chomsky's terminology, a theory that selects the best available descriptively adequate grammar for a given language is said to be **explanatorily adequate**.

A theory of this kind is in effect a theory of universal grammar defining the descriptive resources available for constructing the grammars of individual languages. The more powerful such a theory is, the less comprehensive the grammars of particular languages will have to be, because to a very large extent the properties of the rule-systems that constitute natural-language grammars will be automatic consequences of the theory of universal grammar. It is therefore natural that as research within a given framework of assumptions advances, the emphasis will shift from issues of descriptive adequacy to issues of explanatory adequacy. Once there is a reasonably well-established notion of what kinds of rule and principle are likely to be needed to characterise the grammars of the languages of the world it becomes important to try to develop a theory of grammar from which the utilisation of precisely these resources follows. Since Chomsky's theory of grammar has a longer history than either of the rivals described in this book, it is not surprising that his theory has moved further in the direction of addressing questions of explanatory adequacy than these alternative approaches. One needs a reasonable data base of grammars from which to infer candidate universals and it takes a certain amount of time for grammars of sufficient depth and precision to emerge within any given framework of description.

One consequence of this shift of emphasis is that far less attention is paid in current work within the Chomskyan framework to the precise characterisation of rule-systems; as the focus of interest moves from setting up rules to generate the set of well-formed sentences and assign structural descriptions to these, to establishing a general theory of grammar to define the form of grammars needed for the description of particular languages, it is natural that there will be a certain backing-off from the detail of wide-ranging descriptive analysis and a concentration on whatever range of phenomena seems to offer the most promising insights into the organisation of the theory of universal grammar. This is a major theme of Chapter 2 and is discussed again in Chapter 5.

At the outset of the research programme inspired by Chomsky the existence of an interesting theory of universal grammar was little more than an article of faith. But over the last fifteen years a theory has begun to emerge which incorporates quite abstract principles of considerable explanatory power. As a result, a great many of the properties of the grammars of individual languages may now be viewed as consequences of the internal organisation of the theory. The theory also has the very desirable property that proposals or changes in one area have implications elsewhere. It is therefore predicted that certain sets of grammatical properties will typically co-occur. Such a theory is obviously easier to put to the test than one in which each principle stands in isolation from the others. All of these points will be made in detail in Chapter 2. The important issue here is the status of this theory. From an instrumentalist point of view it is, of course, simply a series of higher-level generalisations drawn from careful observation of the grammars of various languages combined with a little speculation. There could be no question of a real-world interpretation without independent evidence that speakers' internalised grammars really were organised according to the principles proposed. For Chomsky, by contrast, it is inconceivable that a theory which incorporates highly abstract principles giving a plausible account of a wide range of grammatical phenomena should have this capacity by accident, with the phenomena in question being in reality organised according to quite different principles. Much obviously depends on whether the principles in question seem to be *sufficiently* abstract, wide-ranging and explanatory to exclude chance. This is a decision which the reader must make after reading Chapter 2 (see especially 2.3.11). If we assume for the moment that a realist interpretation is a reasonable one, where exactly is the real-world analogue of the linguist's general theory of grammar assumed to exist? Chomsky's answer is that, as a result of millions of years of evolution, human beings are endowed genetically with a faculty of language acquisition. The linguist's theory of universal grammar is a model of this genetic endowment. It is because human infants enjoy the benefit of this language-acquisition faculty that they are able to acquire a highly complex system of knowledge long before they have reached intellectual maturity and on the basis of exposure to primary data that is both limited in quantity and often degenerate in quality.

The plausibility of this position is enhanced if Chomsky can effectively demonstrate the 'poverty of the stimulus' by showing that native speakers have knowledge of grammatical principles that simply could not have been learned by each and every native speaker on the basis of generalisation from samples of primary data. Some examples of the sort of phenomenon often discussed in this connection are given in 2.3.11. To the extent that Chomsky is successful first in establishing the explanatory power of the principles of his theory of universal grammar and secondly in showing that no plausible theory of learning from experience could explain how native speakers of a language come to know what these principles embody, he may be said to have an answer to the problem of language acquisition. If children are equipped with minds/brains that are designed to cope only with grammatical systems that have certain highly restricted properties, if, in other words, they are born with an in-built knowledge of universal grammar, the process of language learning will in fact be largely automatic and *language-growth* might be a more appropriate term. From this point of view the function of the primary data is not to provide the basis for learning the grammar of a language *ex nihilo*; it is simply to provide enough information for the in-built theory of universal grammar to be particularised to the grammar of the language of the speech community that the infant lives in. Thus a normal healthy infant brought up in a given linguistic context will have no more choice about learning the grammar of the language in question than he does about learning to walk or to digest food. The acquisition of grammatical knowledge is to be regarded as the growth of a mental organ analogous in all crucial respects to the growth of physical organs. Indeed it is Chomsky's view that the term 'physical' has been extended to describe an ever-broader range of phenomena as science has progressed, and that its use is a function of the level of understanding in a given domain. The study of language for Chomsky is an important way of investigating the structure of the mind and so ultimately of helping to advance knowledge to the point where a mind/brain distinction becomes unnecessary.

Chomsky's theory of universal grammar, then, is a theory of how it comes about that the native speakers of a given language come to share a highly abstract body of knowledge despite great variations in their linguistic experience. There is, furthermore, some psychological evidence to suggest that the early stages of language acquisition in children follow a fixed pattern of development over a more or less fixed time-scale, and that factors such as intelligence and level of encouragement have no marked influence on the process. This could be interpreted as evidence in favour of the operation of a predetermined grammar-specific biological programme. But it is very difficult to show that the pattern of development is not a function of independent maturational factors. Thus the fact that construction A is consistently used by children before construction B *may* be due to the organisation of some innate language acquisition device, but it might equally be due to the fact that the brain has in any case to mature to a certain point before it can handle the greater relative complexity of construction B. Ultimately, then, Chomsky's theory rests upon the plausibility of the account it offers of the linguistic evidence and of the fact that children acquire their first languages rapidly and effectively, without formal instruction and generally ignoring correction and encouragement, long before they have reached intellectual maturity. If it really were the case that children had to learn languages *ex nihilo* on the basis of their experience of primary data, they would be in much the same position as linguists trying to construct grammars without the benefit of a general theory of grammar. Anything might be possible, and a vast number of possibilities would have to be evaluated by the child (according to some criterion of efficiency) before conclusions could be drawn about what constituted a reasonable grammar of the primary data he had experienced. In these circumstances, it would be little short of miraculous if speakers in fact ended up with the same body of internalised knowledge as the high level of agreement in matters of grammatical judgement suggests that they do. Chomsky's theory of universal grammar is, therefore, explanatorily adequate in a broader sense than that introduced above because of the realist framework in which it is embedded. It offers an explanation of how first language acquisition is possible by attributing to the human infant as a species-specific biological endowment a language acquisition device which makes available only a very small set of possible grammers such that the primary data, however meagre, can be assumed to provide sufficient information for the child to have a basis for choosing between them.

As before, it is possible to object that Chomsky's decision to attribute a specifically grammatical innate schema to the human infant is a direct consequence of his limited domain of enquiry, and that it would be much more fruitful to investigate the possibility that many of the properties of grammars are in fact due to much more general innate schemata that have a role to play in other systems of knowledge and belief and perhaps in the operation of other faculties. It may turn out, for example, that many of Chomsky's universals have excellent functional explanations in the sense that they are motivated by a requirement that grammars be designed so as to generate structures whose properties can most readily be handled by various processing devices and strategies. There is, of course, a very real possibility that by delimiting the field in the way that he does, Chomsky has overestimated the scope of formal grammar and seeks to explain by grammatical principle phenomena that have more general explanations when a broader view is taken. The only way to decide this issue is for those who disagree with Chomsky to try to develop formal theories which embody their ideas and to see if superior explanations of the domain of grammar as defined by Chomsky fall out from the broader perspective taken. Much current work in pragmatics (the study of how language is used as an instrument of communication rather than of grammar as a formal system) is motivated by considerations of this sort, and to some extent the rival theories of Generalised Phrase Structure Grammar and Lexical-Functional Grammar discussed in Chapters 3 and 4 of this book represent an attempt to broaden the data base of linguistic theory so as to open the way for a more comprehensive general theory of language use. To the extent that advocates of Generalised Phrase Structure Grammar tend to be instrumentalists, however, the issues raised tend not to be given any psychological significance, and it is the proponents of

Lexical-Functional Grammar who are most actively seeking to widen the field while retaining a realist stance. In comparison with the Chomskyan framework, though, both of these approaches seem more concerned with issues of descriptive adequacy and relatively little attention has yet been paid to the articulation of a general theory of grammar consistent with the representational assumptions and descriptive apparatus they employ. To this extent, direct comparison in terms of explanatory adequacy is difficult.

1.6 The scope of the book

The grammar of a language may be regarded as a system of rules which relates stretches of sound (or sequences of marks on a flat surface) with meanings. All linguists agree that the sound–meaning correspondences cannot be described 'in one go', and in practice several different levels of grammatical representation are deemed to be necessary.

Phonetics deals with the actual speech sounds employed in utterances (their articulation, their physical properties and their perception), phonology with the sound-system of a given language, *ie* with the ways in which the available physical resources are utilised to make the contrasts which allow for the conveyance of meaning. For example, the initial sound in English *top* is strongly aspirated (followed by a puff of breath) while the second sound in *stop* is not. No pair of English words is differentiated by the presence or absence of this kind of aspiration; therefore the phonetic difference has no phonological status in English. In Ancient Greek, however, *teinō* ('I stretch') was differentiated from *tʰeinō* ('I strike') by precisely this factor. So exactly the same phonetic difference was there of considerable phonological importance. Clearly any descriptively adequate grammar must have a phonological component which describes the abstract sound-system of the language and relates phonological representations to their phonetic realisations. Since grammars deal with sentences rather than utterances, however, the characterisation of phonetic form will have to abstract away from the peculiarities of sound that are the consequence of the idiosyncracies of individuals' vocal tracts and express only those phonetic properties that are essential and invariant.

Above the level of phonological structure lies the domain of the lexicon and morphology. The words of a language cannot be defined in terms of the principles of phonological theory. There are, for example, many phonologically possible words which happen not to be real words, such as *splink* and *braddy*, which conform to the rules defining what is phonologically possible in English, but are, to the best of my knowledge, not listed in dictionaries of contemporary English. The lexicon lists all the words of a language, usually in some conventional citation form, and the morphological component of the grammar describes all the various forms these words can take by virtue of undergoing morphological processes such as affixation. Conventionally, a distinction is drawn between derivational morphology, concerned with the formation of new words from existing ones (such as the formation of the noun *happi-ness* by suffixation from the adjective *happy*), and inflectional morphology, concerned with the changes undergone by a given word according as its syntactic role in sentences changes (as, for example, the addition of *-s* to *run* when the subject of the sentence containing this word as its main verb is a singular proper name, a singular noun phrase headed by a common noun, or a third person singular pronoun; *I/you/we/they run* but *Jimbo/the furious linguist/he/she/it runs*).

Syntax is concerned with the principles according to which words can be combined to form larger meaningful units, and by which such larger units can be combined to form sentences. Sentences, by definition, are the units in terms of which all other units can be accounted for, though the possibility of two or more sentences combining, by co-ordination, subordination or apposition, to form a larger sentence has to be allowed for. It is perhaps worth adding here that there is no general agreement about the location of the boundary between morphology and syntax, and at least some linguists would treat as syntactic relationships which in more traditional analyses would certainly be regarded as morphological. Semantics deals with the interpretation of sentences. Once again we are obliged to abstract away from those aspects of meaning which depend upon a sentence being uttered in a particular context. Sentences are theoretical constructs which have no context of use. Thus the utterance of a sentence such as [9],

[9] *Big Jim will be at the party tonight*

may be interpreted as imparting information, issuing a threat or a promise or a boast, and no doubt many other things, depending on who is talking to whom and in what circumstances. But the meaning of the well-formed **sentence** [9] does not change according to such changes of circumstances because consideration of extra-linguistic circumstance is relevant only to the determination of **utterance** meaning. Semantics is concerned with those aspects of meaning that are determined by the internal workings of the linguistic system, specifically the mechanisms by which the senses of words may be combined to form the senses of larger constructs, and pragmatics deals with the additional aspects of meaning that result from the utterance of a sentence in a particular context by a particular person.

At the very least, a descriptively adequate grammar will have to have a phonological component, a lexicon/morphological component, a syntactic component and a semantic component, together with principles for linking the representations of sentences at one level with representations at other levels. The more ambitious might also try to develop a theory of pragmatics and explore its relationship with the theory of grammar. The nature of the interactions between these various components, and indeed, as already noted, the demarcation of the boundaries between them, is by no means self-evident, and many different theoretical positions are possible. The only rational approach to the problem is to investigate plausible-seeming possibilities in sufficient depth to enable them to be tested for empirical adequacy and to be compared in terms of their empirical consequences. As we shall see, different approaches have been tried and abandoned in the course of the development of Chomsky's theory (Ch. 2), and Generalised Phrase Structure Grammar and Lexical-Functional Grammar (Chs. 3 and 4, respectively) adopt different positions from that currently assumed in the Chomskyan framework, and indeed from each other.

In this book nothing will be said about phonology and very little about semantics. It follows that the central concerns will be the lexicon (though I shall say very little about morphology) and syntax. This choice is dictated by the limitations of my professional competence but it fortunately correlates directly with Chomsky's own interests. The development of Chomsky's theory can only be appreciated in terms of its contribution to the study of syntax, and the significance of rival theories of generative grammar can only be determined by reference to the alternative treatments they propose for phenomena which are treated as syntactic in character in Chomsky's theory. The burden may, of course, be shifted to another component, or a syntactic solution may be adopted which employs assumptions and apparatus quite different from those used by Chomsky. But the details must wait until the essentials of Chomsky's theory have been explained. The first two sections of Chapter 2 (2.1 and 2.2) introduce some important technical apparatus and set the scene historically and conceptually for the third section (2.3), which deals with the current Chomskyan framework.

1.7 Relevant reading

For general discussion of all the issues raised in this chapter see Chomsky (1972a, 1975, 1980a, and 1986a). This series of works is devoted to defending various aspects of the philosophical position outlined in this chapter, and each includes some relatively non-technical exposition of the framework of description and analysis assumed at the time. The last of these presents some innovations which have not been discussed in this book. Chomsky, Huybregts and van Riemsdijk (1982) is a readable introduction to some of the leading ideas of the Chomskyan programme presented in the form of a dialogue, with Chomsky taking the Socratic part.

Popper (1972 and 1973) are the classic works in which he develops the idea that empirical theories can never be confirmed but only refuted. Lass (1976: epilogue) puts forward the view that linguistics is not a 'science' at all, but rather what Popper has called a metaphysical discipline (*ie* one that cannot be interpreted as dealing with matters of fact), and Lass (1980) is a critical evaluation of the notion of 'explanation' that is adopted in the Chomskyan framework.

In support of Chomsky's modular conception of the structure of the mind see J. A. Fodor (1983), and for some elegant arguments to the effect that psychology has nothing to do with linguistics at all see Matthews (1979).

There are some who think that Chomsky has incorporated within 'grammar' a range of phenomena which can be better explained in terms of pragmatics; see in particular Farmer (1984) and many of the papers in Papi and Verscheuren (1986).

Chapter 2

Chomsky's theory of grammar

2.1 The standard theory

2.1.1 Introduction

In the decade from 1955 to 1965 the foundations of generative grammar were laid and a complex technical formalism was developed. In his book *Aspects of the Theory of Syntax*, published in 1965, Chomsky presented the then current state of the art. The formal machinery proposed at that time came later to be known as the 'standard theory' of transformational generative grammar. It is important to have a clear understanding of this, and of its limitations, as a preliminary to an appreciation of later developments, both direct developments of Chomsky's approach and reactions to it. This section attempts to give a concise picture of its salient characteristics.

The various 'components' of a standard-theory grammar and their interrelations may be represented as in [1].

[1]

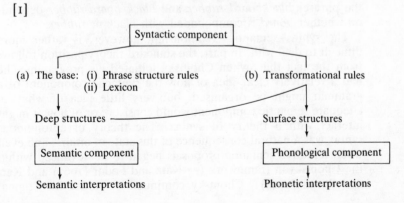

Notice first of all that the rules of the semantic and phonological components are taken to be interpretative of syntactic structures, and that the rules of syntax are at the heart of the system. The view was taken at the time that the syntax should be capable of generating all and only the sentences of a given language without reference to semantic or phonological information, that syntax was, in other words, a wholly autonomous system. By contrast, it was argued that the rules of the phonological and semantic components required syntactic information to operate on. This position is by no means self-evidently correct, and clearly requires some discussion.

The autonomy of syntax from phonology is perhaps the easier claim to justify, since even though it is possible in principle that certain syntactic properties of sentences follow from particular phonological properties, it is clearly not the case that the rules defining sentencehood and inter-sentential relations operate exclusively, or even primarily, on phonological or phonetic information. To take just one example, an account of the active–passive relationship requires the identification of the class of verbs with passive participles (more or less the class traditionally called 'transitive'), and it is obviously impossible to identify this class by means of some set of phonological features shared by all its members because no such set exists. Let us, then, assume the basic correctness of Chomsky's position and accept that the phonetic representation of a sentence is the product of the application of rules of phonological interpretation to a representation of its surface syntactic structure (*ie* an analysis of the syntactic properties of a sentence reflecting the form in which, once phonetically interpreted, it might be uttered). It is simple enough to point to examples where syntactic structure determines phonetic form; for example, the stress placement in the phrases *blackboard rubber* and *black board-rubber* depends on whether *board* is compounded with *black* or *rubber*.

The syntax–semantics relationship, however, is rather more difficult to deal with. In part, the standard-theory position follows from the fact that, when Chomsky initiated his programme, he had a relatively clear idea of how the syntactic component of a grammar might be organised, but very little idea of what an adequate semantic component would consist of or of how it might interact with a theory of syntax. The theory of autonomous syntax was a natural consequence of this state of affairs, and even when tentative semantic proposals began to be advanced within the Chomskyan framework (*eg* Katz and Fodor (1963) and Katz and Postal (1964)), Chomsky continued to pursue his original

approach in the absence, at that time, of compelling evidence
that an adequate theory could not be constructed on this basis.

It is important to note, however, that the autonomous syntax
position has some initial plausibility. For example, the possibility
of translating a sentence of one language into a sentence of
another presupposes that there is some common 'content' shared
by those sentences. But it is clearly not the case that this shared
content entails identical syntactic structure in the two sentences,
as anyone with experience of translating will testify. Furthermore, it is perfectly possible that sentences of one language have
no grammatical translation equivalents in another. In such
circumstances it seems reasonable to suppose that there is
nothing 'deviant' about the message itself, and the fact that there
is no acceptable form into which this message can be put in a
particular language is a matter of the syntax of that language. As
an example consider the pair of sentences in [2] and [3].

[2] *pyon pístepses   ti   fími óti proíghaye?*
    whom believed-2s the story that promoted-3s

[3] **who did you believe the story that (s)he promoted?*

The first is for most speakers a perfectly grammatical sentence
of Modern Greek; the second, its English translation, is obviously ungrammatical. Clearly the difference here cannot be a
consequence of the semantic structure of these sentences. In any
case the content is perfectly intelligible, namely: 'for which
person x is it the case that you believed the story that (s)he
promoted x?' We must therefore be dealing with a syntactic
difference between the two languages that is unmotivated by
semantic considerations.

Nevertheless, the idea that the form of a sentence is determined, at least in part, by its content is also a reasonable initial
hypothesis, though clearly a hypothesis that can only be put to
the test in the context of a properly developed framework of
semantic description. The so-called 'Generative Semantics' movement of the late 1960s and early 1970s was in fact founded upon
the belief that an adequate set of syntactic rules could be developed to map 'semantic representations' into corresponding
surface syntactic forms, the rules in question being all of the same
formal type, and all ultimately motivated by semantic considerations. This movement represented the opposite extreme from
the standard theory, namely the view that syntactic form is determined by semantic content. The framework was abandoned as
it became increasingly clear that the rule systems that would be

necessary to carry out the mapping operation would have to be enormously complex and riddled with exceptions. This was a sure sign that things were being looked at in the wrong way. A theory that allows new rules and rule-types to be invented *ad hoc* to solve each new problem as it arises clearly has no chance of achieving explanatory adequacy (1.5).

This is not, of course, to say that Chomsky's extreme autonomy thesis has been shown to be correct. There has been, as we shall see, a gradual retreat over the years from the view that the syntax should be capable of generating all and only the sentences of a language without reference to other components of grammar. This is a natural development as research into the properties of other components progresses and a better understanding evolves of what would constitute a reasonable model of the interaction of those components with the syntax. There is thus every reason to expect that the 'borders' between different components will be drawn in different places at different times, and that a phenomenon confidently described as syntactic will come to be regarded as semantic or lexical at a later date. In 1965 the potential of components other than the syntax was only just beginning to be explored and it is not therefore surprising that an extreme position should have been taken on the autonomy thesis; since there was very little in the way of formal machinery outside the domain of syntax, phenomena were classified as syntactic willy-nilly. Much of the subsequent history of generative grammar may be viewed as a testing out of different workload distributions between the different components of a grammar in an attempt to assign to each its proper domain of responsibility. This, of course, presupposes reasonably well-worked-out theories of semantic, lexical and morphological structure, as well as of syntax.

2.1.2 Phrase structure rules and lexicon

It is clear to anyone who gives the matter serious thought that the words of an English sentence are not arranged like beads on a string. Certain groups of words cohere and form building blocks within sentences, and native speakers usually have little difficulty in identifying these. For example, all speakers of English know that the bold sets of words in sentences [4], [5] and [6] could also appear in the vacant position in sentence [7], in other words that these sets of words form mobile building blocks that are capable of fulfilling a range of grammatical functions (those of subject, direct object, etc.).

[4] *Unfortunately.* **your mother** *will not be able to come.*
[5] **That drunken slob she calls her boyfriend** *walked out on her.*
[6] **The truth of the matter,** *as I see it, is that we have a lunatic in charge.*
[7] *I recognised – in the Dog and Duck.*

Clearly the identification of such groups of words is not simply a matter of linear position, since the subject of an English sentence may consist of any number of words from one upwards and may occur in a variety of positions with respect to other words in a sentence, as the examples [4] to [6] make clear. There are in fact several ways in which this coherence might be represented, but the tradition in American linguistics, which Chomsky largely followed, was to regard sentences as objects analysable into ever-smaller constituent parts until the ultimate constituents had been reached. The standard view, then, was that these smallest parts combined to form phrases of various kinds and that each type of phrase had a characteristic **distribution**, or range of contexts of occurrence. Sentences could thus be regarded as the minimal units in terms of which the distribution of every type of phrase could be stated but which themselves had no characteristic distribution in terms of some larger grammatical unit.

Phrase structure rules, which form a part of the 'base' component of the syntax in diagram [1], are simply a formal device for representing the distribution of phrases within sentences. Returning to the sentences in [4], [5] and [6], we might wish to say that all the underlined sets of words were noun phrases, and that the subject of a sentence was necessarily a noun phrase. On the basis of the fact that these same noun phrases could also appear in the vacant slot in [7], we might also want to conclude that the direct object of a transitive verb also had to be a noun phrase. We would then have the job of deciding what the internal structure of a noun phrase could be. Obviously it might consist of just a noun, as in [8].

[8] **John** *thinks his boss is a psychopath.*

But it is equally clear from [4] and [5] that a noun may be preceded by a determiner of some sort (article, possessive 'adjective', demonstrative, etc.) and that an adjective may intervene between the determiner and the noun. [5] and [6] also show that various elements may follow the noun, in these cases a relative clause and a prepositional phrase respectively.

We might try to summarise all this by means of the following set of **phrase structure rules**.

[9i]   S → NP VP
[9ii] VP → V (NP)
[9iii] NP → (DET) (ADJ) N (PP) (RC)

S =	sentence	DET =	determiner
NP =	noun phrase	ADJ =	adjective
VP =	verb phrase	PP =	prepositional phrase
		RC =	relative clause

Informally, each rule is to be interpreted as saying that the element on the left-hand side of the arrow consists of the elements on the right-hand side in that order. In other words the rules express part–whole relationships, and impose an order on the parts. Items which are optional are enclosed in parentheses. It is customary to refer to the parts of some whole as its **constituents** and any given constituent that is itself analysable into constituents is assumed to represent a coherent building block. Rule [9i] therefore states that every sentence consists of a noun phrase (its subject) and a verb phrase (roughly what is traditionally called a predicate). This information is often represented in the form of a tree diagram (or **phrase marker**) as in [10], or as a **labelled bracketing** as in [11].

[10]

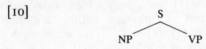

[11] [_S NP VP]

In both cases S **directly dominates** NP and VP, and NP **precedes** VP. Rule [9ii] allows for verb phrases that consist of a verb without complements (an intransitive verb) or a verb with a noun phrase complement (a transitive verb). [9iii] allows for a wide variety of noun phrase types ranging from the simplest (a single noun in isolation) to quite complex structures involving modifiers that both precede and follow. The obligatory element in a given phrase, as the verb in the verb phrase or the noun in the noun phrase, is known as the **head** of that phrase.

Clearly the rules given in [9] could be extended quite considerably by the addition of further categories on the right-hand side so as to allow for an ever wider range of possible sentence types. It might also prove to be necessary to introduce some further stratification; for example, it might be the case that there is

evidence to suggest that a noun and the elements following it
form a constituent, and that the adjective which may precede a
noun forms a constituent with this new constituent, as in [12].

[12]

These are important questions and they will be taken up later
(2.2.2). For the moment it is sufficient to have simply a *general*
appreciation of the principles of phrase structure description, and
the sample rules in [9], though obviously over-simplified, are
adequate for this purpose.

Clearly if we are going to have a set of rules of the general type
illustrated in [9] it is going to be necessary to have a lexicon to
complement them. Such rules **generate** structural descriptions for
sentences, that is objects representable as tree diagrams rooted
in the symbol S, and the more comprehensive the rule system,
the greater the range and variety of structural descriptions it will
generate. But until words are associated with categories such as
DET, V and N these structures are simply formal skeletons,
rather than sentences in the conventional sense. It will be useful,
therefore, at this stage to examine the other half of the base
component of a standard-theory grammar and to see how the two
parts fit together.

Notice first of all that the syntactic categories which the phrase
structure rules operate with fall into two classes, **phrasal** and
lexical. The lexical categories are those which have as members
sets of lexical items. Thus words listed in a lexicon can be
assigned to classes such as noun, verb, adjective or preposition,
but one would not expect to find items assigned to categories
such as noun phrase or prepositional phrase since these are
always analysable further, ultimately into combinations of lexical
categories. The phrasal categories, therefore, are those which do
not have lexical members and which are further analysable
syntactically.

Obviously we need some mechanism which identifies lexical
items of a certain class and arranges for the transfer of an appropriate member of that class into a sentence skeleton under a

lexical category with the correct class label. In the standard
theory each lexical entry is of the form illustrated in [13].

[13] X:$\begin{bmatrix} \text{Category} \\ \text{feature} \end{bmatrix}$ + $\begin{bmatrix} \text{Subcategorisation} \\ \text{feature} \end{bmatrix}$ + $\begin{bmatrix} \text{Selectional} \\ \text{restrictions} \end{bmatrix}$
Semantic representation
Phonological representation

Each lexical item X is associated with a triad of features
expressing its syntactic, semantic and phonological properties.
Since it is the syntactic features which determine the contexts into
which an item may be inserted, nothing further will be said here
about semantic and phonological features. The assignment of a
category feature is straightforward; each lexical item is assigned
to one of the set of lexical categories in a given language
according to its general distributional and morphological properties. Thus if an item can occur in the first position in a verb
phrase and is inflected for tense we can safely assume that it is
a verb.

However it is not the case that every verb can appear wherever
the node V appears in a tree diagram of a sentence structure.
Take, for example, sentences [14], [15], [16] and [17].

[14] *Steve hops.*
[15] *Steve likes girls.*
[16] *Steve puts his money in the bank.*
[17] *Steve says he has never been happier.*

Evidently, it would be impossible to switch the verbs in these
sentences around. *Hop* is an intranitive verb, *like* is a transitive
verb requiring a direct object, *put* is a complex transitive verb
requiring not only a direct object but also a locative complement
(in the form of a prepositional phrase), and *say* is a verb that
here requires a sentential complement. The verb phrases of
sentences [14] to [17] may be represented as in [18] to [21]
respectively.

[18]   VP   [19]   VP   [20]   VP   [21]   VP
        | /\   /|\   /\
        V   V NP   V NP PP   V   S

The four subcategories of verb can readily be identified in terms
of the context in which their members may appear. Each verb
may therefore be given a **subcategorisation feature** in the form
of a specification of the syntactic categories with which it co-
occurs, as in [22].

[22i]   hop: V, + [——]
[22ii] like: V, + [——NP]
[22iii] put: V, + [——NP P]
[22iv] say: V, + [——S]

In each case the categories specified in the subcategorisation feature are those which must co-occur with the verb in question in the VP. The rules of lexical insertion will therefore have to match not only the category feature but also the subcategory feature of a given lexical item with the tree into which the item is to be inserted before the insertion process can take place. Clearly the phrase structure rule defining the possible constituents of VP will in effect have to duplicate the information contained in the subcategorisation features of individual verbs. Consider [23].

[23] VP → V (NP) (PP) (S)

This rule will allow for the VPs in diagrams [18] to [21] but effectively says, albeit in a more compressed form, what is said in [22]. It also allows for other options as verb complements apart from those that have been illustrated, but it would not be difficult to expand [22] with examples of verbs that take a PP complement, or a combination of PP and S, etc. Such duplication of information is obviously redundant and inelegant, and, as we shall see, later versions of the theory seek to eliminate it.

We have not yet, however, exhausted the set of syntactic features associated with each lexical entry in the standard theory. Consider sentences [24], [25] and [26].

[24] *Jimmy Smith elapsed slowly.*
[25] *The bionic woman hacked down the fact with a karate chop.*
[26] *The theorem drank down its soup with a slurp.*

It is undeniable that there is something a little odd about these sentences. Somewhat surprisingly, perhaps, Chomsky decided in *Aspects* that defects of this sort constituted violations of *syntactic* rules and sought to account for them in terms of so-called **selectional restrictions** specified for each item in the lexicon. Thus the verb *elapse*, for example, would be listed as requiring a 'temporal' subject, *hack down* as requiring a 'concrete' object, and *drink (down)* as requiring an 'animate' subject. Since *Jimmy Smith* would not be characterised as a 'temporal' noun phrase, nor *fact* as a 'concrete' noun, nor *theorem* as an 'animate' noun, there would be a violation of the verb's selectional restrictions in each example. It is obviously debatable whether or not sentences like [24], [25] and [26] should be classified as ungrammatical (or ungrammatical to some degree, or whatever). The features in terms of which the selectional restrictions are stated seem to have more to do with semantics than syntax, and indeed could only be regarded as having syntactic import in a theory which required the syntax and lexicon together to generate all the grammatical sentences of a language, and no non-sentences, without assistance from other components. If the absolute autonomy requirement was relaxed, it would be possible to argue that sentences of this sort are syntactically well-formed and leave it, say, to the semantic component to mark them as semantically deviant. But it is debatable even whether we are really dealing with semantic deviance here. It is not unreasonable to argue that the oddness has nothing to do with violation of rules in *any* component of the grammar, and is simply a matter of pragmatics. Thus it is very difficult at first sight to think of situations in which sentences [24], [25] and [26] might reasonably be uttered. This does not necessarily mean that they are ill-formed syntactically or that they violate some fundamental semantic principle, merely that the reader does not have a very fertile imagination. It is almost always the case that after a little thought some fantasy world can be constructed which might truly be described by such sentences, and it is probably true to say that most linguists today are quite happy with the idea that the sort of oddness illustrated in [24] to [26] should be regarded as something to be dealt with outside the domain of grammar. It is certainly true that the proposal to incorporate selectional restrictions among the syntactic features associated with lexical items was very rapidly abandoned.

2.1.3 Deep structures and transformations

Thus far the impression has been given that the base component (phrase structure rules and lexicon) of a standard-theory grammar generates sentences and assigns a syntactic structure (tree diagram or labelled bracketing) to each. This impression is quite erroneous and must now be corrected. Chomsky in fact proposed that the phrase structure rules (and lexicon) generate the **deep structures** of sentences and that the rules of the **transformational component** of the syntax map these into **surface structures**. Thus each sentence has both a deep structure and a surface structure representation. We must therefore consider the role of deep structures and transformations.

In his earliest work on syntax Chomsky argued that a descriptively adequate (1.5) grammar for a natural language could not be constructed if it employed only the apparatus provided by the theory of phrase structure. Many of the arguments employed in early work looked more convincing then than they do now because the potential of components other than the syntax to rescue the phrase structure rules from their supposed inadequacy had only begun to be explored at the time when the standard theory was being developed. (Indeed the potential of the phrase structure rules themselves was underestimated, as the development of Generalised Phrase Structure Grammar has made clear (see Ch. 3)). The result was that many phenomena were taken to provide compelling evidence in favour of a more sophisticated framework of syntactic description, incorporating transformational rules, which large numbers of linguists today would choose to handle by means of more sophisticated phrase structure grammars or by means of various formal devices in the lexicon or semantic component. Some of these alternative approaches are discussed in later chapters. Although Chomsky himself has continued with a transformational approach to syntax, it will become clear below that the domain of transformations within his theory has been somewhat reduced and that the arguments in favour of retaining them have taken on a rather different character (2.3). Nevertheless, it will be useful to examine a typical sample of the problems that were said to arise within a wholly phrase-structure framework, since the motivation for innovative mechanisms in other components advocated by those who wish to reduce the scope of transformations, or even to eliminate them, would otherwise be difficult to appreciate.

A descriptively adequate grammar must, among other things, define the notion 'grammatical sentence', and assign to each and every grammatical sentence a structural description that correctly reflects the native speaker's knowledge of syntactic structure as reflected in his performance. It must, furthermore, offer an account of the native speaker's knowledge of sentential relationships, structural ambiguities, and so on. The key question, therefore, which Chomsky addressed in the mid-1950s was whether phrase structure grammars could be elaborated to meet these requirements. Obviously more and more rules can be added to the list to cover an ever-increasing range of syntactic structures, and the problem of having to define an infinite set of sentences, or of there being no such thing as the longest possible sentence of a language, can be handled by making the rule system **recursive**. Thus if a given symbol appears both on the left-hand side of some rule and on the right-hand side of some rule, the first rule can reapply to the output of the second, and the second can reapply to that of the first, or to that of some rule that depends for its application on the prior application of the first, indefinitely many times. Consider the rules in [27].

[27i] S → NP VP
[27ii] VP → V (NP) (PP) (S)

Since S appears on the left of [27i] and on the right of [27ii], it is possible to generate an infinitely long sentence, or an infinite number of sentences, of the form illustrated in [28].

[28]

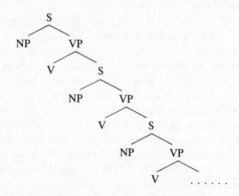

Such sentences as *John said Bill thought Fred believed Mary surmised Jane supposed Chomsky knew Napoleon hinted Plato inferred . . . . . . Ghengis Khan concluded that the earth was a giant egg* are not, of course, on everybody's lips. But this is not a problem from the point of view of defining the grammar (*cf* 1.5).

Nevertheless, some real problems remain. Consider sentences [29] and [30].

[29] *The police believed John put the forged fiver in his pocket.*
[30] *What did the police believe John put in his pocket?*

The lexical entry for the verb *put* would include the syntactic information presented in [31].

[31] *put*: V, + [——NP PP]

and the phrase structure rule [27ii] would provide a suitable syntactic context within a VP for the insertion of this verb.

[32]

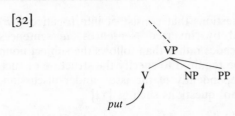

Sentence [29] therefore presents no problems of principle. The verb *put* requires a particular complement structure. In this case the verb and the necessary complements appear adjacent to one another as 'sisters' under a common 'mother'. This, then, is the simplest possible case of the relationship between the verb and its complements. Because all three elements together form a VP, it will always be possible to formulate a phrase structure rule to create an appropriate context of insertion for *put*, and because the complements appear next to the verb, it is possible to specify the required context in a subcategorisation feature as in [31] in a completely straightforward fashion.

The problems begin with sentence [30]. The most obvious characteristic of this sentence is the fact that its direct object NP is not where it would be expected to be on the basis of the subcategorisation feature assigned to *put* in [31]. It is customary for interrogative expressions (most of which begin with *wh-*) to appear at the beginning of a sentence regardless of their grammatical function. Thus in [30] *what* is the direct object of *put*, just as *the forged fiver* is the object of *put* in [29]. However, it stands at the beginning of the sentence and there is simply a 'gap' in the NP position after *put* where we might otherwise expect the direct object to be. Thus one of the tasks of a descriptively adequate grammar is to show that the relationship between *put* and *what* in [30] is simply a more complex version of the relationship between *put* and *the forged fiver* in [29]. Can this be achieved using only the resources of a phrase structure grammar and associated lexicon? The standard answer in 1965 was that it could not. Indeed, it was argued that phrase structure grammars could not even guarantee that the correct set of sentences would be generated, let alone express the nature of the relationship between the two sentence types.

Let us, then, consider the arguments. First of all, it is clear that a new phrase structure rule will be needed to generate sentences like [30]. Consider [33].

[33] Q → NP   S
          [wh] [inv]

This rule allows for questions that consist of interrogative (*wh*) noun phrases followed by 'inverted' sentences, *ie* sentences where the auxiliary precedes rather than follows the subject noun phrase. A rule would be required to specify the structure of such inverted sentences independently of the issue under discussion, because of direct 'yes-no' questions such as [34].

[34] *Will the butler do it?*

The rule itself would be simple enough to formulate, but there is a crucial difference between the inverted sentence [34] and the inverted sentence that follows *what* in [30]; in the latter case the direct object of *put* is 'missing' while in the former case the direct object of *do* is present. Obviously, there is a connection between the presence of a *wh*-word at the beginning of a sentence and the presence of a 'gap' in the inverted sentence that follows; you cannot have one without the other, as the ungrammatical [35] and [36] show.

[35] *What did the police believe John put the rocket plans in his pocket?*

[36] *Did the police believe John put in his pocket?*

Is there any way in which we can guarantee that gaps appear in inverted sentences in just the right places? On the basis of traditional phrase structure rules the answer would appear to be no, because there is no way of linking rules together so that an option exercised in one rule is associated with some particular option in another. The only way to allow for noun phrase gaps in the present framework is to place parentheses around the symbol NP on the right hand side of phrase structure rules. However, *wh*-phrases at the beginning of a sentence can bear the full range of grammatical functions.

[37] *Who did you say* (gap) *bungled the break-in?*

[38] *Who did you say the butler saw* (gap) *in the actress's bedroom?*

[39] *Who did you say Flash Gordon gave the secret formula to* (gap)?

The gaps in these three sentences occur in subject position, direct object position, and in prepositional object position. We would therefore have to allow for phrase structure rules where all NP positions in S, VP or PP were in principle optional.

[40i]   Q →   NP   S
            [wh] [inv]

[40ii] S →   AUX S
        [inv]
[40iii] S →   (NP) VP
[40iv] VP→   V (NP) (PP) (S)
[40v]   PP→   P (NP)

We must now arrange things so that if rule [40i] applies, one, and only one, of the NPs in the inverted sentence is omitted; in other words, we must somehow express the fact that the 'displaced' NP bears the grammatical function normally associated with the position of a unique gap in S. This is very difficult to do, because each of the rules [40iii] to [40v] is an independent object, and there is no obvious way in which the necessary inter-rule links can be established so as to exclude sentences with no gap or with multiple gaps. The problem is compounded by the fact that the relationship between the *wh*-NP and its associated gap is **unbounded**; the gap may occur in any of the potentially infinite number of sentences contained within the topmost (inverted) sentence.

[41] *What did John say the police thought the reporters believed . . . . . . the terrorist put* (gap) *in the bag?*

In the absence of a mechanism for linking choices in otherwise independent rule applications, we end up with a grammar that will generate not only [37], [38] and [39], but also [35] and [36] as well as oddities such as [42].

[42] *What did you say thought believed put in?

This obviously unsatisfactory state of affairs has an equally unsatisfactory analogue in the lexicon. The standard subcategorisation features make reference to strictly 'local' contexts, as we have seen (*cf* [31] above for *put*). Clearly this quality of localness cannot be maintained in the case of 'displaced' constituents such as *wh*-phrases. Thus in the case of a sentence such as [41] it would be necessary to allow for *put* to have a direct object NP indefinitely far removed to the left from the verb which governs it. The main problem with a subcategorisation feature such as [43],

[43] put: V, + $\begin{bmatrix} NP \ldots \ldots \text{———}PP \\ [wh] \end{bmatrix}$

is that this, like the corresponding phrase structure rule introducing *wh*-NPs ([40i]), fails to express the fact that the *wh*-NP bears the same relation to the verb as the NP introduced by the phrase structure rule [40iv] and mentioned in the conventional subcategorisation feature [31]. Yet the expression of this sameness is a task of primary importance if the grammar is correctly to reflect the native speaker's knowledge of the matter. But because the relationship between [31] and [43] is not expressed, any more than the relationship between [40i] and [40iv], we do not even have a way of guaranteeing that the interrogative NP referred to in [43] is a (displaced) direct object; we cannot, therefore guarantee that the verb is correctly inserted. For example, given the phrase structure rules [40iii] and [40iv], it would be possible to have a 'sentence' in which there were two gaps, one in direct object position in a VP and one, say, in subject position in a superordinate clause. [43] would then quite wrongly allow the insertion of *put* (as opposed to a verb like *walked*).

[44] *[NP *Who*] *did they say* (gap) *put* (gap) [PP *in the cupboard*]?

It should be clear that the proposals outlined so far involve the ascription of sets of subcategorisation features to lexical items which simply repeat in different forms the basic contextual requirements of the items in question, *eg* that *put* requires a direct object and a locative prepositional phrase to complement it. But it should also be clear that features such as [43] are incapable of guaranteeing the fulfilment of these requirements. In view of this, we might reasonably ask whether the extension of the power of the formal apparatus involved, allowing features to make reference to indefinitely large 'contexts' for items to be inserted into, and also therefore allowing the lexical insertion rule to scan indefinitely large syntactic structures to see if the specified requirements are met, is warranted. The natural answer, in view of the insufficiency of even this revised apparatus, has to be that it is not.

In response to problems of this sort Chomsky proposed the introduction of transformational rules into the theory of syntax. In his earliest work these did not apply to what later came to be known as **deep structures**, but by 1965 the distinction between deep and surface structure had been clearly drawn, and in this book deep structure and transformations will be dealt with together.

The basic idea is a very simple one. We have already seen that in a sentence such as [45],

[45] *What did Tex Tucker put in his saddlebag?*

there is essentially the same relationship between *put* and *what* as exists between *put* and *his silver-handled six-gun* in [46].

[46] *Tex Tucker put his silver-handled six-gun in his saddlebag.*

Obviously the relationship in [46] is the simple case in that the related items are adjacent to one another as sisters within a VP, while the relationship in [45] is more complex, in that the direct object has been displaced from this 'basic' position. Suppose, then, that every sentence has two syntactic representations; one at which the simple, 'basic', relationship between items holds by definition, and one at which more complex versions of this relationship may optionally be involved. Let us call the first the sentence's deep structure and the second its surface structure. Thus [45] would have the deep structure [47],

[47]

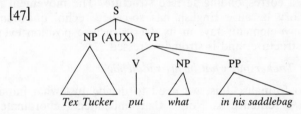

and the surface structure [48].

[48]

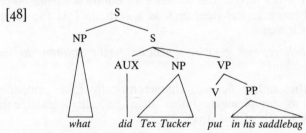

The precise nature of the initial position to which *wh*-expressions move is discussed immediately below.

[46], on the other hand, would have a deep structure identical to its surface structure in the relevant respects, namely [49].

[49]

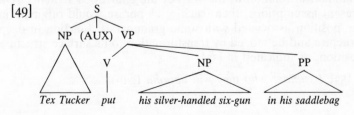

Thus the essential sameness of the relationship between *put* and its direct object in the two sentences is expressed by the fact that the NPs involved appear in precisely the *same* configuration *vis-à-vis* the verb in the deep structures of the two sentences, while the essential difference between the two sentences, the displacement of the object in [45], is expressed by the fact the object appears in two *different* positions in the two surface structures. If we now set up a **transformational rule** to express the nature of the relationship between deep structures such as [47] and surface structures such as [48], all the problems alluded to earlier disappear.

Let us first of all consider the form of the transformational rule. What it has to say is that, if a constituent is marked with the feature *wh* in deep structure, it may be moved to initial position in a corresponding surface structure. The movement is not obligatory because English has so-called 'echo' questions where the *wh*-element stays in its deep-structure position even in surface structure, and is strongly stressed.

[50] *Tex Tucker put **whát** in his saddlebag?*

In order to formalise this, we need to decide just what initial position in a sentence is. Notice that embedded (subordinate) clauses are typically introduced in English by a **complementiser**, *ie* a word which marks the sentence in question as the complement of some lexical item such as a verb. In [51] the complementiser is *that*.

[51] *I believe that general semantics is the solution to our problems.*

Some verbs, unlike *believe*, characteristically take embedded questions as complements rather than embedded statements. *Wonder* is a verb of this sort.

[52] *I wonder whether linguistics is a worthwhile discipline.*

The complementiser in such embedded yes-no questions is *whether*. It is interesting that *wonder* may also take as its complement a question introduced by a *wh*-constituent that bears a grammatical relation to the verb of the embedded sentence. On present assumptions, then, such a *wh*-phrase would originate in the position associated with some grammatical function in deep structure and be moved by transformation to its surface structure position, as indicated in [53].

[53] *I wonder who they will appoint* (gap).

Thus *wh*-phrases may be moved to the beginning of any sentence that is a question, whether the sentence is a main clause or a subordinate clause. Since *whether* in [52] is a complementiser and a *wh*-expression, it seems reasonable to suppose that the position to which *who* is moved in [53] is the complementiser position in the embedded sentence. In the interests of a uniform analysis of questions, therefore, we may also suppose that even main clauses have a complementiser position to which *wh*-expressions may move, even though overt complementisers such as *that* and *whether* never actually appear in such a position in English sentences.

With this background we are now in a position to propose a transformational rule to associate deep structures with *wh*-expressions in subject or object positions with structures with 'displaced' *wh*-expressions. Standard-theory transformations have two parts, a **structural description**, defining the class of (deep) structures to which the rule may apply, and a **structural change**, indicating how the rule affects the class of (deep) structures in question. (The word *deep* is here enclosed in parentheses since, as we shall see, it is possible for a transformation to apply to the output of another transformation, and in such circumstances it is clearly the case that the rule is not applying to a deep structure but rather to some intermediate level of structure between deep and surface structure.) The structural description takes the form of a factorisation of the class of structures affected. In the present case, therefore, we might propose the following structural description.

[54] *Wh-movement* SD: X –   COMP – X – *wh* – X
$$\qquad\qquad\qquad\quad [+Q]$$
$$\qquad\qquad\quad \text{I}\qquad\quad 2\qquad\quad 3\qquad 4\qquad 5$$

This constitutes an instruction to find a structure which can be analysed exhaustively into the five specified factors, namely anything or nothing (X), an interrogative complementiser position ([+Q(uestion)]), anything or nothing, a *wh*-expression and anything or nothing. X is simply a **variable** in such rules and can stand for any sequence of elements including zero. Obviously the relationship essentially involves items 2 and 4, but since the relationship between a moved *wh*-expression and the gap it leaves behind is unbounded, as we have seen (*cf* [41] above), the use of the variable X in position 3 is unavoidable; it is impossible actually to specify what might intervene between the two related items. Similarly in the case of positions 1 and 5, it is impossible

actually to list what might precede and follow the items affected
by the rule. Let us suppose, then, that sentence [45] has the deep
structure [55], and that this may be analysed according to the
structural description of *wh*-movement, as indicated.

[55]

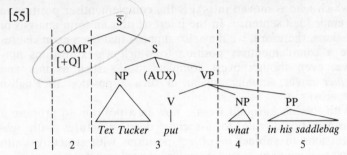

The structure proposed here differs from that in [47] in that we
are now supposing that each sentence is introduced by the node
COMP(lementiser) whether or not an overt complementiser is
present. It is further supposed that COMP and S together form
a constituent $\bar{S}$ (read 'S bar').

We must now specify the relevant structural change.

[56] *Wh-movement* SC: $1 - 4+2 - 3 - \emptyset - 5$ (OPT.)

This tells us that optionally (OPT.) we may move item 4 from
its original position, leaving behind nothing ($\emptyset$), and adjoin it to
the left of item 2, as in [57].

[57]

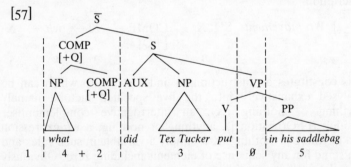

This differs from the surface structure proposed in [48] not only
by the addition of $\bar{S}$ and COMP, but also in the manner in which
the displaced *wh*-NP is adjoined to the tree. For various technical
reasons which are not of great importance in the present context,
it is now generally assumed that adjunction of an item X to the

left or right of an item Y involves the introduction of a 'copy' of Y above the pair in question, so that these then form a constituent of the same type as the constituent to which the moved item has been adjoined. So here a moved NP is adjoined to COMP and a new node COMP dominates the two adjoined elements. The question of the insertion of the auxiliary *do* and its inversion with the subject will not be dealt with here.

Now that the details of the formalism have been dealt with, it remains to examine the benefits. Given a deep structure [55] for sentence [45], a single subcategorisation frame can now be adopted for *put* on the assumption that lexical insertion takes place at deep structure, namely that in [31], repeated here as [58].

[58] *put*: V, +[————NP PP]

This means that *put* will only ever be inserted before a direct object and a prepositional phrase. Whatever happens to the NP subsequently, it will always be associated with a deep structure position identified as that of a direct object. Thus the setting up of deep structure allows the more complex versions of the relationship between a verb and its direct object, which arise when the object is interrogative, to be reduced to the simple case, as expressed in [31]/[58]. The fact that *what* is interpreted as the direct object of *put* in [45] follows from the fact that *what* is the direct object of *put* in the deep structure of that sentence. The setting up of the transformational rule of *wh*-movement confers the additional benefit that there will never be more, or less, than one gap associated with a displaced *wh*-phrase in surface structure. All the problems that arose in a purely phrase structure framework therefore disappear when a distinction is drawn between deep and surface structure and transformational rules are set up to link them.

We have only examined one particular problem in detail, that of expressing basic subcategorisation facts efficiently, but several other potential problems are readily resolved within the transformational approach. Wherever there is a basically 'local' relationship that also has 'long distance' analogues, deep structure and transformations will always allow the long distance dependency to be reduced to the simple case. For example, finite verbs agree with their subjects in person and number, and the subjects of finite verbs, at least when pronominal, must have nominative case. Consider [59] and [60].

[59i] *The Russians are coming.*

[59ii] *The Russians is coming.
[60i]   They are coming.
[60ii] *Them are coming.

In these sentences the subject–verb relationship is local in the
sense that the items affected are adjacent. Obviously there are
sentences in which subjects are displaced, as when they are interrogative. Without deep structure and transformations it is not
easy to see how the requirements of agreement and case-marking
are to be enforced in such cases, because two quite discrete
phrase structure rules will be involved in introducing the two
inter-dependent items, and, as we have seen, there is no obvious
way in which choices made in one rule can be linked with choices
made in another. For example, what is to prevent the choice of
accusative case for the wh-pronoun in [61], or the choice of plural
number for the wh-NP in [62]?

[61]   *Whom did you say set this preposterous examination
       paper?
[62]   *Which examiners did you say sets the essay paper?

Within the phrase structure framework outlined earlier there is,
of course, nothing to prevent these 'sentences' from being
generated. But if we assume a level of deep structure, the wh-
phrases will there be subject NPs adjacent to the finite VPs
headed by the verbs set and sets, and whatever mechanism
enforces agreement and case marking in the simple case will also
operate here. Then whatever happens to these subject NPs
subsequently they will always have the right case and number,
thereby excluding [61] and [62]. Every argument that was ever
advanced in the standard-theory literature for introducing deep
structures and some transformational rule such as wh-movement
ultimately reduces to the claim that the formalism solves the
problem of enforcing a complex or 'long distance' dependency by
reducing it to a simple or 'local' one, thereby allowing the rules
stating the nature of the dependency to operate on adjacent items
in every case.

Let us now examine the notion of deep structure with a little
more care. The arguments for having it have so far all been
essentially syntactic; in other words, deep structures have been
set up as an answer to the question of how we can most efficiently state the rules of subcategorisation, case-marking,
subject–verb agreement, and so on. At this level inter-dependent
items (a lexical head and its complements, a subject NP and a
finite VP, etc.) are adjacent and form a constituent. This local-

ness of relationships at deep structure not only guarantees that deep structures can always be generated by phrase structure rules and that straightforward subcategorisation features can always be devised to guarantee correct lexical insertion, but also that maximally simple mechanisms can be established to handle any kind of syntactic dependency between items. It is important, however, to note that deep structures have intimate semantic connections. Indeed, if diagram [1] at the very beginning of this chapter is examined, it will be seen that in the standard theory deep structure representations are the sole input to the semantic component. It is assumed, in other words, that all the syntactic and lexical information relevant to semantic interpretation is contained at that level. From one point of view, in fact, deep structures might well be regarded as syntactic representations of lexical **predicate–argument structure**. To illustrate and explain this, consider the case of a pair of sentences such as [63] and [64].

[63] *The actress kisses the bishop.*
[64] *The bishop is kissed by the actress.*

Obviously the first is active and the second passive. However, from a semantic point of view, they both describe the same event, albeit with a shift of focus or emphasis. In other words, it would be impossible to conceive of a situation that was truly described by the first but not the second or *vice versa*. The situation described involves two participants, an agent and a patient. In other words 'kissing' is an activity that requires an agent and a patient if it is to be properly performed. To cast this into the usual jargon, the semantic predicate KISS (denoted by the English word *kiss*) is a two-place predicate, a predicate that must be accompanied by two arguments before a proposition is expressed. Let us say, then, that the sentences [63] and [64] both express the same proposition, [65],

[65] a KISS b

where *a* is the individual referred to by the words *the actress* and *b* is the individual referred to by the words *the bishop*. The logical subject (agent) is distinguished from the logical object (patient) by position. Notice that sentence [63] is structurally very closely related to the representation of its predicate–argument structure [65]. In particular the grammatical subject of [63] corresponds to the logical subject of [65] and the grammatical object of [63] corresponds to the logical object of [65]. Sentence [64] by contrast is rather indirectly related in terms of its structure to [65]. Its grammatical subject corresponds to the logical object of [65], and the logical subject of [65] corresponds to the noun phrase governed by the preposition *by* in [64]. It is interesting that purely syntactic arguments can be constructed which lead to the setting up of deep structures for [63] and [64] that reflect more or less directly the relationships expressed in [65]. In other words it is possible to regard deep structures as representations of predicate–argument structure, in the sense that whatever is a grammatical subject in deep structure will always be a logical subject in predicate–argument structure, and whatever is a grammatical object in deep structure will always be a logical object in predicate–argument structure. The grammatical functions of elements at deep structure will always be directly related to issues of semantic interpretation, therefore.

Let us now consider just one argument for setting up a passive transformation, and see what sort of deep structures this leads us to propose for passive surface structures. (I shall assume without argument that active sentences such as [63] have deep structures which reflect the linear and configurational properties of their surface structures.) Consider, first of all, sentence [66].

[66] *MI5 kept close tabs on the Soviet delegation.*

It is clear that the only things one can do with *tabs* is to *keep* them *on* someone; in other words we are here dealing with an idiomatic phrase, and it will be necessary to make it clear in the lexicon that *tabs* must co-occur with *keep* and *on*. This is most conveniently done by means of a subcategorisation feature for the verb *keep* which adds the necessary specific detail to the 'regular' subcategorisation feature.

[67] *keep*: V, +[————NP PP]
            + [————[$_{NP}$ [$_N$ *tabs*]] [$_{PP}$ *on* [$_{NP}$]]]

Thus the idiomatic phrase may be seen as a particular instantiation of the complement structure of *keep*; it has to be listed separately because unlike *keep bikes in (the shed)*, for example, it has a meaning which is not simply 'the sum of its parts'. Once again it is most convenient that the elements of the idiom appear in [67] as adjacent items; this is the simplest possible case of the relationship that binds them. There are, however, cases of sentences where a part (or 'chunk' to use the customary jargon) of the idiom is detached.

[68] *Close tabs, as far as I am aware, were kept on the Soviet delegation by MI5.*

Clearly the presence of *tabs* in [68] is as much dependent upon the presence of *kept* as it is in [66]. Once again, then, we are dealing with a more complex, 'long distance', version of a local dependency, namely that specified in [67] and illustrated in [66]. One obvious way in which this essential unity can be captured is to postulate a deep structure for [68] in which *tabs* relates to *keep* in exactly the same way as it does in the deep structure of [66]. Consider [69] (deep structure for [68]) and [70] (deep structure for [66]).

[69]

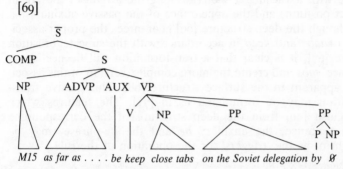

M15   as far as . . . . be keep   close tabs   on the Soviet delegation by Ø

Details of the mechanisms enforcing subject–verb agreement, past tense marking, past participle marking, etc., will be provided only where relevant. At deep structure verbs henceforth appear in their 'basic' forms.

[70]

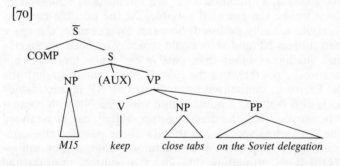

M15   keep   close tabs   on the Soviet delegation

What has been argued for, then, is a deep structure for passive sentences in which the surface grammatical subject appears in direct object (*ie* post-verbal) position. Notice that this deep structure grammatical object is also the logical object or patient. In early versions of transformational grammar, including the standard theory, it was also argued that the NP governed by *by* in surface structure should appear in subject position in deep structure, so that active and passive sentences shared deep structure representations in which the grammatical subject was also the logical subject (usually the agent). The details of the arguments for and against various possible positions are of some interest, but need not detain us here. It is now generally assumed that the 'agent phrase' appears in exactly the same position in deep structure as in surface structure, as we shall see (2.2.4, especially the discussion of example [147]); but for the present the older view will be adopted. The only significant differences between [69] and [70], then, are the presence in the former of a prepositional phrase with a vacant NP slot (awaiting the arrival of the NP in subject position) and the appearance of the passive auxiliary *be*.

Although the deep structure [69] guarantees the proper association of *tabs* and *keep* in accordance with the subcategorisation feature [67], it is clear that a transformation will be needed to 'displace' *tabs* and create the more complex version of this association apparent in the surface structure [68]. This passive transformation may be formulated as in [71]. The features which distinguish [69] from the deep structure of the corresponding active sentence, the auxiliary *be* and the *by*-phrase, may be thought of as the 'triggers' for the operation of the rule.

[71] *Passive* SD: X – NP – . . . – *be* – V – NP – . . . – *by* – np – X
              1   2   3   4   5   6   7   8   9   10 ⇒(OBLIG.)
         SC: 1   6   3   4   5   ∅   7   8   2   10
                               [+PAS]

Factors 3 and 7, symbolised . . ., are intended as **abbreviatory variables**; unlike the essential variables X, the possible contents of . . . could actually be listed. So here, for example, the space between subject NP and verb would typically be filled by adverbials and auxiliaries other than passive *be*. Since these are not relevant to the operation of the rule, it is convenient to omit the details. Factor 9, symbolised np, indicates an NP position which has no lexical content, a position into which an NP with content might be moved. [69], the deep structure of [68], can be analysed into the ten factors specified in the SD of the passive transformation, as in [72] opposite. The structural change is then obligatory (OBLIG.), promoting the object to subject position and demoting the subject into the vacant np slot (see [73]).

It will be useful at this point to summarise what has been said so far about the role of deep structures and transformations. Deep structures are quite simply representations of the syntactic structure of sentences at which all relationships between items are presented in the simplest possible configurational format; *ie* all dependent items are adjacent to the items that condition their appearance, and form constituents with those items. This ensures

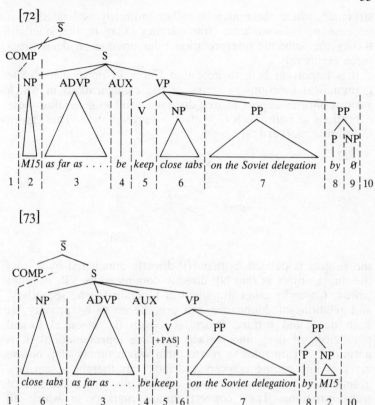

that deep structures are always generable by phrase structure rules, which define the contents of single constituents, and that lexical insertion can always take place with reference to strictly local contexts. Putting the matter slightly differently, deep structures are representations of sentence structure which abstract away from the 'long distance' dependencies of some surface structures, thereby allowing for the formal expression of the identity of these complex dependencies with the dependency of the simple case. From another point of view, however, deep structures can be thought of as representations of the predicate–argument structures of the propositions that sentences express, because there is always a one-to-one relationship of grammatical and logical functions at this level, unlike at surface structure, where these may be rather indirectly associated. It is because of this semantic 'transparency' that in the standard theory the semantic interpretation rules operate on deep structures exclusively.

It is important here to note that Chomsky decided to define grammatical functions in terms of the **configurations** in which various phrases appear in tree diagrams, and to generalise these definitions to both levels of syntactic representation. Thus, given the phrase marker [74],

[74]

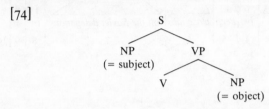

the subject is defined as that NP directly dominated by S, and the direct object as that NP directly dominated by VP. In other words, Chomsky takes grammatical functions to be secondary, and relations of dominance and precedence to be primary, at both deep and surface structure. Given the essential formal parallelism of deep and surface structure representations, it is natural to set up rules to relate them which simply map phrase markers into phrase markers and indirectly thereby assign new grammatical functions to moved constituents; this is the role of transformations. They convert phrase markers in which all dependencies between items are of the 'simple' kind into phrase markers where some at least of these dependencies may be 'complex' in the sense that the items involved in some relationship need not be adjacent to one another or form a constituent together.

This state of affairs is perhaps natural in a theory which stresses the centrality of syntax and in which the structure and potential of other components is relatively unknown. But it must be emphasised that none of the arguments adduced in favour of setting up deep structures and associated transformations is demonstrative. What has been highlighted is a set of problems that arise in the context of simple phrase structure description, to which deep structure and transformations are simply one possible solution. The same results could in principle be obtained in other ways, and, once other components of the grammar are more fully elaborated, it might turn out to be preferable to deal with certain types of phenomena, previously handled transformationally, in other ways. It might even turn out to be the case that the deficiencies of phrase structure description can be overcome by refining the theory of phrase structure, rather than supplementing it, as Chomsky proposed. Much of the development of generative grammar in the 1970s and 1980s has been concerned with the exploration of alternative means of tackling the types of problem outlined in this chapter. Some of these alternatives are examined in Chapters 3 and 4. In the remainder of this Chapter I shall deal with more recent developments in Chomsky's own approach and the motivation behind them. In many ways alternative approaches such as Lexical-Fuctional Grammar and Generalised Phrase Structure Grammar may be viewed as exploiting to the full descriptive apparatus first introduced within the Chomskyan framework as refinements of, and modifications to, the standard theory, so some discussion of these will be a useful preliminary to the chapters that follow.

2.2 Problems with the standard theory and the development of the extended standard theory

2.2.1 More on transformations

There is no doubt that the emphasis in early work in transformational syntax was placed on the attempt to show that the framework was compatible with the requirements of descriptive adequacy. In particular, great efforts were made to devise rules which made explicit the sentential relationships that native speakers of the language under investigation were assumed to 'know'. From the earliest work the task of expressing such relationships fell to transformations. Thus the transformations examined in the previous section, *wh*-movement and passive, might be viewed, in conjunction with the deep structures that they operate on, as devices for expressing the relationship between declarative and interrogative sentences (those not of the yes-no type) and active and passive sentences respectively.

As research progressed, a vast inventory of transformations was accumulated, one for each construction-type that could plausibly be derived from a given deep structure format. In time it became increasingly apparent that these transformations exhibited a wide variety of forms and functions and that very disparate phenomena were all being treated as examples of transformational relationships. The problem, then, was that in the drive to achieve comprehensive coverage of phenomena by means of exploiting the available technical apparatus to the full, the issue of explanatory adequacy had been overlooked. As we have seen,

a theory that is explanatorily adequate has to be a restrictive
theory, a theory that limits the range of technical apparatus to
the minimum compatible with adequate description of the data
(*cf* 1.5). By the late 1960s it was clear that transformations could
be devised to express almost any relationship, and could be given
almost any formal properties that the linguists who devised them
thought necessary for the facts in question to be properly
described. Clearly the time had come for serious developmental
work on the general theory associated with transformational
grammar. What was required was a clear idea of what constituted
a transformational relationship. Phenomena which did not fall
within this properly-defined domain would then have to be
handled by alternative mechanisms elsewhere. And within the
domain of transformational relationships as newly defined, it
would clearly be necessary to try to devise the most general possible set of principles to characterise form and function. Obviously
the boundary between transformational relationships and other
kinds of relationship would be drawn in part on the basis of the
results of this attempt and partly on the basis of work on the
properties of other components, and there would be scope for
progressive readjustments in the light of new developments. In
this section some of the revisions and modifications of the 1970s
will be considered.

2.2.2 X̄-theory and the lexicon
In his paper 'Remarks on nominalization' (1970) Chomsky highlighted a number of problems that arise in attempting to establish
a transformational relationship between sentences of the form
[75] and NPs of the form [76].

[75] *Bresnan criticised Chomsky.*
[76] *Bresnan's criticism of Chomsky*

While it is evidently the case that the same 'logical' relationships
are involved in both, with *Bresnan* interpreted as logical subject
(agent) and *Chomsky* as logical object (patient), it is difficult to
see how a common deep structure could be satisfactorily established. Suppose we take the sentential form of [75] to be basic,
so that the deep structure contains the verb *criticise*. The transformation of 'nominalisation' will then not only have to convert
the verb into something noun-like, it will also have to convert any
adverbial modifiers of the verb (*eg vehemently (criticised)*) into
adjectives (*vehement (criticism)*), make the subject genitive in
form and insert a preposition before the object. This raises a
number of difficulties. In the first place the resultant noun has

potential properties that cannot be plausibly derived from the deep structure proposed. For example, *criticism* can be pluralised and quantified (*Bresnan's three criticisms*), yet the corresponding verb must agree with the singular subject (*Bresnan*) and clearly cannot be associated with a quantifier directly (**Bresnan three criticised Chomsky*). Secondly, neither the form of the nominalisation nor the choice of accompanying preposition is predictable from the form of the associated verb, as the following pairs make clear.

[77i]   *Bertie married Bunty*
[77ii] *Bertie's marriage to Bunty*
[78i]   *Gazdar proposes transformationless grammar*
[78ii] *Gazdar's proposal for transformationless grammar*

It is difficult to see how any general formulation of the relevant rule is possible if there is no regular pattern of word-formation and different prepositions have to be inserted in different cases. Thirdly, there seem to be many cases of nouns that have the appearance of being nominalisations but which have no corresponding verbs, and of verbs that have no corresponding nominalisations.

[79i]   *Dingbat's ignorance of the facts*
[79ii] *Thatcher's contempt for the opposition*
[80i]   *Dingbat ignored the facts*
[80ii] *Thatcher despises the opposition*

The nouns in [79] have no obvious deep structure verbal source, and the verbs in [80] cannot be nominalised because there are no associated nominals. Notice that we cannot plausibly regard *ignorance* as the nominalisation of *ignore* since, despite the formal relationship, their meanings are quite different. Thus [79i] states that *Dingbat* did not know the facts, while [80i] informs us that he did know the facts but chose to disregard them! Since it is assumed in the standard theory that deep structures provide all the syntactic and lexical information necessary for semantic interpretation, it is clear that transformations cannot be allowed to change meaning. Otherwise, the meaning change, not being reflected at deep structure, would go unrecorded. Hence we cannot derive *ignorance* from *ignore* by transformation. But notice that even where there are close formal and semantic correspondences, as in [75] and [76], or in the pairs in [77] and [78], it is usually the case that there are unexpected semantic properties associated with the nominal. For example, a *criticism* could as easily be a physical object as a form of judgement.

[81] *Chomsky's criticism of Israeli policy was burned by the Zionists.*

It is not clear how an example such as this can be satisfactorily related to a deep structure sentence containing the verb *criticise*.

Consider now by way of contrast the examples in [82] and [83].

[82i] *Chomsky criticised Israeli policy.*
[82ii] *Chomsky's criticising Israeli policy*
[83i] *Benn despises Thatcherism.*
[83ii] *Benn's despising Thatcherism*

Once again we are dealing with sentences and related nominal-isations. But here the relationship is much more regular and predictable. Thus the form of the nominal is always the same, and there are no prepositions to be added. Furthermore, there are no accidental 'gaps' in the verb–noun relationship; there is always a corresponding nominal in *-ing* and there are no *-ing* forms that lack corresponding verbs. Finally, the semantic relationship between verb and nominal is always regular; there are no unexpected idiosyncracies. Notice also that an adverbial modifier of the verb in the sentence can remain when the sentence is nominalised (*vehemently criticised/vehemently criticising*).

Chomsky called the first type of nominal (as in [76]/[77ii]/[78ii] etc.) **derived** and the second (as in [82ii] and [83ii]) **gerundive**, and concluded that only gerundive nominals were plausibly regarded as sentence transforms, because of their productive, regular and predictable relationship with sentences. The essence of a transformational relationship, then, is that it should operate regularly on a given type of structure and should not be subject to restrictions that depend upon the choice of lexical material in any given case. It is clear that derived nominals could only be handled transformationally at the cost of introducing highly complex exception mechanisms that depend precisely upon the accidental choice of vocabulary.

This, of course, is not to deny that there is a relationship of some sort between verbs and their derived nominals. The question is where this relationship should be expressed if not in the syntactic component by means of a transformation. Suppose that derived nominals are 'derived' from verbs not by syntactic trans-formation but by an assortment of rules of derivational morphology (or word-formation). These are typically only *partially* productive, and are perhaps best regarded as rules for the analysis of existing forms, which may occasionally be put to use to create new words on old models. For example, in [84],

$$[84i] \begin{bmatrix} \begin{bmatrix} \text{appraise} \\ \text{construe} \\ \text{deny} \\ \vdots \\ \vdots \end{bmatrix}_{N \, V} + \text{al} \end{bmatrix} \quad [84ii] \begin{bmatrix} \begin{bmatrix} \text{abandon} \\ \text{consign} \\ \text{fit} \\ \vdots \\ \vdots \end{bmatrix}_{N \, V} + \text{ment} \end{bmatrix}$$

each example is to be interpreted as saying that nouns can be derived from verbs by the addition of a particular suffix; in general one simply has to learn, as a matter of experience, which suffix to use with a given verb. The nouns so analysed can then be listed in the lexicon alongside their associated verbs. Any noun that has the general appearance of a derived nominal but happens not to have an associated verb would, of course, simply be listed in isolation.

We can now devise a mechanism for expressing the relationship between verbs and derived nominals in terms of their lexical entries. The problem of accidental gaps in the noun–verb relationship now disappears since the relationship will only hold between listed pairs; if only one member of a 'logically possible' pair actually exists, there can be no relationship by definition. The usual mechanism for expressing relationships in the lexicon is a **lexical redundancy rule**, a rule which spells out once and for all information about a particular class of lexical items that is predictable from the properties of some other class. This avoids the need for the information in question to be repeated over and over again in the individual entries for members of the second class. In the case of verbs and their derived nominals we might propose something along the following lines.

$$[85] \quad V, + [\text{---NP}] \rightarrow [_N \, [\text{V-stem}] + \text{suffix}], + [\text{---NP}]$$

Informally, this is to be interpreted as saying that for any pair of items listed in the lexicon such that the first is a verb taking a direct object complement and the second is a noun derived from the verb by the addition of a suffix, it is predictable that the derived nominal will also take a 'direct object' NP. The majority of derived nominals will therefore lack a subcategorisation feature in their individual entries, because the relevant information is supplied by the redundancy rule. Any unpredictable information will, of course, be provided entry by entry.

It is clear, however, that [85], as it stands, is not quite adequate to the task. It provides the information that the transformational analysis of derived nominals provided, namely that derived nominals take complements that are interpreted as 'logical' objects, but it fails to say anything about the surface form of these complements, which, as we have seen, are prepositional phrases. It is possible to have a generalised notion of direct object, expressed in terms of deep structure relationships of dominance and precedence, only if some mechanism is provided to map the rather abstract deep structures involved into appropriate surface structures. We might, then, set up a minor transformation to insert the preposition *of*, since this is the most usual preposition in the complement of derived nominals.

[86] *of-insertion*   SD: X –   N –   NP –   X
                            1   2   3   4   ⇒(OBLIG.)
                      SC: 1   2   *of*+3   4

This transformation simply adjoins *of* to the left of the 'direct object' NP when this is the direct object of a noun; it therefore converts a string such as *criticism Chomsky* into *criticism of Chomsky*. But this procedure in turn is not without its difficulties. First, it requires us to regard *of Chomsky*, for example, as a kind of complex NP, since adjunction does not change category labels but involves simply the creation of a new category of the same type as that to which the specified item is adjoined (see [56] and [57] above, together with the associated discussion). Clearly it would be difficult to put any principled limit on the power of transformations if we allowed them to convert NPs into PPs or insert new categories into phrase markers at random. Obviously we can stipulate what a given rule can do, but as we shall see below in the discussion of explanatory adequacy, it is highly desirable that unmotivated and *ad hoc* stipulations be avoided. The simplest way to avoid this particular problem is to forbid 'structure building' by transformations other than that involved in the adjunction process. But this leaves us with the problem that what is obviously a prepositional phrase is categorised as a noun phrase. Secondly, we still have no answer to the problem of *unpredictable* preposition choice with certain derived nominals. Clearly where the preposition is not *of*, it will have to be given in the individual entry for a given derived nominal. Thus *marriage* would have a subcategorisation feature specifying the co-occurrence of *to*-NP, *proposal* or *contempt* would be listed as requiring *for*-NP, and so on. Now if these collocations are regarded as deep structure prepositional phrases, we instantly lose the obvious parallelism between these and the cases involving *of*; the NPs in question are 'logical objects' whatever the choice of preposition. Thus the relationship between *criticise x* and *criticism of x* is parallel to that between *propose x* and *proposal for x*, in that *x* in each case has the patient role associated with the deep structure object position. If, on the other hand, we treat these collocations as simple NPs in deep structure in order to reflect this parallelism, we once again end up with a host of *ad hoc* preposition–insertion transformations, with no real basis for predicting which rule will apply in any given case. It is clear in fact that the choice of preposition is a property of the individual derived nominal and as such should be listed in the lexicon as something not predictable from the structures in which the nominal appears. Suppose, then, that we treat the collocations in question as complex NPs, parallel in form to those produced by the adjunction of *of*. This immediately undercuts the motivation for the transformation of *of*-insertion. If other prepositions are to appear in lexical entries of individual derived nominals, there is no reason why *of* should not appear in the lexical redundancy rule [85]. But, as we have seen, to treat strings of preposition plus noun phrase as complex noun phrases is syntactically suspect, and in any case the parallelism between verbs and their direct objects and nouns and their direct objects is now very contrived; the NP following V is simple while that following N is complex, and of dubious status.

The real problem here is the fundamental assumption that 'logical' relations can be equated with deep structure grammatical relations defined in terms of the configuration of categories. Thus a deep structure direct object is defined as an NP that is a right sister of V or N in a phrase marker, and such a direct object is taken also to be the 'logical' object to which some semantic role is attached. Unfortunately, as we have seen, an adequate syntactic description does not seem to be compatible with this equation. What is required is a notion of 'logical' object that is distinct from the configurationally defined grammatical relation of direct object. This would allow for the possibility, which is a very real one, that the same 'logical' function might be performed by NPs in different types of configuration. Such a separation naturally has consequences for the notion of deep structure. In Chapter 4, which deals with the development of Lexical-Functional Grammar, these consequences will be examined in detail. Within the context of Chomskyan transformational grammar the problems which have been outlined here have never been satisfactorily resolved. Nevertheless, a number of important developments have followed on from Chomsky's discussion of nominalisations, and it will be useful to examine these briefly here.

First and foremost, the principle was established that transformations do not do derivational morphology, and so cannot change category labels. This represents the first significant reduction in the scope of transformations. Secondly, the realisation that there are types of relationship which are not satisfactorily handled by transformation, and the setting up of an alternative lexical mechanism for handling those relationships, opens up the way for a serious debate as to where the boundary falls between syntax and lexicon. As we shall see, many transformations can be reformulated as lexical redundancy rules, and much of the motivation for deep structure can be undercut, given a slightly more sophisticated version of what a lexical entry should be. Whether such reformulation is desirable is a different and more difficult question, which will also be taken up in later chapters, particularly 4 and 5. Thirdly, the need for a formalism that allows for the expression of cross-category generalisation was highlighted. This is a complex matter that merits careful study. The conclusion that derived nominals are not sentence transforms but deep structure NPs has led us to a position in which notions such as 'subject of' and 'direct object of' have to definable across S and NP. Since Chomsky's definitions of these grammatical relations are configurational, it follows that S and NP will have to be assigned similar 'geometric' properties. And if S and NP both have subject and direct object positions, it should come as no surprise that a rule such as passive may apply in both domains.

[87i]   *Mad Max destroyed the software.*
        The software was destroyed by Mad Max.
[87ii] *Mad Max's destruction of the software.*
        The software's destruction by Mad Max.

What is required, in view of all of this, is a general theory of phrase structure which imposes some degree of uniformity upon the possible configurations of categories, together with a theory of the internal make-up of categories that allows us to predict that a rule will apply in two or more domains because the categories in question have certain characteristics in common. The theory of $\bar{X}$ (read 'X bar') syntax, which is usually thought of as incorporating a theory of syntactic features, has been developed in response to these needs. Unfortunately, different versions of $\bar{X}$-theory have proliferated, together with different feature systems. These are not mutually compatible, and generally have been proposed *ad hoc* (Jackendoff (1977) is an honourable exception) in response to a specific set of problems in the analysis of a particular language. Rather than trying to sort out the merits and demerits of the various proposals, it will be more useful at this stage simply to outline the general *intention* behind them and ignore the details.

The central core of $\overline{X}$-theory is the recognition of the fact that (most) phrasal constituents have 'heads' upon which the other elements of the constituents in question are dependent. Let us then use the cover symbol X to represent the set of lexical categories that can be heads of phrases (*Viz* V(erb), N(oun), ADJ(ective), P(reposition), ADV(erb)). It is clear that these categories may be subcategorised according to whether or not they take a complement and, if so, what kind. Items which are involved in the subcategorisation of lexical heads are almost always interpreted as semantic 'arguments' of the predicates that the lexical heads in question denote. Thus in the sentence in [88]

[88] *Paddington put the cash in the building society on Tuesday.*

or the noun phrase in [89]

[89] *The queen of Ruretania from Birmingham*

it is clear that certain elements are more closely bound to the head than others. In [88] for example, *the cash* and *in the building society* provide information without which the sentence would not be complete or properly interpretable, while *on Tuesday* is a strictly optional adjunct. Similarly in [89], *of Ruretania* is intimately bound up with *queen* (one has to rule, or be ruler of, some territory) while the fact that the queen comes *from Birmingham* is incidental. It is generally assumed that items which are involved in subcategorisation, and which are in most cases interpreted as arguments of the head, appear with the head X in a phrasal category $\overline{X}$, as in [90].

[90]

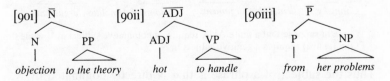

[90i] $\overline{N}$ — N, PP — objection, to the theory
[90ii] $\overline{ADJ}$ — ADJ, VP — hot, to handle
[90iii] $\overline{P}$ — P, NP — from, her problems

For the moment, the complements to N, ADJ and P are given in the old notation; once the exposition of $\overline{X}$-theory is complete, further examples will employ $\overline{X}$ notation consistently.

$\overline{X}$ is called a phrasal 'projection' of X, in this case the smallest constituent containing X as a sub-constituent.

It is equally clear that a given $\overline{X}$ may be further specified. Take the examples in [91].

[91i]   *this – objection to the theory*   ($\overline{\overline{N}}$)
[91ii] *too – hot to handle*   ($\overline{\overline{ADJ}}$)
[91iii] *away – from her problems*   ($\overline{\overline{P}}$)

Let us use the name 'specifier' as a general label for the categories that perform this function, and assume that the specifier together with the $\overline{X}$ that it specifies form a higher phrasal projection of X, namely $\overline{\overline{X}}$, (read 'X double bar'). What we now have is a general *schema* of phrase structure; whatever the value of X, it will always appear in the same basic configurational pattern.

[92]

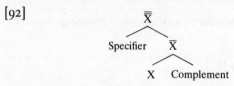

Both 'Specifier' and 'Complement' are to be understood as abbreviations for sets of syntactic categories.

Although this is not a position that Chomsky himself now espouses, one could take the view that V is the head of S, and interpret S as $\overline{\overline{V}}$. If we take NP to be $\overline{\overline{N}}$, the structural parallelism in [93] is obvious, and we have a clear configurational basis for providing a definition of subject and direct object that generalises across the two categories.

[93]

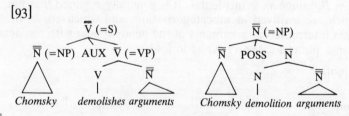

We might suppose that a finite AUX requires a nominative subject in $\overline{\overline{V}}$ while POSS (essive) requires a genitive subject in $\overline{\overline{N}}$.

Thus the subject of a phrase is that $\overline{\overline{N}}$ directly dominated by $\overline{\overline{X}}$, and the direct object of a phrase is that $\overline{\overline{N}}$ directly dominated by $\overline{X}$. (Notice that the phrase markers in [93] are deep structure phrase markers, and it is being assumed that some satisfactory

solution can be found to the preposition insertion problem in
NPs.) The exact number of bar levels that must be supposed is
itself a matter of controversy, as indeed is the issue of whether
the same number of phrasal projections are required for each
lexical category. The majority of linguists have adopted a
uniform system, and most suppose that either two or three levels
are sufficient, but the issues are very complex and technical and
will not be pursued further here.

The largest constituent that has to be set up to account for the
distribution of the dependents of a lexical category is referred to
as a **maximal projection** of that category. In the preceding
discussion it has been assumed that $\bar{\bar{N}}$, $\overline{\overline{ADJ}}$, $\bar{\bar{P}}$, etc. are maximal
projections equivalent to NP, ADJP, PP, etc. If it is thought
desirable to avoid commitment on the question of the number
of bar levels, one can refer to the maximal projection of X as
X^{max}. All complements and most specifiers (apart perhaps from
DET and COMP, though see 5.1, especially the discussion of
[2] & [3]) in fact turn out to be maximal projections in languages
such as English which rely on phrase structure configurations to
signal syntactic relationships (see 4.6 for further discussion).

Turning now to the feature system, the essential idea is that
syntactic categories should be thought of not as atomic objects,
but as objects with internal structure. Thus the conventional
labels such as N, V, $\overline{\overline{ADJ}}$, $\bar{\bar{P}}$, etc. are to be thought of as nothing
more than a convenient shorthand for what are properly bundles
of defining syntactic features. Categories will be more or less
alike according as they have more or fewer features in common,
and rules will be expected to generalise across categories which
share a reasonable number of features. The advantage of this
approach is that the rules themselves can be framed by reference
to the common core of features shared by the categories jointly
affected rather than to a disjunction of these categories viewed
atomically, a formalism that fails to explain why these categories
should be jointly affected by the rules in question.

Once again, unfortunately, there is no orthodoxy that can be
followed here. Much depends on which generalisations a
particular linguist is concerned to express, and different linguists
have different priorities. In a theory which expresses transformational relationships in the form which we have been considering
so far, namely a structural description plus a structural change,
it is clearly desirable that S and NP should be characterised by
feature sets which overlap sufficiently to account for the fact that
the passive transformation applies in both domains. Suppose,
then, that we take S to be $\bar{\bar{V}}$ and NP to be $\bar{\bar{N}}$, and adopt the

proposal that rules which generalise across categories always apply to categories of the same bar level. It remains to decide what the feature composition of V and N should be; these same features will then be projected to higher bar levels. Modifying Jackendoff's (1977) proposals, in some respects quite considerably, a feature system of the following type would give the desired results.

[94]

	Subj	Det	Obj
V	+	−	+
P	−	+	+
N	+	+	+
ADJ	−	+	−

Thus $\bar{\bar{V}}$, for example, is to be interpreted as

$$[95] \begin{bmatrix} + \text{Subj} \\ - \text{Det} \\ + \text{Obj} \end{bmatrix}$$

The features are largely self-explanatory. Thus [+Subj] identifies categories that have a subject, namely V and N. [+Det] picks out a set of categories, excluding V, which allow for a 'determining' element in the specifier slot of their maximal projection; so $\bar{P}$ permits adverbs (*away/down from London*), $\bar{N}$ determiners, demonstratives, etc. (*the/this/that problem*), and $\overline{\text{ADJ}}$ a range of degree modifiers (*so/too/as expensive*), while $\bar{\bar{V}}$ allows only subject $\bar{N}$. [+Obj] is a feature of those categories which may take a simple N complement (direct object), namely V, P and N. Notice that once again it is here assumed that nouns *can* take simple direct object complements, at least in deep structure, and that a satisfactory solution can be found to the preposition insertion problem discussed above. We can now frame the passive rule so that it refers to the features shared by V and N, [+Subj] and [+Obj].

[96] *Passive* SD: $X - \bar{\bar{N}} - \ldots - \begin{bmatrix} +\text{Subj} \\ +\text{Obj} \end{bmatrix} - \bar{\bar{N}} - \ldots - by - \bar{\bar{n}} - X \quad \Rightarrow \text{(OBLIG.)}$

SC:
1 – 5 – 3 – 4 – ø – 6 – 7 – 2 – 9

(SD indices: 1 2 3 4 5 6 7 8 9)

Certain changes *vis-à-vis* the formulation of this rule in [71] follow from the wider scope. In particular, we can no longer refer to the presence of *be*, since this is peculiar to the case where a verb is involved, and we can no longer stipulate that a feature [+PAS] be added, since passive morphology is peculiar to the operation of the rule within $\bar{V}$. Thus factors 3 and 4 of [71] have been amalgamated into factor 3 of the new rule, and some alternative mechanism will have to be found to deal with the modification to the verb's morphology.

As we shall see, however, in the more recent versions of transformational grammar there is no room for rules of this general type, with elaborate structural descriptions and structural changes fully specified, (cf 2.2.4). As a consequence there is now no need to have a feature system that allows for 'common ground' between V and N and thus for the formulation of generalised transformations such as that in [96]. The application of passive in the two relevant domains is a consequence of certain general principles that hold independently of the feature system. Chomsky's feature system, therefore, is quite different from that proposed in [94] and this has now been quite widely adopted, at least as a foundation, not only by transformationalists but also by linguists working in alternative frameworks such as Generalised Phrase Structure Grammar, (cf Ch. 3). Chomsky's system defines categories in terms of the features [±V] and [±N], ie in terms of whether they are 'verbal', 'nominal', neither or both.

[97]

	±V	±N
V	+	−
P	−	−
N	−	+
ADJ	+	+

This allows, for example, for the fact that only [−V] maximal projections ($\bar{\bar{N}}$ and $\bar{\bar{P}}$) appear in the focus position of cleft sentences.

[98i] *It is Chomsky that we all admire.*
[98ii] *It is in linguistics that Chomsky made his reputation.*
[98iii] **It is interesting that linguistics is.*
[98iv] **It is to refute the arguments for transformations that Gazdar wants.*

Similarly, only [+N] lexical categories (N and ADJ) have 'nominal' morphology in languages such as Latin, Greek (ancient and modern), French, German etc. Nevertheless, it is probably true to say that interest in the development of the feature system within transformational grammar has waned in recent years as attention has shifted from the problems of descriptive adequacy to those of explanatory adequacy. It is primarily in Generalized Phrase Structure Grammar that serious work in this area continues, and indeed, within this framework, a properly developed feature system is indispensable. A full discussion is provided in the next chapter.

In what follows, however, conventional category labels will continue to be used for the sake of simplicity, unless the point at issue specifically requires the introduction of $\overline{X}$-notation. This avoids the problem of having to take sides in an area where much is still unresolved, and so of having to introduce much extraneous justificatory argumentation.

2.2.3 Transformational rules and semantic information

In the standard theory of transformational grammar it was supposed that all the syntactic information relevant to semantic interpretation was provided at the level of deep structure. It follows at once that transformations cannot be allowed to change meaning; if the surface structure has a different meaning or interpretation from that assigned to the corresponding deep structure, and if the rules of interpretation operate only on deep structures, there will be crucial aspects of the meaning of a sentence that simply go unrecorded.

Unfortunately it is quite clear that there are many cases where perfectly regular transformations *do* change meaning. Take, for example, the following sentences.

[99] *Beavers build dams.*
      Dams are built by beavers.

These examples, taken from Chomsky, are typical of examples involving quantifiers, whether lexically expressed or not. Thus here it is asserted that it is a property of (all) beavers that they build dams, which is true, and that it is a property of (all) dams that beavers build them, which is false. Ordinarily, in cases which do not involve quantification, active–passive pairs describe the same situation and are truth-conditionally equivalent, that is to say, a situation truly described by the active sentence will also be truly described by the passive sentence. Similar problems arise with respect to the interpretation of pronouns. For example, in [100] the pronoun *his* may be interpreted as referring back to *Oedipus* or to some unspecified male.

[100] *Oedipus loves his mother.*

In [101], on the other hands, *his* can only be interpreted as referring to an unspecified male.

[101] *His mother is loved by Oedipus.*

Evidently there is nothing syntactically aberrant about the operation of the passive transformation in cases such as these. The only possible conclusion therefore, is that surface structure does after all have a role to play in semantic interpretation. In particular, the interpretation of the 'scope' of quantifiers and the reference of pronouns is something that cannot be predicted from deep structure positioning of the relevant items. Thus in [99], it is the left-most NP in surface structure that receives the 'wide scope' generic interpretation; and in [100] and [101] it is clear that a pronominal element may be interpreted as co-referential with a surface subject, but that a subject containing a pronominal determiner cannot have its pronominal interpreted as coreferential with some other noun phrase elsewhere in the sentence. The simplest solution, therefore, is to allow transformations to apply when their structural descriptions are met and to drop the requirement that they do not change meaning. What they do not change are the basic semantic roles of the participants in a given action or event; but other aspects of meaning may well be subject to change. Consequently, we have to allow for rules of the semantic component to operate on deep structures, to determine semantic roles, and on surface structures, to determine quantifier scope and pronominal reference.

As we shall see, in more recent work the introduction of so-called 'trace theory' has permitted the reunification of the process of semantic interpretation, but now at the level of surface structure, (*cf* 2.3). For the moment it is sufficient to note that the standard theory position with respect to deep structure and semantic interpretation had to be abandoned, but that examples such as [99] and [100/101] add a little extra force to the thesis of the autonomy of syntax.

If it seems to be correct to remove general semantic conditions on the operation of transformations, it is necessary for the sake of consistency to remove specific semantic conditions also. In the standard theory arguments had been advanced that the distribution of reflexive pronouns should be handled by transformation. On the basis of examples such as those in [102],

[102i] *Jimbo loves himself.*
[102ii] **Jimbo says [that Sue Ellen loves himself].*

it was concluded that reflexives must have an antecedent in their own clause. Furthermore, the reflexive will ordinarily follow its antecedent, as the ungrammatical status of [103] shows.

[103] *Himself loves Jimbo.

The simplest way, it was argued, to guarantee that reflexives appear only in permissible positions was to introduce them by transformation.

[104] Reflexive SD: X – NP$_i$ – . . . – NP$_i$ – X
                      1   2   3   4   5   ⇒(OBLIG.)
                    (Condition: 2 and 4 are clause mates)
              SC: 1   2   3   4   5
                                        ⎡+PRO⎤
                                        ⎣+self⎦

This rule achieves the correct results by stipulating that if two NPs appear in the same clause ('are clause mates'), and the second refers to the same individual as the first, indicated by the ascription of the same 'referential index' (an arbitrary digit noted here by subscript i) to both NPs, then the second must become a reflexive pronoun. Quite apart from the fact that, as things stand, there is nothing to prevent passive applying to the output of this rule to generate ungrammatical strings such as *herself is loved*, this analysis obviously depends crucially not merely on structural information but also on semantic (or perhaps pragmatic) information; the rule only applies when the two NPs involved are co-referential.

   Consider also the case of so-called **equivalent noun phrase deletion**, or **equi**. It was argued that a transformation was the neatest way to handle the 'gap in the paradigm' apparent in [105].

[105] I want Lex Luther to boil an egg.
      " "   you   " "   "   "
      " "   them   " "   "   "
      " "   him   " "   "   "
      " "   Fay Wray   " "   "   "
    * " "   me   " "   "   "

The only NP denoting an entity capable of boiling an egg that cannot appear between *want* and *to* is *me*, and the reason is that this NP is coreferential with the subject of the main verb *I*. Assuming that these sentences have a deep structure of the following form,

[106]

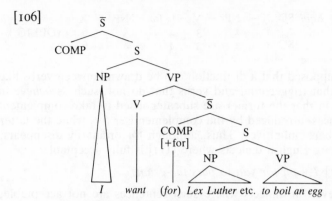

The significance of *for* is explained immediately below.

where *Lex Luther* etc. are subjects of sentences which complement *want*, there are two possibilities. Either we can have a phrase structure rule for S which allows subject NPs to be optional:

[107] S →(NP) VP

or we can allow deep structures in which coreferential NPs appear in the subject position of both the main clause and the subordinate clause, and introduce a transformation to eliminate the second occurrence. In favour of the second option it might be observed that it would be difficult to guarantee that the option permitted in [107] was exercised properly. Nothing, for example, would prevent the omission of the subject in main clauses; and even if we could somehow guarantee that the option of omitting the subject was taken only in subordinate infinitival clauses, it would still be hard to exclude sentences such as [108].

[108] *We all believe to be mad as hatters.

Furthermore, given our observation about reflexives appearing only when an antecedent occurs in the same clause, it is actually convenient to suppose the presence of a subject in the embedded clause, at least in deep structure, in order to account for sentences such as

[109] *Timothy Turtle wants [to teach himself to swim].

If *teach* has a subject NP in deep structure, the reflexivisation rule can apply in the normal fashion on clause mates. Let us then set up a rule to delete the subjects of infinitival complements when these are co-referential with an external NP.

[110] *Equi* SD: X − NP$_i$ − V − [$_{\bar{s}}$ *for*− NP$_i$ − X
        I   2   3   4   5   6 ⇒ (OBLIG.)
     SC: I   2   3   4   ∅   6

It is supposed that a distinction can be drawn between verbs like *want* that trigger equi and verbs that do not, such as *believe* in [108], in that the former are subcategorised to take complement sentences introduced by the complementiser *for*, while the latter take 'bare' infinitives. Thus, although *for* ordinarily disappears, there are English dialects where [111] is fully acceptable.

[111] *I want for you to pass the exam.*

And even in dialects where such sentences are not acceptable, it is usual for the *for* to be retained when adverbials intervene between *want* and the complement sentence.

[112] *I want very much for you to pass the exam.*

By contrast, there are no dialects in which *for* may appear with verbs such as *believe*.

[113] **I believe for them to be seeking promotion.*

The crucial thing about [110], however, is that once again, over and above the syntactic requirements specified, there is the semantic (or pragmatic) requirement that the two NPs involved must be co-referential.

As was observed in 2.2.1, one of the problems with the standard theory was that the conception of transformation was too liberal. In the drive for descriptive adequacy too few constraints were imposed on the form and function of such rules for the resulting grammars to be compatible with the requirements of explanatory adequacy. One obvious way of constraining the transformational component was to eliminate reference to non-syntactic information in the formulation of what were supposed to be syntactic rules, and to handle essentially semantic matters in the semantic component. One of the most important developments in the so-called extended standard theory, therefore, was the disappearance of rules such as reflexive and equi, and the setting up of corresponding interpretative mechanisms. These were designed to co-index (*ie* mark as co-referential by the ascription of identical referential indices) reflexive pronouns and empty subjects with some lexical NP only if the necessary syntactic conditions for successful anaphoric interpretation (*ie* those spelled out in the transformations that these rules replaced) were met. We thus arrive at a situation in which the syntactic rules no longer generated all and only the sentences of a given language, even as an ideal. The syntax was now thought of as embodying only those principles that were *purely* syntactic. As such it would generate as syntactically well-formed many strings that would subsequently be marked as ill-formed ('filtered out' in the jargon) by interpretative devices. It was now the grammar *as a whole* that generated the set of sentences, as tasks previously thought of as syntactic and handled in the transformational component were reassigned elsewhere. For example, NP positions could now be left empty at deep structure and reflexive pronouns could be freely inserted. Thus sentences such as,

[114i] *I expected [Amanda to like np].
[114ii] *I want [Amanda to like myself].

would now be generated by the syntactic rules and lexicon but filtered out by the interpretative analogues of equi and reflexive, on the grounds that neither the empty NP nor the reflexive is in a position to be successfully interpreted as a (null or overt) anaphor of I.

The overall result of this kind of redistribution of workload was a more principled theory, with each component performing a limited range of tasks and subject to restrictive principles determining its internal make-up and role in the grammar. Transformational grammar in the mid-1970s thus began to evolve into a theory involving complex interactions between subcomponents, and there was a great deal of debate about where the boundaries should be drawn between these. Since, however, the details of the mechanisms of interpretation proposed at that time to replace rules such as reflexive and equi are now of only historical interest, no treatment of them will be offered here. It is clearly desirable that the proper distribution of reflexive pronouns and of infinitival complements with 'understood' subjects should follow from general principles concerning the interpretation of anaphoric elements, rather than, as was originally the case, being stipulated *ad hoc* in the individual interpretative rules, much as they had been in the individual transformations that these rules supplanted. A full account of the most recent proposals designed to meet this objective is given in 2.3 below. The important point to note here is that there is now a *second* alternative to transformational analysis, and as we shall see in Chapter 4, when lexical analysis is combined with the use of rules of semantic interpretation, and the potential of these mechanisms is exploited to the full, the result is a system of grammatical description that has no use for deep structures and transformations.

2.2.4 Constraints on transformations

From the earliest work on the development of the standard theory it was recognised that rules which incorporatad an essential variable in their structural descriptions had to be constrained. Consider once again the rule of *wh*-movement ([54] and [56]) repeated here as [115].

[115] *Wh-movement* SD: X – COMP – X – *wh* – X
                            [+Q]
                        1   2   3   4   5   ⇒ (OPT.)
                    SC: 1   4+2   3   ∅   5

The essential variable here is factor 3; there is no grammatically imposed limit on the extent of the movement of a *wh*-expression leftwards into COMP. Ross (1967) observed that if the material in a given phrase marker assigned to this factor had certain attributes, the result of the application of *wh*-movement was ungrammatical, at least in English. Consider the following ungrammatical strings.

[116i]   *Who do you believe the story that Maggie sacked?*
[116ii] *Who is that Maggie sacked unbelievable?*
[116iii] *What did Maggie chew gum and blow?*
[116iv] *What did Maggie wonder who said?*

Parallel sentences with non-*wh*-expressions that remain in their deep structure positions are fully grammatical.

[117i]   *Do you believe the story that Maggie sacked the Chancellor?*
[117ii] *That Maggie sacked the Chancellor is unbelievable.*
[117iii] *Did Maggie chew gum and blow bubbles?*
[117iv] *Did Maggie, wonder who said that?*

In order to account for the ungrammaticality of sentences such as those in [116] a series of constraints were proposed on the contents of the essential variable in rules such as *wh*-movement involving the statement of so-called unbounded dependencies. These constraints were simply a conjunction of a context and an instruction not to move *wh*-expressions outside the specified context. Let us first of all provide phrase markers for [116i–iv] ignoring here the issue of subject–auxiliary inversion. See [118] opposite and over the page. In each case the crucial contextual feature identified as causing the problem has been enclosed in a box. In [118i] this consists of a so-called 'complex NP', *ie* a noun phrase with a lexical head (*story*) and a complement sentence dependent upon that lexical head. The **Complex Noun Phrase**

[118i]

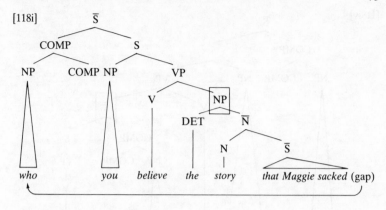

[118ii]

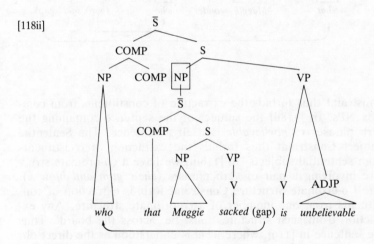

[118iii]

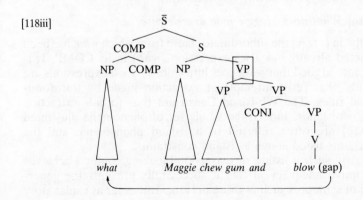

[118iv]

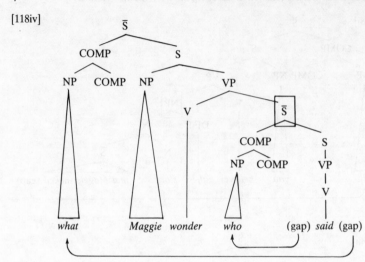

Constraint thus forbids the extraction of constituents from complex NPs. In [118ii] the subject of the sentence containing the verb phrase *is unbelievable* is itself a sentence. The **Sentential Subject Constraint** thus forbids the extraction of constituents from sentential subjects. In [118iii] we have a co-ordinate structure involving a pair of verb phrases (*chew gum and blow x*). The **Co-ordinate Structure Constraint** forbids extraction of constituents from one member of a co-ordinate structure. Any extraction from such structures must be 'across the board'. Thus the sentence in [119], where *what* is understood as the direct object of both verbs, is fully grammatical.

[119] *What does Maggie hate and despise?*

Finally, in [118iv] the subordinate clause from which *what* has been extracted already has a *wh*-expression (*who*) in its COMP. It is therefore argued that sentences introduced by *wh*-expressions are 'islands' that resist attempts at extraction made by transformational rules. The **Wh-island Constraint** thus forbids extraction from *wh*-islands. Indeed the whole set of phenomena illustrated in [116] are often referred to as island phenomena, and the constraints listed above as island constraints.

Clearly such a listing of extraction-blocking contexts achieves descriptive adequacy in that it successfully prevents the generation of sentences such as those in [116]. But as far as explanatory adequacy is concerned, everything is still to be done, since we as yet have no idea what it is that the listed contexts have in common (if anything) that makes them all barriers to extraction, what general principle is at work in these cases. It is only when the particulars fall out as specific cases of some general organisational property of grammars defined by general linguistic theory that we can claim to have an explanation of the phenomena under investigation.

Before considering Chomsky's attempt to provide such an explanation, it will be worthwhile considering the nature of transformations as conceived within the framework of the standard theory in a little more detail. As work progressed, it fairly soon became apparent that all transformations fell into one of three major types; clause-bound operations, operations involving the crossing of one clause boundary, and unbounded operations. As an example of each, we might take reflexive, which, it will be recalled (*cf* [104]), was subject to a clause-mate condition, equi, which involved the deletion of the subject of one clause under identity with a noun phrase in the next higher clause, and *wh*-movement, which operated across an indefinitely large domain. Another example of a clause-bound rule is passive, though this was not specified as such above. If the original formulation in [71] is examined, it will be seen that the key factors required for the operation of this rule are: NP – *be* – V – NP – . . . – *by* – np. But it is crucial that the two NPs be clause mates, since it is not possible for the rule to apply to a string such as [120],

[120] *Chomsky – be –   know –   [Gazdar –   is wrong]– by – np*
      NP   V   NP   . . .

because the product is ungrammatical.

[121] **Gazdar is known is wrong by Chomsky.*

Clearly, then, we must exclude the case where the NP following V is the subject of a subordinate clause.

In view of the ungrammaticality of [121], however, it might reasonably be asked what account can be given of the analogous but fully grammatical [122].

[122] *Gazdar is known to be wrong by Chomsky.*

The answer is provided by a rule of the second type, involving an operation across one clause boundary, known as **subject-to-object raising.** The difference between the two examples in [123]

[123i] *Chomsky knows [Gazdar is wrong.].*
[123ii] *Chomsky knows Gazdar [to be wrong.].*

is supposed to be that in the second case, but not the first, the deep structure subject of the embedded sentence has been 'raised' to become the surface structure (direct) object of the verb of the main clause. It is assumed that finite verbs agree with subjects when present, as in [123i], but that when the subject is removed, as in [123ii], the verb has nothing to agree with and so has to be infinitival. In support of the proposed surface structure, attention is drawn to the fact that when a pronoun is involved in the raising process, it typically appears in accusative form, the case of the direct object.

[124] *Chomsky knows him (*he) [to be wrong.]*.

Suppose, then, that we have a rule of subject-to-object raising. The effect is to make the subject of an embedded clause into the object of the next higher clause, and as a result this NP becomes a clausemate of the subject of the higher clause. Consequently passive can now apply to give us examples such as [122].

1/23/92   Clearly, the three-way typology, just as much as the existence of constraints on variables in rules of the unbounded type, is a fact looking for an explanation. Can this classification of rules in fact be shown to be a consequence of some general organisational principle? Once again, before considering Chomsky's attempt to provide an answer to this question, we have to look at a further distinction that was drawn between transformations that are bounded (*ie* that operate either within a single clause or at most across one clause boundary) and transformations that are unbounded.

Consider first of all the interaction of subject-to-object raising and reflexive as applied to a deep structure such as that in [125], where the brackets indicate clause boundaries.

[125] ¹   ²   ³
       *Chomsky*ᵢ *believe* [*Chomsky*ᵢ *have prove* [*Chomsky*ᵢ *be a genius*]]

Details of verb morphology are here ignored as usual. Let us identify the three occurrences of *Chomsky* from left to right as *Chomsky*-1, *Chomsky*-2 and *Chomsky*-3. As things stand, it is impossible for reflexive to apply, because no two of the three co-referential NPs are clausemates. Suppose then, that subject-to-object raising applies first. It could apply either to *Chomsky*-2 or to *Chomsky*-3. Suppose it applies first to *Chomsky*-2. The result is [126].

[126] ¹   ²   ³
       *Chomsky*ᵢ *believe   Chomsky*ᵢ [*have prove*   [*Chomsky*ᵢ *be a genius*]]

Reflexive can now apply to convert *Chomsky-2* into an appropriate reflexive pronoun, since the two *Chomskys* are clausemates as required.

[127] 1   3
       Chomsky_i believe himself_i [have prove [Chomsky_i be a genius]]

If subject-to-object raising now reapplies to this string and makes *Chomsky-3* the object of *prove*, we obtain [128].

[128] 1   3
       Chomsky_i believe himself_i [have prove Chomsky_i [be a genius]]

Unfortunately, there is now no way in which *Chomsky-3* can be reflexivised, because there is no co-referential NP within its clause to trigger the operation. We thus predict the grammaticality of [129].

[129] *Chomsky believes himself to have proved Chomsky to be a genius.*

On the understanding that the two *Chomskys* refer to the same individual, this is highly doubtful; at best, the structure is most unusual on the intended reading, and at worst is ungrammatical. It is certainly true that the use of a second reflexive pronoun would be the usual way of expressing the intended proposition.

In response to problems of this kind the principle of the **transformational cycle** was proposed. The idea is simply that those transformational rules deemed to be *cyclic* should apply sentence by sentence, beginning with the most deeply embedded clause and working progressively through the intermediate embedded clauses until the main, or root, clause is reached. There is the further stipulation that once a sentence has been passed in the cycle of transformational applications there should be no 'going back' to that clause later, in the sense that no rule should be allowed subsequently to apply wholly within that domain. Assuming that reflexive and subject-to-object raising are cyclic rules, the effect of the principle of cyclic application is to guarantee that these rules interact in such a way as to give the surface structure [130].

[130] *Chomsky believes himself to have proved himself to be a genius.*

Thus, returning to [125], it is now the case that subject-to-object raising will apply necessarily to *Chomsky-3* before it applies to *Chomsky-2*. Reflexive can now apply on the same cycle, followed

by subject-to-object raising and reflexive on the next cycle. This
is illustrated in [131].

[131]

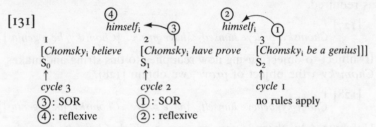

	1	2	3
	[*Chomsky*$_i$ believe	[*Chomsky*$_i$ have prove	[*Chomsky*$_i$ be a genius*]]]
	S_0	S_1	S_2
	↑	↑	↑
	cycle 3	cycle 2	cycle 1
	③: SOR	①: SOR	no rules apply
	④: reflexive	②: reflexive	

Notice that there is no need for these two rules to be ordered
with respect to one another since, given the clausemate constraint
on reflexive, subject-to-object raising will always have to apply
first. Recall that the prohibition on 'going back' to a sentence
that has already been passed in the cycle is designed to prevent
rules applying wholly and exclusively within such sentences.
There is thus no objection to subject-to-object raising affecting
S_2 on the S_1 cycle, since the rule has an effect on both domains
(*viz* removing the subject of the former and making it the object
of the latter).

Having established the cyclic principle as a device for getting
rules to interact correctly, it is possible to argue that any rule is
cyclic if it can be shown to interact with rules that are already
known to be cyclic. Since this is no longer an issue of any great
theoretical significance, the details of specific arguments about
specific rules will not be gone into here. It is sufficient to note
that within the standard theory the set of bounded transformations (*ie* those operating within a single clause or at most across
one clause boundary) were regarded as cyclic rules. By contrast,
any rule that could not be shown to interact with some cyclic rule
or rules in an interesting way was regarded as **postcyclic.** This
meant that after all the cyclic rules had applied in the prescribed
fashion, the postcyclic rules could apply without being subject to
the constraints imposed by the cyclic principle. Typically, rules
involving unbounded dependencies such as *wh*-movement were
put into the postcyclic category because no interesting interactions with the cyclic rules could be found.

Once again then, we have a situation where an explanation is
called for. It is one thing to fix the rule system so that it correctly
describes the data to be accounted for, but quite another to
answer the question of why the rule system has to be fixed that
way. It is thus desirable to investigate whether transformations
have to be divided into these two categories (cyclic and
postcyclic), or whether the same results could be obtained within
a theory that did not make this distinction.

It should be clear from the preceding discussion that the theory of transformations within the standard model of transformational grammar was highly complex, with conditions and stipulations built in here and there in response to particular problems that arose in the process of devising grammars that approached the goal of descriptive adequacy. In an important paper entitled 'Conditions on Transformations' (1973) Chomsky sought to streamline and simplify this baroque construct. Chomsky's goal here was to eliminate as far as possible the rather *ad hoc* and rule-specific conditions that had been imposed in earlier work and to set up a series of general conditions which guaranteed the effects previously obtained by stipulation. In other words, Chomsky now began to address the question not of what the rule system for a grammar of English must be like but rather of why the rule system has the properties that it does. To the extent that the particular features of the rule system follow from general principle they may be said to be 'explained'.

Naturally the success of such a venture could be interpreted as a step towards achieving the goal of explanatory adequacy, particularly important from the point of view of those who adopt a realist interpretation of the grammars devised by linguists. Thus if the general principles that determine the form of grammars are regarded as a model of the human infant's innate language acquisition device, it follows that the task of 'learning a language' is rendered that much easier in that the essential properties of the rule system of the grammar of some language do not have to be 'learned' at all. All the child requires is for his innate schematism to be set into motion by exposure to a reasonable sample of linguistic data. The form of the grammar that is required to account for these and similar data then follows automatically, and we might then be said to have an 'explanation' of the speed and efficiency of acquisition in children despite wide differences in intelligence, parental interest and encouragement, etc. But even if one is unwilling to go along with such a realist line of argument, and feels sceptical about the postulation of innate language acquisition devices, it is still nevertheless highly desirable to have a maximally restrictive general framework within which to operate for the simple reason that a theory which allows grammars to make use of any and every descriptive device that linguists can think up excludes nothing as impossible and so necessarily fails to explain anything. It is a desirable goal to have a theory of the limits within which the grammars of natural languages may vary, a theory of what is a possible natural language grammar, even if one declines to give such a theory an interpretation in terms of the real world.

With this much background, we are now in a position to

consider the proposals advanced by Chomsky in his 'Conditions' paper. Of primary importance is the abolition of the three-way typology of transformations, together with the distinction between cyclic and postcyclic transformations, discussed above. To take the case of unbounded dependencies first, it was argued that these were in fact chains of bounded dependencies, and that a rule such as *wh*-movement should in fact be regarded as cyclic and subject to the cyclic principle of application. As evidence Chomsky pointed to cases where the rule applied in subordinate clauses (cases of indirect questions) such as that in [132].

[132] *I wonder [who they chose to give elocution lessons to Maggie?]*

Clearly *who* is the deep structure direct object of *chose* and is moved into the COMP position of the embedded sentence by *wh*-movement. If this rule were a postcyclic rule, as had earlier been argued, there would of course be no violation of the principle that rules do not operate exclusively within sentence cycles that have already been passed, since this applies only to cyclic rules. But it is a characteristic of cyclic rules that they apply in subordinate clauses as well as main clauses, and by this criterion there is no reason to regard *wh*-movement as anything other than a cyclic rule, even though it cannot be shown to interact with other rules that are ordinarily put into this class. (As will be seen in the next section, there are good reasons why such interaction should not take place.) Chomsky's proposal, then, was that a sentence such as [133],

[133] *Who do you think the umpire believes the tennis authorities should ban?*

should be analysed as involving **successive cyclic** *wh*-movement as indicated in [134] opposite.

We have already seen that bounded rules seem to operate either within a single clause or, at most, across one clause boundary. Chomsky now therefore proposed the general condition of **subjacency** on all transformational rule applications, including applications of *wh*-movement. The effect of this condition is to prevent the displacement of constituents across more than one 'barrier' in a single movement. Consider the diagram [135] on the next page, where the relevant barriers are indicated by the Greek letters α and β (*alpha* and *beta*). Notice that, if only one barrier at most may intervene between source

[134]

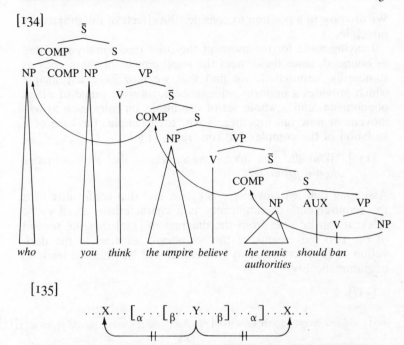

who   you   think   the umpire   believe   the tennis   should ban
                                                  authorities

[135]

$$...X...[_\alpha...[_\beta...Y..._\beta]..._\alpha]...X...$$

The subjacency principle: no rule may move a constituent from position Y to either position X (*ie* across more than one barrier) in a single application.

and destination positions in a given movement, the positions involved will be in the same or adjacent domains. In the case of adjacent domains the source position will, however, always be in a domain *embedded* within the domain containing the destination position. The source position will, therefore, be *subjacent* to the destination position, a fact which gives the principle its name.

The question immediately arises, of course, of what the relevant barriers defining domains ought to be, and of whether these vary from language to language. These are highly complex technical questions which cannot be pursued in detail here. Simply to illustrate the intention of the principle, we can take the view that the set of boundaries for English should be equated with the set of domains within which transformations may apply, *viz* S̄, S and NP. Suppose further that S̄ and NP are the primary barriers, with S assuming barrier status only in certain specified circumstances, details of which will be provided in due course.

We are now in a position to consider the effects of the subjacency principle.

Leaving aside for the moment the rules traditionally regarded as bounded, since these meet the requirements of subjacency as standardly formulated, we find that we now have a principle which provides a uniform explanation for a wide range of island phenomena, and a whole set of conditions on rules such as *wh*-movement now fall together. Take, for example, the case of a violation of the complex NP constraint, [136].

[136] *Who did you accept the argument that the committee should promote?*

Assuming that *wh*-movement is cyclic, and that conformity with the requirements of subjacency is a characteristic of all cyclic rules, it can be seen from the diagram in [137] that the second of the two movements of the *wh*-phrase involved in the derivation of [136] crosses two barriers ($\overline{S}$ and NP) and so leads to ungrammaticality.

[137]

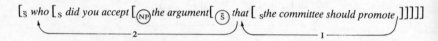

Similarly in the case of [138].

[138] *Who was for MI5 to vet ridiculous?*

which involves a violation of the sentential subject constraint, it is clear from the labelled bracketing in [139] that once again the second movement of *who* violates subjacency by crossing $\overline{S}$ and NP.

[139]

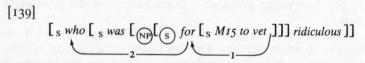

Notice that in neither of these cases has S been taken to be a barrier. In the case of *wh*-island constraint violations, however, it seems that we have to regard it as one. Take sentence [140].

[140] *What did she ask who did?*

The movements required in the derivation of this sentence are indicated in [141].

[141]

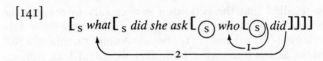

Since the sentence is clearly ungrammatical, and since no movement crosses more than one $\overline{S}$ (no NPs are involved), the most
natural conclusion to come to is that S becomes a barrier when
the preceding COMP position in $\overline{S}$ contains a *wh*-phrase. The
movement of *what* now violates subjacency on the assumption
that no COMP position in English can contain at any time in the
course of a derivation more than one *wh*-phrase. This seems
reasonable enough in view of the ungrammaticality of [142],

[142] *I wonder who what John gave to?*

and if correct, precludes the possibility that *what* in [140] is
moved first into the embedded COMP position containing *who*,
thereby avoiding the subjacency violation. Nor is it possible that
what is moved twice before *who* is moved, because this last
movement violates the principle that no cyclic rule applies exclusively in domains that have already been passed in the cycle.

The same results could have been obtained, as the reader can
easily check, if S and NP have taken to be barriers
throughout, and $\overline{S}$ had been taken to be a non-barrier. Many
scholars have advocated this analysis, which might indeed be
thought preferable since no special adjustment of the definition
of barrier would be required to account for the ungrammaticality
of [140]. The reason why this course was not taken is twofold;
first, there are good reasons to think that $\overline{S}$ is a barrier in the
grammars of many other languages and that from the point of
view of universal grammar it is S which has the more 'fluid'
status, and secondly, as we shall see below in 2.3, it is necessary
to regard $\overline{S}$ and NP as barriers in another context, and it is
desirable that the notion of barrier should be as uniform as possible in all the domains where it appears to be relevant.

Let us turn now to the rules traditionally thought of as
bounded. In the standard theory the boundedness is stipulated
for each rule, either in its structural description or by means of
a special condition. To take an example of a clause-bound rule,
consider the formulation of passive in [143].

[143] SD: X — NP — ... — V — NP — ... — by — np — X
      1   2   3   4 5   6   7   8   9 ⇒ (OBLIG.)
    SC: 1   5   3   4 *ø*   6   7   2   9

Condition: 2 and 5 are clausemates

It will be recalled that the condition is necessary to prevent the rule applying in cases where factor 5 is the subject of a subordinate clause (*cf* [120] and [121] above). As an example of a rule that operates across one clause boundary we might take subject-to-subject raising. This rule is designed to account for the relationship that holds between sentence pairs such as [144i] and [144ii].

> [144i] *It seems that Ronnie is a robot.*
> [144ii] *Ronnie seems to be a robot.*

In deep structure, where constituents bear grammatical functions that reflect predicate–argument structure directly, it is clear that *seem* must be subcategorised as taking a clausal complement. In other words what *seems* to be the case is *that Ronnie is a robot.* Evidently *it* in [144i] is a non-referential 'dummy' element that simply anticipates the logical subject, *viz* the clausal complement of *seem*. Let us suppose, then, that the deep structure of [144i] is as in [145].

[145]

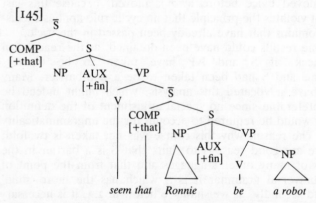

It is assumed here that [+that] COMPs are (optionally) realised as *that* in subordinate clauses but have no realisation in root (or main) clauses. The choice of [+that] entails that the following S will be finite. Finiteness manifests itself inflectionally on the first of a series of auxiliaries, or in the absence of an overt auxiliary, on the main verb. At deep structure it is convenient to indicate finiteness on the node AUX, which may be thought of as an obligatory constituent of S (rather as COMP is of S̄), even when the sentence has no surface auxiliary elements.

Since the subject of such a sentence in surface structure has to be *it*, and since *it* clearly has no semantic role with respect to *seem*, *ie* is not, from the semantic point of view, one of its arguments, the subject position is left empty at deep structure. As we have seen, deep structures can be thought of as configurational representations of predicate–argument structure, so it is natural that non-arguments should not appear, or equivalently, that non-argument positions should not be filled with items from the lexicon. *It* can now be inserted by a minor transformation; all English main-clause sentences have to have subjects in surface structure (with the exception of imperatives), and *it* is regularly used to 'fill the gap'. Sentence [144ii] obviously expresses the same proposition as [144i] and may be supposed to have virtually the same deep structure as [144i]. The only difference between the two is that the clausal complement in [144i] is finite, while that in [144ii] is not. When the clausal complement is infinitival, the subject of the embedded sentence in deep structure becomes the subject of the main clause in surface structure. Once again the non-argument position is filled at surface structure, but this time by a lexical NP present elsewhere in deep structure rather than by the dummy element *it*. The rule of subject-to-subject raising might be formulated as follows:

[146]   *SSR*   SD: X — np — V — [ₛ COMP —   NP — . . . — X
                              [−*that*]

              1   2   3   4   5   6   7 ⇒ (OBLIG.)
          SC: 1   5   3   4   ∅   6   7

This rule operates on the complements of verbs that take empty NP subjects at deep structure (*ie* subjects which lack a semantic role) and infinitival complements. Thus *seem* falls into this category, but not *believe*, because the subject position of sentences containing this verb is an argument position and is lexically filled at deep structure, or *want*, because its subject too is assigned a semantic role, and further, verbs of this class are assumed to take infinitival complements introduced by the complementiser *for* at deep structure (*cf* [111] and [112] above). The feature [−*that*] in factor 4 is thus intended to mark a complement clause not introduced by *that*, *ie* an infinitival clause, which, in the absence of [+*for*], becomes a bare infinitival at surface structure. The rule simply takes the subject of the infinitive and makes it the subject of the main verb by filling in the empty position. The important thing to note about [146] is that the boundedness of the operation is built into the formulation of the rule. It is stipulated that two adjacent clauses are involved, one in fact subjacent to the other, and that the movement takes place across just one clause boundary.

Now if subjacency is adopted as a general condition on all transformational rules, the boundedness of rules like passive and subject-to-subject raising follows at once and the stipulation can

be dropped. This in fact opens the way towards a unified statement of these rules (since both involve the movement of a NP),
provided that the apparent differences in domain of application
can be accounted for. Passive, as we have seen, is seemingly
clause-bound, while subject-to-subject raising necessarily involves
movement across a clause boundary. As a first step we might take
the view that the subject position of passive sentences in deep
structure, contrary to what has been assumed so far, should not
be lexically filled. It is clear that the surface subject of a passive
sentence receives its semantic interpretation by virtue of the
semantic role assigned to the position it occupies as deep structure direct object. In [147], for example,

[147] *Ronnie's batteries are re-charged nightly.*

the NP *Ronnie's batteries* is interpreted as the 'patient' of the re-
charging process, and this is the role associated with the direct
object of the verb *re-charge*. It is therefore the object position
and not the subject position of the passive verb that must contain
Ronnie's batteries at deep structure. But what about the NP
(often 'understood') that is interpreted as the 'agent'? Should this
not appear in deep structure subject position in the case of
passive participles just as it would in the case of the deep structure of a sentence containing the active transitive verb *re-charge*?
Since the whole point of passive sentences is to allow for the
identification of the agent to be suppressed, it is arguable that
passive participles should in fact appear in deep structure representations as one-place predicates with empty subjects, and that
the agent phrase should be treated as an optional adjunct to the
verb. A prepositional phrase of the form *by*-NP may or may not
appear in deep structure in the complement position of a verb
marked with passive morphology. If it does, a rule of semantic
interpretation can readily be devised to assign to this the agent
role.

   Let us accept this line of argumentation, and suppose that not
only sentences derived by subject-to-subject raising but also
sentences derived by passive have deep structure representations
with empty subjects. Both rules can now be expressed in the
same simple form, namely [148].

[148] *NP-movement* SD: X — np — . . . — NP — X
                          1   2   3   4   5   ⇒ (OBLIG.)
                     SC: 1   4   3   ∅   5

In other words, both rules can be interpreted as involving the
filling of empty NP positions by the movement of lexical NPs to

the left. Notice that there is no need to specify that the empty NP should be a subject because only subject positions can ever be left empty at deep structure; all other NP positions are necessarily associated with some semantic role, *ie* are argument positions, and so are lexically filled. Nor is there any danger that sentences such as those in [149] will be generated.

[149i] *Ronnie is believed [s̄ that it is certain [s̄ (to fluff his lines]]

Deep structure: np *be believed* [s̄ *that* np *be certain* [s̄ *Ronnie to fluff his lines*]]

[149ii] *Ronnie seems [s̄ that it is likely [s̄ to punch the button]]

Deep structure: np *seem* [s̄ *that* np *be likely* [s̄ *Ronnie to punch the button*]

In each case subjacency allows movement only across one boundary (S̄); note that the sentences become grammatical if the first empty NP is filled with *it* and *Ronnie* moves into the empty subject position in the embedded clause, as in [150].

[150] *It is believed/seems that Ronnie is certain/likely to . . . .*

There are, however, some unresolved problems with this new analysis of subject-to-subject raising and passive as NP-movement. The most obvious is that, as things stand, there is nothing to prevent the *successive cyclic* movement of *Ronnie* from his deep structure position in examples such as [149i] and [149ii] to the position he occupies in the associated, and ungrammatical, surface structures. Thus the same strings could after all be generated without violation of subjacency.

To handle this problem Chomsky proposed a **Tensed Sentence Condition** which prohibits the extraction of constituents from sentences with tensed (*ie* finite) verbs. Notice that in the examples in [149] the most deeply embedded sentences are infinitival while the next most deeply embedded sentences are introduced by *that* and are finite. Consequently *Ronnie* can move only once, from the infinitival clauses, because any further movement would violate the Tensed Sentence Condition (TSC). An added bonus of adopting the TSC is that the rule of subject-to-object raising can now be dispensed with. Recall that the difference between the two examples in [151],

[151i] *Chomsky is believed to be a genius.*
[151ii] *Chomsky is believed is a genius.*

was supposed to be that subject-to-object raising had applied to

the first, making *Chomsky* a clausemate of the subject NP of
believe (cf examples [122] to [124] and the associated discussion).
On the assumption that passive was a clause-bound rule, it could
only apply after subject-to-object raising. Since this rule had not
applied in [151ii], passive could not apply either. The condition
of subjacency, however, does not allow us to draw a distinction
between clause-bound rules and rules that operate across a clause
boundary. Consequently there is nothing to prevent passive
operating within a single clause or across S. But, given the TSC,
this is exactly what we want. Thus, dispensing altogether with
subject-to-object raising, we can allow passive to extract
Chomsky across the clause boundary into the empty subject
position of the deep structure underlying [151i], because this
involves a non-finite complement, but the extraction is prohibited
in the deep structure underlying [151ii], because here the complement clause is finite. Consider the diagrams in [152].

[152]

[152i]

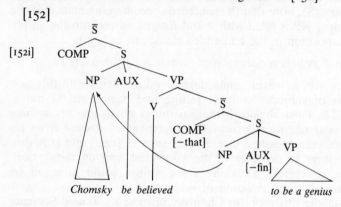

[152ii]

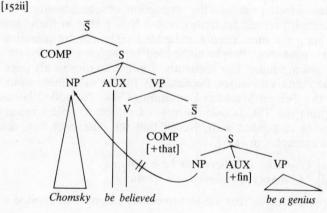

Similarly, there is now no need to stipulate that subject-to-subject raising moves only the subjects of infinitival complements (cf [146]). Movements of finite clause subjects are automatically blocked by the TSC (cf *John seems is happy).

Consider now the sentences in [153].

[153i] *Maggie seems Ronnie to admire.
[153ii] *Maggie is believed Ronnie to admire.

In the original formulations of subject-to-subject raising and passive it was made quite clear in the precisely specified structural descriptions of the rules which NPs were supposed to move, and where to. Given the new formulation in [148], there is nothing to prevent the movements illustrated in [153] – ie the movement in each case of the deep structure direct object of *admire* into the empty subject position of the main clause. Neither subjacency nor the TSC is violated. To handle this problem Chomsky introduced a further condition called the **Specified Subject Condition.** This prohibits the extraction of constituents out of a sentence across a specified subject; for present purposes this can be thought of as being a lexically filled subject NP position. Thus in the examples in [153] *Maggie* has been moved out of a complement clause across the specified subject *Ronnie* in violation of the Specified Subject Condition (SSC).

Notice that the combined effect of the TSC and the SSC is to restrict extraction from sentences to cases involving the movement of the subject of an infinitive. The formulation of the conditions is not ideal, because there is clearly an element of overkill. The TSC prohibits extraction from any position in a tensed sentence, and the SSC prohibits extraction from any position other than subject position, in both finite and non-finite clauses. Thus both conditions prohibit extraction from, say, the direct object position of a finite clause. Nevertheless, the setting up of these general conditions, and the attendant simplification in the formulation of rules illustrated in [148] represents a significant step towards the attainment of explanatory adequacy. Either we can write the rules and add *ad hoc* conditions to them in such a way that they do not permit extraction of anything other than the subject of an infinitive, as in the standard theory, or we can express the rules in general form, allowing NPs *in principle* to move from any position to any position, but rule out the impossible cases by general principles. These can be interpreted as part of the child's language acquisition device. Consequently a child learning English and equipped with the TSC, SSC and perhaps other principles (*eg* subjacency) has only to learn that English has a rule moving NPs. Which NPs to move and where to move them to he 'knows' already, thereby facilitating the learning process enormously.

Needless to say, all sorts of problems remain. For example, it is clear that the TSC and SSC are not very convincing as general conditions on all transformations since an exception has to be made for *wh*-movement. Thus in [154] the movement of *who* involves extraction from the direct object position of a finite clause, in violation of both conditions. Yet the sentence is fully grammatical.

[154] *Who did you say that you saw?*

Clearly the major difference between NP-movement and *wh*-movement is the fact that the latter involves movement to COMP while the former involves movement from one NP position to another. The easiest way to state the exception, therefore, is to add an appendix to each of the two conditions stating that COMP is an 'escape hatch' from sentences with finite verbs and/or specified subjects. But once again this is simply stipulation, and better formulations of the relevant principles are clearly required.

Nevertheless, significant advances were made in the 'Conditions' paper towards the goal of simplifying the statement of transformations by identifying general principles governing the manner of their application. Further refinements will be discussed in 2.3. It is particularly important to note that we are now moving towards a reasonably well-defined notion of 'possible transformation' as an operation subject to certain general conditions. In particular, we now have a theory which predicts rather than merely stipulates rule-by-rule the requirement that non-*wh* NPs can be extracted from sentences only if they are the subjects of non-finite verbs. This curious fact will be the subject of further discussion below (*cf* 2.3.6).

2.2.5 Conclusion

The development of the extended standard theory may be thought of as a process whereby the almost exclusively trans-formational-syntactic approach of the standard theory became less monolithic as research into the properties of the lexicon and rules of interpretation progressed. From the point of view of explanatory adequacy, it is clearly preferable to have a theory which envisages grammars as comprising sets of interacting subcomponents, each restrictively defined in terms of the form and function of its elements, than to have an apparently 'simple' theory which treats a wide range of phenomena in a uniform fashion, but which does so at the expense of making the rules employed irreducible to any general definition and which precludes the statement of a principled delimitation of their properties. By redistributing the task of expressing relationships whose transformational formulation inhibited the development of a restrictive theory of transformational rules, the way was opened up for the more uniform residue to be reanalysed as involving simple operations such as 'move NP' or 'move *wh*' which were subject to general principles of rule application. These general principles could be thought of as forming the beginnings of a theory of universal grammar, or alternatively as a model of the language acquisition device assumed to be a part of the human infant's genetic endowment. The emphasis of work within transformational grammar thus shifted away from the development of (more or less) descriptively adequate rule systems, as models of the grammars of languages internalised by native speakers, to the development of (more or less) explanatorily adequate theories of universal grammar, which sought to explain why the rule systems needed to explain the competence of native speakers had the properties that they appeared to have.

The ideal, of course, would be a theory of universal grammar which allowed for those parts of the grammars of natural languages that are not the product of historical or cultural accident to be derived automatically, given certain basic information about the languages in question, specifically the sort that could be obtained without fail from limited exposure to random samples of data. We would then have an explanation of the process of language acquisition in children; the child's **core grammar**, *ie* that part of his grammar determined by biological necessity, could be viewed as simply 'growing' in the mind as a result of the interaction of his language acquisition device and the primary linguistic data to which he is exposed, and only the marked periphery of exceptions and irregularities would have to be learned consciously in the conventional sense.

Once again, it is worth emphasising that, even if Chomsky's realism and nativism are unacceptable to many, it is nevertheless worthwhile to try to construct as restrictive a metatheory as possible within which to work, to try, in other words, to develop a notion of 'possible natural-language grammar' that allows for only as many options as are absolutely necessary for the proper description of the data. Very few, possibly none, of Chomsky's proposals depend crucially for their existence in his system on their being interpreted as models of some psychological reality.

On the contrary, Chomsky justifies the introduction of new apparatus by appeal to exactly the same set of criteria that the most committed agnostic would appeal to, namely accuracy of prediction, elegance and generality of formulation, and so on. Of course Chomsky would argue that to refuse to adopt a realist interpretation of the linguist's grammar, or to deny that the linguist's theory of universal grammar is a model of the human infant's innate language acquisition device, is to deprive the study of linguistics of its primary importance as a scholarly discipline, namely as a major source of information about the structure of the mind. Nevertheless, if the realism and nativism are abandoned, the same theory of universal grammar could still stand. Only its interpretation would have to change.

It would be possible at this point to outline chronologically the major innovations, over and above those already mentioned in this section, in the further development of the extended standard theory. However, the scene has now been set for the presentation of Chomsky's theory of universal grammar, and no damage will be done if a framework which evolved over a number of years is described in its final form. The last section of this chapter therefore deals with Chomsky's current framework, Government-Binding theory.

2.3 Government-Binding theory

2.3.1 Introduction

The plausibility of Chomsky's position depends on the successful development of a theory of universal grammar that embodies principles that are, as far as we can determine, purely linguistic (*ie* without relevance in other domains of enquiry), that lack convincing motivation in terms of functional notions such as efficiency of communication (not an altogether difficult task in view of the absence of any compelling independently definable measure of this quality), and which attain a level of explanatory power that makes it at least highly unlikely that they hold by accident of systems that are 'really' quite differently constituted. If Chomsky can construct such a theory, and also provide evidence that its principles could not, on reasonable assumptions, be learned, (because, for example, no reasonable sample of ordinary performance data would supply enough relevant information to guarantee that all speakers would be able to learn them), his position is not an implausible one. He is simply suggesting that the capacity to master the grammar of a natural language is the product of millions of years of evolution, and further is actually providing a model of what that genetic endowment might be. Nevertheless, it is matter of judgement whether Chomsky's theory of universal grammar is 'sufficiently' abstract, wide-ranging and explanatory for chance to be excluded, or whether Chomsky's arguments based on the poverty of the stimulus are convincing 'enough' to show that the principles of what he regards as innate universal grammar are not simply learned piecemeal by each speaker. On these matters readers will have to make up their own minds when they have read what follows.

2.3.2 The theory of universal grammar: an overview

In the previous section we have seen that Chomsky views the grammar of a natural language as something best described as a set of interacting components. The only major difference between the general organisation of a grammar presented in [1], the standard theory conception, and that currently supposed is that the rules of the 'semantic component' now operate on 'surface structures' exclusively. We have already seen that deep structure is not the level of representation at which matters such as possibilities of pronominal co-reference can be determined, even though other aspects of semantic structure such as the determination of so-called 'thematic' (*ie* semantic) roles are best handled there. As we shall see, there is a mechanism in Government-Binding theory (henceforth GB theory) which carries over certain aspects of deep structure into 'surface' structure thereby permitting *all* the rules of interpretation to operate at this level.

There have also been some terminological changes. Perhaps most important is the distinction drawn between **S-structure** (what has been called 'surface' structure so far in this book) and **surface structure** (what was previously called phonetic representation). S-structures are the product of the application of transformational rules to **D-structures** (as deep structures are now called), and surface structures are phonetically interpreted S-structures, the product of the application of the **PF rules** (rules determining **Phonetic Form**, roughly the old rules of the phonological component plus rules that effect various optional permutations and deletions that might reasonably be called 'stylistic' rather than strictly grammatical) to S-structures.

The notion of 'semantic interpretation' has also undergone some changes. Strictly speaking there has never been any real semantic interpretation mechanism within the theory of transformational grammar. Semantic interpretation properly refers to a process whereby an uninterpreted string of symbols, *eg* a

sentence of some language, is put into correspondence with some
non-linguistic object, *eg* a particular state of affairs in the world,
which is its interpretation. What the rules of the semantic
component in the standard theory actually did was provide a kind
of **logical form** which made explicit not only such matters as
which NPs were co-referential, or what the scope of some quantifier was, but also, via the technique of lexical decomposition or
componential analysis, sought to reveal the contribution made by
each word in a sentence to the entailments of that sentence. Thus
in sentence [155],

[155] *Edgar is a man.*

if the word *man* is assumed to have a sense that can be
represented by the conjunction of the sense components 'human',
'adult' and 'male', it follows that anyone who asserts [155] is also
committing himself to the truth of the propositions expressed by
the sentences in [156], on the assumption that *human, adult* and
male mean 'human', 'adult' and 'male' respectively.

[156] *Edgar is human.*
Edgar is adult.
Edgar is male.

The proposition expressed by a sentence X entails that expressed
by a sentence Y if it is impossible consistently to assert the truth
of the first and deny the truth of the second. Thus the propositions expressed by the sentences in [156] are entailments of that
expressed by [155], and these can be 'read off' from the logical
form of [155] which, amongst other things, incorporates the
componential definition of *man*. Notice that the entailments of
[155] in effect constitute conditions that the world would have to
meet if [155] were to be a true description of it. The meaning of
a declarative sentence might then be regarded as the state of
affairs described by the totality of its entailments. What the rules
of the semantic component did was to derive logical forms from
deep structures (the objects in question being referred to as
'semantic representations') from which entailments, or truth
conditions could be derived; in other words they translated the
deep structure representations of English sentences into
sentences of the language of semantic components and referential
indices, a language constructed to be more semantically perspicu-
ous and more readily interpretable than English, but they did
not actually *interpret* this translation in the strict sense.

It has to be said that Chomsky's personal interest in this enterprise was never very great, and indeed in recent years the whole

approach of componential analysis has been called into question by semanticists of various persuasions. Within GB theory the rules of the 'semantic component' are now called **LF rules** (*ie* rules determining **Logical Form**), and these apply to S-structures to derive representations at which matters such as quantifier scope are determined. Logical Form is thus no more than a further, rather abstract, level of syntactic representation. The whole componential framework of earlier models has simply been abandoned. To give a simple example, given an S-structure such as [157],

[157] [$_\overline{s}$[$_s$ *Everyone loves his mother*]]

rules of the LF component, quantifier movement and quantifier interpretation, will operate to derive [158i] or [158ii].

[158i] [$_\overline{s}$ *For all x* [$_s$ *x loves x's mother*]]
[158ii] [$_\overline{s}$ *For all x* [$_s$ *x loves his mother*]]

The first, of course, corresponds to the case where *his* in [157] is understood as a variable ('each person loves his own mother'), and the second to the case where *his* is understood as having specific reference (*eg* 'each person loves Bilbo Baggins' mother'). Once again, there are no rules of 'real' interpretation, though doubtless these would apply to representations at the level of LF if anyone thought it worthwhile to devise them. It is worth adding, as a final remark, that any aspects of D-structure or S-structure that are deemed to be relevant to LF are simply carried over from one level to another as a part of the mapping process. Thus referential indices, for example, may be assigned at D-structure, or as part of the mapping process from D-structure to S-structure, and then the NPs in question will simply turn up in LF with the relevant indices assigned.

Summarising, the grammar of some language is assumed to consist of the components listed in [159].

[159] (i)   lexicon
      (ii) categorial component (*ie* PS rules constrained by $\overline{X}$-theory)
      (iii) transformational component
      (iv) PF component
      (v)   LF component

The rules of (i) and (ii) together form the **base** and generate D-structures, which are mapped into S-structures by the rules of (iii). S-structures are then mapped into PF and LF by the rules of the PF and LF components.

[160]

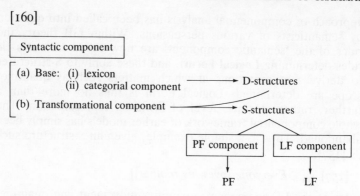

What has been said so far has been designed to provide a link between this and the preceding two sections, but it is misleading in that the ultimate objective of GB theory is to reduce the content of the components of [159] to a minimum. Most of the properties of the system and the manner of the interaction of its subcomponents are supposed to follow from general principle rather than having to be spelled out within the system itself. Only the unpredictable should appear in the rule system proper, and the assignment of representations (D-structure, S-structure, PF and LF) to sentences is now carried out only in part by the rules of [159]. Thus rather than building conditions into the rules themselves (as in the standard theory), or even imposing general conditions on the operation and interaction of simplified rules within the system (as in the early stages of the extended standard theory), Chomsky has now developed a theory of conditions on *the representations themselves*. The rules of [159] are a mere residue of the systems proposed in the standard theory and do no more than specify those aspects of representations that do not follow from general principle. It is only in conjunction with the overall theory of universal grammar that complete representations can be assigned to sentences, and only a sentence assigned four well-formed representations will be grammatical. In this way, transformational grammar has evolved from being a theory of how representations are derived by rule into a theory of the conditions that representations must meet. In the process, the rule system as traditionally conceived has all but withered away.

We may take two simple examples to illustrate the point. Suppose there are general conditions on D-structure, on S-structure and on the relationship between them such that, once it is known which constituents may move in principle, the actual choice of what to move and where to move it to in a given case is predetermined. In these circumstances one might say that universal grammar makes available a transformational component consisting of the single rule schema *Move* α (*ie* 'move anything anywhere'). The child 'learning' the grammar of some particular language then simply has to find out what the permissible values of α are in that language; in English, for example, α would include at least NP and *wh*. Everything else should then follow from the interaction of this information and the child's knowledge of universal grammar. The need for elaborately formulated structural descriptions and structural changes disappears; the transformational component of the grammar of English is no more than a list of values for α. As a second example we may take the PS rules of the categorial component. It was noted above (2.1.2, see especially the discussion of example [22] and [23]) that in the standard theory information was redundantly reduplicated in PS rules and in subcategorisation features in the lexical entries of particular words. Suppose, then, we establish a general principle, the **Projection Principle**, which requires lexical properties to be 'projected' to all levels of syntactic representation. This has wide-ranging consequences, as we shall see, but in the present context the most important is that it renders much of the system of PS rules otiose. Take the case of a verb like *put*, which is given the following lexical entry (with irrelevant information suppressed).

[161] *put*: V, + [$\bar{\bar{N}}$, $\bar{\bar{P}}$] ($\bar{\bar{N}}$ = NP, $\bar{\bar{P}}$ = PP)

The Projection Principle requires *put* to appear with the specified complement structure at all levels of representation, including D-structure. $\bar{X}$-theory tells us that a lexical head X and its complements form a constituent $\bar{X}$, and that any specifiers of this form with it a higher-level constituent $\bar{\bar{X}}$. There is thus no need for rules to spell this out in the case of *put*; it is automatic that *put the gun to his head* is a $\bar{V}$, and that *reluctantly put the gun to his head* is a $\bar{\bar{V}}$ (here assuming that S is not a projection of V, and that the maximal projection of V is equivalent to VP).

It will have been noticed that the order of elements in $\bar{X}$ has not been specified in [161] – the comma between the elements in square brackets is intended to show the absence of a linear precedence requirement. As a consequence no ordering of constituents can be projected from such a lexical entry to D-structures. The child learning English has to find out by experience not only what the complement structures of given words are, but also what the rule is for ordering lexical heads with respect to their complements. The rule for English, of course, is that heads precede their complements. Once learned, this information functions as a lexical redundancy rule; there is no need for an ordering statement to be included in every entry of the general form of [161]. As for the order of the complements themselves, Chomsky proposes an **adjacency principle** which requires complements capable of being case-marked to precede those which are not, and thus to be adjacent to the head of the phrase in question. Case-marking is residual in English, but it is clearly a property of pronominal NPs overtly (and possibly of NPs in general covertly, see 2.3.5 below). Thus by general principle, NP will precede PP in syntactic projections of the subcategorisation information in [161]. The only information that the child learning English has to acquire, therefore, is the complement structure of individual words and the order of lexical heads *vis-à-vis* their complements. Everything else follows from general principle. Since both pieces of information are lexical (expressed as a fact about individual words, as in [161], or as a redundancy rule, as in [162], much of the categorial component can be dispensed with.

[162] H precedes $\bar{\bar{\text{X}}}$ (*ie* a lexical head precedes its complements)

Before proceeding any further with illustrations of this sort, it will obviously be useful to have some overall idea of what Chomskyan universal grammar looks like. Just as his conception of the structure of individual language grammars is modular, so is his conception of universal grammar. Chomsky postulates a set of interacting subtheories each of which deals with some central area of grammatical enquiry. Each of these theories comprises a principle or set of principles, and each of these may be subject to **parametric variation**. That is to say, it is assumed that the grammars of languages vary in only finitely many ways with respect to the domain covered by a given subtheory. In the majority of cases the number of variants will be small. Assuming that this is a model of the child's language acquisition device, it is supposed that ordinary linguistic experience in the form of exposure to random samples of performance data is sufficient for the parameters of each subtheory to be set. They will obviously be set in different ways for different languages. The **core grammar** of a given language is then derived automatically from the interaction of the subtheories of universal grammar with their parameters set. Different kinds of grammar will follow from different kinds of interaction resulting from different parametric settings, but in general the typology of grammars is assumed to be quite restricted. It is particularly important that the theory should have an essentially deductive structure, so that choices made in one area have repercussions in others. In this way it is predicted that whole clusters of grammatical properties will typically occur together in the grammars of languages of a certain 'type', and if this turns out to be the case, the chances that the theory of universal grammar holds only accidentally of the systems whose properties it seeks to delimit are considerably reduced. The subtheories assumed are the following.

[163]   (i) X̄-theory
        (ii) θ (read 'theta')-theory
        (iii) Case theory
        (iv) Binding theory
        (v) Bounding theory
        (vi) Control theory
        (vii) Government theory

It may, of course, turn out that other subtheories are required, or that some of the members of [163] can be dispensed with. [163] is simply a working hypothesis that may well have to be modified in the light of further research. Each of these sub-theories will be examined in the sections which follow.

2.3.3 X̄-theory
The basic principles of X̄-theory have already been dealt with in 2.2.2. To recapitulate, it provides principles for the projection of phrasal categories from lexical categories and imposes con-ditions on the hierarchical organisation of categories in the form of general schemata. Crucially, it makes explicit the notion 'head of a phrase'. It may be that grammars vary according to the extent to which they utilise the resources made available by X̄-theory. Chomsky himself has entertained the idea that there are languages (W* (read 'word star') languages) in which sentences consist simply of a string of words without any higher-level organisation. This highly complex and controversial matter cannot be dealt with here, though it is an issue of some interest for general linguistic theory (cf 4.6). Once again, in what follows X̄-notation will only be employed where the discussion necessi-tates it, since no generally agreed system is yet available.

2.3.4 θ-theory
θ-theory is concerned with the assignment of what Chomsky calls 'thematic' roles to sentential constituents. The Greek letter *theta* is a form of shorthand for **thematic.** By thematic roles Chomsky

means what have been called semantic roles in the preceding sections, roles such as agent, patient (or theme), beneficiary, etc. It is assumed that these are assigned to the complements of lexical items as a lexical property. Thus in the entry for *put*, for example, the NP complement is assigned the role of patient (or theme) and the PP complement the role of location. It is further assumed that the majority of verbs 'θ-mark' the subject position of sentences containing them. Thus the subject NP of a sentence containing *put* is assigned the agent role. Any constituent assigned a θ-role by definition denotes a predicate argument.

Certain verbs, of course, do not θ-mark the subject position; for example, the verbs traditionally thought of as associated with subject-to-subject raising typically take 'dummy' subjects because the position is not an argument position (in predicate–argument structure) and so lacks a θ-role (see the discussion of [144], [145] and [146] above). By the Projection Principle (see 2.3.2, the discussion of [161]) and the principles of X̄-theory (2.2.2 and 2.3.3) the categories assigned θ-roles in lexical entries are projected from the lexicon to become constituents of D-structure, S-structure and LF. The main principle of θ-theory is the **θ-criterion**, which requires each thematic role to be uniquely assigned; *ie* each constituent denoting an argument is assigned just one θ-role and each θ-role is assigned to just one argument-denoting constituent. No sentence, for example, can have two (non-co-ordinate) agents or themes, and strings such as those in [164] are ungrammatical.

[164i]   *Johnny (was) smashed his racked by Jimbo.*
[164ii] *What did Johnny smash his racket?*

The Projection Principle guarantees that the θ-criterion applies at all levels of syntactic representation, though it properly applies to LF, the level at which all the syntactic and lexical information relevant to semantic interpretation, including θ-role assignment, is brought together. The effects of the θ-criterion on D-structure and S-structure representations will be dealt with below, (see especially 2.3.6 and 2.3.10).

2.3.5 Case theory

Case theory deals with the principles of case assignment to contituents. Although, as noted earlier, case is an overt property only of pronominal NPs in English (*cf I/me, she/her, he/him/his, we/us, they/them/their*), Chomsky assumes that *all* NPs with lexical content are assigned (abstract) case. (Abstract Case is usually distinguished from case as an overt inflectional category

by the use of an initial capital, and this convention will henceforth be followed here). Chomsky's reasons for assigning Case
in this way are quite complex and will become apparent in due
course. For the moment we must establish the principles involved
in Case assignment. The basic idea is that Case is assigned under
government, the choice of Case being determined by the
governor in any given example. Government is a traditional
notion involving the delimitation of the sphere of influence of a
particular category with respect to adjacent categories. For
example, familiar statements from grammars of Latin or Russian
that some verb or preposition 'governs the accusative' may be
interpreted in GB terms as saying that certain lexical heads have
the power to determine the Case (and in some languages the
case) of NPs that are their complements. In more general terms,
a lexical head X may be said to govern its sisters in $\bar{X}$, and certain
lexical heads also have the power to Case-mark certain of their
complements. Thus V or P, for example, may by virtue of
governing NP assign, say, accusative Case (or case) to that
constituent. In the context of GB theory the essential point is
that there can be no Case-marking without government; ungoverned positions cannot receive Case. Governed positions may
or may not be Case-marked according to the properties of the
governing and governed categories in any given example. Thus
Case assignment to the NP complements of a lexical head is
straightforward, and entirely traditional. *Accusative*, or *objective*,
Case will be assigned in English to any NP governed by V or P,
but not to NPs governed by N or ADJ. (It is sometimes argued
that P assigns *oblique* Case, but this possibility will be ignored
here.)

[165]

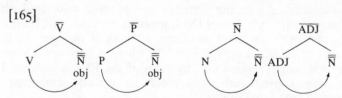

Lexical heads govern their complements. Case is assigned to governed
complements if the governor has the power of Case assignment; in English V and
P assign objective Case, N and ADJ do not.

The absence of overt NP complements to N and ADJ in English
now follows from Case theory on the assumption that all lexical
NPs must have Case in S-structure.

Following on from this, one of the most important principles

of Case theory is the **Case filter**, which states that any S-structure
that contains an NP with lexical content but no Case is ungrammatical. Thus if N cannot assign Case, it follows that the NP *the
city* in the D-structure [166] will have to move for any associated
S-structure to be grammatical. (In the D-structure *the destruction
the city*, *of*-insertion would be obligatory, again because of the
Case filter).

[166] np *destruction the city by the Visigoths*

Thus the obligatoriness of the passive case of NP-movement no
longer has to be specified, at least for movement within NP as
here, because this follows from the Case filter. It also follows that
Case assignment takes place at S-structure. On the assumption
that the participial verb forms that appear in passive sentences,
unlike their active transitive counterparts, also lack the power of
Case assignment, the obligatoriness of NP-movement in [167] also
follows from the Case filter.

[167] np *be destroyed the city by the Visigoths*

This leaves the problem of Case assignment to subjects. To
handle this, Chomsky now proposes that the subject position in
a finite S is governed by an abstract element INFL (generally
pronounced as written, but short for INFL(ection)). INFL may
be marked [+tense] if the sentence is finite, or [−tense] if the
sentence contains an infinitive. A [+tense] INFL is assumed to
contain an agreement element (AGR, also pronounced as
written!) which may be thought of as a kind of abstract pronominal marked with the same features as those associated with
the subject NP. A [+tense] INFL together with its AGR is either
associated with an overt auxiliary, if there is one, or, in the
absense of AUX, is moved into VP, where it becomes a verbal
inflection, once 'spelled out' by rules of the PF component. In
this way subject–verb agreement in tensed sentences is
expressed (see [168] opposite).

But if INFL finally ends up as a verbal inflection, why should
it originate as an independent element? The answer has in part
to do with Case-marking. The finiteness or non-finiteness of a
verb has consequences for the Case of subject NPs but has no
bearing whatever on the Case-marking of its complements. The
latter is determined by the verb-stem irrespective of its inflectional ending.

[168]

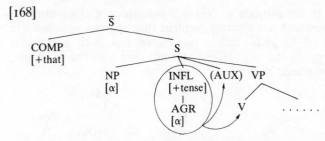

α represents a set of person and number features which subject NP and AGR must share. AUX can now be treated as an optional node, appearing only when the sentence contains an overt auxiliary. The agreement element appears as an inflection on the first AUX or V to its right in surface structure.

[169i] *Jo* [*kisses Bo*]
      Jo is [*kissing Bo*]
      Jo has [*kissed Bo*]
[169ii] *Jo's kissing Bo* (*caused a scandal*).

In [169i] we have a present indicative, a present participle and a past participle all governing *Bo* and all assigning objective Case to it. In [169ii] there is a gerund governing *Bo*, and once again objective Case is assigned. But the subject of the examples in [169i] is nominative in all three cases because in each it is followed by a finite verb form (*kisses*, *is* and *has*). In other words, it is the finiteness of the immediately following verb (or auxiliary) and not the choice of verb-stem (or auxiliary) that controls the assignment of nominative Case. In [169ii] the verb-form following the subject is a non-finite gerund, and here the subject is *genitive* (or *possessive*). This Case assignment once again is characteristic of all gerunds and (though objective Case is sometimes used as an alternative, *cf I hate him/his doing this*) has nothing to do with choice of verb. In these circumstances it is not unreasonable to split off the inflectional element of the verb (or auxiliary) following the subject at the more abstract levels of representation and make this the governor, and Case-marker, of the subject NP, leaving a verb stem in the VP as the governor of the verb's complements. In Chomsky's framework INFL appears in S as governor of the subject NP and assigns nominative Case if it is [+tense]. If it is [−tense], *ie* if the verb is an infinitive, INFL is assumed not to have the power of government or Case assignment. The reasons for this will again become apparent in due course. The assignment of genitive Case to the subjects of gerunds and more generally to the subjects of NPs is a consequence of government by POSS(essive), an abstract element that appears optionally in the case of gerunds and is associated not with agreement morphology on the verb (like [+tense]), but with the suffix-*ing*. This is illustrated in [170].

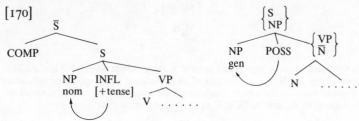

INFL [+tense] governs the subject position in S and assigns nominative Case, POSS governs the subject position in gerundive constructions and in NP and assigns genitive (possessive) Case (*cf* [93] above).

For objective Case assignment in the absence of POSS, see below.

As just noted, there is nothing at present to Case-mark the subject NP of infinitival complements such as that in [171].

[171] *My colleagues believe [her to have gone stark staring bonkers]*

The NP *her* is clearly marked with objective Case, but neither *believe* nor the [−tense] INFL of the complement sentence can be responsible for this on present assumptions. It is argued that NP and S̄, besides being barriers for movement (recall the discussion of subjacency in 2.2.4, beginning with example [135]), are also barriers to government, the difference being that two barriers block movement while only one barrier blocks government. This assumption is necessary in order to block, for example, the assignment of objective Case under government to *John's* in [172],

[172] *They criticised John's decipherment of the tablets.*

which may be assigned the phrase marker given in [173] opposite. Clearly we want objective Case to be assigned to the higher NP but not to its subject. To prevent this, NP is taken to be a barrier blocking the government of *John* by *criticise*. Similarly, in [174],

[174] *They believe the government is about to fall.*

we do not want the NP *the government* to receive objective Case

[173]

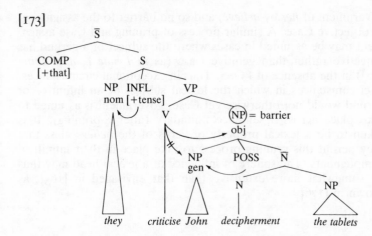

because governed by *believe*, but rather nominative Case because governed by the INFL[+tense] of its own clause. External government is prevented if it is assumed that $\bar{S}$ is a barrier.

[175]

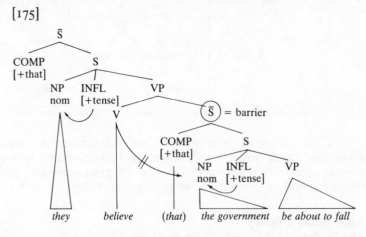

Notice, however, that there is a crucial difference between examples such as [171] and examples such as [174]. In the former there is no complementiser that can ever appear between *believe* and the complement sentence, while in the latter *that* may always optionally appear. In view of the obligatory absence of complementisers in [171] Chomsky supposes that here $\bar{S}$ has been 'pruned', thereby eliminating the COMP position. Once this pruning process has taken place, there is now no barrier to the government of *her* by *believe*, and so no barrier to the assignment of objective Case. A similar process of pruning and Case assignment may be assumed in cases where the subject of a gerund has objective rather than genitive Case (as in *I hate* [s *him doing this*]) in the absence of POSS. Thus in exceptional circumstances, *ie* circumstances in which the lexical subject of an infinitive or gerund would not otherwise get Case, government is assumed to take place across a sentence boundary (after S̄-pruning). It is taken to be a lexical property of verbs of the *believe* class that they permit this pruning process to take place in their infinitival complements. The sphere of influence of a lexical head may thus be somewhat more extensive than that envisaged in [165], as shown in [176].

[176]

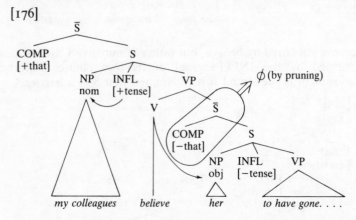

Now that the basic principles of Case assignment have been established, their wider implications are best examined in the context of certain other subtheories of universal grammar, and discussion will be introduced, as appropriate, below.

2.3.6 Binding theory
The binding theory is one of the most important constructs in the system. It is concerned primarily with the conditions under which NPs are interpreted as co-referential with other NPs in the same sentence. For the purposes of the binding theory NPs that are arguments are assumed to fall into one of the three categories listed in [177].

[177] (i) anaphors
       (ii) pronominals
       (iii) referential expressions

Non-argument NPs, such as expletive *it* in *it seems that the end is nigh*, or existential *there* in *there is a fundamental flaw in the government's economic policy*, are outside the system.

Taking each of the categories of [177] in turn, we may define **anaphors** as NPs whose reference is necessarily determined sentence-internally and which cannot have independent reference. In English reflexive and reciprocal pronouns fall into this class. In [178i], for example, *herself* must be taken as referring back to the individual denoted by *Wonderwoman*, and in [178ii] *each other* must refer to the individuals denoted by *Godzilla* and *The Thing*.

[178i] *Wonderwoman projected herself into the 24th century.*
[178ii] *Godzilla and The Thing fought each other on Sunset Boulevard.*

Pronominals are NPs that lack specific lexical content and have only the features person, number, gender and Case; unlike anaphors, they may either refer to individuals independently or co-refer to individuals already named in a given sentence. In [179] the pronominal *he* may refer to the individual denoted by the name *Milton Friedman* or to some other individual not mentioned in the sentence.

[179] *Milton Friedman says he is a genius.*

In certain circumstances the possibility of co-reference is excluded, as in [180].

[180] *Milton Friedman believes him to be a genius.*

R-expressions (the customary abbreviation for referential expressions with specific lexical content), as their name implies, are noun phrases with lexical hands which potentially refer to something. Co-reference is here excluded. Thus in [181] *Big Jim* and *Tiny Tim* must denote two different individuals.

[181] *Big Jim says Tiny Tim should be boiled in oil.*

Even where the same name is used twice, the most natural interpretation is one where two different people are involved.

[182] *Hopkins says Hopkins must be promoted.*

It must, however, be admitted that co-referentiality is here a possibility, but the sentence so interpreted is stylistically highly 'marked', revealing something of the speaker's attitude to Hopkins' pronouncement and Hopkins himself. In these special circumstances the second R-expression has to be taken as a kind of pronominal. Similar remarks apply to such NPs as *the bastard* in [183].

[183] *I know Hopkins and I can't stand the bastard.*

Ordinarily, however, R-expressions are not co-referential with other R-expressions in the same sentence.

The binding theory has three subclauses, one for each of the three subcategories of NP argument.

[184i] An anaphor must be bound in its governing category.
[184ii] A pronominal must be free in its governing category.
[184iii] An R-expression must be free everywhere.

We may begin with the definition of **bound** in [184i]. The term here means not simply co-indexed (*ie* marked with the same referential index as some other NP), but co-indexed with a **c-commanding argument**. A constituent X c-commands (= constituent-commands) a constituent Y if neither directly dominates the other and the first branching node above X in the phrase marker that contains them also dominates (not necessarily immediately) Y. This is subject to the condition that no item can c-command constituents outside the maximal projection that contains it. Thus V, if intransitive, does not c-command its subject NP even though the containing VP node does not branch, given that VP is analysed as V^{max}. On the other hand the subject NP *does* c-command such an intransitive verb because the maximal projection containing the subject, S, also contains the VP containing the intransitive verb. The examples in [185] should help to clarify the definition.

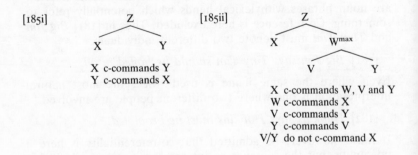

[185iii]

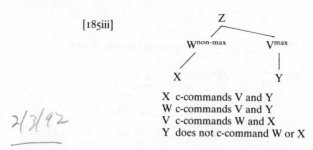

X c-commands V and Y
W c-commands V and Y
V c-commands W and X
Y does not c-command W or X

An argument is an NP in a position associated with a θ-role, as we have seen; roughly speaking, then, an NP within S or NP other than dummy elements such as *it* and *there*. Spelling out the principle [184i] as far as *bound*, an anaphor must be co-indexed with a lexical NP that bears a θ-role by virtue of its position within S (or NP) as subject, direct object or object of preposition, and that c-commands it.

The governing category of some element is the minimal S or NP that contains the governor of that element. Taking the examples in [186],

[186i] *The destruction of the manuscript was a tragedy.*
[186ii] *She loves me.*
[186iii] *I believe her to be the worst Prime Minister ever.*

the governing category of *the manuscript* in [186i] is the NP indicated in [187], because this is the minimal NP or S containing the governor of *the manuscript* (the preposition *of* at S-structure).

[187]

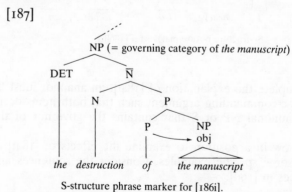

S-structure phrase marker for [186i].

The governing category of *me* in [186ii] is the S indicated in [188], because this is the minimal, and only, NP or S that contains the governor of *me*, namely the verb *loves*.

[188]

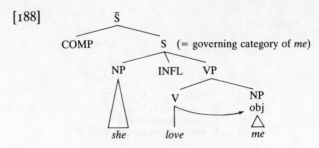

S-structure phrase marker for [186ii]

And finally, the governing category of *her* in [186iii] is the 'root'
S rather than the embedded S, as indicated in [189], because the
governor of *her* is the verb *believe* (after S̄ pruning, as discussed
above).

[189]

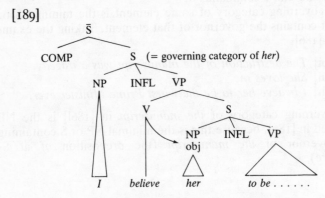

S-structure phrase marker for [186iii].

Thus to complete the explanation of [184i], an anaphor must be
bound by a c-commanding argument such that both items occur
within the minimal NP or S that contains the governor of the
anaphor.

We are now in a position to examine the effects of [184i] as
applied to some specific examples. Consider the sentences and
non-sentences in [190].

[190i] *The lady loves herself.*
[190ii] **Themselves are happier than they have ever been.*

[190iii] *Mad Mike believes himself to have defeated the peace campaigners.*

[190iv] **Silly Sally believes Mad Mike to love herself.*

[190v] **Randy Ronnie thinks himself is the world's wiliest womaniser.*

[190i] may be assigned the S-structure phrase marker in [191].

[191]

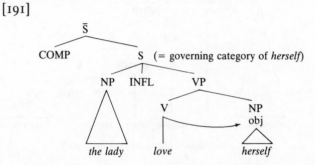

The governing category of *herself* is the whole S, as indicated; this is the minimal NP or S containing the governor of the anaphor, *loves*. The NP *the lady* may bind this anaphor because it is within the governing category of the anaphor, and is an argument (*ie* an NP in a position associated with a θ-role) that c-commands it (the first branching node above *the lady*, S, also dominates the anaphor). The sentence is thus well-formed. Sentence [190ii], however, is ill-formed, because the governing category of the anaphor is the root S (its governor is INFL [+tense]), but the only argument that could give the anaphor its referential index, *they*, cannot bind it properly because it does not c-command it. The first branching node above *they* is the *embedded* S node, and this does *not* dominate *themselves*. Thus the anaphor is not bound within its governing category and the sentence is ungrammatical. This is illustrated in [192] overleaf.

In [190iii] the anaphor *himself* is the subject of the infinitive *to have defeated*. It is governed and Case-marked by *believes* after Š-pruning. The governing category of *himself* is thus the root S and this contains a c-commanding argument *Mad Mike* that can properly bind it. The sentence is therefore well-formed. Consider the diagram in [193] overleaf.

In [190iv] the only argument that could bind *herself* is *Silly Sally* in the root S, but the governing category of the anaphor is the

[192]

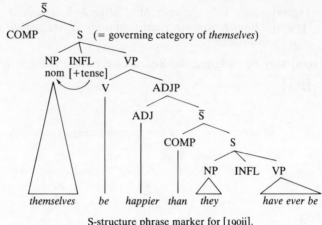

S-structure phrase marker for [190ii].

[193]

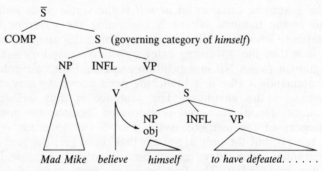

S-structure phrase marker for [190iii].

embedded S. The anaphor is therefore not bound within its governing category, even though *Silly Sally* c-commands it, and the sentence is ill-formed. Compare [194] opposite.

Finally, in [190v] *Randy Ronnie* is the only argument that could bind the anaphor *himself*, but once again the governing category of the anaphor is the embedded sentence (the governor is the INFL element). Thus there is once again no c-commanding argument within the governing category of the anaphor that can bind it and once again the sentence is ungrammatical. Consider [195].

[194]

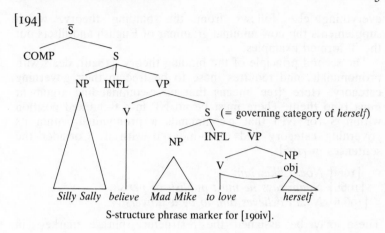

S-structure phrase marker for [190iv].

[195]

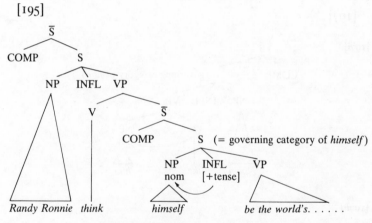

S-structure phrase marker for [190v].

It should be clear from the discussion of these examples that principle [184i] of the binding theory guarantees that only sentences with anaphors in permissible positions will be predicted as being grammatical. The level at which the binding theory applies will be assumed for the moment to be S-structure. The important thing to note is that anaphors, as far as the grammar of English is concerned, can now be inserted freely in NP positions in D-structures that are θ-marked. There is no need for any specific rule of the syntactic or LF components of the grammar of English to say anything about the distribution of reflexives. The lexicon will identify certain nouns as anaphors;

everything else follows from the binding theory, which supplements the now minimal grammar of English and filters out the ill-formed examples.

The second principle of the binding theory, [184ii], deals with pronominals, and requires these to be free in their governing category. Here 'free' means that no c-commanding argument must bind them. There must be no NP in a θ-marked position within S (or NP) that c-commands a pronominal within its governing category and is co-indexed with it. Consider the sentences in [196].

[196i] *Noam likes him.*
[196ii] *Noam says he must publish or perish.*
[196iii] *Noam believes him to be a subversive.*

These may be assigned the S-structure phrase markers in [197i–iii].

[197]

[197i]

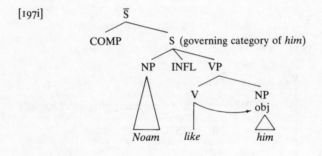

[197ii]

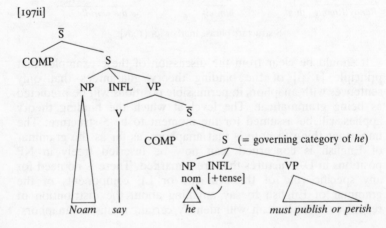

[197iii]

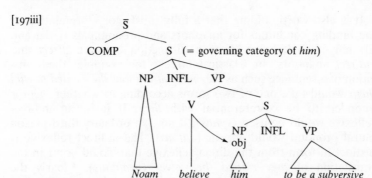

Clearly the governing category of the pronominal *him* in [197i] is the whole S. There must be no c-commanding argument within this S that is co-indexed with *him*. Consequently *Noam* must be assigned a different referential index from that assigned to *him*. In [197ii] the governing category of *he* is the embedded S, the governor being INFL. There must be no c-commanding argument that is co-referential with *he* within that S, and this is the case. The pronoun is, however, free to refer to any suitable individual not referred to within its governing category, including, though not of course necessarily, the individual called *Noam*. In [197iii] the governing category of *him* is the root S (after S̄-pruning), and so *him* cannot refer to *Noam* in this case because *Noam* is a c-commanding argument within its governing category. Once again, then, a very simple general principle provides all the necessary information about the reference possibilities of pro-nominals. One should add here, however, that principle [184ii] is not wholly adequate as presently formulated since there are counterexamples involving prepositional phrases such as *she pushed the offending object away from her*, where *her* may refer to the same individual as *she* (and *herself* is available as an alternative in this case). There are also certain 'formulaic' impera-tives such as *be off with you, go on with you*, etc., where *you* must refer to the same individual as the understood subject but *yourself* is excluded as an option. This suggests that prepositional phrases have a somewhat ambivalent status, in some cases optionally and in others obligatorily analogous to that of S and NP as a governing category, but the full range of facts is quite complex and there is some disagreement amongst speakers as to what the most natural option is in any given case. In view of this no revision of [184ii] will be attempted here, but the reader should be aware of the problem.

It is also worth adding that a fully satisfactory formulation of the binding conditions for anaphors and pronominals ([184i and ii]) may well have to draw a distinction between *direct* and *indirect* anaphors. In Classical Greek, for example, the translation of a sentence such as *they were afraid that she wanted to ruin them* would take one of two forms according to whether *them* is intended to be co-referential with *they*. If it is, an indirect reflexive would be used (*sphas*), if not, an ordinary third person plural pronoun would appear (*autous*). The indirect reflexive is distinct in form from the direct reflexive that would occur in the translation of *they ruined themselves* (*heautous*). Clearly the binding condition for anaphors ([184i]) can only be interpreted as applying to direct anaphors, and indirect anaphors will have to be treated as a type of pronominal. Ordinary pronominals, by contrast, are more like R-expressions (see immediately below) in that they may not be bound (ordinarily) by any c-commanding argument even if that argument is in a higher clause. The situation is even more difficult in Latin where there is no formal distinction at all between direct and indirect reflexives and the translation of a sentence such as *Caesar asks Pompey not to ruin him* may employ either an ordinary third person pronoun (*eum*) or a reflexive (*se*) to translate *him*. In the former case the pronoun may refer neither to *Caesar* nor to *Pompey*, and in the latter the reflexive may co-refer either to *Caesar* or to *Pompey*. This means that ordinary pronominals in Latin also behave rather like R-expressions, and that the anaphor binding condition applies only to a subset of reflexive uses (namely those corresponding to the direct reflexives of Classical Greek). Any fully satisfactory account of binding will have to deal with facts of this sort, but once again a detailed revision is beyond the scope of a book of this sort. For some discussion of the kinds of problem involved see Yang (1983).

Returning now to the final clause of the binding theory, [184iii] is perhaps the simplest of the three conditions. R-expressions must not be bound by a c-commanding argument anywhere else within the same sentence (however long and complex). Thus *Noam* cannot be co-indexed with *Mo* or *he* in any of the examples in [198].

[198i] *Mo(he)/admires Noam.*
[198ii] *Mo(he)/says Noam must go.*
[198iii] *Mo(he)/believes Noam to be an anarchist.*

Consider now the case of NP-movement, illustrated in [199i and ii].

[199i] *I am believed* [– *to be a genius*]
[199ii] **I am believed* [– *is a genius*]

In each case the dash marks the position from which the NP has moved. Compare now the sentences in [200].

[200i] *I believe* [*myself to be a genius*]
[200ii] **I believe* [*myself is a genius*]

The parallelism is obvious. The movement of *I* is blocked when the complement sentence is finite, just as the association of *I* and *myself* is blocked when the complement sentence is finite. A further parallel is illustrated in [201] and [202].

[201i] *I am believed* [– *to love Maggie*]
[201ii] **I am believed* [*Maggie to love* –]
[202i] *I believe* [*myself to love Maggie*]
[202ii] **I believe* [*Maggie to love myself*]

The movement of *I* is blocked when it involves extraction from S across a lexically specified subject, and the association of *I* and *myself* is blocked by an intervening specified subject.

Temporarily ignoring principle [184i] of the binding theory, the differences between the pairs in [199] and [201], it will be recalled (see 2.2.4, especially the discussion of examples [150] to [154], were handled by reference to the Tensed Sentence and Specified Subject Conditions respectively, both of these being interpreted as conditions on the operation of movement rules. In view of [200] and [202], this is clearly too limited a conception of these conditions, and they should be reformulated as conditions on any rule, transformational or interpretative, that seeks to involve two positions across a sentence boundary where that sentence is either tensed or contains a specified subject. But this immediately raises the question of why the two different types of rule should be subject to the same conditions. One way of explaining this would be to argue that the gaps left by the movement of *I* in [199] and [201] are really not gaps at all, but rather empty NPs, NPs whose lexical contents have been displaced but which themselves remain in place. Suppose now that part of the operation of NP-movement is the automatic co-indexing of the NP position to which the movement takes place and the empty NP position from which the material in question has been displaced. The empty NP position, or **trace** of NP, can now be regarded as a phonetically null anaphor. As such it will naturally be subject to the same conditions as overt anaphors, namely the TSC and SSC. We can thus allow NP-movement to operate quite freely on the

understanding that sentences containing NP-trace pairs that fail
to meet the requirements of the TSC and SSC, now interpreted
as conditions on rules of interpretation exclusively, will be ruled
out.

We may cite two pieces of evidence in support of this formulation. First the distribution of traces and overt anaphors is
exactly parallel in [199] and [200] or [201] and [202]; both occur
as subjects of infinitives, and the choice between them is determined by Case theory. The overt anaphor occurs in subject
position of the complement when the verb of the main clause is
capable of Case-marking it and the null anaphor occurs when this
verb is not. Thus active transitive verbs may govern and Case-
mark across S, while the participial verb forms in the passive
analogues may only govern but do not have the power to assign
Case. The movement of the subject is thus obligatory in these
cases if the effects of the Case filter are to be avoided. NPs
without lexical content do not have to have Case, so the Case
filter does not rule out structures with Caseless traces. We may
take it as a general principle, then, that the trace of
NP-movement does not have Case, and that such traces never
occur in positions that are ordinarily Case-marked. NP traces will
thus never be found in direct object position, unlike overt
anaphors. Secondly, if traces are present in S-structure, it follows
that the D-structure positions of NPs will be able to be read off
at that level. This means that the rules of the LF component, as
was noted at the beginning of this section, will now be able to
operate on a single level of representation, because information
about predicate–argument structure and thematic roles, as well
as information pertaining to such matters as quantifier scope
interpretation, will be available at S-structure. This unification of
the operation of LF rules at a single level is a highly desirable
consequence of the adoption of the trace theory of movement
rules.

It is also worth pointing out that trace theory is in any case a
consequence of the adoption of the Projection Principle (2.3.2,
the discussion of [162]). Thus if *believe(d)*, for example, is
subcategorised as the sort of verb that may take a clausal complement, it will have to have a clausal complement at all levels of
representation, D-structure, S-structure and LF. The movement
of the subject NP in [199] or [201] cannot, therefore, be allowed
to leave behind a 'bare' VP; there must always be a subject as
well, albeit an empty one in S-structure (and LF). This issue will
be discussed further in 2.3.10.

The reader will recall from the earlier discussion of the TSC and SSC that the formulation of these conditions was less than ideal (see 2.2.4, especially the discussion of [151] to [154]). In the first place there was overlap between them, in that movement from, say, the direct object position of a finite clause violated both conditions. Secondly, since these were supposed to be general conditions on the operation of all transformations, an exception clause had to be built in to allow extraction of constituents from tensed Ss and Ss with specified subjects if the operation took place via COMP (as in the case of *wh*-movement). We are now in a position to eliminate these problems.

Returning to [200] and [202], the difference between the members of each pair is in fact accounted for by condition [184i] of the binding theory, the binding condition for anaphors. Thus the reflexive pronouns in the subject position of the finite complement clause and the object position of the infinitival complement clause are not bound in their governing categories. But given our new approach to movement, interpreting the traces of NP-movement as anaphors, it follows that principle [184i] of the binding theory will *also* rule out the ungrammatical members of the pairs in [199] and [201]. The anaphor binding condition may therefore be seen as a unification of the provisions of the TSC and SSC. A *single* statement now gives the same effects but without the overkill.

Consider again [199ii] and [201ii], repeated here as [203] and [204].

[203] *I am believed [t *is a genius*]
[204] *I am believed [*Maggie to love* t]

Here *t* is the trace of the moved NP *I*. Taking this to be a null anaphor, it is clear that in [203] its governing category is the embedded S (the governor being INFL), and that within this there is no c-commanding argument co-indexed with it. Similarly in [204], the governing category is once again the embedded S (the governor here being the verb *love*), and once again there is no c-commanding argument within this S that is co-indexed with the trace. Both sentences are therefore ungrammatical.

By contrast the requirements of [184i] are met in [199i] and [201i], repeated here as [205] and [206].

[205] I am believed [t *to be a genius*]
[206] I am believed [t *to love Maggie*]

In both cases the trace is governed by *believed* after S̄-pruning; the governing category is therefore the root S, and this contains a co-indexed c-commanding argument (*I*), as required. Principle

[184i] therefore restricts movement from an embedded S to cases
involving the subject of an infinitive. We now have an explanation for the restrictions previously built into the rule system
(via subject-to-subject raising and the clausemate constraint on
passive); NP-movement is only possible between two positions
such that the element in the destination position may bind the
null element in the source position in accordance with the binding
principle for anaphors.

It is important, however, to note that the extension of this
principle from overt anaphors to null anaphors entails a slight
reformulation. In the case of overt anaphors the antecedent will
always have an independent θ-role, *ie* will be an argument. Thus
in the examples in [207] it is clear that *Willy Wonka* and *himself*
are each assigned distinct thematic roles.

[207i] *Willy Wonka stuffed himself with chocolate.*
[207ii] *Willy Wonka wants to stuff himself with Turkish
        delight.*

The reason, of course, is that *stuff* θ-marks both its subject and
object positions (agent and patient/theme respectively), just as
want θ-marks its subject and complement sentence (possibly once
again agent and theme respectively, though this case is somewhat
less clear-cut). In the case of null anaphors, however, the antecedent must be in a non-θ position (henceforth θ̄-position). This
follows from the θ-criterion (*cf* 2.3.4). If a NP in a D-structure
θ-position were moved to a position in S-structure that was also
a θ-position, the same NP would be assigned two different θ-
roles, which would violate the criterion of well-formedness for
LF that each argument be assigned a single θ-role. (In fact such
a movement would be impossible anyway, since in D-structure
only non-argument positions are lexically unfilled and so only
these are available as empty slots for NPs to move into.) Thus
in [208] the position of *Razors McGinty* is a non-argument
position.

[208] *Razors McGinty* $\begin{Bmatrix} seems \\ is\ believed \end{Bmatrix}$ [t *to be a hit-man*]

Neither verbs such as *seem* nor the participles of passive
sentences θ-mark their subject positions, it is assumed. This is
supported by the fact that these positions may be filled by
'dummy' elements such as *it* or *there*.

[209i] *It* $\begin{Bmatrix} seems \\ is\ believed \end{Bmatrix}$ [*that Razors is a psychopath*]

[209ii] *There* $\left\{ \begin{array}{l} \textit{seems} \\ \textit{is believed} \end{array} \right\}$ [*to be a psychopath on the loose*]

Consequently, we can no longer require that anaphors be bound by a c-commanding *argument*; the trace in [208] is bound by a *non-argument*. It is useful, therefore, to draw a distinction between NPs in A-positions and NPs that are arguments. A-positions are those positions in S that may *in principle* be θ-marked; subject, direct object, and object of preposition for NPs. Arguments are NPs in A-positions that actually *are* θ-marked in a given case. We can now reformulate the binding condition for anaphors as in [210].

[210] *Binding condition for anaphors*: an anaphor must be A-bound in its governing category.

This requires anaphors to be bound by c-commanding NPs in A-positions, whether or not they are arguments. (As an alternative, we might suggest that the θ-role assigned to an NP in D-structure is transmitted to the new position in S-structure by the movement rule, and that the original θ-position becomes a $\bar{\theta}$-position just as the original $\bar{\theta}$-position becomes a θ-position. This avoids violation of the θ-criterion, and allows us to retain the original formulation of the binding condition. This possibility will not be adopted.)

It is important to note that the extension of the binding theory to null anaphors also eliminates the possibility that the theory should apply at D-structure; since there are no traces at this level by definition, the theory could not operate as intended there, a fact which lends support to the working hypothesis that the binding theory is a condition of well-formedness on S-structures. The possibility remains open that it should apply at LF, but there are reasons why this should not be so, and these will be discussed below.

The other problem with the TSC and SSC was that, though intended as general conditions, they did not in fact constrain the operation of *wh*-movement. The replacement of these conditions by principle [210] also eliminates this problem. It is clear that the relationship between a moved NP and its trace is conceptually quite distinct from that between a moved *wh*-phrase and its trace. The first, A-binding, is simply a matter of co-reference marking at LF, derived without change from S-structure. The latter involves **operator binding**. In a logical formula an operator is an element outside a proposition that binds a variable element within the proposition. The sentence [211], for example,

[211] *All men are mortal.*

expresses a proposition which is conventionally represented in the so-called predicate calculus as in [212].

[212] $\forall$ x [MAN (x) $\supset$ MORTAL (x)]

Informally, this is to be read 'for all *x*, if *x* is a man then *x* is mortal'. Notice that the quantifier *all* is represented as an operator ($\forall$), outside the proposition proper, which binds the variable *x* (denoting a random member of the set of individuals in the universe of discourse). If we now take the S-structure [213]

[213] [*Who*[*you* INFL *tip t for the post*]] (*Who do you tip for the post?*)
    S̄   S

where *t* represents the position from which *who* has moved, it seems reasonable to argue that its LF representation should be something like [214].

[214] [*For which x, x a person* [*you* INFL *tip x for the post*]]
    S̄   S

In other words, *who* is best interpreted as a kind of quantifier and its trace as a kind of variable at LF. Notice that both in S-structure [213] and in LF [214] the interrogative/quantifier is peripheral to S (specifically in COMP).

Given this distinction between the case of NP-movement and *wh*-movement, it is not surprising that they should be subject to different conditions. The attempt to make the TSC and SSC into general conditions subject to a COMP escape hatch (see the discussion of [154] above) should be abandoned in favour of separate conditions, one for anaphors (doing the work of the TSC and SSC) and one for variables. We already have a binding condition for anaphors. The question therefore arises whether either of the binding conditions of [184] other than that for anaphors generalises to variables. (*Bound* and *free* are now taken to mean 'A-bound' and 'A-free' respectively in all three conditions).

Notice first that pronominals may be bound by c-commanding NPs in A-positions provided that these are outside their governing category. Thus *Joan* and *she* may be co-referential in [215].

[215] *Joan said that she had all the answers.*

Variables, by contrast, will never be bound by c-commanding NPs in A-positions by definition; variables will always be bound by operators in non-A (henceforth A̅) positions, *ie* positions peripheral to S (specifically COMP). It follows that the binding condition for R-expressions, [184iii], does indeed generalise to variables. Just as NP-traces are phonetically null anaphors, so variables are phonetically null R-expressions for the purposes of the binding theory. Condition [184iii] requires that no R-expression, including now variables, should be bound anywhere by a c-commanding NP in an A-position. This does not, it must be emphasisied, preclude the possibility of A̅-binding of variables, *ie* the binding of variables by c-commanding operator-like elements in A̅-positions like COMP. This type of binding is precisely what is involved in [213]/[214] above. If movement necessarily involves co-indexing, whether we are dealing with *wh*-movement or NP-movement, and if the trace of *wh*-movement is a variable, the effect of the binding condition for R-expressions is to restrict the operation of *wh*-movement to those cases where the *wh*-phrase is moved to an A̅-position (COMP), *ie* to those cases where the trace is bound by an element interpreted as an operator. There is thus no need to specify that *wh*-expressions have to be moved to COMP within the rule system.

The crucial question, of course, is how we know whether a given trace is an anaphor or a variable; with this information we know which binding condition it is subject to. It was observed earlier that NP-traces lack Case; indeed, the motivation for NP-movement is the need to shift lexical NPs from deep structure positions that are not Case-marked to positions which are Case-marked in order to avoid violations of the Case filter (*cf* 2.3.5). By contrast, variables, including the traces of *wh*-movement, are always Case-marked. Thus the movement of subjects of finite clauses, direct objects or objects of prepositions presents no problems since all these positions are automatically Case-marked; though note that, because COMP is not a position to which Case is assigned, items moved there must be assumed somehow to inherit Case from their traces. But what of examples such as [216],

[216] np *be believed [who to be the most likely successor]*

where in D-structure *who* is in a non-Case-marked position? If *who* were to move directly to the COMP position of the root clause, it would not receive Case there either, as there is no governing element capable of assigning it. There is thus an immediate problem in that the S-structure would contain a Caseless lexical NP and be ruled out by the Case filter. But notice further that the empty NP position (np) in [216] would remain empty even in S-structure, and that this position is Case-marked nominative (as subject of a finite clause). The only cases where the subject position of a finite clause may be empty are those where a *wh*-phrase has been moved. In all other cases there must be a lexical subject, if only a dummy element such as *it*. Consider the examples in [217].

[217i] *Who did you say [came]*

[217ii] **Came*

[217iii] *It seems that Chomsky got it wrong.*

[217iv] **Seems that Chomsky got it wrong.*

This suggests that in [216] *who* is moved first into the empty NP position by virtue of being an NP. As the subject of a finite verb it is assigned nominative Case. It may then be moved into COMP by virtue of being a *wh*-phrase, leaving a finite clause with an empty subject just as in the case of the embedded sentence in [217i]. The S-structure would thus be [218].

[218] $[_{\bar{S}}$ *Who* $[_S$ t_1 *is believed* $[_{S}t_0$ *to be the most likely successor*$]]]$

Such an analysis allows us to retain our generalisation that Case-less traces are anaphors and Case-marked traces are variables. In [218] t_0 is an anaphor A-bound by the variable t_1, which is Ā-bound by the operator *who*. Only the variable is Case-marked. Assuming then that the distinction between anaphors and variables can be drawn in terms of Case as suggested, we know immediately for any given empty NP which of the binding conditions it is subject to.

Having discovered the existence of phonetically null anaphors and R-expressions, we might ask whether there are not also phonetically null pronominals. The answer to this is that there are, but since the standard examples of these do not fall under the provisions of the binding theory (at least in standard formulations of GB theory), unlike overt pronominals, they will be dealt with below under the heading of control theory (2.3.8). Other null pronominals are discussed in 2.3.9 (the discussion of examples [240] to [245]).

There is, however, the outstanding question of whether the binding theory should apply at S-structure or LF. Consider [219i and ii].

[219i] *Which book that John wrote did he throw in the fire?*

[219ii] *He threw every book that John wrote in the fire.*

Suppose that these have the S-structures illustrated in [220].

[220]

[220i]

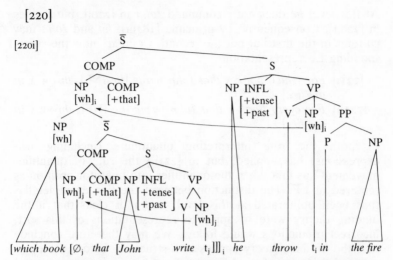

[which book [∅ᵢ that [John write tⱼ]]]ᵢ he throw tᵢ in the fire

It is here supposed that the gap in relative clauses is created by *wh*-movement, exactly as in *wh*-questions; if, however, *that* appears in COMP, as here, the *wh*-phrase has no surface realisation. The trace tᵢ is the trace of the NP *which book that John* INFL *write*, and tⱼ is the trace of the 'invisible' relative pronoun moved into COMP alongside *that*. A rule of predication in the LF component interprets the relative clause as making a statement about the head NP by associating the gap in the former with the latter.

[220ii]

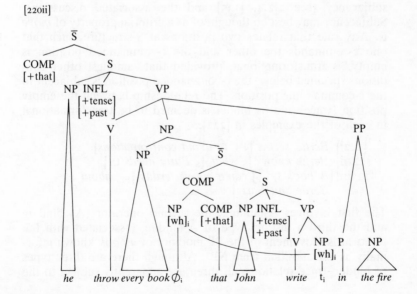

he throw every book ∅ᵢ that John write tᵢ in the fire

At this level *he* does not c-command *John* in [220i], but it does in [220ii]. Consequently, by principle [184iii], *he* and *John* may co-refer in the first but not the second. Compare now the corresponding LF representations.

[221i] *For which book x that John wrote* [*he* INFL *throw x in the fire*]

[221ii] *For every book x that John wrote* [*he* INFL *throw x in the fire*]

In both the rule interpreting quantifiers (including *wh*-expressions) has applied, but in [221ii] the rule of quantifier movement has first taken the quantifier into operator position as required at LF. The distinction between the two examples has thus been obliterated at this level, and it is clear that if the binding theory were to apply to representations of this sort, incorrect predictions would follow. We may therefore conclude that the binding theory applies at S-structure, before the operation of the rules of the LF component.

2.3.7 Bounding theory

Returning now to the subtheories of universal grammar listed in [163], we come to bounding theory. This is concerned with the limitations to be placed on the displacement of constituents by the transformational rule schema *move* α (see 2.3.2, beginning with the discussion of [159] and [160]), and its chief principle is subjacency (see 2.2.4, [135] and the associated discussion). Subjacency may best be thought of as a criterial property of *move* α. Any rule that relates two positions at S-structure, such that one c-commands the other and the c-commanded position is empty, is transformational, provided that, amongst other conditions specified below, the c-commanded position is subjacent to the c-commanding position. The relationship between the empty position (trace) and its binder is deemed to be transformational in each of the examples in [222].

[222i] *Bertie*ᵢ *seems* [s tᵢ *to avoid confrontations*]

[222ii] *Bertie knows* [s̄ *what*ᵢ [s *Barty needs* tᵢ]]

[222iii] [*A book* tᵢ ₙₚ] *came out yesterday* [ₚₚᵢ *about Bertie and Barty*]

The first involves A-binding, the second operator ($\overline{A}$) binding and the third a distinct type of $\overline{A}$-binding (associated with the rightwards movement of the PP modifier of *a book* known informally as **extraposition from NP**). Although there are three types of binder–trace relations, all three are apparently subject to the

subjacency condition (though see 5.2. for further discussion).
Consider the ungrammatical examples in [223].

[223i] *Bertie_i seems [_s̄ that [_⑤ it is likely [_st_i to avoid confrontations]]]

[223ii] *Bertie knows [_s̄ what_i [_s you believe [_NPthe story[_s̄t_i that[_sBarty needs t_i]]]]]]

[223iii] *[A review of [a book t_i NP]NP] came out yesterday [_PP_i about Bertie and Barty]

It was assumed in the earlier discussion of subjacency that NP and S̄ were the main barriers for subjacency, but that S could become a barrier in certain circumstances. Amongst these is the situation illustrated in [223i]. Recall that traces, as anaphors, must be bound in their governing category, and so have a governor. *Likely* when accompanied by an infinitival complement does not select an overt complementiser, and in this is distinct from, say, *possible* which may select *for* (cf: *it is possible for students to begin their courses in November*). The absence of *for* in [223i] might be explained by the process of S̄-pruning discussed in connection with the Case-marking of subjects of infinitives after verbs such as *believe* (cf 2.3.5, [171] to [176]). If S̄ is missing, there can be no overt complementiser and further, the way is now opened up for the government of the trace in subject position of the complement by *likely*. The difference between this case and the case involving verbs of the *believe* class is that only the latter have the power to assign objective Case. The trace in [223i] is thus Caseless, one of the distinguishing characteristics of null anaphors. Without the assumption of S̄-pruning here the trace would be ungoverned, and so lack a governing category; there is nothing within the infinitival complement that can assume the role of governor, and S̄ is a barrier to external government. Assuming that S̄-pruning is necessary to allow the necessary proper government of the trace, it also becomes necessary to assume that the ringed S inherits barrierhood from the pruned S̄ in some way, and so becomes a barrier to movement. It would be difficult to make the other S a barrier to movement because it is not a barrier to government. Without this assumption the movement illustrated would pass only one barrier (S̄), and there would be no subjacency violation to explain the ungrammaticality. If, however, the ringed S is also a barrier, subjacency is violated and the sentence is predicted to be ungrammatical. The other two examples in [223] are straightforward violations of subjacency. The second successive cyclic

movement of *what* in [223ii] crosses $\bar{S}$ and NP, and the extraposition of the PP in [223iii] crosses two NPs.

Obviously, it would not be difficult to invent rules of interpretation which co-indexed empty categories with their binders
subject to certain conditions. We could, then, dispense with D-
structure and *move* α, and operate with a system that had only
S-structure and LF. S-structures would contain empty categories
and would be well-formed only if some interpretative principle
co-indexed each of these with some other element. In the case
of principles co-indexing such S-structures as [222i–iii], these
would be no more than a notational variant of the mechanisms
of transformational grammar, assuming that the generalisation
about all three types of relationship being subject to subjacency
could somehow be taken into account. The important thing is
that generalisations should be expressed where they exist to be
expressed, and the main argument for transformations in GB
theory is that they represent a rule-type defined by a set of properties that distinguishes it from other rule-types. Provided this is
recognised, it makes little difference whether the formulation is
syntactic (*move* α) or interpretative. At a certain level of abstraction, the debate about whether we need transformations or not
is not now a terribly exciting one. The real issue is whether the
generalisation they purport to express, namely that all the
binder–trace relations in examples [222i–iii] are subject to a
common set of conditions, is a genuine one.

This issue will be taken up again in the final chapter (5.2). For
the moment, let us simply repeat what the conditions are. First,
as was noted earlier in the discussion of [207], [208] and [209],
move α requires the binder of a trace to be in a θ-position. This
follows from the θ-criterion and the Projection Principle. Thus
in [222i] *Bertie* is in the subject position of *seems*, a verb which
does not θ-mark its subject (*cf: it seems that. . . . . .*). In [222ii]
what is in COMP, a position that is not θ-marked by any verb by
definition; verbs may θ-mark only A-positions. And in [222iii] the
extraposed $\bar{S}$ is an adjunct of the main clause, loosely attached
to it, and obviously not in a position which an argument of *came
out* could occupy. Secondly, the binder–trace relation is subject
to subjacency, as has been discussed immediately above. Finally,
as was also mentioned, NP traces (and, in fact, *wh*-traces) must
be properly governed, a notion to which we return in the
discussion of government theory (2.3.9). These are the three
defining characteristics of *move* α. It is open to critics to try to
show that the generalisation expressed by this rule schema is
spurious, or to try to show that the same information could be

expressed in alternative ways which have more desirable overall consequences.

2.3.8 Control theory

We come now to control theory. It was observed earlier (2.2.3, beginning with the discussion of [105]) that the transformational analysis of sentences with verbs taking infinitival complements that have null subjects understood as being co-referential with an NP in the main clause was abandoned in favour of an analysis employing interpretative rules. In [224], for example, it is clear that in the first example the empty subject is 'controlled' by the subject of the main clause and in the second example by the object of the main clause. Rules are needed to express these facts.

> [224i] *Ted promised his wife to drop the divorce suit.*
> [224ii] *Ted persuaded his wife to drop the divorce suit.*

Obviously the complement of *promise* or *persuade* is propositional at LF; *ie* the empty subject must be supplied as part of the interpretation, because the empty subject in each case is an argument which is assigned a θ-role (in this case that of agent). The Projection Principle requires that complement structure at one level of representation should also recur at all other levels. Thus *promise* and *persuade* will have clausal complements at D-structure and S-structure as well as at LF. (In the case of D-structure this is entirely natural, since it is simply a configurational representation of predicate-argument structure abstracted from the effects of *move α*.) Furthermore both verbs may take overtly clausal complements when the verb of the embedded clause is finite.

> [225i] *Ted promised his wife that he would drop the divorce*
> *suit.*
> [225ii] *Ted persuaded his wife that she should drop the divorce*
> *suit.*

Let us assume, then, that both verbs take clausal complements as a lexical property, and that the complement may or may not be finite. The question now is why the subject cannot be lexically expressed when the complement is infinitival, and, in the absence of lexical content, what sort of empty category we are dealing with. This immediately raises the further question of what sort of mechanism we need to express the control relations involved; *ie* how does the empty category get co-indexed and under what conditions?

One thing is immediately clear. The empty category in these cases cannot be a trace, and there is no question of its being created by the rule *move* α. First of all the antecedent has an independent θ-role in each of the examples in [224], agent in the case of *Ted* in [224i] and patient/theme in the case of *his wife* in [224ii]. The antecedent of trace can never be in a θ-position, as we have seen. Secondly, the relationship in this type of construction is not subject to subjacency. Consider the example in [226] where the understood subject of *to learn Chinese* can be *Nurdley*, despite the fact that three barriers intervene (S̄, NP and S̄).

[226] *Nurdley thinks*[S̄*that*[S[NP[S̄ – *to learn Chinese*]]*will be easy*.]]

Thirdly, there is good reason to think that the position in question is not governed. Take the case of [226]. Within the GB framework INFL[−tense] cannot govern (or assign Case to) a subject NP (*cf* 2.3.5). So the subject of *to learn Chinese* cannot be governed internally. Nor in this case is there any possibility of external government. As we have seen, S̄ and NP are barriers to government, and there is no basis for assuming that these nodes are pruned here to allow government by *thinks*. The most obvious reason against such a move is the presence of the complementiser *that*, which shows that the higher S̄ is retained.

Suppose, then, that these are the defining characteristics of the empty subject in cases involving control. Consider now the examples in [227].

[227i] *We do not know* [S̄*what* [S – *to do*]]
[227ii] *We tried* [– *to revive some interest in the subject*]
[227iii] *It is important* [S̄ *for* [S *you to learn your lesson*]]
[227iv] *It is important* [– *to leave at once*]

Clearly the empty subject in the complement sentence in [227i] is not governed; there is no possible internal governor and S̄ is a barrier to external government. Since the missing subject in [227ii] is of the same type as that in [227i], *ie* is clearly not a trace, it seems reasonable to assume that there must be an S̄ barrier between *tried* and the empty category. Let us suppose, then, that the major syntactic difference between verbs of the *believe* class and verbs of the *try* class is that only the former allow S̄-pruning, and thereby external government. It is this external government that allows Case-marking or movement of the subject of the complement. Certain verbs and adjectives that prohibit S̄-pruning allow an overt complementiser *for* to appear. *Try* is not of this type, but *important* is, as can be seen from

[227iii]. Notice that when *for* is present in these cases there must be a lexical subject of the infinitive and that when *for* is absent there can be no lexical subject, as in [227iv]. Those verbs like *try* that do not take *for* never allow lexical subjects to appear in their infinitival complements. Where *for* does appear it is clearly the governor and Case-marker of the subject, because INFL cannot govern internally and $\overline{S}$ is a barrier to external government. There is, therefore, a straightforward correlation. Where there is a governor there may be a lexical NP, and the lexical NP can remain *in situ* so long as the governor has the power to Case-mark it. Where there is no governor there must be an empty subject. This follows from the Case filter. If a lexical NP occurred in an ungoverned, and so non-Case-marked, position, the sentence would be ungrammatical. Recall that if the position is ungoverned, the NP cannot move elsewhere, because the resultant trace would not be governed, contrary to the requirements of government theory (on which see 2.3.9 below; see also the final paragraph of 2.3.7).

Thus far we have established that the controller–gap relation in [224] is not correctly analysed as an example of *move α*, and we have an explanation of why the subject has to be empty in such cases. In particular, it was noted that the position in which this empty category occurs cannot be governed. This in fact is not surprising. The item is often rather like an anaphor in that it lacks the potential for independent reference, but is like a pronominal in that its antecedent apparently can never be in the same clause. The binding conditions require anaphors to be A-bound in their governing category and pronominals to be A-free in their governing category. The only way in which the empty category in the subject position of complement sentences such as those in [224] can avoid falling prey to contradictory requirements, therefore, is not to be governed and so not to have a governing category. The only A-position which is ungoverned in the required way is the subject position of an infinitive that is protected by an $\overline{S}$ barrier. Any verb or adjective, therefore, that takes an infinitival complement but does not allow $\overline{S}$-pruning will, in the absence of *for*, have a complement with an empty subject. The distribution of this element is automatic, and does not need to be specified anywhere in the grammar of English. If the verb or adjective takes an NP complement in addition to the clausal complement, or if it θ-marks its subject, one or other or these NPs will be specified as the controller of the empty subject of the complement as a lexical property.

Ideally the choice of controller should be an automatic consequence of principles of the theory of control, but there are numerous difficulties to be overcome before such principles will be forthcoming. Syntactic position (*eg* proximity to the complement sentence) is not a reliable guide to choice of controller, as the case of *Sally promised Bill to give up the booze* (versus *Sally persuaded Bill to give up the booze*) shows; and there are similar problems with *Sally asked Bill to leave*, where speakers of some dialects take *Bill* and speakers of others take *Sally* to be the controller of *to leave*. The solution to this kind of difficulty may lie in the specification of the **semantic type** of control verbs in their lexical entries; this might then provide a basis for predicting the controller that does not depend upon syntactic representations which are incapable of making the necessary discriminations. For some discussion of this possibility in a different framework see Chapter 3, section 6.

There are further difficulties where an infinitive or gerund without an overt subject appears as the subject of an embedded clause, as in [228].

[228i] *John thinks that [teaching theoretical physics] is easy.*

[228ii] *John thinks that [teaching yourself theoretical physics] is easy.*

[228iii] *John thinks that [teaching himself theoretical physics] is easy.*

[228iv] *John thinks that [teaching theoretical physics] will be easy.*

[228v] *John thinks that [teaching theoretical physics] will be easy for you.*

In [228i] the embedded clause may equally naturally denote a generic proposition, with the missing subject interpreted as arbitrary in reference, or as denoting a proposition whose subject is *John*. Notice that the gerund may occur with either *yourself* [228ii], or *himself* [228iii]. But when the modal *will* is employed, the generic reading becomes much more difficult and the reading where *John* is taken to be the subject is the most natural one, as [228iv] makes clear. Nevertheless, [228v] shows that this subject position may in principle be controlled by some NP other than *John*. The point about these control relations involving infinitives and gerunds in subject position is that the interpretation of the missing subject is much more fluid than that involved in examples such as [229],

[229i] *John tried to teach himself theoretical physics.*

[229ii] *It is unclear how best to teach theoretical physics.*

where, in the first case, control by *John* is obligatory and, in the second, we necessarily have the arbitrary interpretation of the empty subject. Any satisfactory theory of control is going to have to specify the conditions under which interpretations become less fixed and also outline what the range of possible interpretations is in these cases. (For further discussion in a framework which distinguishes cases like [228] from those in [229], see Chapter 4, section 7).

For the present, we have at least a basis for predicting the distribution of the null element subject to control, even if we have no fully developed theory of possible control relations. But what exactly is this element? It cannot be a trace, as we saw, because *inter alia* traces must be governed, and this is not true of the empty subjects in question. Is it, then, a pronominal? It cannot in fact be subject to the pronominal binding condition [184ii], any more than it is subject to that for anaphors [184i]/[210], because it does not have a governing category. Accordingly the binding theory has no bearing on the distribution of this element, and it is therefore quite proper that the relationship(s) in question should be assigned to a distinct subtheory of universal grammar, namely control theory. It was suggested earlier that the item in question is sometimes rather like an anaphor; thus in [229i] the empty subject must take its referential index from *John* and has no capacity for independent reference. It also has some of the properties of pronominals; again in [229i], the antecedent *John* has an independent θ-role, as would be the case with the antecedent of a co-indexed pronominal (*cf: John$_j$ loves it when Mary kisses him$_i$*). The antecedent of trace cannot, of course, have an independent θ-role because of the θ-criterion. Furthermore, in [229ii] the empty subject has a referent *not* identified by any other constituent in the sentence (like *he* in *he dreams of wealth and power*). On balance, then, it would seem reasonable to argue that the null element in question is an empty pronominal which, in certain specified circumstances, *viz* those requiring control by a lexical NP, loses the characteristic pronominal property of capacity for independent reference and takes on something of the character of an anaphor. In support of the basically pronominal nature of these empty subjects, note that even when there is a potential controller to determine their reference, they may still behave like pronominals in that their antecedents need not c-command them. Consider the sentences in [230].

[230i] *It is by* [np$_i$ *mastering the facts*] *that John$_i$ will progress.*

[230ii] *It is because [Mary helped him_i] that John_i passed the exam.*

It is clear that neither the antecedent of the empty subject in [230i] nor the antecedent of *him* in [230ii] c-commands the relevant co-indexed category because each occurs in a clause that is subordinate to the clause containing the co-indexed category. It will be recalled (see 2.3.6, beginning with the discussion of [184]) that c-command is an indispensable precondition for anaphoric binding, in contrast with the situation exemplified in [230]. On this analysis, one of the central problems of control theory is to offer an account of why these null pronominals sometimes *have* to be controlled by some other NP rather than having independent (arbitrary) reference. One possibility is that we are in fact dealing with two different kinds of empty category, one of which is essentially anaphoric, the other essentially pronominal. This possibility is discussed at length in 4.7, and again in 5.2.

Assuming that what has been said so far is broadly along the right lines, we may refer to this kind of empty subject as PRO; this is to be thought of as a pronominal element to which the usual features of person, number and gender may be assigned (though not Case, presumably, since this is assigned under government and PRO must be ungoverned), but which lacks phonetic specification. It may be regarded as a lexical item (just like *he*, *they*, *we*, etc.) which is inserted freely into NP positions in D-structures and assigned an appropriate θ-role. Its proper distribution is determined not by rules of the grammar of English but by general principles of universal grammar, which 'filter out' the impossible cases. Assuming that each lexical NP, including PRO, is assigned a referential index at D-structure, the rules of control, once properly developed, can be interpreted as checking that those NPs that must function as controllers share the same index as the PROs they control, and as assigning to PRO the person, number and gender features of the relevant controlling categories.

2.3.9 Government theory
We come finally to government theory. This has played a role in the discussion of several other subtheories of universal grammar and is, therefore, at least in part, already familiar. It remains here to pull together some of the ideas already put forward and to complete the characterisation of this subtheory.

The first task is to establish the set of items that may govern other items, and the second is to delimit the sphere of influence of those items. Let us suppose for the moment that the set of governors comprises lexical heads of phrases, INFL [+tense] and POSS (the abstract element in NPs that governs and assigns possessive/genitive Case to their subjects, as in *Chomsky's theory of grammar, John's rejection of the autonomy hypothesis*, etc.). This preliminary definition will be revised in due course. The domain of a lexical head, INFL or POSS may then be taken as all those elements that it c-commands that are not protected by a barrier. We assumed above that the relevant barriers were NP and $\overline{S}$, the principal barriers also in the definition of subjacency. There is, however, evidence that the definition of barrier should be generalised to comprise all maximal projections in the sense of $\overline{X}$-theory. Thus in the case of government across a sentence boundary, after $\overline{S}$-pruning, we want the verb of the higher clause to govern the subject of the lower sentence but nothing within its VP, since this is the domain of V. Consider [231].

[231]

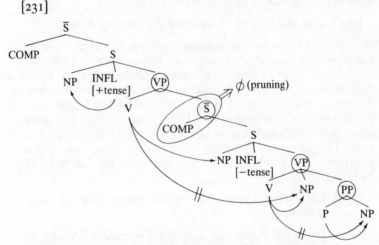

Taking maximal projections (NP, ADJP, VP and PP) as barriers (relevant examples are ringed), the possibilities of government, after $\overline{S}$-pruning, are as indicated.

If VP is analysed as $\overline{\overline{V}}$, and we taken double-bar categories to be maximal projections, the contents of the VP are protected from government by the higher verb in the required way. Similarly, within the VP of the embedded clause of [231] we do not want to say that the verb governs the object of the preposition, since this is obviously the domain of P. Once again, if PP is analysed as $\bar{\bar{P}}$, we have the barrier we need. (If this extension of the notion of barrier is assumed to be relevant also in bounding theory, we will, of course, obtain different predictions about the operation of subjacency. The consequences will not be investigated here).

Consider now the ungrammatical sentence [232].

[232] *Who did you say that t criticised the binding theory?*

Ordinarily, there is nothing to prevent the extraction of a *wh*-phrase from an embedded sentence introduced by *that*. Compare the examples in [233].

[233i] *What did you say that Chomsky criticised t?*
[233ii] *What did you say that Chomsky approved of t?*

Here it makes no difference whether *that* is present or not; the sentences are grammatical. But sentences such as [232] are grammatical only if *that* is missing, as in [234].

[234] *Who did you say t criticised the binding theory?*

Why should there be this asymmetry between subject and other positions with regard to extraction of *wh*-expressions? Chomsky's explanation derives from government theory. First, he draws a distinction between *proper* government and government. Among the governors considered so far only lexical heads are deemed to be proper governors, so INFL and POSS, as abstract elements, are excluded from the set. He then proposes as a principle of government theory that traces must be properly governed. The principle is known as the **Empty Category Principle** (ECP).

[235] *The Empty Category Principle*: traces must be properly governed.

Thus in [233] the traces are properly governed by V and P, as required; and the difference between [232] and [234] is now explained on the grounds that the trace in the former is not properly governed. This requires some explanation.

Consider first of all the S-structure phrase markers of the two examples opposite, [236i and ii] respectively. Notice that, when fully elaborated, both examples involve a trace of *who* adjoined to the embedded COMP; *ie* the movement is assumed to be successive cyclic, as discussed in earlier sections. In both cases the trace in subject position in the embedded sentence is governed by INFL, but not properly governed. What

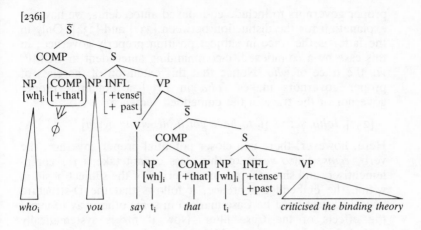

[236i]

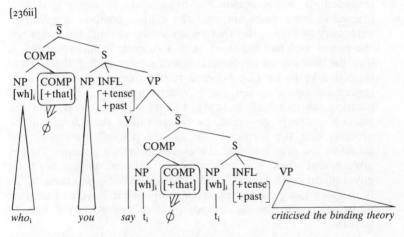

[236ii]

distinguishes the two cases is the structure of COMP. In [236i] *that* has been selected. As a result the trace in COMP does not c-command the trace in subject position. In [236ii] on the other hand, *that* has not been selected and the original COMP position is empty. If we assume a convention that branches terminating in such empty COMPs are pruned (or invisible), then the first branching node above the trace of *who* is no longer the higher COMP (the product of adjunction) but S̄, and this dominates the trace in subject position within the embedded S. We have already seen that c-command is an essential prerequisite to government (including c-proper government). If we now extend the set of proper governors to include co-indexed antecedents, we have an explanation for the distinction between [232] and [234]. Only in the latter is the trace in subject position properly governed; in this case by a co-indexed, c-commanding antecedent in COMP, *viz* the trace of *who*. Notice that this extension of the class of proper governors makes *John* in [237] a potential proper governor of the trace in the embedded sentence.

[237] *John*$_i$ *seems* [t$_i$ *to have got it all wrong again*]

Here, however, there is a closer potential proper governor, the verb *seems*. Since verbs of this class cannot take a *for* complementiser, and since there is no governor of the subject position within the embedded sentence, it follows that the D-structure lexical subject must be Case-marked in some other way to avoid the effects of the Case filter. Now if *for* is systematically excluded, it seems reasonable once again to argue that $\bar{S}$ is pruned in these cases and that the subject position is governed externally by *seems*. But there is no reason to think that *seem* has the power also to Case-mark such a subject; in this respect it is like the participles of passive constructions rather than active transitive verbs (*ie* like *believed* rather than *believe*). The only remaining option, then, is NP-movement to a Case-marked position, as indicated in [237]. Let us suppose, then, that the trace is properly governed by *seems* rather than *John* on the grounds that the former is the closest possible governor, and establish the principle that the closest governor governs. Proper government thus has two subcases, lexical government (*ie* government by a lexical head) and antecedent government. In both cases the governor must c-command the governed item or items, and only the closest potential proper governor actually governs.

Returning briefly to the examples in [233], it is worth pointing out that because the trace is here properly governed by a lexical head within the VP, there is in fact no reason to suppose that *wh*-movement is here successive cyclic, depositing a trace in the embedded COMP. 'Long-distance' *wh*-movement direct to the COMP position of the matrix clause does not violate subjacency if $\bar{S}$ is the only relevant barrier, and no other condition or principle is violated by such a movement. By contrast, 'long-distance' movement from subject position will always leave a subject trace that is not properly governed, since in a case such as [234]/[236ii] the only available position for a proper governor is the embedded COMP. Here *wh*-movement must be successive cyclic and the absence of an overt complementiser follows from the requirement that the trace in COMP c-command, and govern, the trace in subject position. In other words, the interaction of subjacency and the ECP means that there is no need to stipulate the successive cyclicity of *wh*-movement (or indeed any movement operation). The range of permissible movements, some of which may not now be strictly successive cyclic, follows automatically from the organisation of the principles of universal grammar.

Turning now to the ECP, the reader may feel, with some justification, that the requirement that traces be properly governed is met only at the cost of some 'fixing'. Where there is movement from direct object position, or object of preposition position, it is obviously the case that the resultant trace will be properly governed. But subjects, because of their special position within S, pose problems. In certain cases, as with the infinitival complements of verbs like *seem* or participles such as *believed*, the proper government requirement for subject traces is met by assuming S-pruning and allowing lexical government across S. This is perhaps not unreasonable in view of the obligatory absence of *for* in these cases, and crucially allows for the subject trace to be bound in its governing category, as required by the anaphor binding condition (though see 5.2). But in other cases, as with the movement of *wh*-phrases from the subject position of finite clauses, the adjustments are more questionable. Here the proper government requirement is met by taking a *wh*-phrase or its trace in COMP to have the same 'proper governor' relationship with a subject as, say, a transitive verb has with its direct object. It is, however, far from self-evident that the relationship between a phrasal antecedent and the element it binds is parallel in any significant sense to that between a lexical head and its complements; indeed the parallelism seems to be one of nomenclature only, an *ad hoc* stipulation designed to solve a particular problem. It would seem to be worthwhile to explore the consequences of alternative analyses that avoid this rather dubious conjunction. For example, we might argue that in a sentence such as *who said that?* *who* is still in argument position in S-structure and that there is no trace to be governed. And in a sentence such as *who did you say* t *said that?* it would not be unreasonable to suggest that the trace is properly governed by *say* across S after S-pruning, and explain the obligatory absence of *that* on this basis. These proposals cannot be pursued here, but we should note that there is a further problem that arises in connection with sentences such as [234]. Even if we allow that the subject trace is properly governed by the trace in COMP, it is not clear what governs the latter (properly or otherwise). Do we argue that traces in COMP are not subject to the ECP, or do we take $\overline{S}$ to be a barrier in some cases but not others, allowing here for the proper government of the trace by the verb of the higher clause? At the very least, we have to conclude that there are some outstanding issues to be resolved.

The final question to be tackled is the determination of the level of representation at which the ECP applies. Consider the sentences in [238].

[238i] *I don't know* [$_{\overline{S}}$ *who*$_i$ [$_S$ *t*$_i$ *said what*]]

[238ii] **I don't know* [$_{\overline{S}}$ *what*$_i$ [$_S$ *who said* t$_i$]]

At S-structure no condition is violated in either of these sentences, yet the second is ungrammatical. Compare now the LF representations (prior to *wh*-interpretation) associated with these S-structures (see [239i] and [239ii] opposite). Since *wh*-phrases are interpreted as quantifier-like expressions, it follows that at LF they will all appear in COMP even though some may occupy argument positions at S-structure. The movement in the LF component, let us assume, involves adjunction to COMP in the familiar way, as indicated. It is important to note that the sequence of *wh*-phrases in COMP in [238ii], namely *who* + *what*, is ungrammatical, and that the structure involved, [$_{\overline{S}}$ *who*$_i$ *what* [$_S$ t$_i$. . .]] is parallel to that involved in the familiar *that*-trace cases, [$_{\overline{S}}$ *who*$_i$ *that* [$_S$ t$_i$. . .]], in that *who* is prevented from properly governing the subject trace because of the co-presence of some other element in COMP to its right. It seems natural, therefore, to explain the ungrammaticality of [238ii] by reference to the ECP, and conclude that the ECP must apply at LF. This analysis in fact presupposes a slight modification of the definition of c-command, a prerequisite for proper government, in order to allow *who* to c-command the subject trace in [239i]. Thus we must suppose that 'the first branching node above X' is defined differently according to whether X is the item to which something has been adjoined or is itself the adjoined item. In [239i] the first branching node above *who* must be $\overline{S}$, so that *who* can c-command and properly govern the empty subject position, while in [239ii] the first branching node above *who* must be COMP, so that it does not c-command or properly govern the empty subject position. Let us suppose, then, that the c-command relations obtaining prior to adjunction continue in force after adjunction. The effect of this is to make the branching node created by adjunction relevant in the definition of c-command relations for the adjoined item, but 'invisible' in the definition of c-command

[239i]

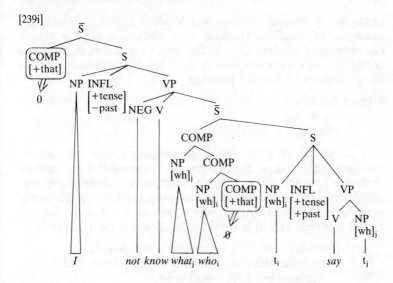

[239ii]

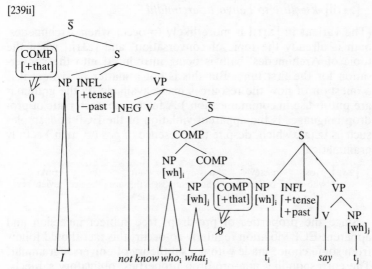

relations for the item to which the adjunction is made.

A number of issues relating to the theory of government and the operation of the ECP arise in connection with the so-called **pro-drop parameter**. It is well-known that in many languages complete sentences may lack overt subjects. This is true, for example, of Spanish, Italian and Modern Greek, but not, for example, of English, German or French. To take a simple example from Modern Greek, the single verb-form in [240] is a complete sentence even though its English translation requires the presence of a subject pronoun.

[240] ðulévi
      work-3sg
      'he/she/it is working'

It is typical of such 'pro-drop' languages that they allow, amongst other things, free inversion of the subject in ordinary declarative sentences. In English inversion is grammatically triggered, as in questions, or following certain emphatically positioned adverbials (*never have I seen such a fiasco*), but the Greek sentence [241ii] is simply an optional variant of [241i].

[241i] *to bányo tu   arçimídhi   kseçílise*
        the bath the-gen Archimedes-gen overflowed-3sg
        'Archimedes' bath overflowed'
[241ii] *kseçílise to bányo tu arçimídhi*

(The variant in [241i] is more likely to occur when Archimedes' bath is already the topic of conversation, and [241ii] when the topic of Archimedes' bath is being introduced into the conversation for the first time. But this is not a matter of syntax; it is a question of how the resources made available by the grammar are put to use in communication.) A further characteristic of pro-drop languages is the apparent violation of the ECP in examples such as [242], which, despite the presence of *pos* (= 'that') is fully grammatical.

[242] pyos   pistévis   pos éγrapse   aftí   tin   gritikí
       who-nom believe-2sg that wrote-3sg this-acc the-acc review-acc
       'who do you think (that) wrote this review?'

Since the properties of pro-drop, free subject inversion and apparent ECP violation regularly co-occur, this fact should follow from some choice made within a subtheory of universal grammar. The corresponding non-pro-drop properties, obligatory subjects, no free inversion and clear conformity with the requirements of the ECP, should follow from the alternative choice within that subtheory. Let us suppose, then, that it is specifically the AGR(eement) element within a [+tense] INFL (*cf* 2.3.5, diagram [168]) that governs the subject of a finite clause, and that the subject position may be left empty when the AGR element is overtly 'rich enough' to guarantee that an empty subject is interpretable. This will be the case in Modern Greek, where there is an elaborate system of verbal inflection such that person and number features are apparent from verb-forms, but not true of English, where verbal morphology is very limited. Compare the paradigms in [243].

[243i]			[243ii]		
	(*I*)	*wrote*		(*eγó*)	*éγrapsa*
	(*you*)	*wrote*		(*esí*)	*éγrapses*
	(*he/she/it*)	*wrote*		(*aftós/aftí/aftó*)	*éγrapse*
	(*we*)	*wrote*		(*emís*)	*γrápsame*
	(*you*)	*wrote*		(*esís*)	*γrápsate*
	(*they*)	*wrote*		(*aftí/aftés/aftá*)	*éγrapsan*

Leaving aside for the moment the question of the nature of the null subject in pro-drop languages, let us first consider the consequences of allowing the subject position to be 'filled' by an element lacking phonetic features. If such a subject is selected rather than a NP with phonetic realisation, the sentence will ordinarily lack an overt subject altogether. But if an overt subject does appear, and the regular subject position is already 'filled' by a null element, it follows that the overt subject will be in an alternative position. Since COMP is excluded, because subject NPs are not logical operators, the only available options are within VP or as adjunct to VP. Let us assume that both these options are available in principle. If a subject appears inside VP, it will follow V, because lexical heads come first in $\overline{X}$ in Spanish, Italian and Modern Greek. If the subject is adjoined to VP, it will naturally appear to the right of it in accordance with the principle that adjuncts are peripheral (*cf* the case of *wh*-phrases which are moved to the left and adjoined to the left of COMP). The normal positions for an additional lexical subject in a sentence with a null (pre-VP) subject are therefore those in [244].

[244]

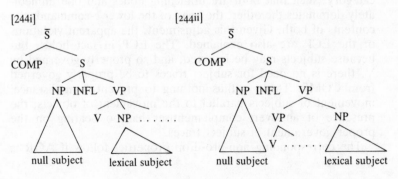

[244i]	[244ii]

$\overline{S}$

COMP — S

NP INFL VP

V NP ......

null subject   lexical subject

$\overline{S}$

COMP — S

NP INFL VP

VP NP

V ......

null subject   lexical subject

The free inversion of subjects in pro-drop languages is thus a consequence of allowing the subject position to be filled by elements lacking phonetic realisation.

Notice further that if *wh*-movement of subjects takes place from within VP or from this adjunct position, the presence or absence of a complementiser in an embedded clause is irrelevant to the issue of whether or not the resulting trace is properly governed. Consider the diagrams in [245].

[245]

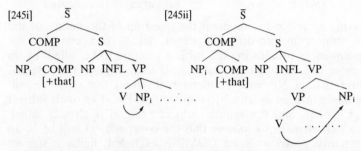

Lexical government of the trace of an 'inverted' subject in pro-drop languages.

We must, of course, adjust the definition of c-command in such a way that the verb c-commands, and so properly governs, the subject trace when this is in adjunct position. Let us suppose, then, that when adjunction takes place, and a duplicate superordinate category is created, the adjoined element within that superordinate category is c-commanded by the head of the subordinate category. This is entirely analogous to the adjustment proposed to account for the data in [239]. Putting the matter a little more simply, where there are two instances of a category, such that both are branching nodes and one immediately dominates the other, the head of the lower c-commands the contents of both. Given this adjustment, the apparent violations of the ECP are also explained. The ECP in fact holds, but because subjects may be inverted, and so properly governed by V, there is no need for subject traces to be properly governed from COMP. There is thus nothing to prevent 'long-distance' movement of subjects parallel to the movement of objects; the presence of an overt complementiser has no bearing on the proper government of subject traces.

The corresponding non-pro-drop properties follow if AGR is

not overtly expressed in the form of distinctive suffixes on verb stems. In this case, a phonetically null subject would be uninterpretable because there would be no concrete basis for assigning features of person, number (and possibly gender) to it. Consequently subjects must have phonetic realisation. In the absence of null subjects there is no motivation for the appearance of subjects in post-verbal positions, and given that subjects will always appear to the left of VP in S, it follows that *wh*-traces in subject position will have to be properly governed from COMP, thereby entailing the absence of complementisers.

As for the nature of the empty subject in pro-drop languages, it seems natural to regard this as a null pronominal like PRO, but which, unlike PRO, is not controlled and has the normal pronominal capacity for independent reference. It is straightforwardly subject to the pronominal binding condition [184ii], that it should be A-free in its governing category. In recent work Chomsky has referred to this non-anaphoric null pronominal as **pro**. The distribution of pro is normally limited to subject position if we require its contents to be determined by its governor; thus within S there are several positions in which pro might in principle occur, but only in the case of subject position is there a governor (AGR in INFL) that is capable of specifying its feature composition, since neither V nor P ordinarily carries a set of object agreement features. The clitic pronouns of the Romance languages, Modern Greek, etc., might however, be analysed as the realisation of such object agreement features, thus allowing for a wider distribution of pro.

2.3.10 Empty categories
In the discussion of the subtheories of universal grammar, four types of empty category have been distinguished, NP-trace, variable (= *wh*-trace), PRO and pro. The first is anaphoric but not pronominal, the second neither anaphoric nor pronominal, the third anaphoric and pronominal, and the fourth pronominal but not anaphoric. As we have seen, the distribution of each of these types is a consequence of the interaction of various principles of universal grammar. At any given level of representation we know which, if any, NP positions may be empty, and if so, what the properties of that empty category will be in terms of the four-way typology above. This state of affairs permits the adoption of the Projection Principle, a desirable consequence, since languages are presumably easier to acquire if lexical properties are automatically projected to all levels of syntactic representation and

the positions in each where gaps may or must occur do not have to be worked out by the learner on the basis of his experience. Let us now take a specific example to illustrate the point.

[246] *Who said that Sidney seems to talk too much?*

This sentence has the D-structure representation [247],

[247]

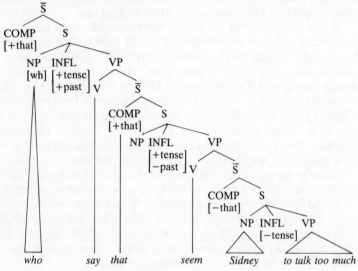

D-structure phrase marker for [246].

the S-structure representation [248] (opposite), and the LF representation [249] (opposite). The Projection Principle requires the θ-marking properties of lexical items to be represented categorially at each level of syntactic representation. Where the subject position is θ-marked, there will always be a subject NP in clauses at all levels, therefore. But, as we have seen, there are cases where a subject NP is not an argument, as in the case of the subjects of verbs like *seem*, or of *be* + past participle combinations in passives. In English, pleonastic elements such as *it* or *there* must fill the subject position in these cases (at least when movement of an argument is impossible). It seems, then, that clauses must have subject positions, even when these are not θ-marked. Let us suppose a further principle

[248]

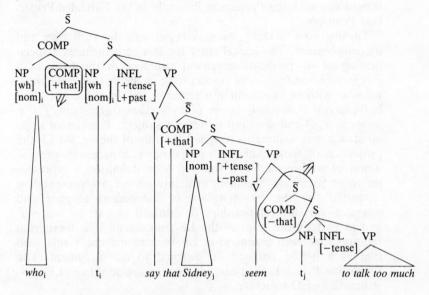

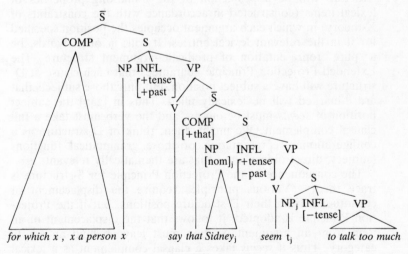

S-structure phrase marker for [246].

[249]

LF representation for [246].

that requires clauses to have subjects, and refer to the conjunction of this with the Projection Principle as the **Extended Projection Principle**.

Turning now to [246], we may begin with the verb *seem* and its complement. The lexical entry for this verb includes a specification of its predicate–argument structure in the form of a categorial identification of co-occurring elements that it θ-marks, together with an indication of whether or not the subject position is θ-marked. Obviously, *seem* takes a clausal argument, (*cf: it seems that X*) and does not θ-mark its subject. The clausal argument, we may assume, is assigned the role of theme. At LF the projection of these θ-marking properties is a necessary precondition of well-formedness, since it is by definition a representation of predicate–argument structure, albeit a representation 'distorted' by the incorporation of antecedent–anaphor and operator–variable relationships determined in part by *move α*, and in part by the rules of the LF component. The θ-criterion requires that each argument at LF be assigned one θ-role, and that each θ-role assigned be assigned to one argument. The Projection Principle then extends this requirement from LF to S-structure and D-structure.

Before examining the LF representation [249] in detail, let us first consider the consequences for D-structure of adopting the Projection Principle. Since this level has no traces by definition, as an abstraction from the effects of *move α*, it follows that D-structure will be a projection of the θ-marking properties of lexical items (constructed in accordance with the constraints of X̄-theory) in which each argument occupies the position specified for it in the relevant lexical entries. It will, in other words, be a 'pure' representation of predicate–argument structure. The Extended Projection Principle guarantees that each clause at D-structure will have a subject position, but only those subjects that are θ-marked will be lexically filled. Thus in [247] the subject position of *seems* must be empty, and the verb must take a full clausal complement. We might, then, think of D-structure as a configurational representation of those grammatical functions (subject, direct object, etc.) that are thematically relevant.

The consequence of the Projection Principle for S-structure is trace theory. Various principles require the displacement of constituents from their D-structure positions, but if the Projection Principle is adopted, it follows that the displacement of an item from an argument position must leave behind an empty category. Thus if *seems* takes a clausal complement as a lexical property, it must have a clausal complement at S-structure, even if the D-structure subject NP has been moved. It follows that the clause in question will remain syntactically complete and have an empty subject. The θ-criterion, however, guarantees that any such movement will be to a θ̄-position, otherwise more than one θ-role would be assigned to the same argument. Moved constituents are thus assigned a sequence, or chain, of grammatical functions, but only the first, the D-structure function, will be thematically relevant. In [248] the D-structure subject *Sidney* appears in the non-argument subject position of *seem*, leaving behind a trace in the subject position of *talk too much*.

It remains to show that the movements involved in the mapping of [247] into [248] do in fact follow from general principles. In [247] all the argument positions are lexically filled and the non-argument position is empty, as required. The movement of *Sidney* is necessary because of the Case filter; at D-structure there is no item that governs this NP, since INFL [−tense] is not a governor and S̄ is a barrier to external government, so it cannot receive Case. Nor can it move, because the resultant trace would not be governed. However, *seem* belongs to the class of verbs that permits S̄-pruning. Once this has taken place *Sidney* is free to move, because *seem* can now properly govern the trace in accordance with the ECP (a principle that in fact applies at LF). *Sidney* might in theory move either to the empty subject position of *seem* or to the COMP of the root clause, since both are θ̄-positions. But in fact only the first is possible, because the trace that is left by the movement is Caseless (*seem* does not assign Case), and as a Caseless trace is interpreted as an anaphor. The binding condition for anaphors requires that the trace be A-bound in its governing category, and only movement to subject position would permit this.

The movement of *who*, by contrast, leaves behind a Case-marked trace, since the subject position of a finite clause is governed by INFL (perhaps more accurately the AGR element in INFL) and assigned nominative Case. Case-marked traces are interpreted as variables and must be Ā-bound. The movement to the peripheral θ̄-position of COMP is thus automatic. It may take place either in the syntax, as here, or in the LF component if the *wh*-NP remains in argument position in S-structure, as in echo questions. The trace in subject position is properly governed by the co-indexed *wh*-NP in COMP in accordance with the ECP (once again this applies properly at LF). Notice in particular that the positions where the traces occur in S-structure could not be occupied by lexical NPs or by PRO. PRO is instantly excluded because both positions are properly governed, and PRO must be ungoverned by definition. Furthermore the antecedent of PRO must have an independent θ-role, and both *who* and *Sidney* occupy θ̄-positions. Lexical NPs are also impossible because, if lexical items are inserted at D-structure and D-structure is a pure projection of lexical semantics, no item could ever be inserted in the subject position of *seem* as well as in the subject position of *talk*, nor could *who* be inserted directly into COMP, leaving room for some other NP in the subject position of *said*. Neither of these positions is an argument position, and must be left empty by definition. If left empty, the movements described above must take place.

The properties of LF, as seen in [249], are carried over from S-structure. If the θ-criterion is met in the latter it will also be met in the former, at least as far as the effects of *move α* in the syntax are concerned. (If movement of quantifiers takes place in the LF component, the movement will also have to be to COMP for the same reasons outlined above in the case of *wh*-movement in the syntax, and the requirements of the θ-criterion will also necessarily be met.) The only difference between [248] and [249], therefore, is the fact that in the latter the rule of *wh*-interpretation has applied, introducing the logical variable x in place of the trace of *who*. Notice that both this position and the position occupied by the trace of *Sidney* are properly governed in accordance with the ECP, as was pointed out above.

It may reasonably be concluded, in the light of the discussion of [246], and in view of the earlier discussion of the subtheories of universal grammar, that Chomsky's goal of developing a system of interacting general principles that determine in large measure the conditions of well-formedness for syntactic representations at all levels is now well on the way to being accomplished. In other words we now have the makings of a theory which predicts the essential properties of the relationship between predicate–argument structures and possible surface syntactic realisations with a minimum of language-specific stipulation.

This is not, of course, to say that improvements in formulation cannot be made. The essential point is that a theory of this sort represents a significant advance over the purely descriptive work of early transformational grammar. In particular, the theory now has a degree of 'deductive structure' in the sense that changes made in one area have repercussions in others because the subtheories of universal grammar interact and complex sets of grammatical properties follow from this interaction. Given that each subtheory is characterised by a limited range of choices (so-called parametric variation), it can be seen that different choices lead to different interactions and different sets of grammatical properties. The theory is correct to the extent that it predicts the co-occurrence of grammatical properties that actually do co-occur with some regularity in the world's languages. The case of the pro-drop parameter discussed above is just one example of such a clustering of properties that the theory more or less successfully accounts for. It is to be hoped that, as work progresses, it will be possible not merely to specify the parameters within which grammars may vary with respect to some subtheory, but actually to define a typology of (core) grammars that follows from a formulation of the theory of universal grammar constructed to predict the necessary implicational relationships between choices in different subtheories.

It is worth emphasising that much of the success of the enterprise to date stems from the study of empty categories and the discovery that these have properties analogous to those of various overt categories. The establishment of the principles for predicting the distribution of empty categories was the crucial step that paved the way for the removal of *ad hoc* conditions on the operation of rules and made possible the development of a powerful model of universal grammar.

2.3.11 Universal grammar and learnability

Let us for the moment accept that Chomsky's view, that the internalised grammars of native speakers really are constituted in accordance with the principles of his theory, is a reasonable one. Given that the grammars he constructs have properties determined by highly abstract principles of considerable explanatory power over the range of data to be accounted for, and given that none of these principles is *a priori* necessary, he can at the very least argue that the chances that speakers' grammars are in reality quite differently constituted have been significantly reduced.

The question now arises of how the theory of universal grammar is to be interpreted in realist terms. The key issue is whether children can plausibly be supposed to have learned the sorts of grammar that Chomsky's theory requires them to know by means of some protracted analysis and induction operation on the primary linguistic data encountered in the first few years of life. In other words, is the stimulus rich enough to guarantee that each and every child will end up with the same core grammatical knowledge? Obviously Chomsky must first of all establish that native speakers of a language do indeed share the same core linguistic knowledge. But having argued for this, Chomsky's answer to the question is that much of this shared knowledge is not plausibly regarded as learned because the relevant information is simply not accessible in representative samples of primary data; *ie* the stimulus is not rich enough to support an analysis and induction theory of language acquisition. In order to account for the fact that speakers share detailed knowledge of the principles of grammatical organisation Chomsky therefore supposes, as we have seen (1.5), that human beings are equipped with knowledge of universal grammar as a part of their genetic endowment, and interprets his theory of universal grammar as a model of this. His theory is explanatorily adequate to the extent that it offers a principled explanation of the speed and efficiency of language acquisition in children as well as accounting for the high level of agreement among speakers as to the properties of the system acquired despite the randomness of the data to which they are exposed and the difficulty of extracting the relevant grammatical principles by simple observation.

At this point the best way to proceed will be to offer a few examples of the sort of linguistic fact that Chomsky highlights in his efforts to establish the existence of shared grammatical knowledge and to show that the stimulus is too impoverished to provide a basis for the induction of the relevant principles. Consider sentence [250].

[250] *Graball found a new set of clients to fleece.*

Speakers of English agree that this can only mean 'Graball found a new set of clients for him, Graball, to fleece them, the clients'. How have all speakers learned to interpret the missing subject and object of *fleece* in this way? The actual physical stimulus provided by utterances of sentences of this sort obviously provides no clues. Either, then, each and every speaker has worked this out for himself in some way, or each and every speaker has been told to interpret such utterances this way, or each and every speaker has learned by one or the other of these methods. We can instantly discount the formal instruction possibility; it is clearly not the case that first languages are acquired on this basis. All parents come very quickly to realise the futility of telling their pre-school children that something is or is not the case. And in any case it is hard to imagine that children start to use sentences of this sort, *eg I haven't found a friend to play with, Mummy,* but intend to convey a message quite distinct from that which adults extract from the utterance, (*eg* 'I haven't found a friend such that he/she can play with me', or 'I haven't found a friend for children in general round here to play with him/her', or whatever), and then have to be corrected. Quite apart from the general lack of effect of offering corrections, it would be very difficult for a parent to know that an error had been made. It is thus surely not the case that an error and correction explanation can be taken seriously. What, then, of the possibility that the correct interpretation is 'worked out' in some way by children? Without any prior knowledge of principles of interpretation it is difficult to see how the correct interpretation would necessarily be extracted from sentences of this sort by all children, or how, if they got it wrong, they would know that they had got it wrong, and correct themselves. In any case, can it really be true that every two-year old has gone through a conscious process of working out what sentences of this sort might mean in principle and then discounting all but the correct interpretation? This seems most unlikely, and if the process is subconscious, or automatic, we have to ask how it turns out that every child comes up with the same answer. Chomsky has an explanation. To attack Chomsky effectively, a critic would have to come up with a better one.

Phenomena of this sort are not hard to find. How do we all know that [251i] is grammatical but that [251ii] is not? Were we told, did we work it out, or did we just know all along?

[251i] *I wonder which report Peter filed without reading?*
[251ii] **I wonder who filed that report without reading?*

(And there is here again the question of the interpretation of the missing subject and object of *reading*.) In [252i] it is clear that *his* may or may not refer to *Wally*, but that in [252ii] it must not.

[252i] *Wally submitted his resignation.*
[252ii] *His resignation was submitted by Wally.*

In [253i] the reflexive *himself* is permitted in the object position of the complement sentence but not in [253ii].

[253i] *Jimbo seemed to us to like himself.*
[253ii] **Jimbo pleaded with us to like himself.*

Have we all been taught the principles of pronominal interpretation and reflexive distribution, or determined them on the basis of our experience? To take just the case of [253], it seems most unlikely that the superficial form of utterances offers enough information to guarantee that the relevant principles will be successfully learned; the two examples here are *exactly* parallel in surface structure but *differ* with respect to the possibility of a reflexive object in the complement sentence. And the notion that we have all been told how to discriminate between the two types is manifestly preposterous.

To take one final example, if children learn the rule of *wh*-movement, why is this rule not routinely over-generalised in violation of island constraints, so that each child can be corrected and taught the constraints in question? We know that children regularly over-generalise the rules of their developing grammars; *cf: I goed to school today and Sarah hitted me*, etc. Is it because they have worked it out for themselves that questions such as *Who do you love me and, Mummy?* are odd? It is hard to imagine that any conceivable corpus of utterances would contain information relevant to the child's coming to this conclusion. It is not enough to say that there are no examples of this sort for the child to imitate and that therefore they are not employed, because forms such as *goed* and *hitted* do not occur in adult speech but regularly occur in the speech of children who are in the process of mastering English. Similarly, how do children learn that overt complementisers have to be omitted when a subject *wh*-phrase is extracted from a finite complement sentence? It is not the case that children regularly say things like *Who did you say that bought me this present?* and then have to be corrected. But in view of the optionality of the complementiser in cases of object extraction, it is surely natural to assume the same optionality principle for all extractions and interpret the absence of examples with *that* in adult speech as an accidental gap in the corpus. This appears not to be what happens. It is very hard to believe that there is something in the random linguistic experience of every child that leads him inexorably to the conclusion that the grammar of English must contain something like the empty category principle, but if he comes to this conclusion subconsciously, we must ask how. Chomsky's answer is that the child 'knows' the principle even before exposure to primary linguistic data. (Some people have objected to the use of *know* in this context, on the grounds that the knowledge in question is 'tacit', but the issue is purely terminological, and some other verb (Chomsky has suggested *cognise*) can be employed to convey the intended meaning.)

Obviously none of these arguments is demonstrative, but cumulatively they constitute a more or less plausible case. Each reader must make up his own mind on the question of whether or not the fact that grammars of natural languages seem to employ rules that conform to the requirements of abstract principles such as those embodied in the binding theory is 'accidental'. If it seems that the binding theory, and the various other principles outlined above, constitute a coherent system that predicts the possible organisation of grammars in a compelling way, the answer will have to be that the observed conformity is not accidental, and that linguists' grammars constructed in accordance with the principles of such a theory are plausibly interpreted as models of the internalised grammars of native speakers. If one accepts this conclusion, one has then to ask whether the relevant principles could have been learned in any conventional sense of that term. If it seems unlikely that the available stimulus is powerful enough to guarantee successful learning, and one believes that the principles in question are indeed common knowledge, then a nativist interpretation of the principles of universal grammar will be the natural outcome. If, on the other hand, the binding theory etc. seem to be simply descriptive principles that provide an account of data that could, in principle, be described equally well in many other ways, employing quite different formal apparatus, one will incline to the view that linguists' grammars are purely mathematical constructs designed to give an elegant account of the data and that they are not to be interpreted as models of anything in the 'real' world. The theory of universal grammar is then nothing more than a set of higher-level generalisations extracted from grammars constructed in conformity with some set of descriptive proposals, and it too will lack any real-world interpretation. But it is important to note that the development of a theory of universal grammar is just as important on these assumptions as it is in Chomsky's theory, for the simple reason that a theory which allows anything explains nothing. We do not want to operate in a context where any descriptive proposal, however *ad hoc*, is regarded as being as good as any other descriptive proposal. To the extent that one believes rational choices between options can be made on some principled basis (*eg* elegance and generality of formulation, etc.), one is subscribing to the view that a constrained theory of grammar is both possible and necessary. In the next chapter a rival theory of grammar, whose exponents reject Chomsky's realism and nativism, will be examined. It is, however, important to appreciate the fact that there is nothing to prevent those who feel so inclined from interpreting Chomsky's proposals as a purely formal theory of grammar or from interpreting the theory presented in Chapter 3 in realist/nativist terms. The issue is not a theory-bound one; it is a question of whether or not one believes that present-day linguistic methodology provides constructs that can in principle provide explanations of how it is, on the basis of diverse, often degenerate, and certainly limited, experience we all come to share a common perception and understanding of linguistic phenomena. Chomsky's view is that those who reject realist interpretations diminish the interest and significance of the subject; Chomsky's critics regard his views as speculative and pretentious, and believe that the conclusions he reaches are not supported by the data and analytic methods at his, or anyone else's, disposal. Neither party, of course, is demonstrably wrong.

2.4 Relevant reading

Chomsky (1957) is the earliest, and many say the most readable, of his books on the theory of syntax. A central theme is the inadequacy of phrase structure description and the need for transformations, and there is some discussion of the goals of linguistic theory. The deep structure/surface structure distinction had not yet been elaborated at this time. Chomsky (1964) includes further discussion of objectives and levels of adequacy.

The classic exposition of the standard theory is Chomsky (1965). The introductory chapter deals with the competence/performance distinction, the evaluation of grammars and the role of universals, and the relevance of notions of generative capacity. The book then continues with a presentation of the deep structure/surface structure distinction together with a detailed discussion of the structure of the base component and the role of transformations, and rounds off with a review of some residual problems.

There is no comparable monograph for the early stages of the extended standard theory, but Chomsky (1972b, 1977a and b and 1980b) are key works in the transition to Government-Binding theory. The first includes the paper 'Remarks on nominalization', first published in 1970, which deals with the need for lexical rules and a framework of phrase structure description that allows for the statement of cross-category generalisations ($\overline{\text{X}}$-theory), and a discussion of the role of both deep and surface structure in semantic interpretation together with a critical survey of rival approaches current at the time (particularly generative semantics). Chomsky (1977a) begins with some general discussion of form and interpretation and the nature of language, and includes the paper 'Conditions on transformations', first published in 1973, which deals with the need to reduce the expressive power of the transformational component by eliminating rule-specific conditions on application in favour of general conditions such as the TSC, SSC and subjacency. A second paper entitled 'Conditions on rules of grammar', first published in 1976, continues the theme. Chomsky (1977b) seeks to show that *wh*-movement is involved in a wide range of 'unbounded dependency' constructions beyond the obvious constituent question and relative clause cases, and thereby seeks to reduce the array of 'long-distance' operations to one. Particularly important is the insistence that this rule is cyclic and so meets the subjacency requirement; this accounts for a range of 'island constraints' in a uniform way, as we have seen. Chomsky (1980b) involves a revision of the TSC and SSC in the direction of the binding theory.

The basic text for Government-Binding theory is Chomsky (1981a), and Chomsky (1982) is a simpler presentation of the leading ideas combined with some discussion of new developments. Both of these deal with the shift of emphasis away from rule-systems towards systems of principles that account for the properties of rule-systems. The former, after an outline of the theory of (core) grammar, includes sections dealing with the various subsystems and principles involved, the notions of government and binding, the specification of empty categories and the role of *move* α. The latter, after a general introduction to GB theory, discusses empty categories in great detail, and in particular elaborates the typology of empty categories (PRO, pro, NP-trace and *wh*-trace), and considers the possibility that all empty categories are inherently alike but receive different characterisations contextually (the so-called 'functional definition' approach). Chomsky (1981b) deals with the notion of 'core grammar' and the idea that there may be 'natural' (unmarked) combinations of parametric settings, an idea taken up again in Chomsky (1981c). Some of the latest technical innovations are presented in Chomsky (1986a), and Chomsky (1986b) is an attempt to provide a principled and uniform definition of barrierhood for both bounding and government theory.

There are a number of textbooks which seek to explain the various stages of development of transformational grammar, most of the earlier ones now largely of historical interest. For the standard theory, sometimes with discussion of modifications pertaining to early stages of the extended standard theory, Akmajian and Heny (1975), Bach (1974), Culicover (1976), Huddleston (1976), Keyser and Postal (1976) and Soames and Perlmutter (1979) can be recommended. For the later stages of the extended standard theory, just prior to the emergence of GB theory, Radford (1981) is excellent. GB theory itself is now beginning to receive adequate coverage in works such as

Jacobsen (1986), van Riemsdijk and Williams (1986), and Sells (1985). This last is particularly useful for two reasons. First the exposition is elementary, concise and (at least for the most part) clear, and secondly it is conducted in a comparative context, with sections on GPSG and LFG to complement the presentation of GB theory. The postscript by Wasow, which seeks to evaluate the merits of these three theories and to establish major points of agreement, is also very helpful for those who do not yet feel ready to commit themselves to any one theoretical framework.

It is also worth mentioning a number of collections of papers which deal with various modifications and extensions of the theory of government and binding such as Belletti, Brandi and Rizzi (1981) and Kayne (1984). In general the series of monographs *Studies in Generative Grammar* (published by Foris), to which some of the works already mentioned belong and to which new titles are constantly being added, is a useful source of information on recent advances, as are the journals *Linguistic Inquiry*, *Linguistic Analysis*, and *The Linguistic Review* (among others).

On specific topics the following are useful.

2.1.1: Of purely historical interest now, Katz and Fodor (1963) and Katz and Postal (1964) outline the basis for a semantic component in a standard theory transformational grammar, and the collection of papers in Seuren (1974) gives something of the flavour of the ill-fated generative semantics movement.

2.1.2: For an alternative to phrase structure description (*viz* dependency theory) see Matthews (1981: Ch. 4) where the two approaches are presented and compared.

2.2.2: The foundations of X̄-theory were laid by Chomsky (1970), and these ideas were further developed by Emonds (1976: Ch. 1) and Jackendoff (1977). For some contemporary views on the role and status of syntactic features see Muysken and van Riemsdijk (1985).

2.2.3: Jackendoff (1972) gives a very good idea of the types of interpretative rules and principles that were proposed in the early days of the extended standard theory to compensate for the reduced role of transformational rules in handling matters such as bound anaphora, pronominal reference, equi constructions, etc.

2.2.4: The key paper in the history of work on constraints on transformations is Ross (1967). This has never been published in full, but useful extracts appear in Harman (1974: pp. 165–200).

The three-way typology of transformations discussed in this section was first introduced by Rosenbaum (1967). Postal (1974) is an extended defence of the raising (to object) transformation undermined and then eliminated from the extended standard theory by the proposals in Chomsky (1973). Discussion and defence of the cyclic principle of rule application in a standard theory grammar is provided by Pullum (1976/79); the example of SOR-Reflexive interaction ([125] to [131]) is taken from this work.

The subjacency condition along with the TSC and SSC were introduced in Chomsky (1973), a paper first written in 1970. Postal (1972) is an attack on the successive cyclic analysis of 'long-distance' dependencies which the subjacency principle presupposes, Chomsky and Lasnik (1977) (in part) a defence. For some recent ideas on bounding theory, in a broader context, see Chomsky (1986b). The view that phenomena handled by NP-movement are better treated in the lexicon by lexical redundancy rules (see also Chapter 4) is discussed in the introduction to (and in several of the papers contained in) Hoekstra, van der Hulst and Moortgat (1980).

2.3.3: See 2.2.2. Hale (1979 and 1983) deal with the problems raised by 'non-configurational' (W*) languages. See also Chomsky (1981a: pp. 127–135) and 4.3 and 4.6 below for further discussion.

2.3.4: Gruber (1965/76) and Jackendoff (1972) have extensive treatments of semantic roles (or θ-roles) from a substantive as well as a purely formal point of view. The θ-criterion ultimately derives from Freidin (1978), where it is called the Argument Uniqueness Condition.

2.3.5: Case theory within the context of GB theory owes its development to Rouveret and Vergnaud (1980) and Vergnaud (1982). Van Riemsdijk (1983) discusses the relationship between abstract Case and case as an overt morphological category, and Aoun and Sportiche (1983) assess a variety of formulations of government, a concept central to Case-assignment.

2.3.6: The binding theory has its origins in earlier work on the interpretation of (bound) anaphors and pronominals such as Postal (1969), Dougherty (1969 and 1970), Helke (1971), Chomsky (1973), Lasnik (1976) and Reinhart (1976). Chomsky (1980b) is a forerunner of the binding theory presented here. The view that the binding theory applies at S-structure is defended in Chomsky (1981a: Ch. 3).

Alternatives to the binding theory are suggested in Huang (1982), Higginbotham (1983), Brody (1984) and Koster (1984). A theory of 'generalised binding', involving the reduction of the ECP to a generalised version of the anaphor binding condition that applies both to A-binding and Ā-binding, has been developed by Aoun (1981), and further developed by Finer (1985).

Yang (1983) discusses phenomena from several languages involving the apparent binding of anaphors outside their governing categories.

Trace theory as described in this section is a development of earlier work by Wasow (1972/79), Fiengo (1974 and 1977) and Chomsky (1976), reprinted in Chomsky (1977a).

The definition of c-command is due to Reinhart (1976), though various modifications have been advanced by different scholars since then; a number of proposals, for example, are advanced in the course of the discussion in Chomsky (1981a).

On government see Aoun and Sportiche (1983).

2.3.7: See 2.2.4. The idea that the choice of bounding nodes for subjacency may vary from language to language (be subject to parametric variation) originates with Rizzi (1982). The need for caution in assuming such parametric variation is a major theme of Horrocks and Stavrou (1987).

Huang (1982) discusses the question of whether movement in the LF component is subject to subjacency as it is in the syntax, and Kayne (1981b) seeks to derive the effects of subjacency from the ECP.

2.3.8: The approach to the distribution of PRO presented here is that of Chomsky and Lasnik (1977), updated in line with the more recent development of GB theory in connection with the specification of empty categories. Recent advances in control theory are presented in Manzini (1983), Bouchard (1984) and Koster (1984).

2.3.9: For a recent discussion of government and proper government see Lasnik and Saito (1984). The view that the ECP should apply at LF is advanced in Chomsky (1981a: Ch. 4) and the extension of this principle to certain classes of LF phenomena is further discussed in Kayne (1981a).

Apart from the discussion of the pro-drop parameter in Chomsky (1981a: Ch. 4 and 1982), two important contributions to the debate are Jaeggli (1982) and Rizzi (1982: Ch. 4). For a discussion of the pro-drop parameter in the context of GPSG (the framework presented in Chapter 3), see Horrocks (1984).

2.3.11: The kind of data discussed here are treated at greater length in the references to Chomsky's work in 1.7. For a completely different approach to universals, emphasising functional explanations for their existence, see Butterworth, Comrie and Dahl (1984). To the extent that this kind of account is successful, it constitutes a challenge to the Chomskyan nativist position.

Chapter 3

Generalised Phrase Structure Grammar

3.1 Introduction

The theory of Generalised Phrase Structure Grammar (henceforth GPSG), developed principally by Gerald Gazdar, Ewan Klein, Geoffrey Pullum and Ivan Sag, represents a deliberate reaction to work within the transformational paradigm of generative grammar based on the conviction that the introduction of transformational rules into grammatical theory was thoroughly undermotivated. Much of the earliest work in this framework in the late 1970s was concerned to show that the adoption of a purely phrase structure model of syntactic description, coupled with a properly developed semantic theory, would allow the construction of descriptively adequate grammars that did not employ any transformational rules at all, contrary to standard assumptions. But from a slightly different point of view this framework might be interpreted as carrying to its extreme Chomsky's strategy (*cf* 2.2.5) of constraining the power of the transformational component by redistributing to other components the task of expressing relationships that do not meet the criterial properties of *move* α (on this rule schema see 2.3.2 (the discussion of [159], [160]), 2.3.7, and for a final evaluation, 5.2). The GPSG position is that when this redistribution is done, there is no transformational component left; in other words, the generalisation that *move* α purports to express, that there is a linguistically significant class of 'transformational' rules with certain specified properties (2.3.7), is bogus, and the rule schema is itself redundant.

Naturally, as time has passed and a reasonably clear picture has begun to emerge of what grammars of particular languages constructed in this framework are like, attention has begun to shift from questions of descriptive adequacy to the issue of universals (see 1.5, and 2.2.1, 2.2.5 and 2.3.1 for a similar development in Chomsky's theory). However, proponents of GPSG are for the most part very cautious about attributing psychological reality to grammars or assuming the innateness of universal constructs. The view is taken that in the absence of independent evidence claims of this sort are simply pretentious. The analogy which Chomsky seeks to press with the 'hard' sciences is dismissed as methodological prejudice, and proposed grammatical constructs are regarded as the artefacts of particular theoretical perspectives whose merits can be assessed in terms of how well they fit the facts and by reference to the usual criteria of elegance and simplicity, but which have no analogues in the real world.

Those who accept such a position will naturally regard Chomsky's competence and innateness hypotheses as linguistically beside the point. For them they fall outside the scope of ordinary linguistic research and are untestable in that context. It may or may not be the case that human beings operate with various knowledge-stores that underlie their performance abilities, and furthermore that these are in part determined by biological endowment, but the data and methods available to linguists are not thought to provide any basis for investigating these issues. The primary task of the linguist is taken to be the development of mathematically precise and fully specified theories of grammar which *may*, once elaborated, prove useful to psychologists and computer scientists working on the problems of language acquisition and language processing.

There is, therefore, a certain irony in the fact that some psycholinguists have been willing to argue that GPSG, a purely mathematical construct in the eyes of its developers, does indeed have important implications for psycholinguistic concerns, and that many computer scientists striving to model human parsing abilities have found this framework particularly useful. This is in marked contrast with Chomsky's realist theory which has had relatively little influence in recent years on the development of psycholinguistic research. Indeed, as was pointed out in Chapter 1, Chomsky has consistently argued in favour of constraining the domain of data which his theory addresses to the now traditional area of introspective judgement, deliberately ignoring work in neighbouring disciplines that might well have a bearing on the choice between competing theories. Given the difficulty of finding decisive 'linguistic' evidence in favour of one theory over another (some of the problems are discussed in detail in Chapter

5), there is likely to be some value in investigating the possibility that aspects of grammatical organisation are determined by production, perception or communication factors. In particular the extended domain of data might provide a better means of choosing between competing analyses of the purely linguistic facts. From this point of view, the fact that GPSG has facilitated a fruitful interchange of ideas between linguists, psychologists and those working in artificial intelligence would constitute a powerful argument in its favour.

That said, as a theory of grammar it stands or falls on its linguistic merits, and the bulk of this chapter will deal with the formal machinery which the theory employs and the motivation for it. One aspect of this framework that will become immediately apparent to anyone who tries to tackle the primary literature is the great emphasis placed on mathematical precision and formal rigour. This is in marked contrast with the relatively informal and sometimes rather speculative style of argumentation that has come to characterise much recent work in GB theory. All constructs are carefully defined, definitions are rigidly adhered to, and argument based on notions that cannot be made mathematically precise is eschewed. The result is a somewhat forbidding framework. As far as possible the presentation in this chapter will be informal, but it should always be borne in mind that some 'hard' mathematics lies behind what is being said. The first section below outlines some of the problems that face phrase structure description, and then the various solutions which have been proposed are presented. The final section deals with some of the implications of GPSG for work in neighbouring disciplines.

3.2 Obstacles to phrase structure description

Phrase structure grammars may be context-sensitive or context-free. Both employ rules of the familiar type, with expansion restricted to single elements on the left of the arrow in order to guarantee that phrase markers are unambiguously constructed. But context-sensitive grammars allow for the possibility that certain expansions are permitted only in certain contexts, while context-free grammars do not. Thus rules of the general format in [1], where ———Z defines the context in which W expands as X and Y, cannot be employed in a context-free grammar, though rules without a context specification *may* be employed in a context-sensitive grammar.

[1] $W \rightarrow X \ Y \ / \ ———Z$

The class of GPSGs normally discussed in the literature is *weakly equivalent* to a subset of the context-free phrase structure grammars (CFPSGs); *ie* they define as grammatical, or generate, the same sets of strings (sentences) as 'equivalent' CFPSGs. Since the mathematically defined class of CFPSGs is an infinite class, it is clearly necessary to impose empirically motivated constraints on the class of possible GPSGs if the framework is to be taken seriously as a theory of the structure of natural languages. The effect, however, as we shall see, is not merely to restrict the weak equivalence of GPSGs to a *subset* of CFPSGs. The restrictions imposed may also guarantee that GPSGs and CFPSGs are not *strongly equivalent; ie* GPSGs may be incapable of assigning structural descriptions to strings that unconstrained CFPSGs can assign, or *vice versa*.

Since the theory of GPSG may be interpreted as a constrained version of the theory of CFPSG, the first task its proponents have to tackle is to show that such a theory is indeed compatible with the requirements of descriptive adequacy, contrary to standard assumptions. Since a GPSG assigns just *one* level of syntactic representation to sentences (a level roughly analogous to S-structure in GB theory, though somewhat less abstract), this may seem a near-impossible task in view of problems such as the following.

Let us assume that the syntactic component of a grammar consists exclusively of context-free phrase structure rules. It is clear that fully specified rules will be required to generate fully specified phrase markers, since there is no other mechanism for assigning such things as agreement features. But if this is the case, a vast number of rules will be required. To take a simple example, the features of a subject noun phrase include, amongst others, a person feature (choice of three), a number feature (choice of two), and, in the case of third person singular nouns and pronouns, a gender feature (choice of three). All of these are necessarily or potentially relevant to agreement within a co-occurring VP. Suppose the subject NP in a given sentence is *she*; then the head of the VP, the verb, must be marked for the features third person and singular, and, just in case the VP contains a transitive verb with a reflexive object, that NP will have to be assigned the features third person, singular and feminine. In order to accommodate all the possible feature combinations and agreement facts, there would have to be one distinct rule for each permissible feature combination. This would mean a whole *set* of rules all telling us that a sentence consists of a subject NP and a VP. This is manifestly unsatisfactory, and it was indeed facts of this sort which constituted part of the case against purely phrase structure description and for the introduction of transformations. Thus, in this case, a simple feature-free phrase structure schema could be adopted provided there was some transformation which could pick out relevant subject–verb pairs and assign identical sets of agreement features to both members. (This is, of course, a traditionaι, standard-theory formulation; in GB theory agreement is between subject NPs and the AGR element in INFL, which is subsequently moved to the VP).

A different kind of problem arose in the case of systematic phrasal or sentential syntactic relations. Consider the VP rules in [2].

[2i] VP → V NP (*kiss*)   [2ii] VP → V (*kissed*)
                                              [PAS]

      VP → V NP PP (*give*)   VP → V PP (*given*)
                                                [PAS]

      VP → V NP S̄ (*persuade*)   VP → V S̄ (*persuaded*)
                                                [PAS]

The rules in [2i] are a sample of the rules needed to introduce transitive verbs and their complements (*eg: kisses his mistress, gives the forged fiver to Freddie, persuades Maggie that Keith should go*). The rules in [2ii] are among those required to generate 'passive' VPs (*eg: (was) kissed, (was) given to Freddie, (was) persuaded that Keith should go*). The two sets of rules are obviously in a systematic relationship; for every transitive verb that takes a direct object and possibly other complements, there is a corresponding PAS(sive) participle that occurs without the direct object but with the other complements, if any. In a conventional phrase structure grammar such as that in [2], which is defined simply as a list of rules, there is no way in which this correspondence can be expressed. Thus quite apart from the fact that there is no indication that the direct object of the transitive verb has the same thematic role as the subject of the (*be* plus) passive participle that corresponds to it, even this syntactic correspondence goes unexpressed. In the standard theory the combination of deep structure and the passive transformation solved both of these problems. Each verb was given a single subcategorisation feature relating to deep structure configurations designed as categorially specified representations of predicate-argument structure. Thus active and passive surface structures would be derived from a common source (at least in the relevant respects), the former directly and the latter via the application of the passive transformation. This rule expressed the fact, therefore, that the subject of a passive sentence, like the object of an active one, is interpreted as a logical object, and simultaneously introduced the required NP gap in VP.

Transformations were also introduced in the standard theory to handle the infinitival complements of raising and control (or equi) verbs. Consider the examples in [3].

[3i]   *Chomsky seems to be content.*
[3ii] *There seems to be a flaw in the argument.*
[3iii] *Chomsky tries to be content.*
[3iv] **There tries to be a flaw in the argument.*

It is a characteristic of verbs such as *seem* that they denote predicates that take a propositional argument; as such they may take dummy subjects such as *there* (*cf* [3ii]). Verbs like *try* by contrast denote a relationship between individuals and propositions, and do not therefore, allow dummy subjects (*cf* [3iv]). Moreover, the subject of such a verb and the 'understood' subject of its infinitival complement must be interpreted as denoting the same individual (as in [3iii]). The subject of a verb like *seem*, however, must be interpreted as an argument of the predicate denoted by its infinitival complement and not as an argument of the predicate denoted by *seem* at all (*cf*: *it seems that Chomsky is content* with [3i]). The original solution to the problem presented by the fact that surface structures such as [3i] and [3iii] are formally indistinguishable, despite these major differences of interpretation reflected in the possibility or impossibility of the occurrence of dummy subjects, was to set up distinct deep structures and two distinct transformations to map them into congruent surface structures. In the deep structure representation of a sentence containing *seem* this verb would lack a lexical subject NP and be assigned only a clausal complement, while the surface subject of *seem* would appear as the deep subject of this clause. This indicated the relevant predicate–argument structure, and the transformation of subject-to-subject raising put the surface subject in place. In the deep structure of sentences containing *try* identical (or equivalent) NPs would occupy both this verb's subject position and the subject position within its clausal complement, thereby once again making explicit the predicate–argument structure. The transformation of equivalent noun phrase deletion then deleted the complement subject to give the associated surface structure. (In GB theory, of course, only the first type is now handled by *move* α; the second type (the control case) involves the interpretation of the null element PRO, which appears at all levels of representation, its distribution being determined by general principles of syntactic well-formedness, cf 2.3.8). Clearly any single-level theory of syntax based upon phrase structure description must be able to do more than assign parallel structural descriptions to sentences such as [3i] and [3iii].

Finally, there is the problem of unbounded dependencies already discussed in some detail in Chapter 2 (2.1.3, especially the discussion of examples [29] and [30]). Summarising briefly, within a traditional CFPSG there is no mechanism to guarantee that the implications of a choice made in the application of one rule will be taken into account when choices are made in the application of others. Thus, for example, if a sentence begins with a *wh*-phrase of some category, there will always be a gap of the same category in the sentence that follows this *wh*-phrase, even though there is no principled finite bound that can be placed on the extent of the syntactic material intervening between the two dependent items. In the absence of a linking mechanism to ensure the presence of just one gap of the appropriate type in this infinitely large domain, and then only when there is an appropriate *wh*-phrase at the beginning of the sentence, a CFPSG will overgenerate in a hopeless fashion predicting the well-formedness of monsters such as those in [4].

[4i]   *Who did you think . . . . . . MI5 arrested the spy?*
[4ii] *Who did you think . . . . . . arrested?*
[4iii] *Who did think . . . . . . arrested?*
[4iv] *Did think . . . . . . arrested?*

In the first example there is no gap corresponding to *who*, and in [4ii] and [4iii] there are too many gaps. In [4iv] there are as many gaps as there are NP positions but no justification for any of them because there is no *wh*-phrase at the beginning of the clause. Here, then, is another major descriptive problem that GPSG must overcome.

But before we examine in detail the proposals advanced within this framework to meet these difficulties, it will be worthwhile to consider in general terms the theory of syntactic features as it has evolved within GPSG. The key to the solutions offered lies in a proper understanding of the feature-system.

3.3 Features

It is certainly true to say that the theory of syntactic features in GPSG has attained a level of development that far and away exceeds that attained in any other framework. This, of course, is entirely in line with the declared objective of formal precision, but as we shall see, a highly developed theory of features is an essential link in the mapping between highly schematic rules and fully specified phrase markers.

Let us begin with some preliminary notions. A syntactic category is conceived, in accordance with most versions of $\bar{X}$-theory, as a complex of features, in fact as a set of feature specifications each of which consists of a feature name and a value for that name. For example, a NP that is third person singular and inflected in the genitive could be represented as in [5].

[5] $\begin{bmatrix} \text{BAR,} & 2 \\ \text{N,} & + \\ \text{V,} & - \\ \text{PER,} & 3 \\ \text{PLU,} & - \\ \text{CASE,} & \text{GEN} \end{bmatrix}$

This assumes that double-bar categories are maximal projections, and, reasonably enough, that nouns are nominal but not verbal. The rest is self-explanatory.

A certain subset of the totality of syntactic features is defined as the set of HEAD features, *ie* features which may well characterise a whole phrasal category via various agreement requirements but which are necessary properties of the head of that phrase. All the features in [5] are HEAD features, and others will be introduced as we proceed.

A further subset of features, which in fact partly overlaps with the set of HEAD features, are the FOOT features. These are features which may characterise a whole phrasal category because of agreement requirements, but which are essentially properties of a non-head constituent within such a category. A good example is *wh*. Consider the sentence in [6].

[6] *The house the colour of the paint on the front door of which caused all but the hardiest to don sunglasses was sold for £65,000.*

Clearly the NP *the colour of the paint on the front door of which* is a *wh*-NP because of its role in the formation of the relative clause. But it is equally clear that *wh* is not a property of the head of the phrase but rather a property of a NP deeply embedded within its complement structure. Again, other FOOT features will be introduced as we proceed.

It should be noted that a syntactic category in this framework does not have to be a fully specified category. In other words there may be situations where it is useful to have a rule that refers to something as vague as [7].

[7] [BAR, 2]

This is to be understood as referring to any maximal projection. Nevertheless all categories in phrase markers, in so far as these represent the syntactic structure of actual sentences, will have to be fully specified by definition, so it will be necessary to have principles determining the ways in which partially specified categories may legitimately be extended. It is obviously not the case that features can be added at random. Part of the task of defining the possible extensions of categories (in this sense) is accomplished by **feature co-occurrence restrictions** (FCRs) and **feature specification defaults** (FSDs). These can be thought of as providing part of the definition of 'fully-specified syntactic category'. Again, a few illustrations will be sufficient at this point to give these concepts some intuitive content. For example, verbs may have different forms in English; finite, infinitival, participial, etc. Let us suppose that one of features of V is VFORM, which has as its values the set of possible verb forms. Clearly what we do not want is the random ascription of VFORM values to prepositions or adjectives. This limitation can be accomplished by a FCR, as in [8].

[8] [VFORM] ⊃ [+V, −N]

This is to be read 'if a category has the feature VFORM then it must be verbal and non-nominal'. On the assumption that adjectives are [+V, +N], and prepositions [−V, −N], this has the desired result. Others FCRs that are needed can readily be thought up. Thus any category that is PAST must be FIN(ite) and non-SUBJ(unctive), *ie* tense is a property of indicatives in English, and since FIN is a value of VFORM, any category that is PAST will also be verbal and non-nominal in accordance with [8].

Feature specification defaults (FSDs) operate in a slightly different way. The basic idea is that, if there is no *specified* value for some feature in a given category, there will always be some default value representing the 'normal' case. To take a specific example, the inversion of subject and auxiliary in English is grammatically triggered, and a precisely formulated grammar will have to specify the conditions under which this takes place, perhaps by adding the feature [+INV(erted)] to the node S in the relevant rules, (*ie* specifying the value of INV as +). But what about other S nodes? Rather than stipulating in every rule that makes reference to a non-inverted S that the value of INV is −, an FSD of the form in [9] can do the job once and for all.

[9] [−INV]

This is to be interpreted as saying that in the absence of a specification to the contrary the value of INV will be −.

This brings us to the question of lexical subcategorisation. It was noted in Chapter 2 that in the standard theory of transformational grammar there was massive redundancy in that the phrase structure rules of the base and the subcategorisation features of lexical entries both specified the possible contexts of lexical insertion. This redundancy was eliminated in GB theory by the adoption of the Projection Principle which in effect renders the phrase structure rules redundant to the extent that the properties of D-structure phrase markers are predictable from lexical entries. In GPSG the opposite solution is adopted. Lexical entries make no reference to syntactic contexts in phrase markers, and subcategorisation is accomplished in a different way. Let us assume for the moment that the rules of a GPSG are simply conventional (context-free) phrase structure rules of the sort familiar from Chapter 2. We might then have in our grammar rules such as those in [10].

[10] VP → V
      VP → V NP
      VP → V NP PP

Obviously the categories listed to the right of V (including ∅) correspond in each case to the conventional subcategorisation frames in a standard theory grammar for intransitive, transitive, and ditransitive verbs respectively. Each lexical item belonging to a given word-class is assigned to a particular subcategory, identified by a numeral, and rules of the type in [10] make reference to those numerals, as in [11i] and [11ii] respectively.

[11i] *weep*: [[−N], [+V], [BAR 0], [SUBCAT 1]] [11ii] VP → V[SUBCAT 1]
      slap: [[−N], [+V], [BAR 0], [SUBCAT 2]]   VP → V[SUBCAT 2] NP
      hand: [[−N], [+V], [BAR 0], [SUBCAT 3]]   VP → V[SUBCAT 3] NP PP

Thus V1 (this will be employed henceforth as an abbreviation for V[SUBCAT 1]) in a phrase marker can dominate *weep* but not *slap* or *hand*, and so on.

One immediate advantage of the GPSG system is that the problems presented by sentences such as [12] within a context-sensitive system of lexical insertion simply do not arise.

[12] *This company has manufactured and marketed plastic paperweights for twenty-five years.*

In the GPSG system *manufacture* and *market* are both V2; so given a rule [13],

[13] VP → V2 NP

and a schema for co-ordination which allows a category to dominate a set of identical categories, such that all may, and the last two must, be conjoined by some overt conjunction, we derive a tree diagram such as that in [14].

[14]

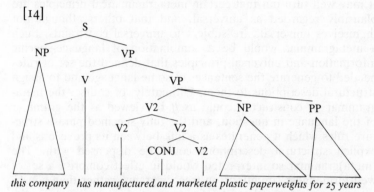

this company   has manufactured and marketed plastic paperweights for 25 years

For a combination of reasons which cannot be detailed here, auxiliaries, such as perfective *have* in this example, are not regarded as forming a word-class distinct from V in GPSG.

In a context-sensitive framework, however, *manufacture* and *market* are both specified as members of the subcategory +[————————NP], but only *market* actually occurs in the re-quired context in sentences such as [12].

The solution to some of the alleged problems facing phrase structure description has in part been hinted at in the preceding paragraphs. Let us now consider explicitly how a single-level theory can cope with the issues that led to the introduction of deep structure and transformations into Chomsky's theory. It should be borne in mind throughout that category names such as NP, VP, ADJ, etc. (or their $\overline{\text{X}}$ equivalents) are intended as abbreviations for sets of feature specifications of the sort discussed in this section.

3.4 Grammars and metagrammars

Most of the difficulties alluded to in 3.2 derive directly from the fact that defining a CFPSG by means of listing the rules it contains provides no opportunity for stating any generalisations about those rules or the structures they generate. Information that could be stated once and for all is repeated over and over again in each individual rule. Suppose, then, that we adopt a more sophisticated conception of a grammar-definition. If all the relevant generalisations about a list-grammar could be expressed in the form of general principles of phrase structure, then these principles could be allowed to interact with basic information about subcategorisation to generate the rule list. We would then have a grammar for generating the grammar, or a metagrammar. It may well turn out that certain metagrammatical principles are plausibly regarded as universal, and that others, though not themselves universal, are subject to universal constraints. Such a metagrammar would be a combination of language-specific information and universal principles that defined the set of rules needed to generate the sentences of some language and to assign structural descriptions to them. Ultimately, of course, the meta-grammar so constructed could *itself* be viewed as the grammar of the language in question, and the fully specified phrase structure rules which it generates as a link between its provisions and explicit structural descriptions could be dispensed with. The (meta)grammar so interpreted would in effect comprise a set of well-formedness conditions on tree diagrams, rather than consti-tute a definition of the rules for generating such objects in the traditional sense.

Before attempting any comparison between such a framework and that embodied in GB theory, it will be useful to flesh out this (meta)grammatical skeleton with some specific proposals and examples.

3.4.1 Immediate dominance and linear precedence

Consider first of all the problem for phrase structure description that arises in the case of a language like Modern Greek where the order of the complements to a lexical head is relatively free. In principle any order is possible provided the head comes first and any clausal complement comes last. For example, the verb *stiçimatízo* (= 'bet') takes an NP complement (the sum), a PP complement (the person with whom the bet is made being denoted by the NP within it) and an $\bar{\text{S}}$ complement (specifying the nature of the bet). Both the VPs in [15] are well-formed. (Note that both could be interpreted as sentences since Greek is a pro-drop language (*cf* 2.3.9, example [240] *ff*)).

[15i] *stiçimatízi   ekató   dhrakhmés   me   ton   Andréa   pos* S
      bet-3s   100   drachmas   with the-acc   Andreas-acc   that S
[15ii] *stiçimatízi me ton Andréa ekató dhrakhmés pos* S
      '((s)he) bets Andreas 100 drachmas that . . . . . .'

Since conventional phrase structure rules specify both immediate dominance and linear precedence facts simultaneously, it follows that there will have to be two rules introducing verbs such as *stiçimatízo*.

[16i] VP → V NP PP [PFORM *me*] S̄
[16ii] VP → V PP [PFORM *me*] NP S̄

In both cases VP dominates the set of constituents V, NP, PP, S̄; it is simply that the order of NP and PP changes. (Note that the form of the preposition is specified as *me* (= 'with'). Many verbs in many languages require prepositional complements with specific prepositional heads (*cf*: *rely on*, *give to*, etc.), and the assignment of a specific preposition name as value for the feature PFORM is a very neat way of tackling the problem.) There is a similar situation in English in the case of verbs taking two PP complements, where the order is usually free (*cf*: *I argued with Noam about GPSG*, *I argued about GPSG with Noam*). Thus it should be clear that, from the point of view of universal grammar, the freer the order of constituents in a given language the greater the number of rules there will have to be to state the basic subcategorisation facts about lexical heads. Since these will in any given case simply repeat the immediate dominance facts within the range of variation of linear precedence permitted by the grammar of the language, the need for a better formalisation is self-evident.

In a transformational account, it would, of course, be possible to choose one order as basic and to derive the others from this by a combination of grammatical transformations (if the ordering change is grammatically triggered) and stylistic 'scrambling' rules (if the ordering change is free). Such a solution is not open in a one-level theory. The obvious solution in such a framework, then, is to state immediate dominance and linear precedence facts separately. Within GPSG the relevant rules are called ID rules and LP rules respectively. The basic subcategorisation facts are expressed, therefore, by the ID rules, and the set of possible permutations of categories mentioned in a given ID rule is determined by the LP statements. The latter express the ordering facts for the language once and for all rather than having these built into each and every phrase structure rule over and over again. The ID rule for *stiçimatízo* is therefore [17i] and that for *argue* is [17ii].

[17i] VP → V, NP, PP[*me*], S̄
[17ii] VP → V, PP[*about*], PP[*with*]

The commas between constituents on the right-hand side show
that no statement of precedence relations is intended. The actually occurring orders of constituents are determined by the LP
statements for Greek and English, [18i] and [18ii].

[18i] $H < \alpha < \bar{S}$
[18ii] $H < NP < PP < \bar{S}$

Both languages require lexical heads (H) to come first among
sisters and clauses to come last. Within the limits of this requirement Greek allows any order of unspecified categories (α is in
practice a variable over NP and PP) while English imposes
further requirements, namely that NPs should precede PPs (*cf:
gives the bone to the dog/?gives to the dog the bone*).

It is particularly important to note that the formulation of the
LP statements in [18] is neutral with respect to the value of H;
the ordering requirements may be partial or total over the
domain of categories involved, but they are exhaustive in that
they apply to any lexical head and its complements, and constant
in that they apply in the same way whatever the category of the
head. This property of 'exhaustive constant partial ordering' is
a powerful constraint on the class of grammars admitted by the
theory of GPSG, because only those CFPSGs which have this
property can be put into ID/LP format, and ID/LP format is a
defining characteristic of GPSGs. The adoption of this format
constitutes the incorporation into the formalism of description of
a universal principle that languages do not operate with ordering
principles that can vary with changes of lexical governor. If this
turns out to be false, a high price will have to paid within the
context of GPSG, and it is worth contrasting this situation with
that which arises in the case of some of the principles of universal
grammar in GB theory. Take, for example, the empty category
principle (*cf* 2.3.9, [235]) that requires traces to be properly
governed. The notion of proper government was adjusted several
times in the course of the discussion of government theory in
order to accommodate new configurations that seemed as if they
ought to fall within its definition. The price of such readjustments
in terms of their consequences for the theory as a whole was very
small, other than to render the definition of proper government
suspiciously broad, comprising as it did, subclauses that seemed
to have little in common. Obviously, precise formulations that
express the relevant generalisations cannot be achieved until
something approaching the full range of relevant phenomena is
known. But once that happy stage is reached, it is arguably in
the interests of linguistic research that linguists strive to frame

universal principles of grammatical organisation in such a way that their abandonment carries a price in terms of repercussions through the system.

Returning to the adoption of ID/LP format in a GPSG, it should be clear that LP rules can be interpreted in one of two different ways. Either they can be seen as a device for mapping ID rules into phrase structure rules (*ie* rules expressing dominance and precedence relations simultaneously), or they can be thought of as imposing a further set of well-formedness conditions on phrase markers over and above those imposed by ID rules. On the first interpretation ID/LP format is one aspect of the metagrammatical definition of the context-free phrase structure grammar needed to generate a given language. On the second interpretation ID/LP format is a property of the grammar of that language, which is no longer conceived as a list of phrase structure rules at all. A well-formed sentence is thus, amongst other things, one to which a structural description is assigned which meets the requirements of some subset of ID rules (obviously not every ID rule is involved in defining the structure of every sentence) and the requirements of the LP rules as a whole. Henceforth, the second interpretation will be adopted, and the notion of a GPSG as a metagrammatical definition of a more or less conventional CFPSG will be abandoned. A GPSG is therefore to be thought of as a theory of the grammatical structure of some language which is distinct from a CFPSG in several respects but most obviously in the fact that it contains no phrase structure rules. It is in fact a statement of the general principles, both universal and language-specific, that determine the properties of fully-specified structural descriptions of the surface structures of sentences in the language under investigation.

Nevertheless, the possibility of the alternative interpretation guarantees the weak equivalence of GPSGs with (a subset of) CFPSGs, even though the exhaustive constant partial ordering property that follows from the adoption of ID/LP format means that in terms of strong generative capacity (*ie* the assignment of structural descriptions to strings) the theory of GPSG is more restrictive than the theory of CFPSG. There is nothing in the latter to prevent the writing of rules with orderings of constituents that vary according to the choice of lexical head, for example.

3.4.2 Metarules

It will be recalled from the discussion of transformations in Chapter 2 that one major reason for their introduction into syntactic theory was a desire to simplify statements of subcategorisation. Thus if a particular lexical item appeared in two or more syntactic contexts that seemed to be systematically related both in terms of their structural properties and semantic interpretation, a common deep structure could be set up allowing for a single subcategorisation statement for the item in question together with a single representation of its predicate–argument structure, provided transformations were introduced to derive the superficial diversity of constructions from this common source. In 3.2 the active–passive relation was given as an example of the problems that the existence of systematic syntactic relations (or equivalently, regularly corresponding multiple contexts of lexical insertion for given word classes) present for phrase structure grammars. It was made clear there that the passive transformation performed a dual function; it expressed the fact that the surface subject of a passive sentence has the thematic role of the direct object of the transitive verb whose passive participle it contains, and it simultaneously expressed the fact that there is a systematic syntactic relationship between active and passive sentences, perhaps more accurately VPs, in that the latter lack an NP that is always present in the former.

In a GPSG the task of expressing those syntactic relationships that are interpretable as generalisations about the subcategorisation of lexical heads falls to **metarules**. The semantic part of the relationship is handled, reasonably enough, by semantic rules whose properties are briefly dealt with in 3.6 below.

Clearly, not every ID rule will introduce a lexical head and its complements. There will, for example, have to be an ID role for S which expands this category as two phrasal categories, (the traditional S → NP VP rule, however these categories are interpreted in $\bar{X}$ terms, though no linear precedence relations will be specified of course). Let us call the subset of ID rules that does involve the introduction of a lexical head **lexical ID rules**. Now it will often be the case that a lexical item that can appear in one context can also appear in another, and that this dual appearance is predictable and regular. Consider again the PS rules for active and passive VPs introduced in 3.2 (see [2] and the associated discussion). These are repeated here in the form of ID rules.

[19i] VP → V, NP (*kiss*) [19ii] VP → V (*kissed*)
  [PAS]

  VP → V, NP, PP (*give*)   VP → V , PP (*given*)
  [PAS]

  VP → V, NP, $\bar{S}$ (*persuade*)   VP → V , $\bar{S}$ (*persuaded*)
  [PAS]

The existence of the class of rules in [19ii] can be predicted on the basis of the class of rules in [19i]. Suppose, then, we establish a class of metarules which by definition take as input one class of lexical ID rules and give as output a related class of lexical ID rules; in other words, metarules are subject to a **Lexical Head Constraint** (LHC). Given this, the second class of ID rules would not then have to be listed one-by-one, and furthermore the existence of a systematic relationship between the two classes would be formally expressed. In the case of the rule sets in [19], we might propose the metarule in [20], which allows for the possibility of an agent phrase in passive VPs by including PP[*by*] in parentheses.

[20] *Passive metarule*: VP → W, NP
$$\Downarrow$$
VP → W, (PP[*by*])
[PAS]

Here W is intended as a variable over the expansion of VP excluding NP. The metarule thus says that any VP rule involving the introduction of a direct object NP has a corresponding passive VP rule in which everything else remains the same but the direct object NP is missing; optionally, there may be a prepositional phrase headed by the preposition *by*. The rules of [19i] are all potential input rules, and the rules of [19ii] are all potential output rules (ignoring for the moment the positioning of the feature PAS); a further set of three output rules containing PP[*by*] has not been illustrated.

Recall now that subcategorisation in GPSG is handled in a context-free manner by the introduction of numerals as values for the feature SUBCAT that is part of the feature make-up of lexical heads. Suppose, then, that the rules in [19i] are more fully specified as in [21].

[21] VP → V2, NP
VP → V3, NP, PP
VP → V4, NP, S̄

The verbs *kiss*, *give* and *persuade* would be listed in the lexicon as members of the subcategories of verb V2, V3 and V4 respectively. If we now adopt the convention that the subcategorisation feature on a lexical head is not affected by the application of metarules, the class of output rules [19ii] will all have a subcategorisation feature assigned to the head category of the expansion they authorise that is identical to that of the head category of the expansion authorised by the corresponding input rule in

[19i]. The rules in [19ii] would then appear as in [22], which now show explicitly that the same subcategories of verb are involved as in [19i]/[21].

[22] $\text{VP} \rightarrow \text{V}_2$
$\quad\quad$ [PAS]
$\quad$ $\text{VP} \rightarrow \text{V}_3, \quad \text{PP}$
$\quad\quad$ [PAS]
$\quad$ $\text{VP} \rightarrow \text{V}_4, \quad \bar{\text{S}}$
$\quad\quad$ [PAS]

In this way metarules express the fact that it is no accident that the same verbs turn up in active VPs with direct objects and passive VPs without. They are perhaps best interpreted, then, as devices for expressing generalisations about the subcategorisation of (classes of) lexical heads.

It is worthwhile at this point to pause and consider the differences between metarules and transformations. First and foremost, metarules map rule sets into rule sets, while transformations map phrase markers into phrase markers and involve the ascription of (at least) two levels of representation to sentences. Metarules are simply devices for adding to the stock of ID rules in a principled way. This difference has two immediate consequences. We know that GPSGs are weakly equivalent to (a subset of) CFPSGs, and there is no reason to suppose that the use of metarules affects this result, since they only add more rules of a type already employed. The use of transformations, on the other hand, may well change the expressive power of the theory in question, since the new rules are both directly involved in the determination of the well-formedness of sentences and the assignment of structural descriptions, and clearly of a formal type distinct from phrase structure rules. The importance of this will be discussed below in 3.8. It also follows that metarules, unlike transformations, will not have access to representations of predicate-argument structure (eg deep structures), and so will be unable to play any role in the statement of generalisations about the assignment of thematic roles etc. The fact that the subject of passive sentences is assigned the same thematic role as the direct object of corresponding sentences with active transitive verbs must be expressed elsewhere.

A second difference between metarules and transformations is that they do not operate within parallel domains. The former can only make reference to the complement structure of lexical heads, while the latter necessarily affect positions over a wider domain. So, for example, since all the NP positions in the subcategorisation frames of verbs (more generally of all lexical heads) are θ-marked, it follows that any movement of an NP from such a position must be to a position outside VP that is not θ-marked. Because of the built-in restrictions on their domain of application, metarules are more like lexical redundancy rules (see 2.2.2, especially the discussion of [84] and [85]); both express relationships by reference to the subcategorisation frames of lexical heads, whether these are represented as ID rules in the syntactic component of the grammar or as context-sensitive subcategorisation features in the lexicon. The boundedness of the relationships they describe is thus an automatic consequence of their formal properties and does not have to be stipulated independently. This contrasts quite clearly with the imposition of the subjacency requirement on *move* α.

This comparison, incidentally, provides one example of how the conception of universal grammar is determined by the view taken of what the properties of the grammars of individual languages must be. A theory based on the assumption that grammars contain transformations will look quite different from one based on the assumption that they do not, not least in terms of the status accorded to 'bounding' theory, which may or may not have analogues in non-transformational frameworks, but which clearly cannot be there interpreted as comprising constraints on movement. In these circumstances it is proper to ask just how much of a given theory of universal grammar is artefactual, and how much of it represents a rather theory-specific way of saying what would have to be said in any adequate framework. The more optimistic might like to suppose that as research within different frameworks progresses a consensus may begin to emerge as to what the essential characteristics of grammars are, and that some notation will be developed that will allow these to be represented in ways that do not tie them to the purely artefactual constructs of rival theories. It may be noted in passing that those who are more optimistic in this regard tend towards realism and those who are more pessimistic incline to instrumentalism in their interpretations of the fruits of linguistic labour.

Continuing a little further with the comparison between metarules and transformations, it is important to note that within GPSG there is as yet no theory of what constitutes a possible metarule. The situation is in some ways analogous to that which obtained in the period of the development of the standard theory when there was no satisfactory definition of possible transformation. The major difference, of course, is the one already alluded to, that metarules are inherently less 'powerful' in scope and demonstrably do not affect the expressive power of the theory they belong to. Nevertheless, the fact remains that there is in a GPSG one metarule for every pair of corresponding rule-sets like that in [19], just as in the standard theory there was one transformation for every construction that could be interpreted as a de-formed version of a comparable simple, active, declarative structure. To the extent that general principles have emerged which allow for the tranformational component to be represented schematically as *move α*, it is reasonable to ask whether there might not be general principles which all, or at least a subset of, existing metarules embody, but which as yet remain unexpressed. Assuming that such a set of principles did indeed come to light, they would presumably be different, at least in part, from those defining *move α*, because metarules and transformations as currently conceived, are not in a one-to-one correspondence. Thus, over and above the differences already mentioned, while *move α* represents a generalisation about the properties of NP-movement (passive and raising), *wh*-movement and extraposition (*cf* 2.3.7), there is in GPSG a passive metarule, but no corresponding metarules for raising, *wh*-movement or extraposition constructions (involving displacement of NP modifiers). A serious attempt to provide a theory of metarules would give us some basis for deciding whether or not their criterial properties really *were* different from those that define *move α*, or aspects of *move α*, in other than superficial ways. If, for example, it turned out that existing metarules were rather like transformations at some level of abstraction, then it might be the case that the fact that GPSG does not need an analogue of subjacency to constrain its passive metarule is outweighed by the fact that the framework is treating in a non-unified way relationships that should be treated uniformly, and that metarule analyses should be extended to cover the same range as *move α*. This would make the two approaches notational variants in the relevant respects (always assuming that an appropriate degree of formal precision is attainable in GB theory, at least in principle). On the other hand, if it turned out that metarules had quite different criterial properties from those of *move α*, then it would certainly be worth looking for evidence that the generalisation that *move α* is supposed to capture is artefactual, and that the non-uniform GPSG approach might therefore be preferable. In the absence of an explicitly formulated theory of metarules, however, comparisons that go beyond the superficially obvious are hard to make (though see 5.2 for some preliminary thoughts).

3.4.3 Feature instantiation principles

Clearly the theory of GPSG must seek to avoid the problem outlined in 3.2, whereby whole sets of rules making identical categorial statements are required in order to express relevant agreement patterns. What is needed are general principles determining the distribution of features in phrase markers. The basic ID rules can then be largely feature-free. A well-formed structural description will be one which conforms to the requirements of a subset of ID rules and the set of LP rules, and is fully specified featurally in accordance with these agreement principles.

Obviously some ID rules will have to make reference to certain syntactic features. These features are said to be *stipulated* as an essential property of the construction in question. For example, the ID rule introducing the constituents of a root *wh*-question will have to require the S following the *wh*-phrase to be inverted (amongst other things). Thus [23] is ungrammatical.

[23] *Who Gerald has implied that the reviewers savaged?*

Similarly, although VPs in complements may contain various types of verb form according to the choice of complement-taking verb or adjective, root sentences must contain finite verb forms. The ID rules introducing root and embedded structures must allow for relevant features to be placed on S (or VP) to ensure the correct results. In other cases, of course, features not explicitly stipulated can have values assigned by virtue of feature specification defaults (*cf* 3.3); thus embedded sentences will all be marked −INV, for example.

But this leaves the main body of agreement facts virtually untouched. Features not stipulated by rule or filled in by default are said to be (freely) **instantiated**. Thus, if an ID rule allows S to dominate NP and VP, we are free to ascribe any permissible combination of person, number, gender features (as determined by the feature co-occurrence restrictions, *cf* 3.3) to, say, the head noun of the subject NP. The crucial thing is that these features recur in all the right places, that the necessary agreement patterns are enforced when features are instantiated elsewhere. The three feature instantiation principles that will be considered in this section are held to be universal, and are designed to ensure that feature instantiation in phrase markers is not haphazard. In earlier versions of GPSG feature instantiation was assumed to take place on ID rules, but since we are here interpreting the metagrammar as a set of well-formedness conditions on syntactic representations rather than as a definition of a phrase structure grammar, feature instantiation will be illustrated directly on phrase markers.

We may begin with the **Head Feature Convention** (HFC). As a preliminary, consider the ID rules in [24].

[24i] $\bar{\bar{N}} \to$ DET, $\bar{N}$ [24ii] $\bar{\bar{A}} \to$ DEG, $\bar{A}$
$\bar{N} \to$ N6, $\bar{\bar{P}}$ $\bar{A} \to$ A4, $\bar{\bar{P}}$
         [PFORM *at*]   [PFORM *with*]

[24iii] $\bar{\bar{V}} \to$ $\bar{\bar{N}}$, $\bar{V}$ [24iv] $\bar{\bar{P}} \to \overline{ADV}$, $\bar{P}$
[VFORM FIN] $\bar{P} \to$ P1, $\bar{\bar{N}}$
$\bar{V} \to$ V2, $\bar{\bar{N}}$

It is assumed that double bar categories are maximal projections and that $\bar{\bar{V}}$ = S. Given suitable LP rules (*eg.* $\alpha <$ H, and H $<$ $\bar{N} < \bar{P} < \bar{V}$, which guarantee that specifiers precede and complements follow the head), these ID statements define the phrase markers in [25] as well-formed.

[25]

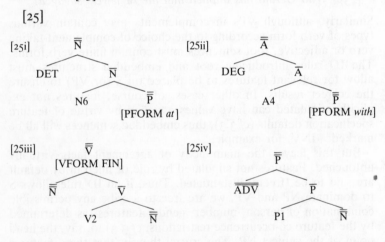

[25i] $\bar{\bar{N}}$ [25ii] $\bar{\bar{A}}$

    DET $\bar{N}$ DEG $\bar{A}$

      N6 $\bar{\bar{P}}$ A4 $\bar{\bar{P}}$
      [PFORM *at*]   [PFORM *with*]

[25iii] $\bar{\bar{V}}$ [25iv] $\bar{\bar{P}}$
    [VFORM FIN]

    $\bar{\bar{N}}$ $\bar{V}$ $\overline{ADV}$ $\bar{P}$

      V2 $\bar{\bar{N}}$ P1 $\bar{\bar{N}}$

Within the general schema which these exemplify, it is clearly necessary that the HEAD features of $\bar{X}$ should agree with those of $\bar{\bar{X}}$, and that those of $\bar{X}$ should agree with those of X.

It is also clear that this agreement requirement extends not only to features such as person, number, gender, case, or verb form, but even to the major category features N(ominal) and V(erbal). This latter agreement is guaranteed by stipulation in the rules in [24]; the former is not, and indeed could not be, if we are to avoid a proliferation of rules making identical ID statements and varying only in terms of feature combinations assigned to relevant categories. The result of this situation is that whatever device is set up to guarantee agreement of person, number and gender, some HEAD features will be transmitted from mother to daughter by stipulation, others by this feature instantiation principle. In view of the inelegance of such a treatment of HEAD features, the best solution is to allow ID rules to stipulate which of the categories in an expansion is the head category but not to stipulate its feature composition further beyond an indication of the required bar level. This could be achieved by the use of the symbols H̄ and H, which are to be interpreted as [BAR, 1] and [BAR, 0] respectively. In practice H will always be accompanied by a SUBCAT feature. The rules in [24i], for example, would now be of the form [26].

[26] $\overline{\overline{N}}$ → DET, H̄
    $\overline{N}$ → H6,   P̄
                [PFORM *at*]

If we now set up a head feature convention which requires all the free HEAD features of a head daughter to agree with the HEAD features of its mother, the agreements of major category features and of features such as person, number and gender will be accounted for in a uniform manner.

The restriction to *free* HEAD features is necessitated by the fact that it may be necessary in particular cases to allow the stipulation of a HEAD feature on a daughter in an ID rule. For example, it might be convenient to take BAR as a HEAD feature because of cases where the head category of an expansion is of the same bar level as the mother (see the treatment of unbounded dependencies in 3.4.4). If the head is indicated simply by H, then the bar level of the mother will automatically be copied onto the head daughter. Notice that H will always be distinct in this use from that in which it marks a lexical head, because in the latter, as noted, it will have an associated sub-categorisation feature. The rules in [26] thus incorporate a stipulated HEAD feature on the head daughter in the form of a bar level requirement. We do not want the head feature convention to override this and assign the value 2 to the BAR feature of the head daughter in the expansion of $\overline{N}$.

The HFC, as observed earlier, is best viewed as a part of the mapping between ID rules and structures; it imposes severe restrictions on the class of trees compatible with a given ID rule in that only those with permissible mother–daughter agreements of HEAD features will be well-formed. Further restrictions are imposed by the **Foot Feature Principle** (FFP). This is particularly important in the analysis of unbounded dependency constructions such as *wh*-questions, where a FOOT feature SLASH plays a major role (*cf* 3.4.4). Other FOOT features include WH and RE(flexive). Let us begin with WH. As noted above, it may be necessary to mark a constituent as a *wh*-phrase in order to account for its syntactic distribution (*eg* clause initially), even though its head may not itself be a *wh*-word. The NP *the writing in the margins of which* (as in *the manuscript the writing in the margins of which Dr Thring deciphered was deposited in the British Museum*) has the structure given in [27].

[27]

Somehow the feature WH must be transmitted to the root $\overline{\overline{N}}$ node. The simplest formulation of the foot feature principle (FFP) would be to require that any FOOT feature specification instantiated on a daughter category in a tree must also be instantiated on its mother category. In [27] this would have the effect of 'transmitting' WH from the *wh*-word along the chain of categories indicated in [28] (opposite).

Similarly in the case of reflexives, if a feature-driven theory of their distribution is adopted, it will be necessary in some cases to mark certain constituents as *containing* a reflexive even though the heads of these constituents are not themselves reflexive. Consider [29].

[29] *Ronnie talks to himself.*

[28]

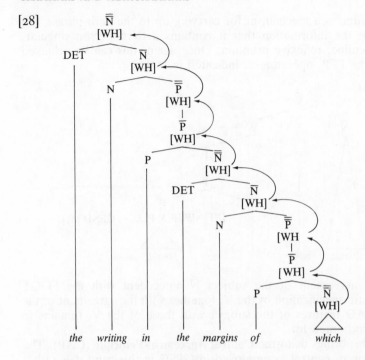

the writing in the margins of which

The non-occurrence of reflexives in subject position in tensed sentences might reasonably be accounted for by the fact that they are necessarily non-nominative in form. Whether there are deeper reasons for the non-existence of nominative reflexives (such as Chomsky's anaphor binding condition, 2.3.6, [184i] and [210]) is a question that will be left to one side for the moment. The feature RE thus occurs on objects. The metarule [30] defines a class of output rules with the feature RE added to the objects of verbs and prepositions.

[30] $\bar{X}[-N] \to W, \bar{\bar{N}}$
$\Downarrow$
$\bar{X}[-N] \to W, \bar{\bar{N}}[RE]$

Here $\bar{X}[-N]$ is either $\bar{V}$ or $\bar{P}$, and W includes at least a lexical head. The value assigned to RE is the category $\bar{\bar{N}}$ marked for the agreement details of the relevant anaphoric element, here [PER 3, PLU −, GEND M]. Assuming that some mechanism can be found for enforcing agreement between sisters in the relevant respects, as here between subject noun phrase and verb phrase (see on the Control Agreement Principle below), what is required is a mechanism for carrying up to the verb phrase ($\bar{\bar{V}}$) node the information that it contains a third person singular, masculine, reflexive pronoun. Once again, this can be achieved by the FFP, operating as indicated in [31].

[31]

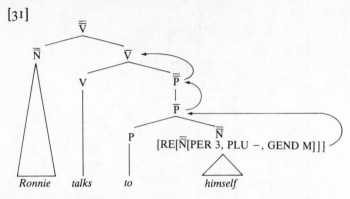

Ronnie   talks   to   himself

The agreement of the subject $\bar{\bar{N}}$ antecedent with the FOOT feature specification of the $\bar{V}$, together with the agreement of the HEAD features of the subject with those of the $\bar{V}$, remains to be accounted for.

This brings us to the **Control Agreement Principle** (CAP). The notion of control as employed in GPSG in this context is rather different from that introduced in the presentation of GB theory, which concerned the determination of the reference of the null (anaphoric) pronominal PRO (*cf* 2.3.8). As a preliminary, let us consider the notion of **semantic type**. Semantic interpretation in GPSG will be considered in more detail in 3.6; for the moment let us simply assume that each syntactic category is associated with a semantic type that determines the set of possible denotations for expressions of that category. Suppose that sentences are of type *t* (truth values) and noun phrases of type *e* (entities or individuals), so that sentences denote truth values and noun phrases denote individuals; these are not in fact the denotations assigned to these categories in semantic work in GPSG, but the simple type-assignment assumed here is adequate for the purpose of explaining the CAP. Given a 'world' or 'state of affairs' populated by individuals with various properties, in various states, performing various actions, each sentence of some language will describe (some aspect of) that world truly or falsely. Each NP in a sentence of some language will denote one or more of the individuals in that world. But what should the denotation of a verb phrase be? Consider the diagram in [32].

[32]

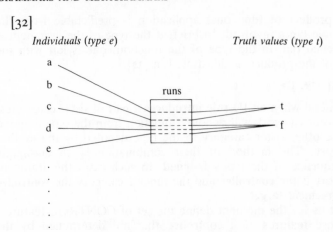

Individuals (*type e*)   Truth values (*type t*)

On the left we have the domain of individuals, each identified by a letter of the alphabet. On the right we have the domain of truth values, *t* and *f*. In the centre we have a typical verb phrase, one consisting of the single intransitive verb-form *runs*. If we now consider each individual in turn, it will be either true or false that that individual is running in our world. *Run* might, therefore, be interpreted as something which, when applied to individuals, gives a truth value as output. In the technical terminology, *run* could be regarded as a function from individuals to truth values. More generally, any verb phrase (including those consisting of intransitive verbs) may be so interpreted. Notice that the application of the function denoted by *run* to the set of individuals divides the set into two, those who are running and those who are not. As an alternative, therefore, to regarding *run* as a function from individuals to truth values, we might interpret it as denoting a set of individuals (the runners in our world). Either way, VPs are assigned the type <e, t>: expressions of this form denote functions from the type on the left to the type on the right, or, if the type on the right is *t*, sets of the type on the left.

The relation of control holds between pairs of categories in a tree that combine semantically as function and argument. Take the case of a singular subject NP and VP. We know that the first denotes an individual and that the second denotes a function from individuals to truth values. The 'meaning' of the sentence is simply the product of the application of the function to the individual which is its argument, as in [33].

[33] <e, t> (e)

The product of functional application is predictable from the semantic types involved. In brief, if the type of the argument is 'cancelled out' in the type of the function, one is left with the type of the product, as illustrated in [34].

[34] $<\!\!¢, t\!\!>$ $(¢)$ = t

In general when an ID rule introduces a pair of sister categories, one sister category will denote a function from the type denoted by the other sister category to the type denoted by the mother category. The method of their combination is an automatic consequence of the types assigned. In such cases the argument category is the **controller** and the functor category the **controllee** or **agreement target**.

Let us for the moment define the set of CONTROL features, *ie* those features of a controllee that are determined by the controller, as consisting of the single member AGR, and suppose that any constituent that can be marked for morphological agreement will have this feature among the set of those for which it may have a value defined. The CAP requires that the value of the CONTROL feature (*ie* AGR) of a controllee must be equal to the controller. In the case of a sentence such as *he runs*, the structure of which may be represented as in [35],

[35]

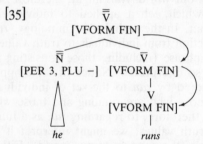

The features [VFORM FIN], together with the major category features
[+V, −N], are carried down onto the phrasal and lexical head by the HFC.

we know that $\overline{\overline{N}}$ is the controller of $\overline{V}$ because $\overline{\overline{N}}$ denotes the argument of the function denoted by $\overline{V}$. Assuming that V and its projection $\overline{V}$ may be marked for morphological agreement, both will require a value to be assigned to the feature AGR. By the CAP the value of AGR in $\overline{V}$ must be equal to the controller; since the subject is $\overline{\overline{N}}$ [PER 3, PLU−] the value of AGR in $\overline{V}$ will be $\overline{\overline{N}}$ [PER 3, PLU−]. By the HFC this feature specification is passed down to the head V as required. This is summarised in [36].

[36]

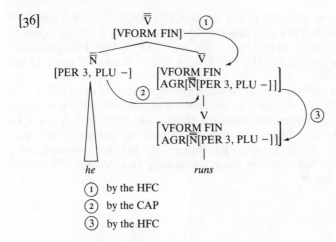

① by the HFC
② by the CAP
③ by the HFC

Returning now to sentence [29], *Ronnie talks to himself*, the agreement between *Ronnie* and *talks* will be handled exactly as in [36] *mutatis mutandis*. But what of the agreement between *Ronnie* and *himself*? It will be recalled that the FFP assigns the FOOT feature RE N̄ [PER 3, PLU−, GEND M] to P̄, P̄ and V̄ (*cf* [31] repeated here as [37] but with all agreement processes made explicit).

[37]

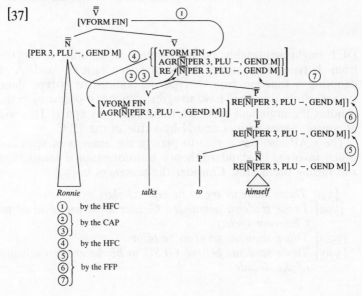

① by the HFC
②
③ } by the CAP
④ by the HFC
⑤
⑥ } by the FFP
⑦

If we now add RE to the set of CONTROL features, the CAP will also require the value assigned to this in $\bar{V}$ to be equal to the controller. In this case, then, the CAP and the FFP guarantee that the features of the reflexive in $\bar{V}$ match up with those of the subject $\bar{\bar{N}}$.

The CAP can be put to work more generally if need arises. For example, in languages in which determiners and adjectives agree with head nouns the relevant categories, DET and $\bar{\bar{A}}$, may be assigned semantic types that are functions, and have the value of their AGR feature determined by the argument-denoting category that controls them. Assuming the structure illustrated in [38] for $\bar{\bar{N}}$,

[38]

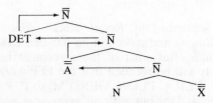

DET denotes a function from $\bar{N}$-type denotations to $\bar{\bar{N}}$-type denotations.
$\bar{\bar{A}}$ denotes a function from $\bar{N}$-type denotations to $\bar{N}$-type denotations.

DET might reasonably be interpreted as denoting a function from $\bar{N}$-type denotations to $\bar{\bar{N}}$-type denotations, and $\bar{\bar{A}}$ as denoting a function from $\bar{N}$-type denotations to $\bar{N}$-type denotations. Both, then, will have to agree with the co-occurring $\bar{N}$ that denotes the argument to which these functions apply. This will, of course, agree with $\bar{\bar{N}}$ and N by virtue of the HFC.

The CAP also has a role to play in the analysis of sentences which involve, in standard-theory transformational terms, equi and raising predicates. Consider the sentences in [39].

[39i]   *Those students try to be real scholars.*
[39ii] *Those students persuaded Gazdar to be president of the Chomsky society.*
[39iii] *Those students seem to be idiots.*
[39iv] *Those students believe GPSG to be the greatest advance of the decade.*

The first point to emphasise is that the verbs in [39i] and [39iii] are assumed to take $\bar{V}$ complements, and the verbs in [39ii] and [39iv] to take $\bar{\bar{N}}$ plus $\bar{V}$ complements, as illustrated in [40].

[40]

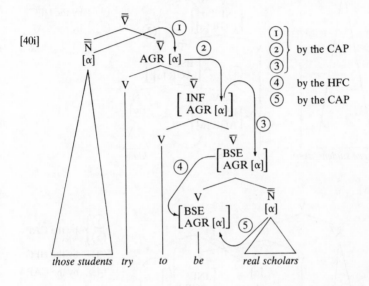

[40i]

those students   try   to   be   real scholars

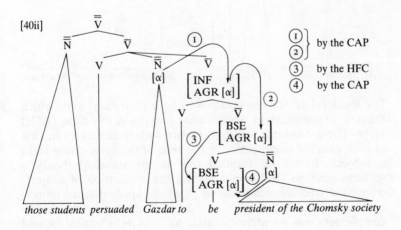

[40ii]

those students persuaded Gazdar to   be   president of the Chomsky society

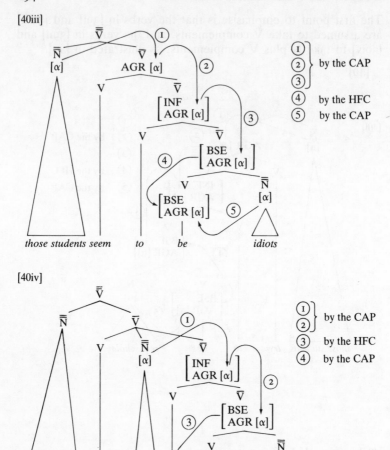

For technical reasons *to* is taken to be a (defective) verb which takes a V̄ complement whose head has the verb's base (BSE) form. These resemble standard theory surface structures in that in each case the complement of the verb of the main clause lacks a subject. It will be recalled that in the standard theory a sentence such as [39i] would involve the application of subject-controlled equi-NP deletion and [39ii] the application of object-controlled equi-NP deletion to deep structures in which the complement was a sentence containing a subject identical to, and co-referential with, the subject of the main verb. By contrast [39iii] and [39iv] would involve the application of subject-to-subject raising and subject-to-object raising to deep structures in which once again the complement was sentential, the subject in the case of [39iii] being *those students* and in the case of [39iv] *GPSG*. The result of all these processes was to leave a bare VP complement in surface structure.

In GB theory, however, all of these sentences have sentential complements at all levels of representation. PRO is the D-structure and the S-structure subject of [39i] and [39ii]. In [39iii] the D-structure subject is *those students* and the S-structure subject is the trace of *those students*. And in [39iv] *GPSG* is the subject at both levels. It is assumed to be governed and Case-marked across S, after S̄-pruning, by *believe*; it is no longer regarded as the 'surface' object of *believe* at all, and the rule of subject-to-object raising has been abandoned. The GB position is largely the product of the adoption of the Projection Principle, requiring the θ-marking properties of lexical items to be represented categorically at D-structure, S-structure and LF.

There is no analogue of the Projection Principle in GPSG. There is only one level of representation, which is a projection from the set of ID rules, including those involved in subcategorisation. But there is no level of representation at which the θ-marking properties of lexical items, or equivalently their predicate-argument structures, are projected categorically. The contexts relevant to subcategorisation are surface structure contexts and do not reflect predicate–argument structure directly, like D-structure, or indirectly, like S-structure enriched with empty categories. Nevertheless, it is claimed that semantic interpretation in the real sense, *ie* involving the assignment of denotations to linguistic expressions, can be carried out on the basis of the sorts of surface structure generated by a GPSG together with a knowledge of the semantic types assigned to lexical items. The actual interpretation mechanisms required to handle sentences such as those in [39] containing complements with missing subjects will be discussed in 3.6. The important thing to note here is that the noun phrase which appears as the complement of *be* in these sentences has to agree with a noun phrase in the main clause (the subject in [39i] and [39iii], and the object in [39ii] and [39iv]. Assuming that the CAP as already formulated can handle the agreement between a subject and its verb phrase, we now have to deal with the transmission of this agreement down to the predicate nominal in cases of 'subject-controlled equi' and 'subject-to-subject raising', and explain why the predicate nominal agrees with the object in cases of 'object controlled equi' or 'subject-to-object raising'.

Beginning with [40i] (subject-controlled equi) and [40iii] (subject-to-subject_raising), it is clear that the infinitival $\overline{V}$ does not have a sister $\overline{\overline{N}}$ that can be interpreted as its controller. In fact verbs such as *try* and *seem* are most naturally interpreted as denoting functions from $\overline{V}$-type denotations to $\overline{V}$-type denotations, as a glance at the relevant trees will confirm. If we extended the notion of control to these cases, then, it would turn out that the verb is the functor and the infinitival complement its argument. But this is obviously useless since the functor cannot agree with its argument for the simple reason that the argument has no features for the functor to agree with (though the functor has a set of features from the mother $\overline{V}$ by virtue of the HFC). Since it is the argument that is the agreement target here rather than the functor, the simplest solution is to say that the agreement target has no controller and is not itself a controllee, and to add a clause to the CAP which requires a category which includes a CONTROL feature (such as AGR) but lacks a controller (like an infinitival complement to a verb such as *try* or *seem* or the base-form complement to *to*) to have the value of its CONTROL feature set equal to the CONTROL feature of its mother. Thus the infinitival and base-form $\overline{V}$s in [40i] and [40iii] will agree with the $\overline{V}$s that dominate them, and these will agree with the subject $\overline{\overline{N}}$, by virtue of the (extended) CAP. The VFORM and AGR features now descend onto the head verb *be* by the HFC, and if we assume that predicate nominals can be morphologically marked for agreement, as seems quite natural, and that these denote a type which is the argument of the function denoted by the type assigned to *be*, *become* etc. (*ie* functions from the type of predicative expressions to $\overline{V}$-type denotations), the agreement of *lecturers* and *idiots* in [40i] and [40iii] with the head V will also follow from the CAP.

In the case of [40ii] and [40iv] we wish to make the direct object $\overline{\overline{N}}$ the controller of the infinitival $\overline{V}$, since here we are dealing with object-controlled equi and subject-to-object raising in standard theory transformational terms. Suppose, then, that *persuade* and *believe* denote a type that combines with the type of an infinitival $\overline{V}$ to make the type of a 'transitive $\overline{V}$', *ie* a type that combines with the type of a $\overline{\overline{N}}$ to make the type of a $\overline{V}$. To give a simple example, using English words to represent types, *persuade* would combine with an infinitive like *to resign* to form a transitive verb phrase *persuade-to-resign*. This would then combine with a noun phrase object like *Maggie* to form an expression *persuade-to-resign* (*Maggie*), which is of verb-phrase type, because it can combine with a subject noun phrase to form an expression of sentence type, for example, *persuade-to-resign* (*Maggie*) (*Neil*). The corresponding sentence of ordinary English would, of course, be *Neil persuades Maggie to resign*. Returning to [40ii] and [40iv], the V̄s headed by *persuaded* and *believe* will now be assigned the type of functions from V̄-type denotations to functions from N̄-type denotations to V̄-type denotations, and will thus combine semantically first with a V̄-type denotation and then with an N̄-type denotation. Again using English words to represent types, we obtain [41].

[41i] *persuade* (*to be president of the Chomsky society*) (*Gazdar*)

[41ii] *believe* (*to be the greatest advance of the decade*) (*GPSG*)

Notice that in each case there is a functor category (the transitive V̄) with an unspecified AGR feature within it (in the infinitival complement) that applies to a N̄ argument that is its controller. The verbs *persuade* and *believe* thus mediate the control relation between the infinitival V̄ (controllee/agreement target) and object N̄ (controller), though the CAP can apply exactly as before to ensure that the CONTROL feature of the target is equal to the controller. Once the infinitival V̄ has the appropriate value set for AGR, the second clause of the CAP, dealing with cases where there is no controller, will ensure the agreement of the base-form complement as before. The VFORM and AGR features then descend onto the head V (*be*) by the HFC, and the agreement of the predicate nominal follows from the original clause of the CAP.

As suggested at the beginning of this section, the three feature instantiation principles discussed are intended as universals in the mapping between ID rules and structures. Obviously the agreements enforced in any given language will depend on the membership of the sets HEAD, FOOT and CONTROL in that language, but the manner of operation of the principles on the members of these sets is indeed universal. In general one would not expect much variation in the membership of the three sets, though the distribution of AGR, and indeed the internal make-up of AGR, may vary quite considerably according to the extent of overt morphological agreement-marking in a given language and the range of features it applies to.

3.5 Unbounded dependencies

As noted in 3.2, unbounded dependency constructions provide
a major problem for phrase structure description. The name is
in fact something of a misnomer in the context both of GB theory
and of GPSG. In the former, as we have seen, subjacency
constrains the operation of *move* α, and in the latter, as we shall
see, 'unbounded dependencies' turn out likewise to be chains of
bounded dependencies, though for different reasons.

Consider first of all the conjoined phrases in [42].

[42i]   *Ivan wrote **an article and a review**.*
[42ii] *Ivan wrote **to Gerald and to Geoff**.*
[42iii] **Ivan wrote **an article and to Geoff**.*

Although there are many problems concerning the theory of co-
ordination, it seems reasonable to argue on the basis of examples
such as these that when we are dealing with the co-ordination of
constituents, the constituents concerned must be of the same
syntactic category. (The problem that arises in the case of
predicative expressions (*Ronnie is **the chairman of that committee
and quite unscrupulous***) is here ignored, though it does have a
solution in GPSG.) Compare now the sentences in [43].

[43i]   *Did Ivan **draft an article and revise a review**?*
[43ii] **What did Ivan **draft an article and revise**?*
[43iii] *What did Ivan **draft and revise**?*

An obvious explanation for the ungrammaticality of [43ii] is that
it involves the co-ordination of unlike categories, and is therefore
unacceptable for the same reason as [42iii]. In [43i] two complete
verb phrases are conjoined, and in [43iii] two transitive verbs are
conjoined but both have their objects missing. In [43ii], however,
there is an attempt to conjoin a complete verb phrase, in which
the transitive verb has an object, with an incomplete verb phrase,
in which the object of the transitive verb is missing. For the
explanation to go through, it will be necessary to supplement the
set of syntactic categories so that a distinction is drawn between
a category X and a category X with a missing Y. Let us then
introduce the convention that X/Y (read 'X slash Y') is the name
of a category that is like X in all respects bar one; where X
contains within it a category Y, X/Y does not. Thus in [43i] two
$\bar{\bar{V}}$s are conjoined, in [43iii] two $\bar{V}/\bar{N}$s, and in [43ii] a $\bar{V}$ and a
$\bar{V}/\bar{N}$. By the like-category constraint, therefore, only the first two
will be well-formed co-ordinations. Notice too that the adoption
of this new approach to syntactic categories renders the **Co-**

ordinate Structure Constraint assumed in most transformational work redundant (see 2.2.4, especially the discussion of [115] to [119]. There is no need for a constraint blocking extraction from one of a pair of conjuncts, since there is now an independent explanation for the ungrammaticality of the product that derives from the theory of co-ordination.

How exactly should these new slash categories be interpreted? It turns out that exactly the right results are obtained if SLASH is taken to be a member of the set of FOOT features, and its distribution in trees in left to the FFP. The values assigned to SLASH will, of course, be syntactic categories. There is also good reason to make SLASH a member of the set of CONTROL features as well, as we shall see.

Consider first of all a typical example of an unbounded dependency construction.

[44] *Who did you say Gerald showed the manuscript to?*

The rule which introduces such unbounded dependency constructions is [45].

[45] $\bar{\bar{V}} \rightarrow \bar{\bar{X}}, H/\bar{\bar{X}}$

Taking $\bar{\bar{V}}$ as S, this says that a sentence node may dominate a maximal projection and another sentence node (recall that by the HFC H with no stipulated features will be a category whose HEAD features are those of the mother) whose SLASH feature is stipulated as being a maximal projection. This is the GPSG solution to the problem of guaranteeing the presence of a 'gap' in the sentence following a 'displaced' *wh*-phrase. Obviously it remains to explain how the two unspecified maximal projections referred to in [45] are made to agree, and how the information that there is a 'gap' is carried indefinitely far down a tree to the gap itself.

The answer to the first question is straightforward if SLASH is added to the set of CONTROL features. It is natural to interpret slash categories as denoting functions from denotations of the type on the right of the slash to denotations of the type on the left. Take the case of $\bar{\bar{V}}/\bar{\bar{N}}$. This is a sentence with a missing noun phrase; if the function which this denotes is applied to a $\bar{\bar{N}}$-type denotation, the result, naturally enough, is a $\bar{\bar{V}}$-type denotation, because the missing $\bar{\bar{N}}$ (denotation) has been 'replaced'. The independent $\bar{\bar{X}}$ in [45] therefore controls the slash category. By the CAP the CONTROL feature of the slash category must be equal to the controller. Consequently the value of SLASH will always be a category identical to the independent

$\overline{\overline{X}}$. Suppose, then, that this latter is instantiated as $\overline{\overline{N}}$[WH Q]; this will also be the value for the SLASH feature of the sister category.

Consider, now, the tree diagram in [46] which represents the structure of [44].

[46]

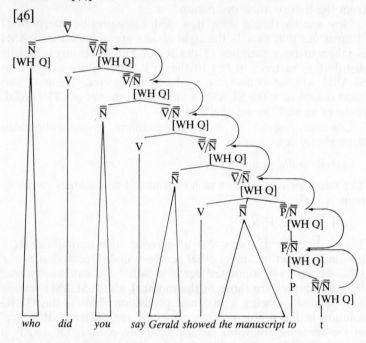

What is required here is the projection of a SLASH feature through the tree from the position of the 'gap', along the path indicated. The set of *possible* projection paths is in fact identifiable by virtue of the FFP, which requires any FOOT feature, including now SLASH, that is instantiated on a daughter also to be instantiated on its mother. The projection path illustrated in [46] is thus only one of a number of possible paths available for the percolation of SLASH in a sentence of this type (*cf What did you say Gerald showed to Geoff?, Who did you say showed the manuscript to Geoff?*), but all of these would conform with the requirements of the FFP. We can exclude the possibility that lexical categories get instantiated with a SLASH feature by means of an FCR.

[47] SUBCAT ⊃ ~SLASH (*ie* if a category has the feature SUBCAT, it will not (~) have SLASH.)

The projected SLASH feature here must, of course, be $\overline{\overline{\text{N}}}$ [WH Q], since the CAP requires this feature to appear on the topmost SLASH category, as we have seen, and the requirements of the CAP and the FFP have to match if the tree is to be well-formed. 'Unbounded' dependencies are thus analysed as linked series of local mother–daughter feature correspondences.

The termination of a projection path is handled by metarule. Suppose that the 'gaps' in unbounded dependency constructions are in fact phonetically null categories, or traces, as suggested in GB theory. If the distribution of such traces is determined by metarule, a restrictive version of the empty category principle (requiring traces to be properly governed) follows at once. Metarules, by virtue of the Lexical Head Constraint, operate only on lexical ID rules and output only lexical ID rules (*cf* 3.4.2). Consequently any trace introduced where a full $\overline{\overline{\text{N}}}$ (or other maximal projection) might otherwise have occurred will necessarily be lexically governed (*ie* be in the subcategorisation frame of a lexical head). The formulation is more restrictive than that in GB theory since there is no question of proper government across S or of proper government by co-indexed categories from COMP (*cf* 2.3.9); lexical government of sisters is the only form of proper government that is definable in a way that can be incorporated into the available descriptive apparatus. Once again, as with the exhaustive constant partial ordering property, the universal is not stated as an autonomous proposition, but actually 'built in' to the framework of description. The penalties for the failure of such universals are correspondingly higher, and they cannot be casually revised or abandoned in the face of new evidence or counter-examples. The testability of the framework is thus enhanced, this being one of the essential properties of an empirical discipline.

It is, however, important to note that the 'range' of this restrictive ECP is less than that of its GB equivalent, because constructions involving NP-movement in GB terms are not analysed in GPSG in terms requiring reference to traces. As we have seen, passives are handled by metarule but the 'gap' in a passive $\overline{\text{V}}$ is taken to be 'real', in the sense that no category, even a null one, is present, and raising constructions involve 'bare' infinitival $\overline{\text{V}}$ complements that have their missing subjects interpreted semantically (details in 3.6 below). The existence of any significant generalisation of the type *move* α is thus denied (see 5.2 for some discussion).

There are two metarules required for the purposes of slash termination, [48i] and [48ii].

$$[48i]\ X \to W, \bar{\bar{X}} \qquad\qquad [48ii]\ X \to W, \bar{\bar{V}}[FIN]$$
$$\Downarrow \qquad\qquad\qquad\qquad\qquad \Downarrow$$
$$X \to W, \bar{\bar{X}}[NULL] \qquad\qquad X/\bar{N} \to W, \bar{V}$$

The second is a consequence of the restrictiveness of the lexical government requirement for traces in GPSG, and it might reasonably be asked whether a more elegant formulation might not be devised that would allow [48ii] to be dispensed with. However, as things stand [48i] deals with all dependencies apart from those into subject position in embedded clauses, which are handled by [48ii]. This formulation of the termination of projection paths in subject position is analogous to the government-from-COMP possibility in the ECP; both are effectively *ad hoc* additions to cope with the peculiarity of subjects, and both are suspect.

Taking [48i] first, this says that for every rule introducing a lexical head and a maximal projection (with or without other elements; W is a variable over a lexical head and its complements other than $\bar{\bar{X}}$) there is a corresponding rule in which the maximal projection has the feature NULL. If we suppose an FCR as in [49],

[49] NULL ⊃ SLASH

we guarantee that NULL categories have a SLASH feature. The FFP, of course, guarantees that any instantiation of that feature on a NULL category will also appear on its mother. In the case of [46], therefore, the fully specified tree for the lower $\bar{V}$ would be as in [50].

[50]

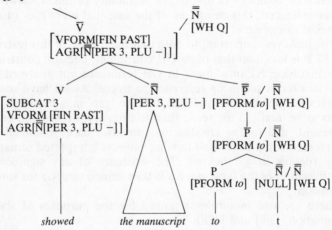

The rule for verbs like *show* is [51].

[51] $\bar{\text{V}} \rightarrow$ V3, $\bar{\bar{\text{N}}}$, $\bar{\bar{\text{P}}}$[PFORM *to*]

This is a possible input to [48i], and the output will be identical except that NULL will have been added to one or other of the maximal projections. If it is added to $\bar{\bar{\text{N}}}$, this must also have the feature SLASH by [49]. As noted, in [46]/[50] the value of SLASH must be $\bar{\bar{\text{N}}}$[WH Q] in order to match the requirements of the CAP. Notice that the output ID rule will still mention verbs of subcategory 3. The generalisation about subcategorisation that motivated the introduction of the transformation of *wh-movement* (*cf* 2.1.3) is thus taken care of.

Rule [48ii] is needed because subject $\bar{\bar{\text{N}}}$ do not fall inside the subcategorisation frames of lexical heads on standard analyses. Take the sentence *You said Gerald showed the manuscript to Geoff*, represented as in [52].

[52]

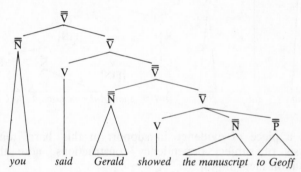

It is clear that neither the rule introducing the complement sentence,

[53] $\bar{\bar{\text{V}}} \rightarrow$ V7, $\bar{\bar{\text{V}}}$[FIN] (*say* S)

nor the rule expanding the complement sentence,

[54] $\bar{\bar{\text{V}}} \rightarrow \bar{\bar{\text{N}}}$, $\bar{\text{V}}$

contains a lexical head that is a sister of the subject of the embedded sentence. Neither of these is therefore a possible input to [48i]. [48ii] allows rules like [53] to be input, and outputs rules where the $\bar{\text{V}}$ is stipulated as containing a missing $\bar{\bar{\text{N}}}$, and this in turn is stipulated as being the subject of the complement sentence. This effect is achieved by turning the sentential complement into a verb phrase complement; a sentence with a missing subject $\overline{\overline{N}}$ is indeed a $\overline{V}$. If [53] is input to [48ii], the output is [55].

[55] $\overline{V}/\overline{\overline{N}} \rightarrow V_7$, $\overline{V}$[FIN]

This is the rule that defines the immediate domination relations in the subordinate clause of a sentence such as [56].

[56] *Who did you say showed the manuscript to Geoff?*

The structural description assigned to [56] would be [57].

[57]

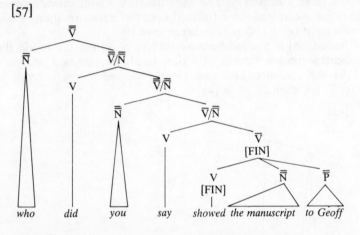

As a piece of evidence in support of this 'bare' tensed $\overline{V}$ analysis of subject dependency constructions, note the co-ordination facts in [58].

[58i] *What did **Ronnie** say and **Maggie** approve of?* $(\overline{\overline{V}}/\overline{N} + \overline{\overline{V}}/\overline{N})$

[58ii] **Who did you say **Maggie invited to the rostrum** and **spoke**?* $(\overline{V}/\overline{N} + \overline{V})$

If the second conjunct in [58ii] were analysed as a sentence with a missing noun phrase $(\overline{V}/\overline{N})$, rather than as a $\overline{V}$ in line with the predictions of metarule [48ii], there would be no basis for explaining the ungrammaticality of the sentence. As it is, the ungrammaticality follows naturally from the like-category constraint on co-ordination. [48ii] also predicts the fact that a bare finite $\overline{V}$ cannot follow an overt complementiser (*cf*: **Who did you say that approves of Maggie?*). As a metarule, [48ii] can only operate on lexical ID rules, rules introducing the lexical head of a phrase that shares the same major category features.

A rule expanding $\bar{\bar{V}}$ [COMP *that*] as COMP [*that*] and $\bar{V}$[FIN] (the equivalent of $\bar{S} \rightarrow$ COMP S) is clearly not a lexical ID rule because COMP is not the lexical head of phrase. It follows that [48ii] cannot apply to such a rule to give a corresponding rule with $\bar{V}$[FIN] in place of $\bar{\bar{V}}$[FIN].

This section on the analysis of unbounded dependencies would not be complete without some discussion of the treatment of island constraints in GPSG. Clearly it would be difficult to incorporate a constraint analogous to subjacency (*cf* 2.2.4 and 2.3.7) in this framework, because this requires reference to quite extensive domains and constraints in GPSG are most naturally expressed in local terms by reference to the categories involved as mother and daughter(s) in individual ID rules. To take an example, consider [59].

[59] *Who do you believe the claim that Ronnie sacked?*

In movement terms, the sentence is ruled out because the second movement of *who* indicated in [60] crosses two barriers, $\bar{S}$ and NP, and so violates subjacency.

[60]

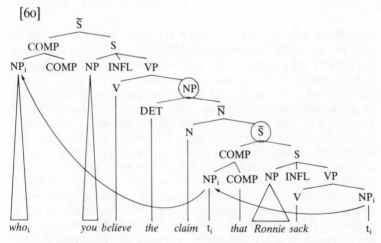

The structure assigned to [59] in GPSG would be that in [61] (overleaf) – assuming that structures can be assigned to ungrammatical strings for the purposes of exposition. What is needed is a constraint on possible projection paths for SLASH. But the only way to replicate the effect of subjacency would be to establish a class of filters with power to scan portions of tree greater

[61]

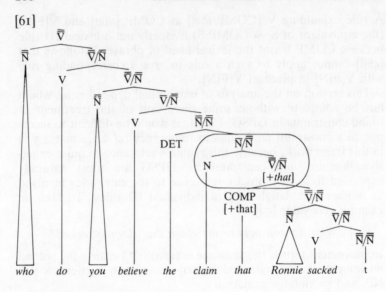

who   do   you   believe   the   claim   that   Ronnie sacked   t

than those admitted by individual ID rules. Otherwise, notions such as 'trees with the feature SLASH passing through sequences of $\overline{\overline{N}}$ and $\overline{\overline{V}}$ on a single projection path are ungrammatical' could not be expressed. Although the imposition of a class of such tree filters would not in fact affect the generative capacity of the class of grammars employing them, such devices are clearly out of keeping with the local character of all the other constraints imposed on the mapping between ID rules and structures. By reverting to a non-unified approach to island phenomena, some at least of Ross's constraints (*cf* 2.2.4, [115] to [119]), could in fact be translated into GPSG terms as local filters. For example, the ungrammaticality of [59]/[61] could be explained by reference to the complex noun phrase constraint, and this could be interpreted in GPSG terms as a requirement that SLASH does not pass through $\overline{\overline{V}}$ when this is the complement of a lexical head noun. That is to say, structural descriptions such as [61] containing subtrees of the form [62],

[62]   *

would be marked ungrammatical.

But the proper formulation of island constraints within GPSG is in fact a largely outstanding problem. Nevertheless, on the credit side there is the fact that the co-ordinate structure constraint is no longer required. Furthermore, the *wh*-island constraint follows from the fact that SLASH is a feature capable of taking only one value. Consider a sentence such as *Who did she ask who Ronnie introduced to?* represented in [63].

[63]

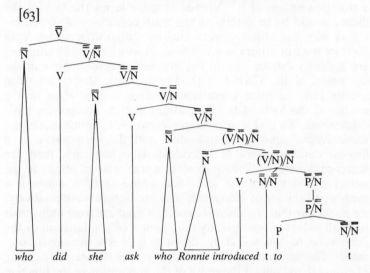

Once we come down to the embedded question, it is clear that the slash value of $\bar{\bar{V}}$ and $\bar{V}$ has to be doubly specified, once in agreement with the sentence initial *who* and once in agreement with the embedded *who*. As things stand, this is impossible; but in the case of languages such as Italian and Modern Greek, which permit (certain) violations of the *wh*-island constraint, it would be possible to relax the requirement that SLASH have only a single value in order to accommodate the relevant cases as a less common alternative to the state of affairs exemplified by English.

3.6 Semantic interpretation and control

A full treatment of the semantic theory employed in GPSG would require a book of its own. Broadly speaking, the approach is that of Richard Montague and is best regarded as a kind of modified Montague semantics. The view is taken that a minimal task for natural language semantics is to define a function which, given an arbitrary sentence of the language to be interpreted and a possible state of affairs, tells us whether the sentence is true or false in that state of affairs. Alternatively, this programme might be thought of as an attempt to determine which possible states of affairs are truly described by given sentences. In other words, the theory would be an attempt to answer the question 'what would the world have to be like for a given sentence to be a true description of it?' Viewed in these terms the task of the theory would be to determine the truth conditions of sentences. Either way, the objective is tackled by setting up a **model**, *ie* an abstract state of affairs in which basic expressions of the language are assigned denotations, in the manner suggested above in the discussion of the CAP (3.4.3). The semantic theory will then specify how complex expressions receive a denotation in the model on the basis of the denotations of their component basic expressions. To give a very simple example, if in our model the name *Noam* denotes an individual and the verb phrase *is a linguist* denotes a set of individuals (the linguists), then the sentence *Noam is a linguist* denotes a true state of affairs in the model if and only if the individual whose name is *Noam* is a member of the set of individuals who are linguists. Alternatively, we might say that *is a linguist* denotes a function from individuals to truth values. Consequently the manner of combination of the denotation of *Noam* and the denotation of *is a linguist* is automatic. The sentence *Noam is a linguist* will denote a true state of affairs if and only if the result of the application of the function to the argument (the individual denoted by *Noam*) gives the value 'true'.

Obviously such a framework of analysis lends itself most readily to the characterisation of the meaning of declarative sentences used to make statements. The extent to which it can be successfully extended to other types of sentence, such as interrogatives and imperatives, is a highly complex and disputed issue that cannot be explored here. Some references are given in 3.9 for those who would like to pursue these matters further.

Confining our attention here exclusively to declarative sentences, two things should be emphasised. First, the clauses of the semantic theory assign denotations in the model directly to expressions of the language being interpreted. There is no level of representation corresponding to Logical Form, nor is there any level of representation that makes explicit the predicate–argument structure associated with a syntactic (surface) structure in the manner of deep structure. There is thus no possibility of rules of the 'semantic component' or 'semantic representations' playing any role in the determination of well-formedness; the rules of the syntax must define grammaticality alone. This position is thus very close to that of the standard theory at the appropriate level of abstraction. Nevertheless, in order to make the semantic claims of the theory as explicit as possible, the way in which denotations are assigned to expressions is via a translation into **intensional logic**, a specially constructed logical language whose elements stand in a totally transparent relationship with their denotations. The logical expressions which translate a constituent of an English sentence determine the model-theoretic interpretation of that constituent by their very nature and we could then say that an interpretation of the constituent is induced by the translation. It might, however, appear that the intensional logic translations are functioning as a kind of logical form, but this is not so. They are totally dispensable and denotations could be assigned to English expressions in ways other than through translation into intensional logic. The only loss would be the explicitness and clarity that the translations bring with them. Secondly, the view is taken that the semantic type assigned to a lexical item of a given subcategory together with the syntactic form of the rules which introduce items of that subcategory are sufficient to determine the form of the translation rule; this determines the set of logical expressions that represent the constituent expanded by the syntactic rule, and therefore the model-theoretic interpretation of that constituent. To take a simple example, consider the ID rule in [64].

[64] $\bar{V} \rightarrow V_2, \bar{\bar{N}}$ (*kiss, shoot, admire, ...*)

Suppose that verbs of subcategory 2 are assigned the semantic type in [65].

[65] $<TYP\ \bar{\bar{N}}, <TYP\ \bar{\bar{N}}, TYP\ \bar{\bar{V}}>>$

That is to say, verbs of this subcategory denote functions from $\bar{\bar{N}}$-type denotations to functions from $\bar{N}$-type denotations to $\bar{\bar{V}}$-type denotations; more succinctly functions from $\bar{\bar{N}}$-type denotations to $\bar{V}$-type denotations. Thus the translation of a transitive verb is something that combines with the translation of a noun phrase to give something that translates a verb phrase (*ie* something whose translation combines with that of a noun phrase to form the translation of a sentence). Since [64] has introduced a verb of subcategory 2 and a noun phrase, we now know that the translation of the $\bar{V}$ constituent that dominates them will be a logical expression formed by applying the function denoted by the verb to the argument denoted by the noun phrase, and we know that this translation has a denotation in the model that is function from $\bar{\bar{N}}$-type denotations to $\bar{\bar{V}}$-type denotations. (In the discussion of the CAP it was assumed that these expressions denoted individuals and truth values respectively; on this assumption, therefore, a verb phrase such as *kisses Ronnie* denotes a function from individuals to truth values, or equivalently a set of individuals, namely those of whom it is true that they are performing the relevant action on the individual assigned the name *Ronnie*. In fact noun phrases and sentences are assumed to denote much more complex objects (properties of sets of individuals and functions from possible worlds to truth values, or propositions, respectively), but the points made above hold good whatever the denotations assigned.)

Those who are interested in pursuing the study of formal semantics in a serious way are recommended to begin by reading Dowty, Wall and Peters (1981). Sufficient has been said here, albeit in rather general terms, to give some impression of the nature and scope of the enterprise. The one remaining task is to give an account of the semantic interpretation of raising and equi verbs. These, it will be recalled, are assumed to take simple infinitival complements and it is clear that some account must be offered of the 'missing' subject and of the basic differences between the two types (*cf* 3.4.3, [39] to [41]).

So far the semantic type assigned to a verb has simply been the type one would expect to be assigned, given the verb's sisters. On the assumption that V, as the lexical head of $\bar{V}$, translates as a functor, the type assigned to V will be that which denotes a function from the type assigned to the verb's complement to $\bar{V}$-type denotations. Consider [66].

[66]

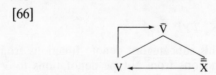

Thus a simple transitive verb, such as *hit*, a complex transitive verb such as *put*, and a verb taking a clausal complement, such as *say*, will be assigned the types indicated in [67],

[67i]   *hit* $<TYP\ \bar{\bar{N}} <TYP\ \bar{\bar{N}},\ TYP\ \bar{\bar{V}}>>$
[67ii] *put* $<TYP\ \bar{\bar{P}} <TYP\ \bar{\bar{N}} <TYP\ \bar{\bar{N}},\ TYP\ \bar{\bar{V}}>>>$
[67iii] *say* $<TYP\ \bar{\bar{V}} <TYP\ \bar{\bar{N}},\ TYP\ \bar{\bar{V}}>>$

where, in each case, $<TYP\ \bar{\bar{N}}, TYP\ \bar{\bar{V}}>$ is the type assigned to $\bar{\bar{V}}$. Notice that where a verb has a complex complement structure, as in [67ii], the denotation of the direct object $\bar{\bar{N}}$ is treated as the second argument to be combined with the denotation of the verb (more accurately, with the denotation of the verb plus prepositional phrase combination). This opens the way for a universal definition of grammatical relations in GPSG that is independent of phrase structure configurations. The indirect object or locative complement or sentence that occurs in addition to the direct object with verbs such as *give*, *put* and *persuade* (as in *persuade John that S*), will always denote the first argument to be combined with the denotation of the verb, the direct object the second argument, and the subject the last argument (since this, properly speaking, combines with the denotation of the whole $\bar{V}$). Unlike those employed in GB theory, these definitions hold good even in languages with relatively free phrase order where grammatical relations are identified by morphological means (case endings, etc.) rather than by the configurations in which $\bar{\bar{N}}$ occurs, (though see 4.5 for some potential problems with this approach).

In all the cases in [67] the basic argument structure of the verb is predictable from the form of the syntactic rule introducing the verb and its complements. Let us call the type indicating a verb's argument structure its **lexical type**, and the type that one predicts will be assigned to a verb on the basis of its complement structure its **head type**. In the cases considered so far, therefore, lexical type and head-type correspond. The crucial thing about raising and equi verbs is that this correspondence does not hold good. Taking the verbs *try*, *seem*, *persuade* and *believe*, the lexical types are as indicated in [68], where standard theory descriptive labels are employed to indicate the relationship between lexical type and head-type, which is, of course, analogous to that between deep and surface structure representations in the relevant respects. For simplicity, $TYP\ \bar{V}$ is represented simply as $\bar{V}$, and so on.

[68i] *try* (subject-controlled equi) $\quad <\bar{\bar{V}} <\bar{\bar{N}}, \bar{V}>>$
[68ii] *seem* (subject-to-subject raising) $\quad <\bar{V}, \bar{V}>$
[68iii] *persuade* (object-controlled equi) $<\bar{\bar{V}} <\bar{\bar{N}} <\bar{\bar{N}}, \bar{V}>>>$
[68iv] *believe* (subject-to-object raising) $<\bar{V} <\bar{\bar{N}}, \bar{V}>>$

The types here assigned are conventional indications of predicate–argument structure analogous to deep structures in terms of the information they provide. Thus *try* denotes a function which takes a $\bar{V}$-type denotation as its argument to give a $\bar{V}$-type denotation.

In standard theory terms, *try* takes a clausal complement in deep structure, the two together forming a verb phrase. *Seem* denotes a function from $\bar{\bar{V}}$-type denotations to $\bar{V}$-type denotations. In standard theory terms, *seem* is a verb that takes only one argument, namely a sentence, which is its logical subject, this information being represented either by making the sentence the subject of *seem* in deep structure, or, as has been assumed in discussion so far in this book, by making the sentence a complement of *seem*, but leaving the verb with an empty subject position; either way, the function denoted by *seem* combines with a proposition to give a proposition. *Persuade* denotes a function from $\bar{V}$-type denotations to a function from $\bar{N}$-type denotations to $\bar{V}$-type denotations. In standard theory terms, *persuade* takes a noun phrase and a sentence as complements in deep structure, the whole forming a verb phrase. *Believe* denotes a function from $\bar{V}$-type denotations to $\bar{V}$-type denotations. In standard theory terms, *believe* takes a clausal complement and forms with it a verb phrase. To make matters completely clear, the lexical type of *believe*, for example, in *I believe Ronnie to have got it wrong* is exactly the same as that assigned to *believe* in *I believe (that) Ronnie has got it wrong*, and the lexical type of *persuade* in *I persuaded Ronnie to throw in the towel* is the same as that of *persuade* in *I persuaded Ronnie that he should throw in the towel*.

The head-types assigned to these verbs, by contrast, are those which one would expect to be assigned on the basis of surface structure syntactic representations. The head-types in question are those in [69].

[69i]   *try* $\langle \bar{V} \langle \bar{\bar{N}}, \bar{\bar{V}} \rangle \rangle$
[69ii]   *seem* $\langle \bar{V} \langle \bar{\bar{N}}, \bar{\bar{V}} \rangle \rangle$
[69iii] *persuade* $\langle \bar{V} \langle \bar{\bar{N}} \langle \bar{\bar{N}}, \bar{\bar{V}} \rangle \rangle \rangle$
[69iv]   *believe* $\langle \bar{V} \langle \bar{\bar{N}} \langle \bar{\bar{N}}, \bar{\bar{V}} \rangle \rangle \rangle$

From this point of view, *try* denotes a function from $\bar{V}$-type denotations to $\bar{V}$-type denotations; the reason for representing this type in two different ways will become apparent in a moment. In surface syntactic terms, *try* combines with a verb phrase to form a verb phrase. *Seem* is identical to *try* in this respect. Similarly both *persuade* and *believe* denote functions from $\bar{V}$-type denotations to functions from $\bar{N}$-type denotations to $\bar{V}$-type denotations. In surface syntactic terms, both combine with a noun phrase and a verb phrase to form a verb phrase.

Compare now the lexical type assignments of [68] with the head-type assignments of [69]. The raising verbs, *seem* and *believe* both have one less N argument in their lexical types than in their head-types. All four verbs have $\overline{\overline{V}}$ in their lexical types where $\overline{V}$ occurs in their head-types. This last fact indicates that we are dealing either with a raising verb or an equi verb. We know which by seeing whether the number of $\overline{\overline{N}}$ arguments in the lexical type corresponds to the number in the head-type (equi verbs) or is one less (raising verbs).

On the basis of this, let us suppose that the types assigned as intensional logic translations to raising and equi verbs are essentially their head-types, but that these are now treated as the arguments of one or other of the functions f_R or f_E according to whether we are dealing with a raising verb or an equi verb. The combination of f_R or f_E with the 'regular' translation of the verb forms a functor which applies to the set of arguments in the usual way. Thus the translations assigned to the verb phrases in [70],

[70i] *tries to sound convincing*
[70ii] *seems to be on the ball*
[70iii] *persuades Maggie to quit*
[70iv] *believes Boris to be bonkers*

would be of the form indicated in [71],

[71i] $f_E(tries')\ (to\ sound\ convincing')$
[71ii] $f_R(seems')\ (to\ be\ on\ the\ ball')$
[71iii] $f_E(persuades')\ (to\ quit')\ (Maggie')$
[71iv] $f_R(believes')\ (to\ be\ bonkers')\ (Boris')$

where in each case a prime (') is employed at the end of an expression to indicate that we are dealing with intensional logic translations rather than words and phrases of English.

These verb phrase translations can naturally combine with (subject) noun phrase translations to form sentence translations such as those in [72].

[72i] $f_E(tries')\ (to\ sound\ convincing')\ (Willie')$
[72ii] $f_R(seems')\ (to\ be\ on\ the\ ball')\ (Willie')$
[72iii] $f_E(persuades')\ (to\ quit')\ (Maggie')\ (Willie')$
[72iv] $f_R(believes')\ (to\ be\ bonkers')\ (Boris')\ (Willie')$

Notice that in each case the 'controller' of the translation of the verb phrase is the noun phrase translation immediately to its right; this may be the translation of either a subject or an object noun phrase, as expected. The essential thing is that these translations are assigned appropriate denotations in the model. In the case of [72i] we require this expression to denote a situation identical to that denoted by an expression in which *Willie'* is the argument not only of *tries'*, but also of (*to sound convincing'*), and in which (*to sound convincing'* (*Willie'*)) is itself an argument of *tries'*, as in [73].

[73] *tries'* (*to sound convincing'* (*Willie'*)) (*Willie'*)

In [72ii] by contrast, we require equivalence with an expression in which *Willie'* is the argument of (*to be on the ball'*), and this whole sentence translation is the (sole) argument of *seems'*, as in [74].

[74] *seems'* (*to be on the ball'* (*Willie'*))

In [72iii] and [72iv], we require equivalence with expressions in which the translation of the object noun phrase functions as controller of the translation of the infinitive; in the equi case, but not, of course, in the raising case, this expression will also be an argument of the translation of the lexical head of the verb phrase. The relevant expressions are those in [75].

[75i] *persuades'* (*to quit'* (*Maggie'*)) (*Maggie'*) (*Willie'*)
[75ii] *believes'* (*to be bonkers'* (*Boris'*)) (*Willie'*)

The expressions in [73], [74], [75i] and [75ii] are, of course, the translations that one would expect on the basis of the lexical types assigned to the verbs in question in [68].

We can now employ a pair of **meaning postulates** to stipulate the required equivalences. Intuitively, these can be thought of as providing an interpretation for f_R and f_E, stating that expressions of one form necessarily have the same denotation as expressions of another form. The meaning postulates in [76] perform the task of relating [72i] with [73], [72ii] with [74], [72iii] with [75i] and [72iv] with [75ii]. Notice that just one meaning postulate covers both cases of equi, and one meaning postulate covers both cases of raising.

$$[76i] \ \forall \overline{V}' \ \forall \overline{\overline{N}}' \ \Box \ [f_E V' \ (\overline{V}') \ (\overline{\overline{N}}'_1). \ldots \ldots (\overline{\overline{N}}'_n) \equiv$$
$$V' \ (\overline{V}'(\overline{\overline{N}}'_1) \ (\overline{\overline{N}}'_1). \ldots (\overline{\overline{N}}'_n)]$$
$$[76ii] \ \forall \overline{V}' \ \forall \overline{\overline{N}}' \Box \ [f_R V' \ (\overline{V}') \ (\overline{\overline{N}}'_1) \ \ldots \ldots (\overline{\overline{N}}'_n) \equiv$$
$$V' \ (\overline{V}'(\overline{\overline{N}}'_1)). \ldots \ldots (\overline{\overline{N}}'_n)]$$

The intention of each of these should be clear from the preceding discussion. The first says that 'for all verb phrase translations and all noun phrase translations, it is necessarily the case (□) that an expression of the form on the left, comprising the translation of an equi verb applying as functor to a verb phrase translation and a series of noun phrase translations, is equivalent (≡) to an expression of the form on the right, in which the $\overline{N}$ translation closest to the $\overline{V}$-translation on the left has become an argument of that $\overline{V}$ translation as well as retaining its original argument position'. The second says that 'for all verb phrase translations and all noun phrase translations, it is necessarily the case that an expression of the form on the left, comprising the translation of a raising verb applying as functor to the translation of a verb phrase and a series of noun phrase translations, is equivalent to an expression of the form on the right, in which the $\overline{\overline{N}}$ translation closest to the $\overline{V}$ translation on the left has become the argument of that $\overline{V}$ translation and has lost its original argument position'. (It is perhaps worth pointing out for the benefit of the purists that [76i] is in fact syntactically ill-formed on its right-hand side, given the type assignments conventionally assumed in GPSG. Since the corresponding well-formed expression is considerably more complex, but in effect says the same thing as the expression actually used, it is hoped that the error will be tolerated in the interests of clarity and simplicity.) The combined effect of these meaning postulates is to ensure that the expressions which translate sentences containing verb phrases headed by equi verbs and raising verbs receive correct denotations in the model, and hence that the sentences themselves are assigned correct denotations.

Without going into details, this section may usefully be concluded with the observation that the semantic aspect of the passive transformation receives its analogue in GPSG in terms of the assignment of a type to passive participles which involves a functor f_P whose interpretation is also established by meaning postulate. Needless to say, the purpose of this meaning postulate is to express the fact that the translation of the subject noun phrase of a passive sentence has a semantic role identical to that of the translation of the direct object noun phrase of the corresponding active sentence, and that if there is a *by*-prepositional phrase, this translates as an expression interpreted analogously to the subject noun phrase of the corresponding active sentence. The passive metarule introduced in 3.4.2 [20] is thereby supplemented in a way that expresses all relevant semantic information; sentence pairs such as *Our friends believe Ronnie to be a raver* and *Ronnie is believed by our friends to be a raver* are related syntactically by virtue of the metarule which derives passive ID rules from active transitive ID rules, and receive identical denotations by virtue of the meaning postulate which stipulates the equivalence of the expressions translating active and passive pairs into intensional logic.

3.7 Summary

GPSG may usefully be thought of as a combination of Montague's approach to the semantics of natural languages and a highly sophisticated version of $\overline{\text{X}}$-theory. It is worth emphasising once again that syntactic structures are assigned semantic interpretations *directly* in the form of denotations in a model without reference to any level of representation other than syntactic surface structure. The task of defining the set of grammatical strings thus necessarily falls exclusively to the syntactic component.

The organisation of a GPSG may be represented as in [77].

[77]

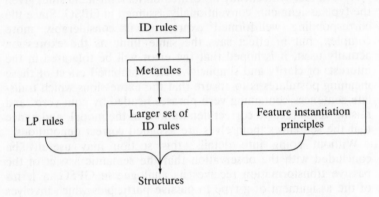

Structures may thus be thought of as fully specified projections of a basic set of schematic ID rules supplemented by the output of metarules applied to this basic set. The set of permissible projections is determined in part by the set of LP rules and in part by feature instantiation principles such as the HFC, FFP and CAP together with a set of FCRs and FSDs. It is the intention that the framework be as explicit as possible, so that precisely formulated claims can be made and tested, and that any universal principles of phrase structure organisation that emerge should be 'built in' to the framework of grammatical description rather than being expressed as autonomous statements. An attempt will be made in Chapter 5 to compare GPSG with GB theory in terms of the goals which generative grammarians have set themselves. Such a comparison is best adjourned until the final grammatical framework to be discussed in this book, Lexical-Functional Grammar, has been dealt with. The strengths and weaknesses of all three approaches can then be dealt with together. This chapter on GPSG is most conveniently rounded off with a survey of the implications of this approach for neighbouring disciplines.

3.8 Implications

A context-free phrase structure grammar generates a context-free language. Generalised phrase structure grammars are different from traditional context-free phrase structure grammars in several respects. For example, they treat syntactic categories as complexes of features rather than as atomic constructs without internal structure, and do not contain phrase structure rules. Nevertheless, the class of GPSGs described above is weakly equivalent to a subject of the CFPSGs. These GPSGs, therefore, generate context-free languages.

It seems, however, that there are certain construction types in natural languages that require the elaboration of the apparatus presented in ways that increase the strong generative capacity of GPSGs beyond that of ordinary CFPSGs. This is the case, for example, if infinite rule schemata are employed to handle flat co-ordinate structures such as *big and handsome and strong and.* . . . . . It is important to note that, though grammars incorporating such devices are no longer strongly equivalent to CFPSGs, their weak equivalence is not affected. Even though certain tree-types cannot be assigned the right sort of structural description by a CFPSG, this does not necessarily mean that no CFPSG could generate the associated strings. Similar arguments apply in the case of the multi-valued SLASH features that are needed to deal with languages (*eg* Danish, Swedish and Norwegian, *cf* 4.9 [80]) where several unbounded dependencies are allowed into a single constituent. If a finite bound is placed on the number of values that can be assigned to SLASH, the grammar will be equivalent to a CFPSG. If, however, no bound is placed on the number of values assignable to SLASH, on the grounds that this is a matter of performance, the grammar will be equivalent to an **indexed grammar**. This class of grammars generates the indexed languages, which are a proper superset of the context-free languages. There is, however, no linguistic evidence to suggest that the full power of the indexed grammars is required in constructing grammars for natural languages. So even if the Scandinavian languages permit indefinitely many unbounded dependencies into a single constituent, there is as yet no reason to suppose that the set of grammatical sentences in those languages is other than a context-free language, even if the grammars of those languages make limited use of the resources of the indexed grammars. In other words, it may be that natural languages are weakly context-free but not strongly context-free, in the sense that they are in principle generable as string-sets by

CFPSGs, but appropriate structural descriptions can be assigned to certain types of string only if the resources of the theory of CFPSG are extended. The task for linguistic theory will then be to discover how the resources of mathematically more powerful theories are to be constrained in linguistically relevant ways.

Let us suppose, then, that there is no good reason to think that natural languages are not weakly context-free, and that large parts of them may be strongly context-free. This has important consequences, because it is known that there is an effective parser for any context-free language, and that parsing times for the sentences of a context-free language are, at worst, proportional to less than the cube of sentence length. A theory of grammatical description which, like GPSG, only allows for the construction of grammars that are probably weakly, and in large part also strongly, equivalent to CFPSGs thus provides a sound basis for constructing that part of a theory of performance that deals with parsing abilities. In particular, it is easy to design a phrase structure parser that incorporates information about a language in a form that is directly derivable from the grammar of that language.

Let us now compare theories which employ only context-free phrase structure rules, or descriptive apparatus that can be shown to be for the most part equivalent in generative capacity, with transformational grammars. One of the problems with the latter as the basis for a theory of performance is that transformationally-defined dependencies may subtend a considerable number of words in a sentence, while the psychological evidence suggests that people make structural decisions more or less word by word as the utterance of a sentence is perceived. Consequently many of the more promising approaches to the parsing of 'transformed' sentences have not attempted to follow the transformational derivations of competence grammar, but have assumed a simple left-to-right phrase-structure parsing device supplemented by additional mechanisms for detecting displaced constituents and storing them until suitable gaps are detected in the left-to-right scanning of an utterance that can be filled by such constituents. If, by contrast, grammars do not employ transformational rules, so that even 'transformed' sentences are assigned structural descriptions by context-free phrase structure rules or some descriptive equivalent, these supplementary devices can be dispensed with, and the description of the grammar will at once tie in with the formal results about the existence of efficient parsers for context-free languages and the psychological discoveries about how people actually use something plausibly representable as phrase structure rules to parse strings of words.

Thus quite apart from the purely linguistic arguments that might be advanced in favour of GPSG, the greater promise of this theory as a basis for explaining parsing can be interpreted as a powerful piece of evidence in its favour, if one is willing to take the view that facts about parsing are performance data which should have a bearing on the form of grammatical description. Assuming that descriptively adequate grammars can be constructed within this framework, it could be interpreted as having the advantage over transformational frameworks in that it predicts a direct relationship between learning the grammar and learning to parse utterances. A GPSG, for example, constitutes an attractive alternative hypothesis concerning the manner in which displaced constituents (fillers) and their traces are stored. Rather than being placed in some special memory, as in most approaches to the analysis of 'transformed' sentences, these are stored as part and parcel of the phrase marker for the sentence via the SLASH feature mechanism. In other words facts about the distribution of fillers and gaps are simply part of the description of phrase structure, and no special devices have to be incorporated into the parser over and above the information supplied by the grammar. There is thus good reason to aim for a theory of grammar that is not merely restrictive in empirically motivated ways, but is also mathematically restrictive in that the formal apparatus employed is weakly, and also in large part strongly, equivalent to that of context-free phrase structure grammars. GB theory clearly meets the former criterion, but the mathematical properties of the grammars constructed in conformity with the requirements of the associated theory of universal grammar are almost wholly unknown. Thus not only do the psychological discoveries about how people set about parsing not relate directly to the formalism of grammar description, the mathematical results about context-free languages and their parsability cannot apply either, because we do not know what kind of languages such grammars generate. This isolation from work in neighbouring disciplines naturally guarantees the absence of any independent evidence in favour of the psychological reality of the constructs of the theory. The evidence for a realist interpretation of work within the GB framework is thus entirely theory-bound, and effectively no more than a reflection of the philosophical commitment of its practitioners that linguistics is analogous to the natural sciences in the relevant respects. To the extent that this is a matter for dispute, so is the issue of interpretation.

Finally, a few words need to be said about the learnability of grammars, and the extent to which different frameworks of grammatical description provide a basis for explaining our ability to pass grammaticality judgements on utterances. It has been claimed, for example, that the class of **recursively enumerable** languages is unlearnable. A language is recursively enumerable if there is some device that can enumerate the members of the set of sentences in the language one by one so that eventually any sentence will turn up in the list, but no such device that is capable of enumerating the set of strings over the same vocabulary that are not sentences of the language. Peters and Ritchie (1973) showed that unconstrained transformational grammars of the standard-theory type generate recursively enumerable languages. On the basis of this, Levelt (1979) sought to show that, given certain technical definitions of learnability, recursively enumerable languages were unlearnable, and that therefore transformational grammars of natural languages were also unlearnable.

This is clearly an unacceptable conclusion for advocates of transformational grammars, but the conclusion in fact rests on extremely dubious foundations. First, no one has ever seriously proposed unconstrained transformational grammars for natural languages of the type whose properties were investigated mathematically by Peters and Ritchie. Secondly, the various technical definitions of learnability upon which Levelt's conclusion rests are sufficiently abstract and far-removed from the likely circumstances of real-world learning as to call the implications of his conclusions for the study of language acquisition in children into question. There is, for example, little reason to suppose that children abstract grammars from a finite set of string/grammaticality judgement pairs, though this assumption is crucial to Levelt's conclusion. As things stand the question of the connection between learnability and the formal class of languages to be learned is wide open. Chomsky is surely right to insist that the crucial factor in learning is that the set of grammars to be considered by the child as possible grammars for his or her language is small. Given this, and that the various options are distinguishable on the basis of a finite amount of data, learning (or in Chomsky's view growth) should be possible in the real-world circumstances of language acquisition. Whether the grammars in this set generate context-free languages, recursively enumerable languages, or completely wild languages seems to have little demonstrable bearing on the issue.

Potentially more important is the question of native speakers' ability to pass grammaticality judgements. If transformational

grammars generate recursively enumerable languages, it is difficult to see how we could know whether any given string was a
sentence of our language or not; the essence of a recursively
enumerable language is that we can never know that a given
string is *not* in the set of sentences that constitute that language
(see the definition given above). A language is **recursive** if both
the set of sentences and the set of non-sentences are enumerable
in a finite amount of time by some formal device, and it seems
reasonable to suppose that natural languages are recursive in
view of the fact that we can generally say whether or not a given
string is well-formed. Context-free languages are a proper subset
of the recursive languages, and this might be thought an argument in favour of a framework that is at least weakly equivalent
to the theory of CFPSG.

However, once again, the facts are not so clear-cut. Apart
from the fact that it is by no means certain that transformational
grammars of the sort actually proposed for the description of
natural languages do in fact generate non-recursive sets, it is also
the case that our ability to pass judgements with any degree of
certainty diminishes as the length and complexity of utterances
increases. In other words the arguments for recursiveness are not
unequivocally supported by speakers' performance capabilities.
It is at least possible to argue, though without compelling
evidence to support the claim, that if the infinite languages
generated by transformational grammars are indeed recursively
enumerable, the actual utterances normally encountered (say,
those of fewer than fifty words in length lacking multiply centre-
embedded and other difficult-to-process constructions) may be
fully accessible to the processing mechanisms because they are
utterances of a recursive subset of the totality of sentences. In
view of the overall uncertainty about the mathematical properties
of transformational grammars, and given the possibility that
those actually proposed for the description of natural languages
in fact generate recursive sets, it seems that the best *independent*
evidence in favour of adopting a formal framework such as
GPSG comes from the fact that its constructs facilitate a direct
link between theoretical linguistics and the work of experimental
psychologists and computer scientists on the investigation and
modelling of human parsing and information-processing abilities,
(though see 4.9 for further discussion).

3.9 Relevant reading

The fullest and most up-to-date description of GPSG is Gazdar,

Klein, Pullum and Sag (1985). See also Sells (1985 Ch. 3).

An early general discussion of the advantages that follow from the mathematical restrictiveness of phrase structure description, together with some detailed implementations of the ideas involved is Gazdar (1982).

The first detailed elaboration of the feature system employed in GPSG is given in Gazdar and Pullum (1982).

Gazdar and Pullum (1981) deals with the context-free approach to lexical insertion and introduces the ID/LP format. The effectiveness of this treatment of constituent order is demonstrated in Pullum (1982), Horrocks (1983) and Stucky (1983). Sag (1985) discusses some difficulties that arise in this framework and proposes an alternative account in a 'head-driven' phrase structure grammar format (see Chapter 5 for some discussion of HPSG; Pollard (1984 and 1985) and Goldberg (1985) provide the background to this approach and some implementations of the leading idea that lexical ID rules should be eliminated in favour of subcategorisation statements in the lexicon).

The idea of using metarules to generate the rules of a grammar goes back to van Wijngaarden (1969), whose work on the computer language ALGOL68 is discussed in Cleveland and Uzgalis (1975). The Lexical Head Constraint on metarule application is due to Flickinger (1983).

The feature instantiation principles of GPSG are first discussed in Gazdar and Pullum (1982)

Gazdar (1981a and b) deal with unbounded dependencies and co-ordinate structure, and explain the slash category concept, which originates with Harris (1962). SLASH is later interpreted as a feature whose distribution is subject to the FFP in Gazdar and Pullum (1982). The ideas involved are developed further in Gazdar, Klein, Pullum and Sag (1982), and a highly detailed account of co-ordination is given in Sag, Gazdar, Wasow and Weisler (1985). Williams (1981) is a review of the GPSG approach to unbounded dependencies from the point of view of GB theory.

The theory of semantic interpretation is ultimately that of Montague (1970a and b, and 1973); see also the collection of Montague's papers in Thomason (1974). Dowty, Wall and Peters (1981) is a beginners' guide to this daunting subject. A variety of modifications to this approach have in fact been proposed, partly in order to enhance its compatibility with phrase structure syntax, but the essential objectives remain intact. The syntactic analysis of control phenomena, involving a bare VP analysis of the complements of raising and equi verbs, has been forcefully defended by Brame (1976 and 1979), and is adopted also in LFG (see Chapter 4). A detailed model-theoretic interpretation of control constructions is offered in Bach (1979). The GPSG treatment of control is a development of the work initiated in Klein and Sag (1982/83). The definition of grammatical functions in terms of the order of composition of semantic arguments is proposed by Dowty (1982). The strengths and limitations (particularly the problems of non-declaratives and of the 'performative' use of declaratives, as in *I (hereby) name this ship 'Titanic'*) of truth-conditional and model-theoretic semantics are discussed in Kempson (1977: Chs. 3, 4 and 5), Lyons (1977:Vol. 1, Ch. 6, especially section 6) and Lyons (1981: Chs. 5, 6 and 7). Karttunen (1977) is a good example of how a committed practitioner seeks to deal with questions in a truth-conditional framework.

For the mathematically defined hierarchy of grammars and languages see Chomsky (1963). Book (1973) is a concise survey of the mathematical properties of CF languages and grammars, and Earley (1970:p 99), Valiant (1975) and Graham (1976) present the parsability results available for languages of this type. That these give a significant computational motivation to linguists to constrain their grammars to CF generative capacity is argued by Sheil (1976) and Kaplan (1980), and Pullum and Gazdar (1982) try to show that the range of arguments standardly advanced to prove that natural languages cannot be CF do not in fact go through. While this obviously does not prove that every natural language is CF, they argue that only minor enhancements of generative power are likely to be necessary to handle potentially problematic data such as the multiple dependencies into a single syntactic constituent permitted by the Scandinavian languages (discussed in Maling and Zaenen (1982)). For some of the difficulties facing those seeking to devise effective parsing strategies that rely on a transformational model of syntactic description see Fodor (1978 and 1980). J. D. Fodor (1983) elaborates the advantages of GPSG in this regard and highlights a number of important psycholinguistic implications of this framework. A defence of GB theory that challenges the conventional wisdom of the superiority of CF description as a basis for explaining speakers' parsing abilities is given in Berwick and Weinberg (1982 and 1984).

A demonstration that unconstrained transformational grammars generate recursively enumerable sets is provided by Peters and Ritchie (1973), a result which Levelt (1979), relying on Gold's (1967) definition of learnability, seeks to exploit to show that transformational grammars are unlearnable. For further discussion of the connection between recursiveness and learnability see Levelt (1974). Lasnik (1980 and 1981), and Chomsky (1980a: Ch. 3) are defences of transformational grammar based on the view that learnability requires the cardinality of the set of grammars available to the learner to be minimised on the basis of empirically motivated constraints, and that recursiveness has nothing to do with the issue.

Chapter 4

Lexical-Functional Grammar

4.1 Introduction

Chomsky and his associates believe that characterisations of
formal grammar shed light on the way in which grammatical
knowledge is represented in the minds of native speakers. Advocates of GPSG, by contrast, take the view that, whatever the
merits of a theory that a common store of grammatical knowledge underlies all forms of verbal behaviour, there are no
grounds for interpreting linguistically motivated formal systems
of the type developed by linguists as representations of this internalised system, and argue that there is no justification for such
realist interpretations without independent evidence that grammatical knowledge is stored in the supposed form. They take the
primary task of linguistics to be the construction of formal grammars within a mathematically restrictive theoretical framework
that provide a basis for fruitful interaction with the results of
psycholinguistic and computational research on mental representations and language processing. Cautious optimism is expressed
that GPSG may be successful in these terms, but no claims are
made for its psychological reality on the basis of its success in
promoting such interdisciplinary co-operation.

The views of leading advocates of Lexical-Functional Grammar
(henceforth LFG), namely Joan Bresnan and her associates, can
perhaps best be characterised as essentially Chomskyan, subject
to an expansion of the domain of enquiry and a corresponding
modification of the apparatus of description. In the first place,
it is argued that the competence hypothesis is desirable in principle, on the grounds that, properly formulated, a linguistic
grammar *could* provide a unified theory of the grammatical

knowledge assumed to underlie verbal behaviour. In other words, the fact that linguistically motivated grammars of the type developed by Chomsky have not been very successfully incorporated in psychologists' models of acquisition, comprehension or production is taken to be an indication not that the competence hypothesis itself is wrong but that Chomsky's notion of the structure of competence is wrong because based on too narrow a domain of evidence. Once again, therefore, the need to develop a linguistically well-motivated theory of grammar whose principles do not conflict with the results of psycholinguistic research is taken to be the major objective for theoretical linguistics. But such a theory, once developed, is assumed to have a clear claim to psychological reality, and this contrasts sharply with the position adopted by advocates of GPSG.

There is obviously an equally sharp contrast with Chomsky's theory in terms of the data to be accounted for. Chomsky has consistently taken the view that the rules and representations of linguistic systems characterise the competence of an *ideal* native speaker, and that the production and comprehension of utterances by *real* native speakers is determined by a combination of this grammatical system and a variety of other systems. Any discrepancies between his theory of competence and psycholinguists' conceptions of the knowledge stores required for processing are assumed to derive from these performance factors which are taken to be irrelevant to grammatical theory. The LFG response is to suggest that this approach involves an illegitimate 'idealisation' of the data the purpose of which is not to facilitate progress by abstracting away from irrelevant aspects of the flux of experience but rather to insulate linguistic research from results obtained in the cognitive sciences which have a direct bearing on the issue of the mental representation of grammatical knowledge. Since we cannot directly observe the native speaker's internalised grammar, its properties must be inferred from the evidence that is observable, and Chomsky is accused of arbitrariness in his decision to restrict the data of linguistics to the domain of introspective judgements when a combination of the formal representation of linguistic theory with the experimental methods of psycholinguistics and the information-processing techniques of computer science provides a set of mutually constraining results that together offer, it is argued, a far superior basis for the development of a psychologically realistic competence-based model of linguistic performance. In other words, if the idea that competence underlies performance is to be taken seriously, it should be acknowledged that psycholinguistic and computational considerations may have important implications for the form in which linguistic representations are cast.

To summarise, proponents of LFG accept that realist interpretations of grammatical constructs are in principle defensible, but argue that Chomsky bases his theory on too narrow a domain of fact to justify a realist interpretation of his particular system. Once the domain is extended such interpretations become fully justified. The ultimate objective of the LFG programme, therefore, is the contruction of a theory of grammar that satisfies the usual internal criteria of adequacy but which is realisable as the central component of a theory of performance and which accordingly unifies work in linguistics with work in neighbouring disciplines on language acquisition and language processing. There is, therefore, a further criterion of adequacy to be met over and above those conventionally imposed in frameworks such as GB theory, namely that the representations of linguistic knowledge assumed to underlie various processing abilities must be isomorphic to the competence grammar, because for as long as it is possible to explain discrepancies by reference to unspecified performance factors, the competence hypothesis remains insulated from important sources of evidence.

Before considering the supposed advantages of LFG and the extent to which this framework has succeeded in bringing together work in linguistics with work in psychology and artificial intelligence, it will be useful to have a clear idea of the formal machinery employed. The essential idea is that a grammar with an expanded lexical and contracted syntactic component, in particular a syntactic component without transformations, promises to have far greater explanatory power than current versions of transformational grammar such as GB theory.

4.2 Transformations and lexical rules

Like GB theory, LFG is concerned to characterise the associations between predicate–argument structure and surface syntactic structure, but the two theories make quite different representational assumptions. A brief summary of the transformational position, and of the role of transformations and lexical rules in such a framework, will provide a useful starting point for comparison.

As was made clear in Chapter 2, the basic representational assumptions of transformational grammar have remained quite constant since the mid-1960s despite many modifications in the formal machinery employed. Grammatical functions such as subject and direct object are defined configurationally at all levels of syntactic representation by reference to the 'geometry' of phrase markers, the subject being that NP directly dominated by S, the direct object that NP directly dominated by VP. On this understanding, it is assumed that the representation of predicate–argument structure can take the form of a representation of grammatical functions (*viz* a constituent structure phrase marker) to which θ-roles are assigned in one-to-one fashion in accordance with the requirements of the θ-criterion. The purpose of D-structures, then, is to represent thematically relevant grammatical functions, and so to represent predicate–argument structure.

This configurational representation of predicate–argument structure has important consequences in view of the fact that S-structures (and ultimately surface structures) also take the form of constituent structure phrase markers. Given the nature of representations at these two levels, the expression of the relationship between them necessarily takes the form of structure-dependent mappings between phrase markers, *viz move* α. Turning to the specific example of passive sentences, the surface subject in each case has the same θ-role as the direct object of the corresponding active sentence, namely patient. At D-structure, therefore, this NP must bear the grammatical function associated with the patient role, and appear in direct object position within VP. The mapping between D-structure and S-structure will obviously now involve NP-movement from direct object position to subject position.

Notice that the rule of NP-movement is bounded (*ie* can move an NP at most over one clause boundary) and structure-preserving (*ie* moves NPs to positions where NPs are generated by the phrase structure rules of the base component – but left empty at D-structure because they are not argument positions – rather than adjoining NPs in positions where the phrase structure rules do not permit them). These requirements follow from subjacency, and, more importantly, the binding condition for anaphors. This latter requires the trace of NP-movement to be bound in its governing category by a c-commanding NP in an A-position, and since A-positions are the canonical NP positions in S, it follows that the movement will always be structure-preserving. Furthermore, the A-position in question must be within the governing category of the associated trace. Since government is essentially a local relationship, involving at most one intervening S (but not S̄) between governor and governed, it also follows that the movement will be bounded, irrespective of the requirements of subjacency. But despite the insight that it embodies about the parallelism between possibilities of movement and possibilities of anaphoric interpretation, it is nevertheless true that the anaphor binding condition is stipulative; it does not follow from any other principles or from the way the grammar is organised. From the point of view of GB theory, therefore, it looks like a good candidate for inclusion in the theory of universal grammar. But it is worth asking whether the relevant properties of NP-movement might not turn out to be an *automatic* consequence of different assumptions about the way a grammar is organised.

It will be recalled (*cf* 2.2.2) that Chomsky himself proposed that certain types of relationship between predicate–argument structures and surface forms might best be handled not syntactically, by transformations, but lexically, by means of redundancy rules. Thus the sentence *Jimbo assaulted the linesman* and the noun phrase *Jimbo's assault on the linesman* clearly involve the same predicate–argument structure, but there are good reasons why they should not be derived from exactly the same D-structure source (even though the geometry of the two distinct D-structures should allow for a generalised definition of subject and object in order to account for the common assignment of θ-roles to the NPs involved). The alternative to a transformation of nominalisation is to allow for two lexical entries, with *assault* listed as both a verb and a noun, but with the omission of those properties of the noun that are predictable by general principle from the properties of the verb. These properties would be stated once and for all for every such verb–noun pair by means of a redundancy rule. In particular, in order to account for the common argument structure of verb and noun, we would want the rule to state that for any pair of items listed in the lexicon such that the first is a verb taking a direct object complement (in D-structure) and the second is a nominalisation of the verb, it is predictable that the derived norminal will also take a direct object complement (in D-structure). Consider [1].

[1] $V_x, + [\text{---} NP] \rightarrow [_N V_x (+ \text{affix})], + [\text{---} NP]$

Such a formulation allows for a generalised definition of direct object in terms of phrase structure configuration, and so guarantees a common assignment of θ-roles and parallel representations of predicate–argument structure apart from the syntactic category assigned to the head of the phrase.

The problem with this formulation, dealt with at some length in 2.2.2, is precisely the representational assumption outlined above, namely the identification of D-structure grammatical functions with 'logical' functions associated with thematic roles. The only way in which a 'logical' direct object associated with the patient role can be represented is as a syntactic D-structure direct object, a NP within the subcategorisation frame of a verb or noun. This causes great problems when, as here, the surface realisation of this D-structure representation involves a shift of category in the complement. Thus, although *assault* as a noun must be subcategorised to take an NP complement in underlying structure, it must somehow be provided with a PP complement headed by *on* in S-structure. The choice of preposition here is obviously an idiosyncratic property of the noun *assault* and the obvious place for this information to be stated is in the lexical entry for that item. But it cannot appear in the subcategorisation frame where it belongs because this would prevent the statement of the generalisation about the assignment of θ-roles in terms of a common complement structure for both verb and noun. The only alternative, therefore, is a wholly undesirable and totally *ad hoc* insertion transformation whose domain of application is determined not by structural considerations but by the choice of lexical items in a given context.

The theory of LFG involves the extended use of lexical rules, but modified in a way that overcomes the problem of category change between D-structure and S-structure representations. These lexical rules not only supplant transformational operations such as NP-movement, but also provide a principled explanation for the bounded and structure-preserving properties of the mapping between predicate–argument structure and surface syntactic representations that have to be stipulated in the case of an NP movement analysis. Before illustrating this, however, we must first examine the role of grammatical functions in GB theory a little more carefully, and contrast this with their role in LFG.

4.3 Grammatical functions

As we have seen, it is a fundamental principle of Chomsky's approach that the definition of grammatical functions is a secondary matter, based upon the primitive notion of direct dominance derived from the theory of phrase structure ($\bar{\text{X}}$-theory). It was, however, pointed out in 2.3.3 that there are nonconfigurational languages (W* languages) which appear not to exploit the resources of $\bar{\text{X}}$-theory and whose sentences appear to consist of strings of words without higher level organisation. A good example of this type of language is Warlpiri, an aboriginal language of Australia, discussed at length by Hale (1979 and 1983). Clearly the definition of grammatical functions in languages of this sort cannot be based on phrase structure configurations. From Chomsky's point of view, therefore, the ideal situation would be one in which nonconfigurational languages do not exhibit processes that involve reference to functions such as subject and direct object, and configurational languages like English allow generalisations potentially associated with grammatical functions (*eg* the movement of NPs from object position to subject position in the case of passive sentences) to be cast in a form which makes reference only to configurations (*eg* in terms of notions such as government, c-command, etc.). If, by contrast, it turns out that there exist various phenomena in natural languages of both types that seem most appropriately described in terms of grammatical functions, it follows that no universal characterisation of the relevant processes will be available in Chomsky's theory. In particular the transformational account of the relationship between predicate–argument structure representations and surface syntactic representations obviously cannot be employed in the analysis of nonconfigurational languages, and distinct syntactic mechanisms will have to be adopted.

Chomsky's analysis of certain aspects of Japanese syntax (1981a: pp 127*ff*) is illuminating. Japanese is taken to be an example of a nonconfigurational language with 'flat' sentence structure. The order of component elements within sentences is fairly free (a characteristic nonconfigurational property) subject to the requirement that the verb comes last. The crucial thing is the existence of sentence pairs such as that in [2].

[2i] NP NP *tabe*   (*tabe* = 'eat')
[2ii] NP *tabe-rare*   (*tabe-rare* = '(be) eaten')

The NPs in [2i] are assigned the θ-roles agent and patient (the order is immaterial), while the NP in [2ii] is assigned the θ-role patient. This is clearly an example of the active–passive relationship in that the NP which is assigned the patient role in [2i] has the postposition *o*, which may be thought of as the direct object marker, while the patient NP in [2ii] has the postposition *ga*, which may be thought of as the subject marker. (The NP assigned the agent role in [2i] also has the postposition *ga*.) The essential difference between this pair and a corresponding English active–passive pair is the manner in which the relevant grammatical functions are identified; the basis of the relationship is constant across the two languages if it is expressed in terms of grammatical functions, namely that the subject of the passive sentence bears the same θ-role as the object of the corresponding active sentence. Putting the matter in GB-theory terms, the subject of the S-structure representation of a passive sentence is the direct object of the corresponding D-structure representation. Yet GB theory provides no way of expressing this cross-linguistic generalisation because the relationship is expressed in terms of movement in a language like English, where grammatical functions are positionally (configurationally) defined, but obviously cannot be so expressed in a language like Japanese, where there is insufficient constituent structure to support such definitions.

Chomsky's solution is to propose that D-structure and S-structure representations are properly to be thought of as *pairs* of objects consisting on the one hand of formal syntactic structures and on the other of representations of the associated grammatical functions. Given this, the definition of grammatical functions can be universally configurational, and English and Japanese can be thought of as differing in that the configurational representation of grammatical functions extends to formal syntactic structures only in the former. To give a simple example, the D-structure for an English sentence containing the verb *eat* would consist of the two elements in [3], omitting irrelevant detail.

[3]

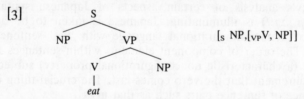

Formal syntactic structure   Representation of GFs

while the D-structure of a Japanese sentence containing *tabe* would consist of the two elements in [4].

[4]

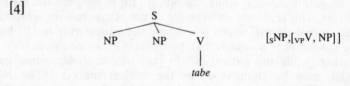

Formal syntactic structure   Representation of GFs

In English there is no real need to distinguish the two members of the pair, since the representation of grammatical functions is straightforwardly derived from the formal syntactic representation by abstracting away from precedence relations. But in Japanese the distinction is crucial, because the formal syntactic representation is flat while the representation of the associated grammatical functions is the same as the corresponding element in English.

If we now concentrate exclusively on the representations of grammatical functions, it is clear that the lexical entries for *eat* and *tabe* can be framed in exactly the same way. Both verbs take direct object NP complements, assigning to them the θ-role of patient and forming with them VPs that assign to the subject NP the θ-role of agent. These properties are projected to the D- and S-structure representations of grammatical functions directly. The passive analogues of these verbs assign the patient role to the object and form a VP with it, but do not assign, via VP, any role to the subject. Since such passive verb forms do not assign Case to their objects, the Case filter will require the movement of the object NP to subject position in S-structure. In this position nominative Case can be assigned, and the requirements of the binding theory are met.

There remains, of course, the problem of the associated representations of formal syntactic structure at D- and S-structure. Here the parallels between English and Japanese resulting from the assumption of independent representations of grammatical functions framed in a universal format cannot, of course, be duplicated. The D-structure representations of the formal syntactic structure of Japanese sentences containing *tabe* and *tabe-rare* must be as in [5] (overleaf); the associated GF-representations are given below.

In both cases, we must suppose that the θ-marking properties of the verbs concerned are projected non-configurationally. Thus in [5i] two NPs must be assigned one θ-role each, the roles of agent and patient being assignable to either NP. In [5ii], the role of patient must be assigned to a single NP. Since the patient role is in fact assigned to the direct object as a lexical property, the NP associated with this role in [5i] will receive objective Case (realised as the postposition *o*) and the other NP, associated with the agent role assigned to the subject, will receive nominative Case (realised as the postposition *ga*). In [5ii], however, no Case will be assigned because passive verb forms cannot Case-mark

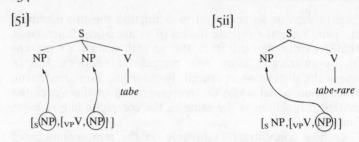

The active verb θ-marks both its subject and its object; both therefore appear in the formal syntactic representation of D-structure, the order being free, and the determination of subject/agent and object/patient at S-structure following from Case-marking.

The passive verb θ-marks only its object; only one NP therefore appears in the formal syntactic representation of D-structure. Since this cannot be Case-marked it must assume an S-structure function that permits Case-marking, *viz* subject.

their objects. To avoid the effects of the Case filter therefore, the D-structure must be converted to an appropriate S-structure in which the NP can receive Case. This cannot be accomplished by *move α*, of course, so Chomsky proposes an analogue of movement for nonconfigurational languages, namely the rule in [6].

[6] Assume a grammatical function.

In any given instance the choice of grammatical function will be determined by the requirement that it should lack a θ-role but allow Case-assignment. Since the NP cannot be assigned Case within VP, it follows that the 'assumed' grammatical function will be that of subject, a position not θ-marked by *tabe-rare*, but to which nominative Case (the suffix *–ga*) is assigned. Notice, however, that the crucial identification of grammatical functions, relevant both to θ-marking and Case-assignment, takes place not by reference to the representation of formal syntactic structure but by reference to the configurational representation of the grammatical functions associated with this, as already described. In other words all the crucial properties of the formal syntactic representations of D- and S-structure are determined by reference to grammatical functions which are not definable in terms of those representations themselves. This means that the obvious generalisation about passivisation in English and Japanese, namely 'make the D-structure object the S-structure subject', can be expressed only by reference to the representation of grammatical functions. When the relevant formal syntactic representations in the two languages are examined, it is clear that two different accounts of the relationship will have to be employed, namely *move α* and *assume a grammatical function*. This analysis, therefore, embodies the claim that grammatical functions are central concepts in the theory of syntax, but it concedes that there is no way in which these can be defined universally in terms of formal syntactic representations, and therefore has to adopt alternative syntactic mechanisms for saying something that could be stated in a universal format in *functional* terms.

The solution to this problem in LFG is to treat grammatical functions as primitive notions of syntactic theory, *ie* as not reducible to any general definition in terms of phrase structure configurations or Case-marking, and to seek to give an account in functional terms of the associations between predicate–argument structure and surface syntactic realisations that are handled in GB theory by movement rules or their non-configurational analogues.

4.4 Passive in LFG

Central to the theory of LFG is the fact that lexical entries represent predicate–argument structures independently of phrase structure forms. The verb *eat*, for example, denotes a two-place predicate, and the thematic roles assigned to its two arguments are agent and patient. Consider [7].

[7] eat, V, 'EAT <AGENT PATIENT>'

Here the predicate denoted by the verb *eat* is represented by the use of capitals, and its two arguments are contained within the angled brackets.

The next step is the assignment of grammatical functions to the arguments/thematic roles. This provides the link, as we shall see (4.6), between predicate–argument structure and surface syntactic structure. The assignment is subject to the condition of **function–argument biuniqueness** which requires that a unique function be assigned to each argument that is grammatically interpreted (*ie* has some surface syntactic realisation), and that a unique argument be assigned to each function that is associated with an argument. Notice that this is in some ways analogous to Chomsky's θ-criterion, but allows for the possibility that no function is assigned to a given argument or that a function is associated with no argument. It also allows for the possibility that, where two words denote the same predicate, there may be different assignments of grammatical functions to the arguments involved. The significance of all this will become apparent in due course. In the case of [7], however, the assignment of functions is straightforward; (SUBJ(ect)) is assigned to the agent argument and (OBJ(ect)) is assigned to the patient argument, as in [8].

[8] eat, V 'EAT < (SUBJ)   (OBJ   )>'
                   AGENT   PATIENT

This tells us that a sentence containing the verb *eat* contains a subject that is interpreted as the agent argument of the predicate denoted by *eat*, and a direct object that is interpreted as the patient argument of that predicate. The entry for the Japanese verb *tabe* would be identical in all relevant respects.

Compare now the lexical form for the passive verb *eaten*, given in [9].

[9] eaten, V, 'EAT < (BY-OBJ)   (SUBJ)>'
                     AGENT   PATIENT

Since this denotes the same predicate as *eat*, the same two arguments appear in its lexical form. But here different grammatical functions have been assigned. The subject of (*be*) *eaten* is interpreted as the patient argument of EAT, and the object of *by* is interpreted as the agent argument. Since there are also 'agentless' passives lacking the *by*-phrase altogether, we also have to allow for the case where the agent function is not grammatically interpreted. In the lexical form in [10], therefore, no grammatical function has been assigned to the agent argument.

[10] eaten, V, 'EAT< (∅   ) (SUBJ)>'
                    AGENT   PATIENT

The lexical forms in [9] and [10] can be conflated as in [11].

[11] eaten, V, 'EAT< {(BY-OBJ)} (SUBJ)>'
                        {(∅   )}
                    AGENT   PATIENT

The entry for the passive Japanese verb *tabe-rare* is identical to that for *eaten*, except that (NI-OBJ) appears in place of (BY-OBJ), indicating that the agent, if expressed, takes the form of a noun phrase with the particle *ni* suffixed.

Notice that the lexical entry for *eaten* could readily be derived from that for *eat* by means of an operation on the lexical form that readjusted the assignment of grammatical functions. Such an operation is most naturally carried out by the redundancy rule [12].

[12] *passive*: (SUBJ)   → (BY-OBJ)/(∅)
              (OBJ)   → (SUBJ)

The rule for Japanese would be identical apart, once again, from the substitution of (NI-OBJ) for (BY-OBJ). Since agents in passive sentences are generally associated with some oblique grammatical function in the world's languages (expressed as an oblique case inflection or as a prepositional/postpositional phrase), the most general formulation of passive would be one in which the function name (OBL$_{AG}$), *ie* an oblique function paired with an agent argument, appeared in place of (BY-OBJ) or (NI-OBJ), with the actual realisation of this function to be specified language by language. The crucial thing is that the LFG formulation permits a universal statement of those aspects of passivisation that are universal, namely 'demote or eliminate the subject, make the object the subject'. This is made possible because the rules which express the relationship make reference only to grammatical functions, and the grammatical functions involved are taken to be primitives of syntactic theory which are not reducible to definition in terms of the configurational properties of phrase markers.

4.5 Lexical rules and lexical forms

Some of the differences between the LFG approach and GB theory can now be elaborated in a little more detail. In GB theory a lexical entry includes a strict subcategorisation feature which identifies the arguments of the predicate denoted by the item in question categorially. The Projection Principle requires the specified arguments to appear as complements of the head in syntactic representations, and if the head is a verb, it also requires the presence of a subject in the sentence containing the verb and its complements. The categories involved are assigned grammatical functions according to the configurations in which they appear, with θ-roles assigned to specific functions. An argument is thus identified with a thematically relevant grammatical function, and D-structure is a representation of such functions defined configurationally. This means that a pair of items such as *eat* and *eaten*, which denote the same predicate, must be assigned the same subcategorisation frame in order to express this fact. Both, therefore, take direct object NP complements, to which the patient role is assigned. The Projection Principle guarantees that both will have a direct object NP complement at S-structure as well, though in the case of the passive verb this will be an empty category (trace) because of the effects of *move α*. The θ-criterion guarantees that the subject position to which the contents of the direct object NP have been moved as a $\bar{\theta}$-position.

Contrast now the entry for *eat/eaten*, given in [13],

[13] eat(en), V, $+\left[\begin{array}{cc} \text{------} & \text{NP} \\ & \text{(patient)} \end{array}\right]$

with the entries employed in LFG, repeated here as [14].

[14] eat,   V, 'EAT < (SUBJ)   (OBJ   )>'
                       AGENT   PATIENT
    eaten, V, 'EAT < (ø/BY-OBJ) (SUBJ   )>'
                       AGENT   PATIENT

First, it is clear that one of the arguments specified in [14] is
suppressed in [13]. There is no mention of the subject, because
this is defined as that NP directly dominated by S and the
subcategorisation feature is (by definition) a representation of the
contents of VP. Nevertheless, it is crucial that the θ-marking
properties of verbs with respect to their subjects be specified so
that appropriate D-structure projections can be constructed. In
particular, we need to know that *eat* θ-marks its subject while
eaten does not. This assignment must therefore be determined
by some *ad hoc* addition to lexical entries. In practice it is assumed
that the θ-role of subjects is determined by whole VPs rather
than by their verbal heads, though the exact details are never
elaborated. In LFG, by contrast, the full argument list is
specified. This is possible because the representation of
predicate–argument structure is independent of considerations of
phrase structure configurations. In other words predicate–argument
structures are assumed to be 'flat', in the sense that the argument
assigned the subject role does not have any special status *vis-à-
vis* other arguments. As evidence in favour of the inclusion of the
subject argument in representations of predicate–argument structure in lexical forms, one can point to the existence of subject
idioms, where the choice of subject affects the semantic role of
the object [15i], and to cases where the choice of a non-subject
argument depends upon the choice of subject [15ii].

  [15i] *The cat's got Bill's tongue/The cat's got Bill's tie*
  [15ii] *The roof fell in on Ronnie's plans/??The wall fell in on
      Ronnie's plans*

Theories which omit the subject argument from lexical entries are
hard to reconcile with facts of this sort.

Secondly, because predicate–argument structure is represented
independently of grammatical function assignment (or considerations of phrase structure 'geometry'), it is possible to assign

different grammatical functions to the same set of arguments (*eg* by redundancy rule) without losing the generalisation that two forms denote the same predicate. Thus *eat* and *eaten* are both assigned the same predicate–argument structure in [14], even though different grammatical functions are involved in the two cases. The functions assigned are, of course, surface grammatical functions, which means that the subject is θ-marked for both active and passive verbs. There is, however, no violation of the θ-criterion, because each argument is assigned a unique θ-role as required. The crucial difference between LFG and GB theory here is that arguments are no longer identified with particular grammatical functions; so patienthood is no longer the exclusive property of direct objects. The patient role can, therefore, be associated directly with the subject of a passive sentence by lexical redundancy rule without any need to refer to 'deep' or 'empty' direct objects. In other words the association of predicate–arguments/θ-roles with surface grammatical functions is no longer treated as a matter of phrase structure manipulation and the syntactic apparatus set up to express the association, D-structures, transformations and S-structures enriched with traces, can be dispensed with. This means that simpler and more concrete syntactic representations can be adopted, (*cf* below and 4.6).

Let us first pursue this issue in general terms. Since arguments are identified with thematically relevant grammatical functions in GB theory, it follows that every predicate argument will have to be categorially represented in D-structures, and also, because of the Projection Principle, in S-structures. In LFG predicate arguments are listed independently of grammatical function assignment; this raises the possibility that certain arguments will have no surface grammatical interpretation and that certain surface grammatical functions will have no thematic role. In particular, if there is no *overt* category in surface structures that can be identified with a particular θ-role, there is no need to assume the presence of an empty one. Thus agentless passives, for example, can be represented syntactically as precisely that, because the presence of an (understood) agent follows from the lexical form.

Consider now the more complex case of 'subject-to-subject raising'. A typical GB theory S-structure is given in [16].

[16] *Chomsky*$_i$ *seems* [$_S$ t$_i$ *to like transformations*]

In LFG there is no need to assume the presence of a trace in the subject position of the embedded sentence because the assignment of a θ-role to *Chomsky* can be effected by a redundancy rule. In LFG the entry for *seem* (ignoring the case where the verb is also associated with a perceiver, as in *Chomsky seems to me to like transformations*) would be that in [17].

[17]   seem, V, 'SEEM <(V-COMP)> (SUBJ)'
                      PROP

A lexical form is a conflation of (a) a representation of predicate–argument structure with (b) a list of (surface) grammatical functions that co-occur with the item in question. [17], then, is a conflation of [18],

[18]   (a) 'SEEM <PROP>'
       (b) (V-COMP) (SUBJ)

and represents the fact that this verb co-occurs with two grammatical functions but denotes a predicate that takes only one (propositional) argument. Since the subject function is non-thematic, it appears outside the argument-list of SEEM, which is enclosed within the angled brackets in the usual way. We have here, then, an example of a function that is not associated with a θ-role. The subject cannot be assigned directly to an argument, unlike the subject of a passive verb, because the relevant argument is not an argument of SEEM but of the predicate of the propositional argument of SEEM. This argument has no overt syntactic interpretation; *to like* in [16] does not have a lexical subject. In Chomsky's theory, of course, where arguments are identified with grammatical functions associated with θ-roles, there is a null subject. In LFG, by contrast, *seem* is subcategorised to take a V-COMP, a function which is assigned to infinitival VP complements lacking subjects altogether. But because this function is associated with a propositional argument, it follows that the predicate involved in that proposition will have a subject argument. Since *to like* is assumed not to have its own subject in syntactic representations (*ie* there are no traces), it follows that some other surface grammatical function must be identified as the subject assigned to this argument. This task can be performed by the redundancy rule in [19], which is not a statement of a subcategorisation generalisation but a rule of interpretation.

[19]   *functional control*:
           If V-COMP is assigned as a G(rammatical) F(unction) in a lexical form L, then $(GF_{\bar{\theta}})$ = (V-COMP SUBJ).

This rule identifies the non-thematic grammatical function of a lexical form with the subject of the V-COMP. In [17], therefore, the non-thematic subject of *seem* is identified as the subject assigned to the agent argument of the predicate LIKE. Once again, then, the association of predicate–argument structure and surface syntactic representations is achieved without reference to, or manipulation of, phrase structure representations.

In general, because LFG requires no 'normalised' phrase structure representation (D-structures or trace-enriched S-structures) to represent predicate–argument relations, the syntactic component of the grammar can be vastly simplified. All that is required is a phrase structure representation of surface forms, *ie* a representation without the θ-marked traces or PROs of Chomsky's S-structure. The link between such surface structures and predicate–argument structures is provided via the medium of grammatical function assignments. A constituent identified by position or case-marking as, say, the subject of some sentence in surface structure is associated in a lexical form with that predicate argument to which the subject function has been assigned. The actual formal machinery for carrying out these associations will be dealt with in the next section, but the underlying idea should now be clear.

It should, perhaps, be added here that [19] is deliberately formulated to generalise to cases where the controlling element is a non-thematic function other than subject. In Chomsky's theory, of course, all subcategorising functions are necessarily θ-marked. As subjects are not involved in subcategorisation these may be non-thematic, but all complements to a lexical head must have a θ-role. In LFG, however, because functions and arguments are not in a one-to-one relationship, it is possible for objects as well as subjects to be non-thematic. For example, since passive is a rule that makes reference to the object function (*cf* [14]), and since sentences such as *they believe Chomsky to be wrong* can be passivised, it follows that the post-verbal NP (here *Chomsky*) must be analysed as a (surface) direct object of *believe*, contrary to the assumptions of GB theory. This makes *to be wrong* a VP complement to which the (V-COMP) function is assigned. From the point of view of predicate–argument structure, however, BELIEVE is a two-place predicate involving a believer and a propositional object of belief as arguments. The lexical form for *believe* (when it takes an infinitival complement), therefore, will be [20],

[20] believe, V, 'BELIEVE <(SUBJ) (V-COMP)> (OBJ)'

and [19] will identify the non-thematic *direct object* as the subject assigned to the argument of BE-WRONG.

A good deal more will be said on the subject of control below

(47). For the present it is important to note that the use of lexical rules to express relations that might be analysed as movements of NP in transformational theories provides a natural explanation for why those movements are both bounded and structure-preserving (*cf* 4.2). Assuming that *only* lexical rules can alter the assignment of grammatical functions to thematic roles, and assuming that lexical rules operate on lexical forms of the type that have been discussed, it follows that the domain of such 'relation-changing' rules will be automatically restricted to whatever can properly be included in lexical forms. A lexical form is essentially equivalent to a strict subcategorisation feature in GB theory, except that the co-occurring elements are identified functionally rather than categorially, and the association of functions with predicate arguments may be much less direct than in the lexical entries of GB theory. Since a lexical entry lists just those grammatical properties peculiar to a given lexical item, the only functions which can legitimately be included in a lexical form are those whose presence is required to ensure that sentences containing the item in question are syntactically well-formed and semantically interpretable. In practice this means those functions whose values serve as arguments to the predicate denoted by the lexical item in question, and/or whose surface syntactic exponents have morphological properties (*eg* agreement, case-marking, etc.) determined by that item. The list, therefore, includes subjects, objects and the various types of complement, but does not include adjuncts of any sort. Thus no relation-changing rule can ever operate on a domain greater than that represented by the subject, object(s) and complement(s) of a single lexical head. (In theories employing movement rules, of course, this restriction has to be stipulated.)

Furthermore, since lexical rules make reference only to grammatical functions, it follows that in languages where such functions are uniformly associable with particular configurations within S, the consequence of a lexical readjustment of grammatical function assignments will appear to be a movement from one configurationally definable position in S to another; *ie* in a theory employment movement rules the operations involved will be structure-preserving. Passive, for example, involves the substitution of SUBJ for OBJ in lexical forms. If subjects are always those NPs directly dominated by S, the surface syntactic realisation of a passive lexical form will naturally seem to involve the movement of an NP from the object position it would occupy as the complement to an active transitive verb to the subject position of the corresponding passive sentence. In nonconfigurational languages, of course, where grammatical functions are identified not by the position of constituents but by case-marking, the same lexical substitution of SUBJ for OBJ in a lexical form will have its surface syntactic analogue in the form of a case-change rather than a change of position.

The type of lexical entry envisaged in LFG also provides a solution to the problem noted earlier in 4.2 (and 2.2.2), namely the association of two or more categorially/configurationally distinct surface forms with the same predicate–argument structure. Consider [21].

[21] assault, V, 'ASSAULT < (SUBJ) (OBJ)>'
                 AGENT   PATIENT
    assault, N, 'ASSAULT < (SUBJ) (ON-OBJ)>'
                 AGENT   PATIENT

This represents the fact that in the sentence *Chomsky assaulted Gazdar* and the noun phrase *Chomsky's assault on Gazdar* we are dealing with exactly the same predicate–argument structure. But now there is no need to express this configurationally by allowing nouns as well as verbs to take direct object NP complements in D-structure with all the problems that this entails. Instead different (surface) grammatical functions can be associated with the same argument/thematic role. The formal relationship between verbs and their derived nominals can now be stated quite simply by means of the redundancy rule [22].

[22] *derived nominalisation*: (OBJ) → (OF-OBJ)

This expresses the fact that in the 'normal' case the noun's lexical form can be derived from the verb's by the substitution of OF-OBJ for OBJ (*cf*: *destruction of, fear of, construction of, review of*, etc.) Where there is an unpredictable choice of preposition, as with *assault on*, the noun must be provided with a partial lexical form expressing the relevant idiosyncracy. The remainder of the lexical form, however, is again predictable from that associated with the verb; *ie* except for the stipulated substitution of ON-OBJ, there is no change. Naturally, the more idiosyncratic the relationship in any given case, the more information there will have to be in the entry for the derived nominal.

The advantages of treating grammatical functions as primitives which are not reducible to configurational definitions should now be clear. It remains, however, to assess the proposal advanced within GPSG (3.6) that grammatical functions can be defined in terms of their roles in the semantic composition of sentence interpretations. It will be recalled that the object was defined

within that framework as the NP whose denotation combined
with that of a verb to produce a VP (or intransitive verb) denotation, and the subject as that NP whose denotation combined
with a VP denotation to form a sentence denotation. If such a
proposal proved to be genuinely explanatory, it would lead us to
the conclusion that grammatical functions do not, after all, have
the status of primitives. In order to be successful, proponents of
this view would have to show that the syntactic properties of
grammatical functions (*eg* those outlined above in connection
with passivisation and functional control) follow automatically
from the semantically-based definitions. There are, however,
reasons for thinking that this is not necessarily so. For example,
in terms of semantic composition, the subject plays the same
semantic role with both transitive and intransitive verbs. But it
is clear that in some languages the process of causativisation (*ie*
the formation of verbal expressions meaning 'cause (NP) to V'
by regular morphological or syntactic means) affects the subjects
of transitive and intransitive verbs differently. Thus in Malayalam, a Dravidian language of South India, the subject of an
intransitive base verb behaves syntactically like the object of the
corresponding causative, while the subject of a transitive base
verb behaves syntactically like an oblique instrumental of the
corresponding causative, (*cf* Mohanan (1981)). A similar situation obtains in French, where the subject of a base verb appears
as a direct object of the causativising verb *faire* if the base verb
is intransitive, but as an oblique expression if the base verb is
transitive. Consider the examples in [23].

[23i] *Il   fait   travailler   ses   élèves.*
       he   makes   to-work   his   pupils
[23ii] *Il   fait   travailler l' algèbre   à/par ses élèves*
       he   makes   to-work   the algebra to/by his pupils
       'he makes his pupils work on algebra'

Since the semantic properties of the causativised subjects are the
same whether they function as direct objects or as oblique
expressions, it follows that semantic definitions of grammatical
functions cannot explain the observed syntactic distinctions. The
more facts of this type emerge the more justified is the treatment
of grammatical functions in LFG as syntactic primitives.

4.6 C-structures and F-structures

The mapping between lexical predicate–argument structures and
surface forms in LFG is effected by correlating the grammatical

functions that are assigned to predicate arguments in lexical forms with the grammatical functions that are associated with syntactic representations of surface structures. So far we have dealt formally only with the lexical encoding of grammatical functions. We are now in a position to consider the syntactic encoding of grammatical functions in representations of surface syntactic structure (known as C(onstituent)-structures), and to introduce the F(unctional)-structures which formally represent the functional correlations between C-structure and predicate–argument structure.

C-structure rules are simply context-free rewriting rules of the familiar sort. They are defined over the vocabulary of categories made available by $\overline{X}$-theory, and, for a configurational language such as English, have the basic form illustrated in [24],

[24] $X^n \rightarrow C_1 \ldots X^{n-1} \ldots C_n$

where each C is either a minor category (such as COMP or DET, which are assumed to lack phrasal projections), a maximal projection ($\overline{\overline{X}}$) of a major lexical category (V, P, N and A), or S. The major categories are defined in terms of the features **predicative** and **transitive.** Intuitively, a predicative category is one which does not allow the subject function to be associated with any of the symbols introduced by the PS rules expanding its maximal projection and an intransitive category is one which does not allow the object function to be associated with any of the symbols introduced by the PS rules expanding its $\overline{X}$ projection. One might, then, substitute the features ($\pm$ SUBJ] for [$\pm$ pred], and [$\pm$ OBJ] for [$\pm$ trans], a move which would result in a feature system analogous to that of Jackendoff (1977), discussed briefly and in modified form in 2.2.2 (see especially [94] and [95] with the associated discussion). The feature matrices of the major lexical categories are given in [25].

[25]	pred	trans
V	+	+
P	$\pm$	+
N	$\pm$	−
A	+	−

S and $\overline{S}$ are taken to be non-predicative major categories (undefined for transitivity) which are projections of no lexical category, but all other major categories are phrasal projections of the major lexical categories with the same feature composition and differing only in bar level.

It is, of course, natural that in a theory which stresses the centrality of grammatical functions the categories of natural languages should be defined in terms of their relations to the subject and object functions rather than in terms of the categorial features $[\pm N]$ and $[\pm V]$ of GB theory or GPSG. Once again feature specifications and $\overline{X}$-notation will not be employed below unless there is good reason to do so. VP, PP, etc. are to be interpreted as maximal projections, and $\overline{V}$, $\overline{P}$, etc. will not be included in rules or representations.

The basic rule type given in [24] has to be supplemented by a further type in order to handle exocentric constructions, *ie* constructions where the dominating category is not a phrasal projection of any of its daughters. Exocentric rules have the form given in [26],

[26] $X^n \rightarrow C_1 \ldots \ldots C_n$

where each C is either a minor category or a maximal projection of a lexical category. To illustrate both rule types, consider the set of rules in [27].

[27i] S $\rightarrow$ NP VP
[27ii] NP $\rightarrow$ DET N
[27iii] VP $\rightarrow$ V (NP) (NP)

[27i] is of the general type [26], the other two are of the type given in [24] (ignoring the intermediate categories $\overline{N}$ and $\overline{V}$ as explained above). These rules will assign a C-structure representation to the sentence *a professor gave the student an assignment*, as in [28].

[28]

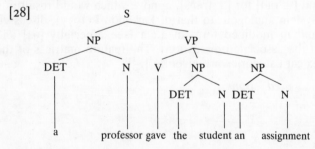

Such representations are the input to the phonological rules which assign a phonetic representation.

Surface grammatical functions, identified positionally or by case-marking at C-structure, play a central role as primitive constructs at the second level of syntactic representation assigned to sentences, namely F-structure. F-structures are the input to the semantic rules which compose the logical formulas which encode the meaning of sentences from the information provided. The F-structure for the sentence whose C-structure is given in [28] would be [29].

[29]

$$
\begin{bmatrix}
\text{SUBJ} & \begin{bmatrix} \text{SPEC} & \text{A} \\ \text{NUM} & \text{SG} \\ \text{PRED} & \text{'PROFESSOR'} \end{bmatrix} \\
\text{TENSE} & \text{PAST} \\
\text{PRED} & \text{'GIVE} \quad <(\text{SUBJ}) \, (\text{OBJ2}) \, (\text{OBJ})>' \\
\text{OBJ} & \begin{bmatrix} \text{SPEC} & \text{THE} \\ \text{NUM} & \text{SG} \\ \text{PRED} & \text{'STUDENT'} \end{bmatrix} \\
\text{OBJ2} & \begin{bmatrix} \text{SPEC} & \text{A} \\ \text{NUM} & \text{SG} \\ \text{PRED} & \text{'ASSIGNMENT'} \end{bmatrix}
\end{bmatrix}
$$

This identifies *a professor* as the subject of the sentence, *the student* as the direct object and *an assignment* as the second object. Taking the case of the SUBJ function as a basis for explaining the notation involved in all three examples, this is to be understood as saying that A is the SPEC(ifier) of the SUBJ(ect), s(in)g(ular) is the NUM(ber) of the SUBJ(ect) and 'PROFESSOR' is the PRED(icate) of the SUBJ(ect) (*ie* 'being a professor' is predicated of the individual denoted by the subject); in other words the value of the SUBJ function is specified in the form of a subsidiary functional structure which comprises the assignment of values to the attributes SPEC NUM and PRED.

Notice that the value for the PRED function of the sentence as a whole, 'GIVE <. . .>,' is a lexical form of the type familiar from the preceding sections. The rules of the semantic component treat these values for PRED as a pattern for composing the interpretation of the sentence. So here, the first argument position of the predicate GIVE (agent) is filled by the formula that results from interpreting the SUBJ function of the sentence, the second (patient) by substituting the interpretation of the OBJ2 function, and the third (goal) by substituting the interpretation of the OBJ function. The formulas for the SUBJ and the two OBJ functions are in turn determined by their PRED values, in this case the simple semantic forms 'PROFESSOR', 'STUDENT' and 'ASSIGN-MENT', which are interpreted as predicates on individuals quantified by the information derived from the values for SPEC and NUM. Obviously all the functions mentioned in a lexical form incorporated as the value of PRED in a functional structure have to appear in that functional structure, and all the functions which have subsidiary F-structures as values (*ie* SUBJ, OBJ, etc.) must be mentioned in the lexical form.

Clearly F-structures are a syntactic projection of the information contained in the lexical forms associated with the words that appear in a given C-structure. If they are to provide an account of the nature of the relationship between lexical predicate–argument structure and surface syntax, it is obvious that the grammatical functions associated with predicate arguments in a structure such as [29] must also be associated with the categories employed in a representation such as [28]. This is done by annotating the phrase structure rules with functional information which is carried over into C-structure representations. Functional structures then associate the functions so defined with the functions assigned to predicate–argument structures and so express the necessary correlations. Consider the annotated set of rules in [30].

$$[\text{30i}] \quad S \rightarrow \quad \underset{(\uparrow \text{SUBJ}) = \downarrow}{\text{NP}} \quad \underset{\uparrow = \downarrow}{\text{VP}}$$

$$[\text{30ii}] \quad NP \rightarrow \quad \underset{\uparrow = \downarrow}{\text{DET}} \quad \underset{\uparrow = \downarrow}{\text{N}}$$

$$[\text{30iii}] \quad VP \rightarrow \quad \underset{\uparrow = \downarrow}{\text{V}} \quad \underset{(\uparrow \text{OBJ}) = \downarrow}{\text{NP}} \quad \underset{(\uparrow \text{OBJ2}) = \downarrow}{\text{NP}}$$

The basic principle is to associate a function-assigning equation (*ie* $(\uparrow \text{GF}) = \downarrow$) with non-head maximal projections and to assign the equation $\uparrow = \downarrow$ elsewhere. Major categories associated with $\uparrow = \downarrow$ are the heads of their phrases; so VP is the head of S, N of NP, V of VP. But what exactly do these symbols mean? Let us first of all provide an appropriately annotated C-structure representation.

[31]

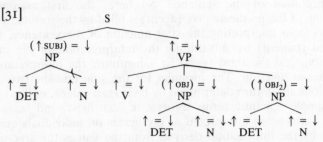

Further functional annotations are derived from the lexical entries of the items inserted. The entries for the vocabulary in our example sentence are those in [32]. Notice that upward arrows have also been added here in various places, and that the semantic forms contained in single quotation marks are now explicitly identified with the PRED function by means of equations; all items which may appear as the lexical head of a phrase have a PRED value.

[32] a, DET, ($\uparrow$ SPEC) = A
         ($\uparrow$ NUM) = SG

professor, N, ($\uparrow$ NUM) = SG
             ($\uparrow$ PRED) = 'PROFESSOR'
gave, V, ($\uparrow$ TENSE) = PAST
         ($\uparrow$ PRED) = 'GIVE <($\uparrow$ SUBJ)($\uparrow$ OBJ2)($\uparrow$ OBJ)>'
the, DET, ($\uparrow$ SPEC) = 'THE'
student, N, ($\uparrow$ NUM) = SG
           ($\uparrow$ PRED) = 'STUDENT'
assignment, N, ($\uparrow$ NUM) = SG
              ($\uparrow$ PRED) = 'ASSIGNMENT'

When these items are inserted into the tree in [31] together with the associated equations, we obtain [33].

[33]

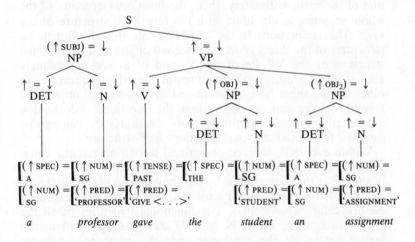

The combination of information from the annotated syntactic rules and the lexicon can now be used to construct a functional structure for the sentence (or equivalently to determine whether a given functional structure has all the necessary properties to be the functional structure of a given sentence). In the process,

GF = grammatical functions?

constituents of C-structure are associated with the functions of F-structure and so with the relevant predicate arguments. Informally, each equation of the form $\uparrow = \downarrow$ is to be read 'my mother's functional structure is equivalent to my functional structure', and each equation of the form $(\uparrow GF) = \downarrow$ is to be read 'my mother's functional structure's GF is equivalent to my functional structure'. Consider first the NP and VP under S. The annotation to the NP says that the subject of the functional structure of the sentence is to be identified with the functional structure of the NP. This is a roundabout way of saying that the NP in question is the subject of the sentence. But more importantly, it tells us that the functional information associated with the constituents of the NP constitutes the value of the SUBJ function in F-structure. We shall return to this in a moment. The annotation to the VP says that the functional structure of the sentence is the same as the functional structure of the VP. This equation simply means that functional structures are 'flat'; in other words, grammatical functions are there associated with predicate–argument representations that do not distinguish the subject argument by assigning it to a higher level of structure than other arguments. Within the VP, the annotation to V once again expresses an identity, this time between the functional structure of the VP and that of the verb. Ultimately, then, the functional structure of the whole sentence is identified with the functional structure of the verb. The annotations to the two NPs state that the functional structures of the direct object and second object of the functional structure of the VP (*ie* of the V, and of S, see immediately above) are the functional structures of the NPs in question. In other words, these NPs are identified as grammatical object and second object, and we know that the functional information associated with their constituent parts constitutes the value to be assigned to the OBJ and OBJ2 functions in F-structure.

Within each NP, subject, object and second object, the equations on DET and N simply tell us that the functional structure of the NP is that determined by the combination of its daughters' functional structures (which must not, therefore, contain contradictory value assignments). The functional structures of all the lexical categories, DET, N and V, are those specified in the lexical entries of the particular examples of these categories inserted in the C-structure representation, as the upwards arrow in each case indicates.

The reader can now check that all information necessary for the construction of the F-structure in [29] has been provided. The combination of functional information originating in the lexicon with the functional information coming from C-structure rules in fact constitutes what is called a **functional description** from which the functional structure must be computed. Clearly a functional structure can only be constructed if the statements of the F-description are consistent. To be grammatical, a sentence must be assigned both a well-formed C-structure and a well-formed F-structure. Many types of ungrammaticality are therefore explained on the basis of functional ill-formedness. If, for example, the NUM attribute of a DET is assigned the value PL and that of its sister N is assigned the value SG, it is obvious that no consistent functional structure can be constructed as the value of the grammatical function assigned to the NP concerned. Three conditions on functional well-formedness are in fact imposed, the **uniqueness, completeness** and **coherence** conditions. The uniqueness condition ensures that the assignment of grammatical functions and features to C-structure configurations and lexical items is globally consistent, *ie* that any given attribute is assigned a unique value and not a set of inconsistent values. Completeness is satisfied if, for every grammatical function assigned to an argument of the PRED of a clause, there is a corresponding grammatical argument in the clause. Thus in [29] the functions SUBJ, OBJ and OBJ2 appear both in the argument list of GIVE and as grammatical arguments in the F-structure representation of the clause as a whole. Coherence is satisfied if every meaningful grammatical argument occurs in a clause whose PRED has a matching grammatical function assigned to one of its arguments. In [29] all the grammatical arguments of the clause are also assigned to arguments of GIVE. Sentences such as *a professors give the student an assignment, *a professor gives* and *a professor gives the student an assignment to his secretary* are ruled out because their functional structures violate the uniqueness, completeness and coherence conditions respectively.

To summarise briefly, F-structures are formal representations of the mapping between lexical predicate–argument structures and C-structures (representations of surface syntactic structure). They express the association between predicate–arguments and syntactic categories via the medium of grammatical functions. These are assigned to predicate arguments in lexical forms and to surface syntactic categories, and F-structures tell us the value of each surface grammatical function and which surface grammatical function is associated with which predicate argument. The relationships involved are expressed in a universal vocabulary, locally with respect to lexical subcategorisation, and compositionally with respect to semantic interpretation.

This representation of predicate–argument/surface syntax relations allows a simplification of the syntactic component of the grammar *vis-à-vis* GB theory. This now comprises a set of context-free phrase structure rules which define a single level of C-structure representation. The form of C-structure rules is in fact largely predictable from the theory of syntactic encoding. It was noted above that function-assigning equations (↑ (GF) = ↓) are associated with non-head maximal projections, and the equation ↑ = ↓ is associated with other categories, the head of a phrase being identified as the major category annotated ↑ = ↓ . Thus only maximal projections bear grammatical functions, every phrase has a (unique) head, and the functional features of a phrase are identified with those of its head. It also follows that in configurational languages only maximal projections will be involved in subcategorisation. Furthermore, if there is only one level of C-structure, there can be no rules mapping C-structures into C-structures; *ie* transformations are eliminated and 'relation-changing' rules must be formulated as lexical redundancy rules modifying the assignment of grammatical functions to predicate arguments prior to the insertion of lexical items and associated lexical forms into C-structures and F-structures.

In support of the central assumption of the theory, that grammatical functions are primitives of syntactic theory, attention is drawn to the fact that many grammatical processes in the world's languages can be neatly expressed by reference to such functions and that these functions are just as central to the grammars of languages which lack sufficient constituent structure to support the conventional configurational definitions. If the dominance and precedence relations of constituent structure are taken to be primitive the appearance in nonconfigurational languages of predicate–argument/C-structure mappings that can be characterised in exactly the same functional terms as the corresponding mappings in configurational languages would be difficult to explain.

To complete this section a brief word is necessary on the subject of syntactic encoding of grammatical functions in non-configurational languages. The basic form of C-structure rules in the grammars of these languages is that in [34],

[34] C → X* (X* = a string of Xs of any length)

where C is a major non-lexical category and X is a lexical or non-lexical category. Thus some non-configurational languages, like Japanese, may lack a VP but have phrasal complements to verbs, others, like Warlpiri, may lack phrase structure almost completely, so that sentences may consist of strings of words. Let us take the case of Japanese, where [35] is a representative expansion rule for S.

[35] S → NP* V

S may dominate a string of NPs followed by a verb. The basic principle of syntactic encoding is to associate pairs of function and feature-assigning equations with each NP, and to associate ↑ = ↓ with the head (*ie* the major lexical category in a given expansion). Consider, for example, the pairs of equations in [36].

$$[36i] \left\{ \begin{array}{l} (\uparrow \text{ SUBJ}) = \downarrow \\ (\downarrow \text{ CASE}) = \text{GA} \end{array} \right\} \qquad [36ii] \left\{ \begin{array}{l} (\uparrow \text{ OBJ}) = \downarrow \\ (\downarrow \text{ CASE}) = \text{O} \end{array} \right\}$$

These can be associated randomly with NPs in C-structure, given that phrase order is free. Each requires that the NP identified as bearing some grammatical function have a daughter that bears the appropriate case-marking. In practice this will be the head of the NP, N, once again the major lexical category in the expansion. The V, of course, is annotated ↑ = ↓. Subjects and objects are now identified in C-structure by case-marking (or the use of postpositions) rather than by position. Obviously well-formed F-structures meeting all three of the conditions stipulated above will only be constructed if the number of NPs in a C-structure corresponds to the number of arguments in the argument list of the predicate denoted by the sentence's verb, and if the same grammatical function assignments are involved in both cases.

The problems are a little more difficult in the case of languages like Warlpiri, where there are typically no constituents above the word level and a basic expansion rule for S would be [37].

[37] S → X AUX X* (X = any lexical category)

The only requirement is that the AUX have a fixed position within the configuration of S (much as V has a fixed position in the configuration of S in Japanese). In cases such as this, pairs of equations like those in [36] are assigned to nouns and their modifiers, and ↑ = ↓ to the head. Since heads by definition have a PRED, and since the uniqueness condition requires a unique value be assigned to the sentence-PRED, it follows that only one category can be the head of the sentence. Ordinarily this will be V, though it seems that the head of S may also be nominal in Warlpiri. In any case a sentence will have at most one main verb if it is to be assigned a well-formed F-structure. Once again, the F-structure will be consistent, coherent and complete only if the non-head elements of the C-structure can be interpreted as constituting a set of arguments that corresponds to that specified in the argument list of the predicate denoted by the head of the sentence. Items which in a language such as English would be grouped together as a phrasal constituent may, of course, be widely separated within the flat structures permitted by [37]. But processes such as case-marking identify the elements that 'belong together' just as efficiently as hierarchical phrasing; so although the manner of syntactic encoding of information is different, the basic relationship between lexical predicate–argument structure and the C-structure of a Warlpiri sentence can be represented by an F-structure of exactly the same type as that employed in the description of a corresponding English sentence. For example, the SUBJ function is syntactically encoded in English sentences by the construction of a noun-headed phrase directly dominated by S, while in Warlpiri it is encoded by the addition of a common ending (ergative or absolutive according to circumstances) to all the elements that would in English form a subject NP but which in Warlpiri may be scattered randomly under S. Since only one of these elements may be interpreted as the PRED of the subject by the uniqueness condition (the element that would be the head of the NP in English) all the others will be interpreted as its modifiers. The whole must, of course, constitute a consistent and coherent subsidiary F-structure if the sentence is to be well-formed.

4.7 Control

Within the framework of Lexical-Functional Grammar, control involves a relationship of referential dependence between an unexpressed subject and some other constituent whereby the properties of that constituent (the controller) determine those of the unexpressed subject (the controllee). A distinction is drawn between **functional control**, which requires that the F-structures of the controller and controllee be identical over and above the requirement of referential identity, and **anaphoric control**, which requires only identity of reference between controller and controllee and also allows for cases where there is no overt controller within the same sentence and the reference of the controllee is therefore arbitrary. The examples in [38] illustrate the former, those in [39] the latter.

[38i]   *Keith seems sad to Maggie.*
[38ii] *Michael regards Maggie as hostile.*
[38iii] *Ronnie tends to shoot from the hip.*
[38iv] *Caspar believes Ronnie to be trigger-happy.*

[38v] *George and Caspar try to impress each other.*
[38vi] *Leon persuaded his colleagues to think again.*

[39i] *Leon decided that selling off the family silver was his only chance.*

[39ii] *Involving herself in the disarmament negotiations was risky for Maggie.*

[39iii] *Mike signalled to Keith to quit while the going was good.*

[39iv] *Pinching bottoms is offensive.*

It will be seen that functional control includes phenomena that would be treated in the standard theory of transformational grammar (see Ch. 2) as involving subject-to-subject raising ([38iii]), subject-to-object raising ([38iv]) and equi-NP deletion ([38v] and [38vi]). The crucial common factor here is the obligatory absence of the infinitival complementiser *for*, and the related absence of overt subjects in the infinitival complement. Anaphoric control deals with cases that are related to the examples [38v] and [38vi], but differs in that overt subjects may in principle always appear. Compare the examples in [39] with those in [40].

[40i] *Leon decided that* $\begin{Bmatrix} his\ selling\ off \\ for\ him\ to\ sell\ off \end{Bmatrix}$ *the family silver was his only chance*

[40ii] $\begin{Bmatrix} Her\ involving\ herself \\ For\ her\ to\ involve\ herself \end{Bmatrix}$ *in the disarmament negotiations was risky for Maggie.*

[40iii] *Mike signalled to Keith for him to quit while the going was good.*

[40iv] $\begin{Bmatrix} Secretaries'\ pinching \\ For\ secretaries\ to\ pinch \end{Bmatrix}$ *(managers') bottoms is offensive.*

Notice that when an overt pronoun occurs there is no need for this to be taken as co-referential with the potential controller in the majority of cases; it is perhaps a little more difficult to obtain a disjoint reference reading in examples such as [40iii], though it is by no means impossible.

Before dealing with the mechanisms employed in LFG to handle functional and anaphoric control, it will be useful to outline once again the approach to these problems adopted in Chomsky's government and binding theory (*cf* 2.3.8) as a basis for comparison. It will be recalled that an NP such as *Ronnie* in [38iv] is treated as the subject of the infinitive at all levels of representation, and that NP-movement is involved only in cases of subject-to-subject raising such as [38iii]. The binding condition for anaphors, requiring that traces be bound in their governing categories, guarantees that only subject positions will be vacated by movement in such cases, and only when the clauses involved are infinitival. The same condition, redundantly supported by the subjacency condition, also guarantees that the dependencies involved are local, in the sense that moved NPs and their traces may be separated by at most a single S boundary (not $\bar{S}$, since this is an absolute barrier to government).

Chomsky's theory of control deals with the distribution of the anaphoric pronominal PRO; since this is supposed to have properties characteristic of both anaphors and pronominals, and since the binding condition for anaphors requires these to be bound in their governing category while that for pronominals requires these to be free in their governing category, it follows that PRO cannot have a governing category, *ie* that PRO is ungoverned. The only ungoverned position is the subject of an infinitive that is protected from external government by $\bar{S}$. This must lack the complementiser *for*, which would act as an internal governor. The cases of equi, [38v] and [38vi], clearly fall under this heading. Chomsky insists that one of the major differences between PRO and trace is the fact that the control relationship, unlike the NP/trace relationship, is not subject to subjacency. So although cases such as [38v] and [38vi] always exhibit a purely local dependency, exactly like [38iii], Chomsky dismisses this parallel in favour of the parallel with examples such as those in [39] which may, as with [39i] and [39ii], exhibit a relationship between controller and controllee that is not constrained by subjacency. This is justified on the grounds that the antecedent in all the relevant cases has an independent θ-role, and cannot, therefore, appear where it does in S-structures as a result of movement.

There is, nevertheless, a further difference between examples such as [38v] and [38vi] and examples of the type seen in [39], namely the possible occurrence in the latter of overt pronominals, as we saw in [40]. This suggests that in Chomsky's terms there is optional government of the subject position in these cases, whereas government is absolutely prohibited in the cases of 'local' equi. LFG, stressing the differences between [38v/vi] and [39], pulls together the local dependencies under a common heading (much as was done in GPSG, see 3.6), so that raising and local equi constructions are distinguished from (potentially) 'long-distance' equi relationships as cases of functional, as opposed to anaphoric, control.

Consider now the S-structure representations of [38iii] and [38iv] given in [41].

[41i] *Ronnie tends* [s t *to shoot from the hip*]
[41ii] *Caspar believes* [s *Ronnie to be trigger-happy*]

Such representations could not be adopted as C-structure representations within the framework of LFG. Full sentential complements can be assigned only 'closed' grammatical functions such as COMP(lement) and the essential property of closed functions is that they cannot be functionally controlled. (The closed functions comprise the full set of functions apart from XCOMP, the function assigned to predicative complements like *angry* in *Maggie seems angry* or *to fume* in *Maggie seems to fume*). Since the complement in [41i] lacks an overt subject, and since *Ronnie* in [41ii] must be analysed as a direct object to account for the fact that such sentences can be passivised, it follows that we are dealing here with cases of functional control and that the complement to *tends* or *believes* cannot be a full clause. The theory requires the complements of lexical heads to be maximal projections in a configurational language such as English, and since the complements in [41] are clearly headed by a verb, it follows that the complements in question must be VPs. Similar considerations apply in the case of local equi. The C-structures for [38iii] to [38vi] are therefore those given in [42].

[42]

[42i]

[42ii]

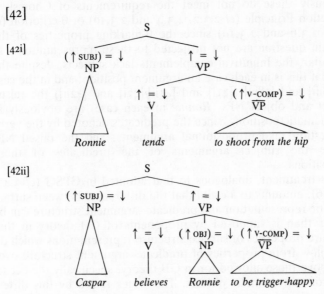

[42iii]

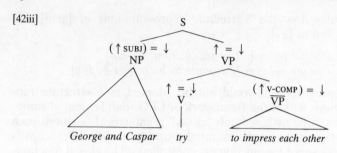

[42iv]

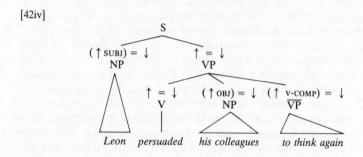

In each case $\overline{VP}$ is assumed to dominate *to* + VP.

Obviously these do not meet the requirements of Chomsky's Projection Principle (*cf* 2.3.2, 2.3.4 and 2.3.10) or θ-criterion (*cf* 2.3.4, 2.3.6 and 2.3.10) since the θ-marking properties of the verbs in question are not projected to these representations. In particular, the infinitival complements lack subjects, despite the fact that this is in each case an argument position; and in the case of [38iii] and [38iv] ([41i] and [41ii]/[42i] and [42ii]) the raised subject and object NPs (*Ronnie* in each case) are obviously in non-thematic positions, since the predicates denoted by the verbs in question take propositional arguments, and the raised NPs denote the subject arguments of the predicates of those propositions.

This treatment, analogous to that adopted in GPSG (*cf* 3.4.3 and 3.6), amounts to a claim that the differences between surface syntactic representation and predicate–argument structure can be greater than is supposed by proponents of GB theory in that there are properties of surface structure representations which do not follow from properties of predicate–argument structure over and above those allowed for in GB theory, specifically the occurrence of non-thematic objects. The issues raised by this difference in representational assumptions will be considered shortly

(*cf* also 5.2). The lexical entries for the verbs in [38i] to [38vi]
would be as follows:

[43i] *seem*   : (↑ PRED) = 'SEEM <(XCOMP) (TO-OBJ)> (SUBJ)'
[43ii] *regard*   : (↑ PRED) = 'REGARD <(SUBJ) (OBJ) (XCOMP)>'
[43iii] *tend*   : (↑ PRED) = 'TEND <(XCOMP)> (SUBJ)'
[43iv] *believe* : (↑ PRED) = 'BELIEVE <(SUBJ) (XCOMP)> (OBJ)'
[43v] *try*   : (↑ PRED) = 'TRY <(SUBJ) (XCOMP)>'
[43vi] *persuade* : (↑ PRED) = 'PERSUADE <(SUBJ) (OBJ) (XCOMP)>'

In each case XCOMP is the function assigned to the 'predicative'
constituent; this is either an adjective (in fact an ADJP) or an
infinitival VP. The distinction between the cases of raising and
the equi examples lies in the by now familiar fact that the former
involve a subcategorising function that is not assigned to any
argument, while the latter have all their subcategorising functions
assigned.

The rule of functional control is simply a lexical redundancy
rule which expands entries such as those in [43] by spelling out
which of the functions listed is to be interpreted as the subject
of the XCOMP function. The relevant rule is given in [44], which
is simply a generalised version of the rule given earlier in [19].

[44]   *Rule of functional control*
       If XCOMP appears in the grammatical function assignment
       of a lexical form, add the following to that lexical form:

       (i)   (↑ OBJ2) = (↑ XCOMP SUBJ) if OBJ2 appears, otherwise
       (ii) (↑ OBJ) = (↑ XCOMP SUBJ) if OBJ appears, otherwise
       (iii) (↑ SUBJ) = (↑ XCOMP SUBJ).

This gives the correct results when applied to each of the entries
in [43]. The effect is that in the functional structure of sentences
such as those in [38] the argument position assigned the function
SUBJ of XCOMP is linked by means of an arrow to the appropriate
controlling function (thematic or non-thematic), thereby marking
the relevant identities. For an example, see [58] below.

Notice that [44] defines the unmarked case; that is, in the
absence of information to the contrary, [44] applies assigning
controller priority as indicated. There are, however, exceptions
to the general rule, as exemplified by the case of *promise*, where,
despite the optional presence of an object, the subject is the
controller.

[45]   *Maggie promised Ron to sell Buckingham Palace to the
       highest bidder.*

The lexical entry for such verbs includes an idiosyncratic control
equation (to the effect that some function other than that

expected on the basis of [44] is the controller), and this blocks the application of the general rule.

Turning now to anaphoric control relations, these involve the presence of an anaphor ('PRO') in functional structure which is not expressed in C-structure. Here 'anaphor' is defined as a grammatical element which may be assigned an antecedent by the rules of sentence grammar. It therefore includes both those pronouns that are obligatorily assigned antecedents by the rules of grammar, such as reciprocals and reflexives (bound anaphors), and those which may optionally be assigned such an antecedent, such as the ordinary definite pronouns *him, her*, etc. 'PRO' is taken to be an anaphor very similar in its interpretation to *him, her*, etc., *ie* an anaphor that need not be bound. It is important to bear in mind that in Chomsky's theory the term anaphor is used exclusively in connection with bound anaphors, and that the term pronominal is employed to deal with those items which may or may not be assigned an antecedent within the same sentence. Chomsky's PRO is assumed to exhibit properties of both (bound) anaphors (in that it has no intrinsic referential content) and pronominals (in that it never has an antecedent within its own clause), from which it follows that it must be ungoverned (since it cannot simultaneously satisfy both the anaphor and pronominal binding conditions), from which it follows that it appears only as the subject of infinitives. By contrast 'PRO' in LFG is not a bound anaphor but, in Chomsky's terminology, a (morphologically unexpressed) pronominal. Since in English it appears as the PRED of a SUBJ function, and since SUBJ is among the functions that may appear in lexical forms as part of the definition of an item's subcategory (see the discussion of [13] and [14] above), it follows that 'PRO' is governed. (This consequence is the result of the identification within LFG of subcategorisation and government; *ie* lexical items are deemed to govern all of their subcategorising functions.) The implications of the different treatments of PRO and 'PRO' in GB theory and LFG will be considered below, and again in 5.2.

The functional anaphor 'PRO' is created by an optional schema of the form [46].

[46] $(\uparrow \text{GF PRED}) = \text{'PRO'}$

The possible occurrence of instantiations of this schema are severely limited. 'PRO' is a semantic form (as the inverted commas make clear) and originates in the lexicon like all other semantic forms. Clearly, then, the optional schema [46] must belong to a lexical entry. Since LFG does not allow for null NPs in C-structure corresponding to Chomsky's PRO or trace, as we have seen, the entry in question cannot be that for a null NP. The schema must, therefore, be introduced as part of some other entry, namely that of a lexical form that governs the GF in question. It will be recalled that the set of lexically induced functional controllers was restricted in [44] to SUBJ, OBJ and OBJ2. The set of lexically introduced functional anaphors in [46] is similarly restricted. This common restriction follows from a distinction which is drawn between semantically restricted and semantically unrestricted GFs. The former (*eg* the various types of oblique function) can be paired only with arguments of specific semantic types. So the BY-OBJ of a passive sentence can only be associated with an AG(ent) argument, and so on. By contrast, the semantically unrestricted GFs (namely SUBJ, OBJ and OBJ2) can be paired with any argument type, or even remain unpaired (as in the case of 'non-logical' subjects and objects). If we now require that every semantically restricted function that occurs in a lexical form be paired with an argument of the appropriate type (by appearing in the argument list at an argument of that type), and stipulate that this is the only possible way for lexical forms to refer to semantically restricted functions, it follows that only the semantically unrestricted GFs can be involved in functional and anaphoric control relations as controllers and controllees respectively. In fact in English the potential set of lexically introduced functional anaphors has to be restricted to the SUBJ function as a language-particular property. Assuming that only [± FIN(ite)] lexical items (*ie* verbs) permit the functional anaphor, and that English, again as a language-particular property, requires [−FIN] to be selected for 'PRO' to appear, the rule for introducing [46] can be given as [47].

[47] *Rule of functional anaphora*
For any verb and any semantically unrestricted GF which it governs, assign optionally the following equations to the verb's lexical entry:
(i) ($\uparrow$ GF PRED) = 'PRO' (For English GF = {SUBJ})
(ii) ($\uparrow$ FIN) =$_c$ α (For English α = −)

The conditions on the right have the effect of confining the appearance of the functional anaphor to the subject position of non-finite clauses (*ie* those whose verbs are infinitives or gerunds). The second equation in [47] is a **constraint** equation (hence the letter *c* adjacent to the equals sign), and is in effect a well-formedness condition on functional structures. Unlike the first equation, it does not result in the addition of information to a functional structure but merely constrains the set of functional structures which may contain 'PRO' as the PRED of SUBJ.

Given [47], any infinitive that may be introduced by *for*, and so have a lexical subject, (this excludes all the cases that fall under the heading of functional control where *for* is obligatorily absent), and any gerund, all of which may have lexical subjects, may also appear without a syntactic subject and have the PREDS of their SUBJ functions interpreted as 'PRO' by [47]. Consider the examples in [48].

[48i] *Maggie wishes (for) her to resign.*
[48ii] *Maggie wishes to resign.*
[48iii] *Maggie likes her writing speeches.*
[48iv] *Maggie likes writing speeches.*

The interpretation of pronominal SUBJ, whether morphologically expressed like *her* in [48i], or unexpressed morphologically, as in [48ii], is determined by the **obviation principle**, given in [49] (Obviation refers to a situation in which co-reference between pronouns and (potential) antecedents is precluded).

[49] *Obviation principle*
    If P is the pronominal SUBJ of an obviative clause (in English this means an infinitival clause that may be introduced by *for*), and A is a potential antecedent of P and the SUBJ of the clause immediately containing the obviative clause, P is bound to A if P is not morphologically expressed, and P is not bound to A if P is morphologically expressed.

So in [48i], *her* is the pronominal subject of an obviative clause and *Maggie*, as the subject of the clause immediately containing the infinitival, qualifies as a potential antecedent. But co-reference is blocked because the pronominal subject of the infinitive is morphologically expressed. In [48ii], by contrast, the pronominal subject has no morphological realisation and so must be interpreted as co-referential with *Maggie*. The restriction to cases where the potential antecedent is the subject of the immediately containing clause is justified by the fact that the interpretation of *her* or 'PRO' in sentences such as (*for her*) *to concede seems silly to Maggie* and *Maggie thinks that* (*for her*) *to withdraw is discreditable* is 'free', *ie* may or may not be bound to *Maggie*. In these cases, then, [49] is simply inapplicable.

It might be thought on the basis of [48iii] and [48iv] that the same principles of interpretation apply for gerunds. Unfortunately the situation here is much more complex. The preferred interpretation of 'PRO' in [48iii] is, of course, the one in which *Maggie* and *her* refer to two different individuals, but as [50] makes clear, the possibility of co-reference in such cases cannot be excluded (The introduction of a modal element enhances the naturalness of such examples.).

[50] *I like my having to write my own speeches.*

Similarly, the absence of an overt subject pronoun with a gerund does not guarantee a co-reference reading, as [51] makes clear.

[51] *Maggie approves of singing round the campfire.*

It seems, then, that there is no straightforward general principle for stating control relations in such cases, and that preferred interpretations depend upon a variety of factors including the lexical meaning of the verb governing the gerund, modality, and a range of pragmatic considerations. The situation becomes clearer, however, in cases where the gerund is in a structural position such that there is no potential subject antecedent in the immediately containing clause.

[52] *Maggie thinks that criticising the opposition is always justified.*

Here the obviation principle could not apply in any case because *Maggie* is too 'remote' from *criticising the opposition*. In these circumstances the interpretation of 'PRO' is free in the sense that [52] may be interpreted as meaning that Maggie thinks her own criticism of the opposition is always justified or that such criticism is always justified regardless of who does the criticising. Similarly, if the lexical subject *her* is inserted, we are free to choose between a reading where *her* = *Maggie* and a reading where *her* refers to someone else.

In all cases where a morphologically unexpressed pronominal is assigned an antecedent, whether obligatorily by [49] or optionally in the case of examples like [52], there is a universal condition on anaphoric control that must be met. This is given in [53].

[53] *The F-command requirement*
The grammatically assigned antecedent of morphologically unexpressed pronominals must f-command those pronominals.

F-command is a relationship between functions in F-structures much as c-command is a relationship between constituents in constituent structures, (cf 2.3.6). Putting the matter as simply as possible, one function f-commands another in a functional structure if (and only if) the first does not contain the second, and every F-structure that contains the first also contains the second. To illustrate the operation of [53] and the definition of f-command consider the sentence in [54].

2/29/92

[54] *Those who met her dislike wearing Chanel No. 72.*

Obviously the wearing of perfume is disliked by *those who met her* and not by *her* (as far as we know). Consider the F-structure for [54], given in [55].

$$[55]\begin{bmatrix} \text{SUBJ}_\alpha & \begin{bmatrix} \text{PRED} & \text{'THOSE'} \\ \text{ADJUNCT} & \begin{bmatrix} \text{TOPIC} & [\text{PRED} \quad \text{'WHO'}] \\ \text{SUBJ} & \rule{1.5cm}{0.4pt} \\ \text{PRED} & \text{'MEET} <(\text{SUBJ}) (\text{OBJ})>' \\ \text{OBJ}_\alpha & [\text{PRED} \quad \text{'HER'}] \end{bmatrix} \end{bmatrix} \\ \text{PRED} & \text{'DISLIKE} <(\text{SUBJ}) (\text{OBJ})>' \\ \text{OBJ} & \begin{bmatrix} \text{SUBJ}_\beta & [\text{PRED} \quad \text{'PRO'}] \\ \text{PRED} & \text{'WEAR} <(\text{SUBJ}) (\text{OBJ})>' \\ \text{OBJ} & [\text{PRED} \quad \text{'CHANEL NO. 72'}] \end{bmatrix} \end{bmatrix}$$

The relative clause is assigned the function ADJUNCT of SUBJ$_\alpha$ and the relative pronoun is treated as the TOPIC of the ADJUNCT, with which the SUBJ function of 'MEET' is equated (by means of the arrow). The main clause OBJ function is assigned to a propositional argument whose SUBJ function (SUBJ$_\beta$) has the PRED 'PRO'. Clearly there are two potential antecedents, SUBJ$_\alpha$ and OBJ$_\alpha$, but for anaphoric control to be possible, the antecendent must f-command the controllee. Neither of the two potential antecedents contains SUBJ$_\beta$, but while the F-structure that contains SUBJ$_\alpha$ (*ie* the whole F-structure for the sentence) also contains SUBJ$_\beta$, the F-structure that contains OBJ$_\alpha$ (*ie* that defining the properties of the ADJUNCT of SUBJ$_\alpha$) does not. Hence only SUBJ$_\alpha$ is a possible antecedent for 'PRO'.

It is important to note that f-command and c-command are not simply notational variants, since it is clear that in the constituent structure of a sentence such as [56],

[56] *Demoting herself seems inconceivable to Maggie.*

given as a Chomskyan S-structure in [57] opposite, *Maggie* does not c-command the subject position in the gerund, while in the F-structure for [56], the OBL(ique) function assigned to *Maggie* does f-command the SUBJ of *demoting herself*. Consider [58] opposite.

[57]

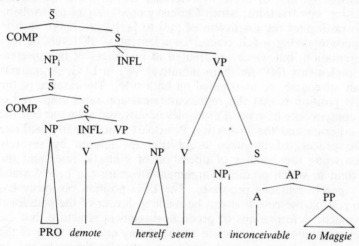

[58]
$$\begin{bmatrix} \text{SUBJ} & \begin{bmatrix} \text{SUBJ}_\alpha & \begin{bmatrix} \text{PRED} & \text{'PRO'} \end{bmatrix} \\ \text{PRED} & \text{'DEMOTE} <(\text{SUBJ}) (\text{OBJ})>\text{'} \\ \text{OBJ} & \begin{bmatrix} \text{PRED} & \text{'HERSELF'} \end{bmatrix} \end{bmatrix} \\ \text{PRED} & \text{'SEEM} <(\text{XCOMP})> (\text{SUBJ})\text{'} \\ \text{XCOMP} & \begin{bmatrix} \text{SUBJ} & \underline{} \\ \text{PRED} & \text{'INCONCEIVABLE-TO} <(\text{SUBJ}) (\text{OBL}_{\text{EX}})>\text{'} \\ (\text{OBL}_{\text{EX}})> & \begin{bmatrix} \text{PRED} & \text{'MAGGIE'} \end{bmatrix} \end{bmatrix} \end{bmatrix}$$

In this example the rule of functional control ([44]) has identified the (non-argument) SUBJ of *seems* as the SUBJ of XCOMP in F-structure, and this is indicated here by the arrow. If we understand the SUBJ of *seems* as filling the argument position SUBJ of XCOMP, then it is clear that the OBL function paired with the EX(periencer) role that has been assigned to *Maggie* is contained within an F-structure (that defining the properties of XCOMP) which also contains SUBJ$_\alpha$. Obviously, then, c-command cannot be stipulated as a requirement for the controller of PRO in Chomsky's theory, but f-command is a general condition on anaphoric control (determining the reference of 'PRO') in LFG, whether optional, as here, or obligatory.

It remains to discuss briefly the two issues raised earlier, namely the rejection of the Chomskyan Projection Principle implied by the use of bare VP complements to raising and equi verbs, and the implications of treating 'PRO' as parallel in most crucial respects to ordinary definite pronouns. It is convenient to discuss the first of these by reference to the 'subject-to-object raising' constructions, which Chomsky now analyses as involving no raising (*cf* the discussion of [38] to [42] above), the verb in question taking a full clausal complement at all levels of representation, but which are treated as sequences of two discrete complements (NP and bare infinitival VP) in LFG. Arguments can, of course, be marshalled on both sides. The essence of the GB position is that the representational apparatus employed is a consequence of general principles of universal grammar (*viz* the θ-criterion and the Projection Principle) which greatly facilitate the process of language acquisition in children by severely restricting the manner of operation of syntactic rules and the extent to which predicate–argument structure can be deformed by purely syntactic processes. The LFG position obviously has to rest on the case that can be made in favour of the additional syntactic deformations of predicate–argument structure that the representational assumptions of the theory embody. Most of the arguments that can be advanced are naturally 'theory-bound' in the sense that the position adopted follows from some general principle forming part of the foundations of the framework. If, for example, it is believed that passivisation is a process that is best described by reference to grammatical functions and that rules which change grammatical relations by assigning a new set of functions to a given set of arguments have to be lexical rules, it follows that passivisation will be a lexical rule stipulating the demotion of a subject and the promotion of an object to subject. And since the 'raised objects' of sentences such as *Ron believes Rambo to be the answer* can in fact become the subjects of passive sentences (*Rambo is believed to be the answer*), it follows that they must indeed be objects in C-structure representations, and appear in English sentences as sisters of a governing verb such as *believe*.

It is in fact doubtful whether decisive evidence is available from a consideration of the facts of English alone; and when one looks farther afield, it is possible to find languages where the facts support the Chomskyan position (Latin, for example) and languages which support the LFG (or GPSG) position (Malayalam, for instance). In view of this, one has to conclude that the 'best' general analysis of these constructions cannot yet be determined on strictly empirical grounds and each linguist must for the present make up his own mind which set of theoretical assumptions most appeal to his sense of elegance and economy in terms of the range of descriptive apparatus permitted. See 5.2 for further discussion.

Turning to the question of PRO/'PRO', it will be recalled that the essential property of PRO for Chomsky is that it is ungoverned. This follows from the fact that it exhibits simultaneously properties of (bound) anaphors and pronominals, but obviously cannot simultaneously satisfy the binding conditions for both types of expression because these are mutually incompatible. Since both conditions make reference to the notion of a 'governing category' (an anaphor must be bound, a pronominal free, in its governing category), the only solution is for PRO to lack a governing category and so be ungoverned. This restricts its distribution, given certain assumptions about barriers and pruning, to the subject position of non-finite clauses.

Against this analysis, it might be argued that PRO is really not very like (bound) anaphors at all. The essential property of a bound anaphor is that it lacks intrinsic referential content and has to be assigned reference by an antecedent. In the case of PRO, however, there is the further option of being assigned an indefinite interpretation in contexts where there is no antecedent to assign specific reference. And it is at least arguable that PRO in certain sorts of sentence has definite reference despite the lack of an antecedent. Consider the examples in [59].

[59i] *Pinching the boss's bottom had been a damn fool thing to do.*

[59ii] *It had been uncertain which would be the best bottom to pinch.*

If one of these was the first sentence of a novel, we would naturally be eagerly awaiting the moment when the identity of the intrepid bottom-pincher would be revealed. Evidently the generic interpretation of PRO in a sentence such as *reading linguistics curdles the brain* follows from its generic temporal/aspectual properties, just as the definite interpretation of PRO in the sentences in [59] is determined by the 'unique occasion' implication of the pluperfect in the main clause in each case. If we conclude that PRO *can* refer independently to specific extra-sentential referents, we must also conclude that it is in this respect exactly like overt pronominals. The basis for assigning it simultaneously to the categories (bound) anaphor and pronominal would then be undermined and the GB-theory explanation for the distribution of PRO would no longer look so convincing. On the other hand, the LFG approach would now be justified in treating 'PRO' as a morphologically unexpressed anaphor. (Recall that in LFG an anaphor is defined as a grammatical element that may be assigned an antecedent by the rules of sentence grammar; in other words 'PRO' is simply a pronoun that lacks its own feature matrix.)

It should, however, be recalled that not all instances of PRO translate as instances of 'PRO'; the controlled subject of an equi clause is PRO in GB theory, but is dealt with as a case of functional control in LFG and no functional anaphor is involved. Yet it is precisely *these* instances of PRO that most clearly exhibit the (bound) anaphoric properties that motivate the GB analysis. Elsewhere, as the subject of a gerund or of an infinitive that could in principle take a *for* complementiser, PRO does indeed look much more like an ordinary pronoun, as evidenced by the possibility of an overt pronominal subject instead of PRO in most such cases. This substitution is possible, for example, in both sentences of [59]. What this means, of course, is that the attack on the characterisation of PRO mounted above does not in fact deal with the central cases, though GB theory has to recognise that PRO in [59] is not quite the same thing as PRO in *he tried to kick the habit*. This problem is considered further in 5.2, where the two theories are compared in more general terms.

A further issue here is whether raising and equi phenomena should be unified as cases of functional control, as in LFG, or treated as distinct phenomena, as in GB theory. The evaluation of this issue is in many ways analogous to that of the treatment of 'subject-to-object raising' constructions given above; the representational frameworks of the two theories follow from different underlying general assumptions, are highly theory-bound, and so are not easily compared for descriptive or explanatory efficiency on the basis of the available empirical evidence. It is, of course, usual for proponents of one particular theory to attack rival approaches as if this were not so, and to assert that adoption of their analysis conveys great advantages that no other theory can match. In reality, some theories do some things better than others, but very often the range of data that falls within the scope of one theory is not strictly comparable to that dealt with by another and comparison with a view to choosing the 'best' theory overall is anything but a straightforward matter. Claims to the contrary are almost always based on methodological commitment and theoretical prejudice rather than compelling empirical evidence. Nevertheless, an attempt is made in 5.2 below to assess the evidence that can be brought forward in support of the different generalisations embodied in the theories discussed in this book. For the present we must complete the characterisation of LFG by dealing with the treatment of unbounded dependencies.

4.8 Unbounded dependencies

Constructions involving unbounded dependencies, such as *wh*-questions and relative clauses, constitute the one class of constructions in which LFG permits the use of null constituent structure. In other words, in a sentence such as [60],

[60] *What did everyone believe the Chancellor would do next?*

there is assumed to be a null NP in C-structure following *do*, as represented in [61].

[61]

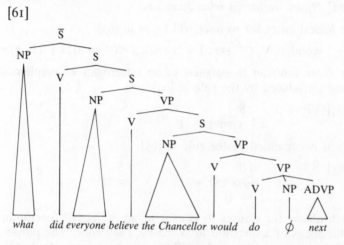

In sentences such as [60] it is obvious that the clause-initial *wh*-phrase must be assigned the clause-internal function (here direct object) that would normally be assigned to a constituent in the position of the gap. This type of dependency is frequently referred to in the LFG literature as **syntactic binding** or **constituent control**. Syntactic binding establishes a syntactic identity between elements that would otherwise be distinct, and in this respect is like functional control. But unlike functional control, which establishes a linkage between entities that fill particular functional roles in adjacent clauses, syntactic binding establishes a linkage on the basis of constituent structure configurations (clearly the initial *wh*-phrase can fulfil a variety of grammatical functions and the relationship is not restricted to any particular one) and does so across indefinitely large stretches of intervening material.

It should be noted that the restrictions on such dependencies (discussed in Chapter 2 under such headings as the Complex

Noun Phrase Constraint, the Sentential Subject Constraint, Subjacency, etc. – *cf* 2.2.4 and 2.3.7) have nothing to do with the functional properties of the predicates that occur in the intervening clauses and everything to do with the particular configurations of nodes that occur on the C-structure path between controller (the *wh*-phrase) and controllee (the gap). The mechanism employed in LFG to deal with unbounded dependencies is a variant of the $\uparrow = \downarrow$ notation familiar from earlier discussion. Consider the sentence in [62].

[62] *Noam wondered what Joan said.*

The lexical entry for *wonder* will be as in [63].

[63] wonder: V, $(\uparrow$ PRED$) = $ 'WONDER $<(\uparrow$ SUBJ$)$ $(\uparrow$ COMP$)>$'

The COMP function is assigned to an interrogative complement clause introduced by the rule in [64].

[64] VP $\rightarrow$ V $\quad \bar{\text{S}}$
$\qquad\qquad\quad (\uparrow$ COMP$) = \downarrow$

$\bar{\text{S}}$ itself is expanded by the rule in [65],

[65] $\bar{\text{S}} \rightarrow \qquad$ NP $\qquad\qquad\qquad$ S
$\qquad\quad (\uparrow$ Q-FOCUS$) = \downarrow \qquad \uparrow = \downarrow$
$\qquad\qquad \downarrow = \Downarrow$

which allows for clauses to consist of an initial NP functioning as the focus of a question followed by a sentence. The purpose of the second equation under NP ($\downarrow = \Downarrow$) is to indicate that the NP is the controller of a gap in the following S. It may be read informally as 'my functional structure is assigned as the functional structure of something below'. The double-shafted arrow differs from the single-shafted arrow in the following way. An equation $\uparrow = \downarrow$ states a relationship of equivalence between the functional structures of two constituents that stand in a relationship of immediate dominance. The one must be the daughter of the other. An equation $\downarrow = \Downarrow$ states a relationship of equivalence between the functional structures of two constituents that may be indefinitely far apart. The first is the constituent to which the equation is attached and the second is identified by a corresponding equation $\uparrow = \Uparrow$, to be read 'my functional structure is specified as the functional structure of something above'. In the case of [62] we must associate this equation with an empty NP, as in [66].

[66] NP $\rightarrow \qquad$ e
$\qquad\qquad \uparrow = \Uparrow$

The equation thus identifies the gap as the controllee in a relationship of syntactic binding.

The annotated C-structure for the subordinate clause of the sentence in [62] can now be given as in [67].

[67]

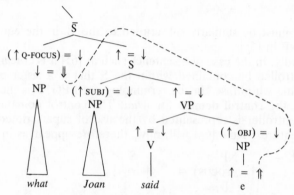

The corresponding F-structure is given in [68], this time for the whole sentence.

[68]
$$
\begin{bmatrix}
\text{SUBJ} & [\text{PRED} \quad \text{'NOAM'}] \\
\text{TENSE} & \text{PAST} \\
\text{PRED} & \text{'WONDER} < (\uparrow \text{SUBJ}) (\uparrow \text{COMP})>' \\
\text{COMP} & \begin{bmatrix}
\text{Q-FOCUS} & [\text{PRED} \quad \text{'WHAT'}] \\
\text{SUBJ} & [\text{PRED 'JOAN'}] \\
\text{TENSE} & \text{PAST} \\
\text{PRED} & \text{'SAY} <(\uparrow \text{SUBJ}) (\uparrow \text{OBJ})>' \\
\text{OBJ} &
\end{bmatrix}
\end{bmatrix}
$$

The dotted line indicates that the semantic form 'WHAT' serves as the PRED in the OBJ F-structure for *said*. The line in other words indicates a relationship of constituent control, the F-structure of the constituent associated with the 'down' equation ($\downarrow = \Downarrow$) being identified with that of the constituent associated with the 'up' equation ($\uparrow = \Uparrow$), on the understanding that every $\Downarrow$ has a 'corresponding' $\Uparrow$.

This notion of correspondence must, of course, be made precise. Obviously there must be categorial correspondence between the constituents involved in the control relationship. An ADJP cannot, for example, control an NP gap, as [69] makes clear.

[69] *How silly did you say the president gave a lecture to?*

We may, therefore, adopt the convention that all $\Downarrow$ and $\Uparrow$ are associated with categorial features and that controllers and controllees must have matching features. The rule in [66] will now appear as in [70],

$$[70] \quad NP \rightarrow \quad e$$
$$\uparrow = \Uparrow_{NP}$$

and NP must be similarly subscripted to the $\Downarrow$ in the equation below NP in [65].

Secondly, in the case of a sentence such as [62] it is crucial that the controllee be contained within the S that is a sister of the controlling wh-phrase. In the terminology of LFG, S is the root node of the **control domain** for *what*. The control domain of a given controller is represented by the use of superscripted category features. Rule [65] will, now, therefore appear as in [71].

$$[71] \quad \bar{S} \rightarrow \quad NP \qquad\qquad S$$
$$(\uparrow \text{ Q-FOCUS}) = \downarrow \quad \uparrow = \downarrow$$
$$\downarrow = \Downarrow_{NP}^{S}$$

The feature S on $\Downarrow$ indicates the control domain of the *wh*-phrase and NP indicates the category of the *wh*-phrase and associated gap.

It is not the case, however, that every example of a constituent of the specified category within a given control domain is a potential controllee. Obviously the familiar 'island constraints' must be accounted for, (*cf* 2.2.4). The solution in LFG is to specify a set of **bounding nodes** and to exclude potential controllees from the control domain of some controller by stipulating that there must be no bounding nodes on the C-structure path from the potential controllee up to, but not including, the root node of the control domain. As an example, we could enforce the *wh*-island condition, violated in [72],

[72] *What did you wonder who approved of?*

by making the S node introduced by the rule in [71] a bounding node. This is indicated by enclosing the node within a box, as in [73].

$$[73] \quad \bar{S} \rightarrow \quad NP \qquad\qquad \boxed{S}$$
$$(\uparrow \text{ Q-FOCUS}) = \downarrow \quad \uparrow = \downarrow$$
$$\downarrow = \Downarrow_{NP}^{S}$$

The C-structure for the sentence in [72] is given in [74].

[74]

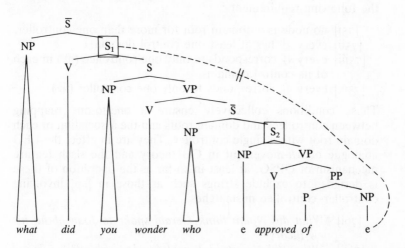

It will be seen that the C-structure path from the root node of *what*'s control domain, S_1, to the gap in PP is 'blocked' by the intervening bounding node S_2. Notice that the root node of a control domain does not itself constitute a barrier to control by its own controller. Thus S_2 does not block control of the gap in subject position by *who*, because the path between the empty constituent *e* and the root of *who*'s control domain S_2 is defined so as not to include the initial element. Thus *did you wonder who approved of this?* is fully grammatical.

Obviously, if bounding nodes are specified rule-by-rule, as in [73], the framework lays itself open to the charge of failing to express relevant generalisations and stipulating conditions in an *ad hoc* manner. It is to be hoped that, as a reasonable sample of phenomena from the world's languages becomes familiar, some general theory of bounding nodes will be advanced which at least specifies what the possible bounding nodes are and what the general principles are, if any, which determine particular choices in particular circumstances from this set in the grammars of individual langauges. In the meantime, one possible advantage of the rule-by-rule approach is that it allows for a given node to be a bounding node in one construction type without requiring it to be a bounding node universally in the grammar.

When the various categorial and phrase-structural conditions which have been mentioned are met, we must finally see to it that all controllers have corresponding controllees and all controllees

have corresponding controllers. This may be achieved by making
the following requirements:

[75i]   no node is a domain root for more than one controller.
[75ii] every ⇓ has at least one control domain.
[75iii] every ⇓ corresponds to only one controllee (⇑) in each
        of its control domains.
[75iv] every ⇑ corresponds to only one controller (⇓).

These conditions collectively ensure a one-to-one mapping
between controllees and domain roots and the association of each
domain root with a single controller. They are in effect the LFG
analogue of *wh*-movement in GB theory and the slash feature
mechanism of GPSG, at least in so far as the operation of these
is designed to exclude strings such as those in [76] involving
controller–controllee mismatches.

[76i]   *What did Noam think Gerald spoke to Joan about his
        new theory?*
[76ii] *What did Noam think spoke to Joan about?*

It will be recalled that the combination of functional information
originating in the lexicon with the functional information coming
from C-structure rules constitutes a functional description from
which a functional structure is computed. For F-structures to be
complete and coherent the F-descriptions they are derived from
must themselves be well-formed, consistent and determinate. The
conditions in [75] may be thought of as contributing to the well-
formedness of F-descriptions by ensuring that each controller has
an appropriate gap to control in its control domain (or domains
in the case, say, of co-ordinate structures) and that each
controllee has its own proper controller.

Finally, before leaving the subject of unbounded dependencies,
it is perhaps worth pointing out that in the most recent work in
LFG the possibility has been investigated that such 'long-
distance' relationships should be analysed as involving chains of
grammatical functions such that the initial thematically relevant
grammatical function assigned to the empty NP is linked by a
functional control equation, via a series of functions, one for
each clause on the path between the gap and its controller, to
the non-thematic grammatical function assigned to the 'displaced'
constituent (*eg* OBJ in COMP . . . . . . in COMP = FOCUS). This
proposal, discussed again in the final chapter, has the effect of
bringing the LFG analysis into line with the GB theory position
that there are no *genuinely* unbounded dependencies, and of
assimilating the treatment of these constructions more closely to
the 'functional' analysis of other phenomena.

4.9 LFG and language processing

The primary motivation behind some of the earliest work on the potential of lexical rules (*eg* Bresnan 1978), work which was eventually to evolve into the theory of Lexical-Functional Grammar, was the desire to develop a linguistically well-motivated theory of generative grammar which could be embedded in an overall theory of performance to provide the basis for an account of language production and language processing. Despite the hopes of theoretical linguists and the efforts of psycholinguists, it was becoming increasingly clear by the early 1970s that there were real difficulties facing those who sought to incorporate transformational grammars (as conceived at that time) into psychologically realistic models of language use.

The chief of these was the fact that there was little or no psychological evidence to support the 'derivational theory of complexity'. It will be recalled that standard-theory transformational grammars employed large numbers of construction-specific transformations (*cf* 2.2.1) and that, as a consequence, the surface structures of many sentences were viewed as the product of a complex series of rule applications, each rule providing an output that served as input to the next. If grammars of this type are interpreted as models of the knowledge-store employed by speakers in processing utterances, and if we suppose that one aspect of such processing is the determination of predicate–argument structure, it follows that speakers should find it more difficult to understand utterances of sentences with a long and complex transformational derivation than utterances of sentences with minimal transformational modification, because in the case of the former the deep structure (*ie* the phrase-structural representation of predicate–argument structure) is much more remote from the immediately accessible surface structure of the stimulus than in the case of the latter. Consider, for example, the sentences in [77].

[77i] *John seems to have been given first prize.*
[77ii] *It seems that someone has given first prize to John.*

The underlying structure for both sentences in standard-theory notation would be as in [78] overleaf. The derivation of [77ii] is a straightforward matter of the application of the transformation of extraposition, repositioning the sentential subject to the right of the main verb and substituting the dummy subject pronoun *it*. Example [77i], by contrast, would require first the application of dative shift in the embedded clause (*someone has given John first prize*), followed by passive (*John has been given first prize*

[78]

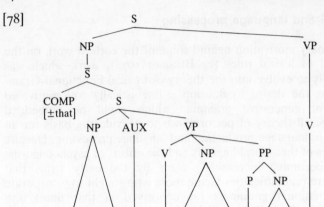

by someone) and unspecified prepositional phrase deletion (*John has been given first prize*), and secondly the application of subject-to-subject raising in the main clause to take *John* up into his surface structure position and to reposition the residue of the sentential subject to the right of VP. Initially, some support was found for the view that decoding sentences such as [77i] was a more difficult task than decoding sentences such as [77ii], but as time went on the vast majority of psychologists came to the view that the derivational theory of complexity was simply false, (*cf* for example, Fodor, Bever and Garrett, 1974). And it must be said that, intuitively, the information-content of [77i] is not perceptibly harder to access than that of [77ii].

Bresnan's early work was motivated by a desire to eliminate the complexity predictions that followed from standard-theory transformational accounts by reanalysing as lexical redundancy rules all the bounded transformations that preserved basic phrase structure but changed grammatical functions. The major consequence of this reanalysis was that all the possible correspondences between an argument and a set of grammatical functions were expressed in the lexicon by finite sets of lexical entries. A verb like *give*, for example, would appear with active, dative, passive and dative-passive entries, thanks to the operation of the dative and passive redundancy rules on the active entry and of the passive rule on the dative entry. Because the output of such redundancy rules could be viewed as part of the stored knowledge of the speaker, he was no longer required to perform dative, passive or raising *computations* in decoding the utterance of a sentence such as [77i]. Instead he was assumed simply to 'look up' the function–argument correspondences for any uses of *seem* and *give* and to combine the products. In the case of [77i], therefore, it is predicted that there should be no perceptibly greater difficulty in accessing the message than is encountered in processing any sentential paraphrase involving the verbs *seem* and *give*.

This approach of Bresnan's may be seen as a response to those psycholinguists who have argued that the failure to incorporate transformational grammars in models of language acquisition, comprehension or production reveals the fundamental inadequacy of the hypothesis, advocated by Chomsky, that characterisations of formal grammar shed light on native speakers' mental representations of linguistic knowledge. Bresnan's view is that the competence hypothesis is desirable in principle because it provides the basis for the development of a unified theory of verbal behaviour. If it is rejected, we move in the direction of a much weaker hypothesis, namely that different bodies of knowledge may be required for different aspects of verbal behaviour. Some philosophers in fact take the view that speaking and understanding are skills which do not rely on structured knowledge-stores at all, but for those who accept the need for some sort of underlying body of knowledge it is surely preferable to investigate the possibility that the same knowledge-store is involved in all forms of language use before retreating to any such weaker position. Obviously if this is to be done successfully, a theory of grammatical representation has to be devised which allows for a fruitful interaction with work in neighbouring disciplines. According to Bresnan, then, a grammar may be regarded as 'psychologically real' if it not only meets the usual linguistically-motivated criteria of adequacy but also provides a basis for explaining a much wider range of data including such things as the performance of verbal tasks in controlled conditions and observations of the linguistic development of children. Since the competence hypothesis requires evidence that linguists' grammars correspond to speakers' internal representations of grammatical knowledge, and since these are not directly observable, it is felt that all potential sources of evidence should be carefully considered, and that the restriction of the data of linguistic theories to the domain of introspective judgements, as advocated by Chomsky, is unwarranted. In particular, it is argued that the formal representations of linguistic theory, the information-processing models of computer science and the experimental techniques of psycholinguistics can be usefully combined to provide a much broader-based set of criteria of adequacy for grammars that purport to characterise the grammatical knowledge that underlies performance. Since LFG is a linguistically well-motivated theory which does not conflict in its representational assumptions with the results of experimental work in psycholinguistics, in particular does not presuppose anything like the derivational theory of complexity, it is regarded by its proponents as a powerful defence of the competence hypothesis.

Further support for lexical-functional grammars can be derived from the results of mathematical investigation of their properties. Although in the early days of the development of generative grammar Chomsky himself was concerned with issues of mathematical linguistics, in particular with the question of where natural languages stand in the hierarchy of mathematically-defined languages, he has recently denied that such investigations have any serious implications for theoretical linguistics, choosing instead to emphasise the need for empirically motivated restrictions on the class of possible natural-language grammars in order to reduce the cardinal value of this set to a minimum and thereby account for the success of language acquisition in children. There has, nevertheless, been a great deal of work done in recent years by computer scientists working in artificial intelligence on the mathematical properties of different types of grammar. Much of this work has proved to be of great value to those trying to devise parsing programs for natural languages. It is to the credit of those working in both GPSG and LFG that the significance of this work for theoretical linguistics has been emphasised. At the end of Chapter 3 it was noted that generalised phrase structure grammars provide an excellent basis for explaining the parsing abilities of speaker-hearers in so far as they have the weak generative capacity of context-free phrase structure grammars. Context-free phrase structure grammars generate context-free languages, the sentences of which are parsable, in the worst case, in a time that is proportional to the cube of sentence-length. Given the various empirically motivated constraints on the form and functioning of generalised phrase structure grammars, it is to be expected that much better results than this can in fact be achieved in practice. The formal precision of the framework is, of course, an important factor in the testing of its capacities as a model for natural-language parsing.

Lexical-functional grammars of the type proposed are in fact rather more powerful than generalised phrase structure grammars in that the formal machinery of the theory can be employed to characterise at least some of the non-context-free context-sensitive languages. The context-free languages are a proper subset of the context-sensitive languages, so the claim is being made that natural languages may exhibit phenomena that require descriptive apparatus of greater power than that made available within the theory of context-free phrase structure grammar. Perhaps the most persuasive argument in favour of this position has to do with the so-called 'cross-serial' dependencies of Dutch, illustrated schematically in [79]. (See the discussion of example [7] in 5.1 for a detailed account.)

[79]

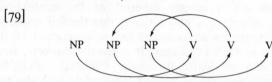

eg X *see* Y *help* Z *walk* ⇒ X Y Z *see help walk*

It has been argued that although sentences exhibiting this type of dependency may in principle be generated by some context-free phrase structure grammar there is no such grammar that will assign the correct type of structural description to those sentences (see Bresnan, Kaplan, Peters and Zaenen 1982). Consequently, while natural languages may be weakly context-free, they are apparently not strongly context-free, and given that cross-serial dependencies of the type illustrated in [79] can in fact be handled neatly by a lexical-functional grammar, we may infer that the additional descriptive power which the theory embodies has *prima facie* justification. It will be recalled that even within the GPSG camp it is acknowledged that there are phenomena which may well require the elaboration of the theory to include descriptive apparatus with greater than context-free power (*cf* 3.8). An important example would be the case of multiple 'long-distance' dependencies into a single constituent in the Scandinavian languages, an illustration of which is given in [80].

[80] *Dette   er   de diktene   som laererin*
    these   are   the poems   that the-teacher

    spurte   oss hvem vi   trodde   hadde skrivet
    asked   us who we thought   had   written

Evidently in this Norwegian sentence there is a double dependency into the most deeply embedded sentence. Assuming that there is no *grammatically* motivated finite bound on the number of such dependencies (*ie* assuming that, given an indefinitely large number of clauses embedded one within another, any number of *wh*-expressions might be 'displaced' from their argument positions), it follows at once that the grammars required to generate such sentences cannot be equivalent in strong generative capacity to context-free phrase structure grammars because the vocabulary they employ is no longer finite (a defining characteristic for context-free grammars). Such grammars are in fact equivalent to indexed grammars; these generate the indexed languages which are a proper superset of the context-free languages. It is, of course, highly unlikely that the full resources of the indexed grammars are required for the description of the properties of the world's languages. It is equally unlikely, from the point of view of lexical-functional grammars, that full context-sensitive power will be needed. Thus while both theories incorporate descriptive apparatus that increases the strong generative capacity of the grammars they licence beyond that of context free phrase structure grammars, it remains possible that the languages those grammars generate are wholly or very largely (weakly) context-free and that the parsability results for context-free languages continue to hold. Obviously a fruitful line of research in both theoretical frameworks will be the precise determination of the extent to which more powerful descriptive apparatus is in fact needed to provide well-motivated structural descriptions for sentence types that resist insightful context-free analysis.

But suppose it turns out, contrary to what might be hoped, that natural languages not only require grammars with non-context-free descriptive apparatus but are themselves (at least in part) non-context-free in the sense that no context free grammar could even generate the strings involved. The parsability results for context-free languages would no longer hold, and the problem of recognising languages with, for example, context sensitivities can be computationally much more complex than the recognition problem for context-free languages. In the worst case, *ie* if full context-sensitive power is exploited, there are no solutions for the recognition problem that require less than exponential resources. But given that any linguistically motivated theory will impose severe constraints on the class of mathematically defined grammars which it permits as grammars of natural languages, it is to be hoped that the worst case computational complexity for the subset of generalised phrase structure grammars or lexical-functional grammars that conform to these empirical constraints will prove to be subexponential. In other words, the retreat from absolute context-freeness need not necessarily lead to the loss of all the advantages that would have followed if natural languages had turned out to be (at least weakly) context-free *in toto*; interesting results may well hold for more powerful grammars, provided the extra power is limited in linguistically relevant ways.

It is instructive at this point to contrast Chomsky's reaction to the failure of the standard theory as a model of the knowledge-store used in language processing with that of Bresnan, which has just been outlined. It is true that many of the objections to the standard theory, in particular the lack of supportive evidence for the derivational theory of complexity, have become increasingly less cogent because of the radical simplification of the transformational component in more recent work and the incorporation of crucial aspects of derivational history in surface syntactic structure through the trace mechanism. And in any case, the abandonment of the derivational theory of complexity, and much of the motivation for adopting a different kind of formalism, such as LFG, was based on a tacit, and quite possibly counterfactual, assumption that the human parser cannot process in parallel (*cf* Berwick and Weinberg (1982, 1984)). Nevertheless, Chomsky himself has persisted in adopting an essentially 'isolationist' position. His view is that grammars are psychologically real if they contribute to the explanation of the linguistic judgements that he takes to be the subject-matter of the discipline, and that the conception of what is real in this domain can be progressively refined, in exactly the same way as conceptions of physical reality have been refined by physicists, by further research aimed at devising an explanatory (*ie* highly restrictive) theory of grammar from which most of the properties of the grammars of individual languages will follow automatically. As we have seen, such a theory would provide an answer to the logical problem of language acquisition in children; instead of having to work out on the basis of fragmentary evidence which of a potentially vast number of logically possible grammars might be the best grammar for the language he is learning, the child equipped with knowledge of universal grammar (as modelled by the linguist's theory of universal grammar) will in fact have very little working out to do. Such a theory would also explain how the native speakers of a language come to share a common system of grammatical knowledge despite widely differing linguistic backgrounds and experiences.

In pursuit of this programme of research, Chomsky has consistently idealised away from what he takes to be performance factors. In other words the behaviour of native speakers in performing various production and processing tasks is assumed to be determined by the interaction of their knowledge of grammar with a variety of other knowledge-systems and devices, and as a result there is no reason to suppose that observation of this behaviour will give the linguist any insight into the nature of the grammatical system which is his primary concern. So while Bresnan is willing to assume that competence is shaped in part by the fact that it is embedded in a network of processing devices with which it must be fully compatible, Chomsky continues to characterise competence in isolation from these. The essential justification for this position is its fruitfulness as a research strategy. By concentrating on the description of the abstract structure of the native speaker's linguistic knowledge the theory of transformational grammar has advanced from being, in its earliest form, little more than an explicit formalisation of some of the central insights of traditional grammar, to become a genuinely explanatory theory (albeit still in a rather rudimentary form) incorporating abstract principles of considerable power. This theory is now structured in such a way that changes made to the composition of one of its subcomponents have repercussions elsewhere, a highly desirable property that enhances the testability of the framework by making complex sets of interrelated predictions about the way grammars work. Obviously it is much easier to falsify an interconnected *set* of claims than it is of falsify an isolated hypothesis; the available data may not be sufficient to decide an individual case, but if there are extensive repercussions elsewhere that follow from adopting this or that position, then false assumptions should be easier to locate and eradicate. Such a theory is also more explanatory from the point of view of language acquisition, since it implies that there are almost certainly 'natural' combinations of parametric settings across the various subtheories of universal grammar. The task of language acquisition is clearly simplified if there are such implicational universals, and it will be a major task of future research to try to determine in detail what these are. The results of such work would then form the basis of an account of many of the facts that form the core subject-matter of linguistic typology.

It is surely not unreasonable to argue that these results and the interesting research possibilities which have been opened up constitute a powerful defence of the Chomskyan position. It is certainly true that a great many of the more interesting and influential theoretical innovations and insights of the last fifteen years have come out of work in transformational grammar. Though this is not to deny that other frameworks have contributed important ideas, it nevertheless remains true that Chomsky has continually been in the forefront of research, setting and revising the agenda of issues of current controversy, while those working in other frameworks have often been put in the position of trying to show that anything he can do they can do better. It is in the end perhaps best to regard the theories which have been discussed in this book as complementing each other, despite the often polemical rhetoric employed by their practitioners. As new ideas are advanced, and rival theorists assess these in the context of their own frameworks, the result is a productive and stimulating debate which serves to highlight the strengths and weaknesses of the different sets of descriptive and theoretical apparatus and to focus the attention of theorists of all persuasions on a range of central issues, thereby paving the way for an embryonic consensus. This will be taken up again in 5.3.

It is, of course, largely thanks to GPSG and LFG that this debate is now being conducted, at least in some circles, in a way that allows for an interchange of ideas between theoretical linguists on the one hand and psycholinguists and computer scientists on the other, and practitioners of GB theory are now beginning to address some of the issues which have been raised in a serious way. A particularly important example of this is the work of Berwick and Weinberg referred to earlier. In response to the alleged advantages of adopting a framework of grammatical description that is demonstrably equivalent to a type of grammar which is 'low' on the hierarchy of mathematically defined systems, such as context-free phrase structure grammar, they have argued that the direct use of computational complexity results without attempting to place these in a realistic biological context is of little value since the determination of relative *cognitive* complexity requires the incorporation of a variety of implementation factors, such as the range of inputs that are likely to be encountered, the size and manner of internal representation of the grammar and the organisation of the parsing device that makes use of the grammar, which the theory of mathematical complexity regularly abstracts away from. According to Berwick and Weinberg, it is the *size* of the grammar which is most significant once these additional factors are taken into account rather than its mathematical type. In other words, a language quite 'high up' in the mathematically-defined hierarchy (for example, a strictly context-sensitive language) may in fact be parsed more rapidly than languages 'lower down' in the hierarchy provided that the exercise is confined to sentences of a length that are likely actually to occur and there is a sufficient gain in the succinctness of the formulation of the (context-sensitive) grammar to offset any possible increase in parsing time that would other-wise have occurred. In general, the same grammar, of whatever type, can be incorporated into parsing devices with vastly different time complexities according as the details of the various implementation factors mentioned above are adjusted. So while they have no objection in principle to wider aspects of perform-ance being used as evidence for constraining the class of possible grammars, they conclude that parsing efficiency as typically defined in a mathematical sense may not be much of a criterion of adequacy. When the factors influencing the implementation of a parsing device are taken into account, and if one confines one's attention to sentences of 'realistic' length, it may be that almost any language is efficiently parsable. From this point of view proof that the apparatus one employs generates context-free languages and claims that natural languages are substantially (at least weakly) context-free are of little interest since they do not advance linguistic theory towards the goal of constraining the class of possible grammars. Berwick and Weinberg therefore endorse the Chomskyan strategy of seeking empirically rather than mathematically motivated criteria of adequacy for possible grammars, and argue that the sort of grammars advocated by GB theorists are perfectly compatible with the need for efficient parsing. Such a line of argumentation would, of course, be interpret-ed by proponents of GPSG and LFG as one more example of GB theorists seeking to insulate themselves from the results of work in neighbouring disciplines. For them it is simply perverse to choose to adopt a framework of description whose mathematical properties are completely unknown when many of the insights and observations of GB theory can be 'translated' into equivalent formulations in frameworks employing apparatus of known generative power which permit serious interdisciplinary interac-tion. If it is possible to impose a set of empirically motivated constraints on the class of generalised phrase structure grammars or the class of lexical-functional grammars similar in effect to those imposed on the grammars sanctioned by GB theory it is possible to have the best of both worlds. The extent to which insights developed in one theory are translatable into another is, not surprisingly, a controversial matter, and in many cases no serious attempt has been made to do this for reasons of practi-cality or theoretical commitment. But in general it is reasonable to suppose there is a high level of *potential* intertranslatability between the three theories which have been discussed in this book, always allowing for the fact that one theory may handle one domain of fact in a more efficient way than another and that the scope of one theory may not be exactly parallel to that of another. Indeed, if GPSG and LFG are of independent linguistic interest it is precisely because they offer analyses of a wider, or at least different, range of facts from GB theory, or account for a familiar range of facts in a novel way that confers some advantage. But in so far as none of these theories is demonstrably superior in all respects to the others, it follows that one's choice of theoretical commitment will be determined in large measure by the range of one's personal interests. In particular, a great deal will depend on the extent to which one believes that linguistics ought to be trying to make its results available in a form which other disciplines can exploit or whether one feels that linguistics should function as an autonomous discipline adopting a range of subject-matter and criteria of relevance which are motivated entirely by 'internal' considerations. In this, as in many other respects, Chomsky's position is more 'traditional' than that of the interdisciplinarians.

We are now in a position to attempt to provide an overall evaluation of the theories which have been described in this and the preceding two chapters and to offer some general assessment of the direction of research in generative grammar. This will be the subject of the next, and final, chapter.

4.10 Relevant reading

The most important reference work for LFG is the collection of papers in Bresnan (1982), which introduces all aspects of the theory, presents a variety of implementations and discusses some of its implications for other disciplines. Levin, Rappaport and Zaenen (1983) is a slightly more recent collection of papers introducing some innovations and extensions. The theory has its origins in Bresnan (1978). See also Sells (1985: Ch. 4).

The papers in Hoekstra, van der Hulst and Moortgat (1980) examine the potential of lexical rules from a number of different points of view and the introduction to this book, a valuable survey of the development of 'lexicalism' beginning with Chomsky (1970), includes a discussion of the movement alternative. An interesting approach to lexical grammar, slightly different from Bresnan's, is developed in Brame (1976, 1978 and 1979).

The centrality of grammatical functions in LFG invites comparison with work in Relational Grammar (see, for example, Johnson (1979), Perlmutter (1980 and 1983). Chomsky's treatment of passivisation in Japanese (1981a; pp. 127–135) also highlights the importance of grammatical functions in the statement of syntactic processes, as the discussion above makes clear, but he refrains from drawing the conclusion that these are primitives of syntactic theory.

For a detailed discussion of the passive in lexical theory see Bresnan (1982: Ch. 1), which illustrates the role of lexical forms and lexical rules particularly clearly. Further discussion of the theory of lexical forms is provided in Bresnan (1982; Ch. 3). Causativisation in Malayalam, discussed briefly in 4.5, is dealt with in detail by Mohanan (1981).

On control see Bresnan (1982: Ch. 5). This chapter also includes a general introduction to LFG with sections on the role of grammatical functions, the lexical and syntactic encoding of grammatical functions and the syntactic representation of grammatical functions and constituent structure. Mohanan (1983) and Simpson and Bresnan (1983) elaborate the theory of control. The latter deals specifically with the advantages of LFG in the analysis of W* languages such as Warlpiri, discussed in detail in Hale (1979 and 1983). Further developments in the theory of anaphoric binding can be found in Kameyama (1984 and 1985).

The treatment of unbounded dependencies in 4.8 is taken from Kaplan and Bresnan (1982) (Chapter 4 of Bresnan (1982), which is the most complete and precise exposition of the formal system of grammatical representation assumed in LFG). The more recent developments alluded to at the end of this section are explained in Kaplan and Zaenen (1985).

Kaplan (1978) shows how the lexical theory can contribute to a computationally simpler model of language processing, and Pinker (1982) (Chapter 10 of Bresnan (1982)) argues that it provides the basis for a psychologically more realistic theory of language acquisition. That the class of grammars defined by the lexical theory can be successfully incorporated in realistic models of perception and production is demonstrated in Ford, Bresnan and Kaplan (1982) (Chapter 11 of Bresnan (1982)) and Ford (1982) (Chapter 12 of Bresnan (1982)) respectively. A discussion of the generative capacity of lexical-functional grammars is provided in Kaplan and Bresnan (1982) (Chapter 4 of Bresnan (1982)). Berwick and Weinberg (1982 and 1984), however, challenge the notion that transformational grammars are incompatible with efficient parsing by arguing that the human parser can process in parallel, thereby undermining the arguments for LFG based on the lack of psychological evidence for the derivational theory of complexity (*cf* Fodor, Bever and Garrett (1974)).

Chapter 5

The theories compared

5.1 Preliminary remarks

To refresh the reader's memory, I begin this chapter with a review of the theories discussed in Chapters 2 to 4, and add some general observations about their strengths and weaknesses.

The essentials of GB theory are given in [1].

[1]

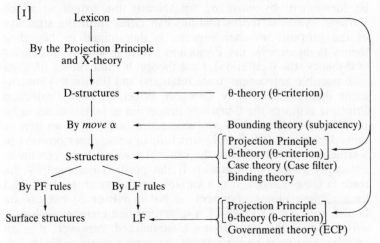

N.B. Both the assignment of Case and the operation of the binding theory at
  S-structure require reference to notions of government

The lexicon defines the subcategory of the word-class that a given item belongs to by reference to the phrasal categories that co-occur with it. Each of these categories is assigned a thematic role so that, in effect, predicate arguments are identified with syntactic categories. D-structure is simply a projection of the θ-marking properties of lexical heads, supplemented by the requirement that sentences must have subjects whether this position is θ-marked or not. Grammatical functions such as subject or direct object are, for a language such as English, configurationally defined, and the configurations in which the categories mentioned in a lexical entry may occur at D-structure are determined by the principles of $\overline{X}$-theory once its parameters have been set. D-structure is therefore a representation of predicate–argument structure in which each argument is identified with a syntactic category whose grammatical function is determined by the configuration of elements in which it occurs. Thus no NP, for example, can occur in a non-argument ($\overline{\theta}$) position, and the only position which can be left empty is the subject position, since all sentences must have subjects whether this is θ-marked or not.

The relationship between the pure projection of predicate–argument structure (D-structure) and the more superficial level of syntactic representation known as S-structure is determined by the operation of the transformational rule-schema *move* α. The extent to which predicate–argument structure can be 'deformed' by *move* α, equivalently the extent to which 'surface' syntactic representations can differ from the structure of the propositions they express, is determined by bounding theory (subjacency), the Projection Principle and the principles of θ-theory (the θ-criterion), Case theory, binding theory (dealing with possible antecedent–trace relations) and (indirectly) government theory (the Empty Category Principle). The Projection Principle requires the θ-marking properties of lexical items to be projected to all levels of syntactic representation. If an item is moved from a position in D-structure to some other position in S-structure, it follows that the original position must remain as an empty category (or trace). If the position occupied by the trace is Case-marked, it is a variable, and it must not be bound by a c-commanding argument (*ie* NP in NP or S) but can be bound only from COMP by a quantifier-like element such as a *wh*-phrase; if the trace is not Case-marked, however, it is an anaphor and must be bound in its governing category (*ie* by a c-commanding argument within the minimal NP or S that contains the item that governs it.) The ECP stipulates that all traces must be properly governed (*ie* by a lexical head or a co-indexed phrase in COMP). The relationship between a trace and the phrase which binds it must meet the requirements of the subjacency condition, and the items which bind traces must be in $\overline{\theta}$-

positions to avoid violation of the θ-criterion (*ie* COMP or a non-argument subject position). Virtually all the properties of 'permissible' transformations follow from these conditions, and the rule itself can be stated in its minimal form.

Transformations in this framework no longer perform their original function, in conjunction with D-structures, of allowing a once-and-for-all statement of subcategorisation possibilities for lexical items, since the inclusion of traces at S-structure, as required by the Projection Principle, allows for the possibility of lexical insertion at that level in conformity with the categorial co-occurrence requirements listed in the lexicon. Transformations and D-structures might, then, actually be dispensed with, and a new type of interpretation rule could be established to operate on S-structures to ensure that any restrictions on binder–trace relations previously guaranteed by the transformational model, specifically the subjacency requirement, were met. The main reason for retaining the time-honoured machinery is that it represents what is taken to be a significant generalisation, namely that there is a set of surface syntactic constructions in which some item appears in a position other than that in which it 'logically' belongs from the point of view of predicate–argument structure, such that the 'logical' position is always subjacent to the 'surface' position, and that the rule schema *move* α, distinguished from all other rules associating one position with another by virtue of the subjacency condition, allows these various constructions to be described in a uniform way (abstracting away from differences that follow from the operation of other principles of universal grammar). I return to this below (5.2).

S-structures are input on the one hand to the rules of the P(honetic) F(orm) component, which derive surface structures (*ie* phonetically interpreted syntactic strings), and on the other to the rules of the L(ogical) F(orm) component. These latter derive a representation of LF from S-structure by making explicit such things as quantifier scope, interpreting *wh*-phrases as quantifier-like elements binding variables, and enforcing control relations between antecedents and the null element PRO. LF is a third level of syntactic representation, albeit a rather abstract one, and since it combines, via the trace mechanism, information about predicate–argument structure with a variety of other semantically relevant information of the sort just mentioned, it may be thought of as the input to whatever rules or mechanisms are involved in semantic interpretation.

Clearly some justification is needed for setting up three levels of syntactic representation for each sentence. The evidence that can be adduced essentially reduces to demonstrations that some explanatory principle of universal grammar must apply to representations with properties characteristic of one of the three levels postulated, or that the level in question has properties which constitute an essential part of the input to some other component of the grammar. To give just a few examples, arguments were presented above to show that the binding theory must apply at something like S-structure. Obviously, if its principles are to generalise to antecedent–trace relations, it cannot apply at D-structure, and certain crucial distinctions would be lost if it were to apply at LF (details are given in 2.3.6, examples [219] to 221]). Furthermore, both D-structures and LF representations are clearly too abstract to be input to the rules of the PF component. Similar arguments can be provided for LF. LF is motivated primarily by the need to have a level of representation at which such things as quantifier-scope is made explicit. Quite apart from the ordinary cases of quantifier movement, however, *move* α must apply both in the syntax and the LF component if the quantifier-like role of *wh*-expressions in both non-echo and echo questions is to be made clear. This means that the θ-criterion must be thought of primarily as a condition of adequacy for LF, checking antecedent–trace pairs for thematic coherence once all movement is complete, and whose requirements are projected to other levels of representation by the Projection Principle. Arguments were also given above to show that the ECP requires LF-type representations if it is to do its job properly (*cf* 2.3.9 [238] and [239]).

From this point of view, according to which levels of representation have to meet certain general conditions of adequacy, it is D-structures which are the hardest constructs to justify. To the extent that GB theory is a theory of the relationship between projections of predicate–argument structure and surface syntax, it is, of course, convenient to have a level of representation at which predicate–argument structure is made explicit. But in reality D-structure is no more than S-structure with the effects of *move* α abstracted away, and all the properties of D-structure are visible at S-structure in any case, thanks to the Projection Principle and the empty categories (traces) which it entails. To a very large extent the whole D-structure/transformations apparatus is a hangover from the early days of transformational grammar, the sole motivation for its retention being, as was pointed out earlier, the fact that it appears to capture a significant generalisation by pulling together an apparently diverse set of construction types. To the extent that transformations are structure-preserving (*ie* move items to positions already allowed for at D-structure), even the principles of X̄-theory can be thought of as defining permissible S-structure configurations rather than D-structure configurations.

In this connection, it is interesting to note that in very recent work in GB theory it has been argued that S is a maximal projection of INFL and S̄ a maximal projection of COMP, as illustrated in [2].

[2]

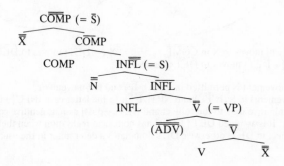

The arguments in favour of this are somewhat complex and theory-bound, but if they are accepted, it should be noted that *wh*-movement now displaces constituents to the X̄ slot in the specifier position in COMP. This in effect makes *wh*-movement a structure-preserving rule rather than an adjunction operation of the type illustrated in Chapter 2, and the notion that the principles of X̄-theory must define some set of basic or canonic structures distinct from S-structures is further undermined. It is perhaps also worth pointing out in passing that there is a growing body of evidence to suggest that what have traditionally been analysed as NPs are in fact better thought of as Determiner Phrases which have Determiners rather than Nouns as their heads, and which have an internal geometry analogous to that of sentences as analysed in [2]. The nature of the parallel is given in [3].

The arguments in favour of this reanalysis of NP are extremely complex and cannot be dealt with here. Suffice it to say that it solves a number of outstanding difficulties and confers a number of descriptive and theoretical advantages. Some references are

[3]

> the structure of ① corresponds to that of ③
> the structure of ② corresponds to that of ④

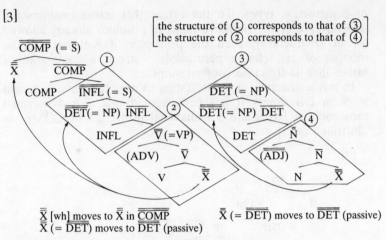

$\overline{\overline{X}}$ [wh] moves to $\overline{\overline{X}}$ in $\overline{\overline{\text{COMP}}}$ $\overline{X}$ (= $\overline{\overline{\text{DET}}}$) moves to $\overline{\overline{\text{DET}}}$ (passive)
$\overline{X}$ (= $\overline{\text{DET}}$) moves to $\overline{\overline{\text{DET}}}$ (passive)

Thus wh-movement is permitted in $\overline{S}$ ($\overline{\overline{\text{COMP}}}$) and NP-movement
($\overline{\overline{\text{DET}}}$-movement) in S ($\overline{\text{INFL}}$) and NP ($\overline{\text{DET}}$). In the latter case INFL [+tense]
assigns nominative case to the subject and DET [+poss] assigns genitive case to
the subject. It is assumed DET [+poss] has no lexical realisation when there is a
lexical subject in $\overline{\overline{\text{DET}}}$; otherwise DET dominates a determiner in the usual way.

given at the end of the chapter for those who would like to
pursue this matter further.

Turning now to GPSG, the essentials are given in [4].

[4]

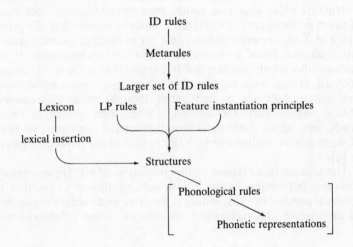

A basic set of Immediate Domination rules provides the canonic subcategorisation information for lexical heads. There are also ID rules which expand a category as a set of phrasal categories, such as that which specifies that S, however analysed, may dominate NP and VP, however analysed. The lexical ID rules are input to the set of metarules which in effect determine the range of subcategorisation possibilities for lexical heads by allowing items which appear in one context also to appear in another. The output of a metarule is a class of ID rules (or an ID rule-schema) which can be added to the basic class to form a larger set. Recall that in the lexicon subcategorisation is handled in a context-free way, by assigning a number to each subclass of lexical heads and associating the same number, either directly, for the basic ID rules, or indirectly via metarules, with all the ID rules that introduce sets of complements with which items of the subclass in question can co-occur. This may be thought of as the (partial) analogue of the Projection Principle, in the sense that duplication of subcategorisation information in both the lexicon and the rule-system is avoided. In GB theory structures are projections of lexical entries, in GPSG structures are projections of schematic ID rules which, if they are lexical ID rules, perform the role of subcategorisation features in GB theory. It should be noted, however, that the categories listed as complements to a lexical head are not necessarily semantic arguments of that head in GPSG, and that the Projection Principle is therefore rejected. So, for example, a verb such as *persuade* will be permitted to co-occur with a NP direct object and a VP (infinitive) complement, even though from the point of view of predicate–argument structure the predicate denoted by *persuade* takes an NP argument and a clausal argument ('persuade NP that NP should VP'). In many cases, of course, the head-type of a particular item, determined by the set of syntactic categories with which it co-occurs, will correspond exactly to its lexical-type, determined by the set of arguments that co-occur with the predicate it denotes, assuming some mechanism for associating semantic types with syntactic categories. But this is not necessarily the case as it would be in GB theory, where the correspondence holds not just at D-structure, but at all levels of syntactic representation thanks to the Projection Principle. The basis for handling the correspondences that do exist in GPSG, and the mechanism for handling cases where the correspondence does not hold, will be discussed below.

For the moment, it is important to point out that the basic properties of ID rules are essentially determined by the principles of $\bar{X}$-theory that are concerned with hierarchical, as opposed to linear, organisation, and that the operation of metarules, besides being inherently restricted by the bounded nature of the potential inputs (the set of ID rules), is further restricted by the Lexical Head Constraint, which allows only *lexical* ID rules as input. This has the effect of enforcing a rather strict version of the ECP; any item 'removed' by metarule will necessarily leave a properly governed gap because it will necessarily occur in the subcategorisation frame of some lexical head. The possibility of proper government by some category in COMP, allowed in GB theory, is excluded. This also entails the rejection of the Projection Principle, since in a sentence such as *who did you say came?* the empty subject position of the embedded clause must be governed not by a trace of *who* in the adjacent COMP but by *say*. In effect, then, *came* has to be analysed as a bare VP complement to *say*, an analysis which is clearly not consistent with the requirement that predicate–argument structure should be projected to all levels of syntactic representation, but which is supported by a number of syntactic considerations (*cf* 3.5).

In general, then, the approach to syntax is much more concrete than in GB theory. In particular, as pointed out in connection with *persuade* above, the subject gaps of equi and raising constructions have no syntactic representation as empty NPs, and what appears to be a VP complement is analysed accordingly (just as *came* was analysed in the 'subject-dependency' sentence above). This, of course, amounts to a claim that the rules of syntax can 'deform' predicate–argument structure to a greater extent than is supposed by advocates of GB theory, by permitting real syntactic gaps (not just empty categories) in what are interpreted as argument positions. But proponents of GPSG could in principle argue that the occurrence of syntactic gaps in certain 'logical' subject positions is a consequence of some general theory of semantic interpretation or syntactic organisation in much the same way as GB theorists do. The fact that they do not, and have so far simply stipulated in the rule system what the possibilities are, is to a very large extent a matter of style and choice of objectives rather than of any fundamental inadequacy. If one's goal is to develop a fully explicit theory of syntax and semantic interpretation that could serve as the basis for a computerised model of certain language-processing capabilities, there are clear advantages in adopting an essentially concrete descriptive model, always assuming, as has so far been the case, that semantic rules can be devised to interpret the syntactic structures postulated in satisfactory ways. This is particularly true if no claims to psychological reality are made, and purely formal considerations are allowed to predominate. Nevertheless, a theoretical defence of the GPSG position can be mounted, as we shall see in 5.2.

The larger set of ID rules that results from the application of the set of metarules together with the set of universal feature instantiation principles (the Head Feature Convention, the Foot Feature Principle and the Control Agreement Principle, which state all the possible agreement patterns between co-occurring items mentioned in ID rules) and the set of Linear Precedence rules (which state linear precedence possibilities among items introduced by ID rules once and for all) define structural descriptions for the well-formed sentences and phrases of the language under investigation.

To summarise, there is just one level of syntactic representation corresponding perhaps most closely to the S-structures of GB theory, but lacking PRO and NP-traces altogether. The grammar in effect consists of a basic set of ID rules, giving amongst other things canonical subcategorisation facts, and a set of rules and principles (metarules, feature instantiation principles and LP rules) which map this set of ID rules into phrase markers. There is thus a projection of lexical information to syntactic structures, but the lexical information in question is not necessarily revealing of lexical semantics, as we have seen. To a great extent the format of the rules and principles involved in the mapping is universal, though parametric variation has to be allowed for to deal with the attested range of agreement patterns, constituent order variations and so on. The single level of syntactic representation assigned to each sentence could potentially be input to a set of phonological rules which would provide phonetic interpretations.

It is particularly important to note that in the mapping from ID rules to structures no use is made, or indeed could be made, of rules which map structures into structures (transformations). Traditionally thorny problems are handled by semantic rule (*eg* equi and raising constructions), or by a combination of semantic rule with metarules (*eg* passive), or the SLASH feature mechanism (*eg* unbounded dependency constructions such as *wh-* movement). The supposed unity of the phenomena that fall under *move* α (in particular the passive and subject-to-subject cases of NP-movement and *wh*-movement) is therefore denied. But while in GB theory the subject and object raising cases are distinguished one from the other, and raising constructions generally are distinguished from cases of 'control' (which covers not only equi phenomena but also what LFG practitioners call

anaphoric control (*cf* 4.7)), in GPSG raising and equi constructions are treated in essentially the same way as exhibiting
'control' relations that are handled in the semantics by meaning
postulates (*cf* 3.6). The evidence for and against the *move* α
generalisation is considered below in 5.2.

GPSG is unique among the theories discussed in this book in
that it provides a model-theoretic interpretation for the syntactic
structures generated. In GB theory it is assumed that LF representations are the subject of semantic interpretation, and in LFG
that F-structures are input to the semantic interpretation rules,
but in neither case are detailed proposals ordinarily given. By
contrast the semantic proposals of GPSG are an integral part of
the framework which cannot be left aside in any presentation of
its organisation. A semantic type is assigned to each syntactic
category, lexical or phrasal, such that the manner of combination
of the denotations of the categories introduced by an ID rule is
automatically predictable. A transitive verb, for example,
denotes a function from NP-type denotations to VP-type denotations. The meaning of a VP containing a transitive verb and its
object will, therefore, be the product of applying the function
denoted by the verb to the argument represented by the denotation of the NP object. Often, the head-type of a given lexical
item, that is the type assigned on the basis of the types assigned
to co-occurring syntactic categories, corresponds to the lexical-
type of that item, that is the type assigned as a part of the lexical
entry to represent its 'logical' argument structure. A transitive
verb, for example, takes a direct object NP complement with
which it forms a VP. Its head-type is a function from NP-type
denotations to VP-type denotations, as explained above, and its
lexical type (ignoring the subject argument) is identical. But
there are, of course, cases where head-types and lexical-types do
not match, as, for example, with passive verbs or verbs
involving infinitival VP complements with missing subjects
(raising and equi constructions). According to the type of
mismatch involved, and each has characteristic properties, the
semantic rule predictable from the head-type is treated as the
argument of one of the functions f_P, f_R or f_E (passive, raising or
equi), and the meaning of each of these is given by means of a
meaning postulate whose purpose is to make sure that the structures with 'displaced' or 'missing' arguments (displaced or missing
from the point of view of conventional predicate–argument structure as represented in an item's lexical type) nevertheless end up
with a model-theoretic interpretation exactly the same as that
which their lexical-type would lead us to expect (*cf* 3.6).

In all cases, then, the way in which the meaning of a syntactic constituent is determined follows from the semantic types assigned to the constituents it dominates; this may be a straightforward process, where head-type and lexical-type match, or may require reference to a meaning postulate, where there is a discrepancy. The meaning of a sentence is therefore built up in model theoretic terms in parallel with the rule-by-rule generation of its syntactic constituents, since each syntactic rule has a corresponding semantic rule whose properties are predictable from the types assigned to the constituents introduced in the syntactic rule and the lexical-type assigned to the head.

One of the leading ideas of GB theory is that clause structure is essentially a projection of the semantic properties of predicates; this is the import of the Projection Principle. This theory of syntax is therefore a theory of how far superficial syntactic structure may differ from predicate–argument structure. GPSG, at least in the form presented in this book, cannot be interpreted in this way because the basic set of lexical ID rules are simply listed as a part of the syntactic component and cannot be regarded as a projection of the lexical-types of the various heads they subcategorise, because there is no one-to-one correspondence between lexical-types and head-types. If, however, the basic subcategorisation information was included in the lexicon along with an indication of predicate–argument structure, we would have something very similar to lexical entries in LFG (except that the subcategorisation information would be given in the form of categories and configurations rather than by reference to grammatical functions). Subcategorisation could now be linked directly with lexical semantics and the ID rules, given the principles of $\bar{X}$-theory, could be regarded as largely predictable from predicate–argument structure (*ie* in the cases where lexical-type and head-type correspond). We would, of course, have to require that syntactic categories mentioned in a subcategorisation frame be paired with predicate arguments mentioned in the specification of an item's lexical type in a unique, coherent and complete fashion, as in LFG (*cf* 4.4, 4.5 and 4.6), always allowing for cases of non-thematic categories in raising constructions and thematic 'missing' categories in equi constructions. Since the basic subcategorisation information is now included in the lexicon, metarules will in effect become lexical redundancy rules, and the new version of GPSG will be largely indistinguishable from LFG except for the fact that there is no formal level of syntactic representation corresponding to F-structures at which categories/ functions are paired with predicate arguments. This type of 'head-driven' phrase structure grammar has been developed in recent work by Pollard (1984, 1985). It must, however, be pointed out that in the absence of a theory of which categories are syntactically present but non-thematic, or syntactically absent but thematically relevant, the head-type/lexical-type mismatches simply have to be listed (much as they are in LFG), and no explanation can be offered of why this mismatch occurs. The theory developed by Chomsky is considerably more ambitious in this regard, since the issue of whether a given 'argument' position is filled or empty in surface syntactic structure is a consequence of the way the theory works and does not have to be stipulated in the rule system.

The point which is being made here is that, if a theory is modified so as to incorporate some supposed advantage of a rival theory, as here GPSG is modified to allow a closer association of subcategorisation and lexical semantics, it is inevitable that the standards of adequacy set for the rival theory become much more obviously applicable to the modified theory, as the frameworks and objectives converge. By this criterion, both GPSG and LFG are deficient in that they adopt unexplained syntactic/semantic mismatches as a central feature of the system. Proponents of these two approaches could, of course, adopt different objectives, so that their theories are judged by different criteria, or seek to undermine the Projection Principle by showing that, however desirable it may be in theory, it is untenable in practice. But once it is accepted that clause structure is largely a projection of lexical semantics, theories of syntax become theories of syntactic/semantic discrepancy, and mere stipulation is not sufficient.

It would, of course, be interesting to see advocates of GPSG and LFG try to develop their frameworks in this direction to see if genuinely different explanations are forthcoming for these discrepancies, and Pollard's work might be seen as a first step in this direction. Traditionally, however, advocates of GPSG have set themselves the objective of developing a formally precise system of syntactic and semantic rules, constrained by considerations of elegance and simplicity, to generate the grammatical sentences of some language and assign model-theoretic interpretations to them. From this point of view, it is not necessary to regard the resultant theory as a theory of how predicate–argument structure relates to surface syntax, and the absence of a Projection Principle analogue need not be thought a serious deficiency. No doubt to proponents of GB theory this will seem a much less interesting theory than their own. But from a different point of view GB theory may seem unsatisfactory because of its failure to offer a comprehensive and precisely formulated account of the recursive function that assigns to each grammatical and meaningful sentence of some language an appropriate structural description and semantic interpretation. The concentration on a highly restricted domain of data whose analysis happens to be compatible with current assumptions about the structure of universal grammar is a clear retreat from the original goal of explicitness in the definition of grammaticality, and in any case, if parsers require access to a rule-system, as many suppose, GB theory must be inadequate as a basis for explaining performance.

In reality, of course, the issue is one of emphasis, and the two directions of research are ultimately complementary. The pursuit of universal principles of grammatical organisation is obviously worthwhile, but it is equally desirable that the scope of such a theory be as wide as possible; and for this to be the case it is necessary, as an indispensable preliminary, to have satisfactory accounts of a reasonably large subset of the grammatical structures of natural languages. There will, of course, be frequent readjustments, both of the rule system and of the theory of grammar that licenses it, in the light of new research in both areas. But the fact that one theory is currently more concerned with issues of descriptive adequacy, while another is preoccupied with the problems of explanatory adequacy, does not mean that one is inherently better than the other in any absolute sense. To the extent that two or more theories accept that the structure of sentences can be adequately described by phrase markers indicating constituency, generalisations about the properties of such phrase markers are usually translatable from one framework to another with more or less satisfactory results, and many of the apparent differences between such theories are often little more than a reflection of different immediate objectives and different styles of presentation within the same general framework of assumptions.

This is not, of course, to deny that there are real differences that follow from different choices of theoretical apparatus and different delimitations of objectives. It is, for example, difficult to see how a belief that the distribution of certain sorts of null syntactic category (or syntactic gaps) follows from the principles determining the distribution of anaphors could be translated into an organising principle of GPSG. The gaps in question (NP traces in GB theory) are introduced into phrase markers (or perhaps more accurately, are not introduced into phrase markers) by stipulation in ID rules and are not distinguished formally from gaps that would be identified as examples of PRO in GB terms. On the other hand raising and equi phenomena are treated in a parallel way in GPSG and there is no way in which this generalisation could be incorporated into (standard) GB theory, since it is crucial that NP-trace and PRO be distinguished, and in any case raising-to-object is prohibited on general theoretical grounds.

The arguments that can be advanced in favour of this or that generalisation are almost always theory-bound in the sense that, if certain co-occurring theoretical assumptions are removed, the arguments in favour of a particular analysis fail to go through. To elaborate our example, if passivisation is a process that must be expressed by metarule, it follows that the affected NP of the active VP must always be a sister of the head V if it is to be accessible to rule. In a sentence such as *Mags believes Ron to be rich*, *Ron* must, therefore be the direct object of *believes*, despite the fact that this is not an argument position. But since there are also non-argument subjects, as in *Ron seems to be rich*, and since a uniform mechanism can be found to pull the two cases together as instances of 'control' (*cf* 3.6), it might be argued that this analysis of object-raising constructions facilitates the statement of a linguistically significant generalisation. But if, on the other hand, it is argued that the accessibility of NPs to passivisation is not clause-bound, and that, subject to certain conditions, subjects of embedded clauses are accessible to rules with greater power than metarules, there is no need to suppose that *Ron* in *Mags believes Ron to be rich* is anything other than the subject of *to be rich*. This prevents any association of subject and object raising constructions but opens the way for a generalisation between subject raising and passivisation based on correspondences between the position of the resulting gap and the distribution of bound anaphors (*cf* 2.3.6), and ultimately, therefore, leads to the principle that NP 'movement' parallels anaphora.

Everything, therefore, hinges on whether or not *Ron* is the object of *believes* in the sentence above, but there is no way of assessing this independently of the conclusions that follow from adopting one of the two analyses, and there is no obvious way of assessing which of the two generalisations that follow from the two analyses is the more important. According to one account, NP gaps occur where the principles of 'control' allow their interpretation, and according to the other NP gaps occur where the principles of 'anaphora' allow their interpretation. The major difference between GPSG and GB is that the spelling out of the relevant generalisation is given considerably more weight, as constituting a principle of universal grammar, in the latter than in the former. But, as we have seen, this is in principle simply a matter of emphasis and presentation, and there is no reason why advocates of GPSG should not devise a notation which makes the distribution of certain types of NP gap in ID rules a consequence of the theory of control, so that the rules themselves do not have to stipulate the facts.

It is, however, true that from the perspective of GB theory the absence of such an account is a deficiency in GPSG, even if it is not a problem from the point of view of the attainment of the immediate objectives of that approach. The real interest of such an account, of course, is that it would constitute a formal challenge to the Projection Principle by sanctioning the occurrence of non-thematic NPs in other than subject position. The ultimate issue, then, is whether or not the generalisation that such a theory would express is a sufficient reason to abandon a principle (at least in part) that would appear to facilitate the process of language acquisition by excluding a range of syntactic distortion of predicate–argument structure that other theories permit. In the absence of such an account and any reliable assessment of its overall consequences, general considerations of restrictiveness may perhaps lead us to favour theories which are compatible with the Projection Principle.

Before continuing with our comparison of the frameworks introduced in the preceding chapters, we must of course complete this review by summarising the essentials of LFG. We may begin with the schematic diagram in [5].

[5]

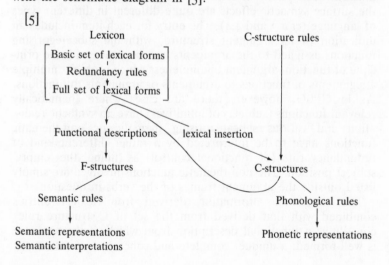

The C-structure rules, whose general properties are determined by the properties of $\overline{X}$-theory, generate C-structures which are input to the phonological rules that determine phonetic interpretations. The C-structure rules are essentially context-free phrase structure rules annotated with functional information. That is to say, the categories introduced by rule are identified as bearing some grammatical function or as playing some specific role in F-structures, and this information is one source of input to the functional description of the sentence whose constituent structure is being described.

The other source of functional information is the lexicon. The lexicon comprises a basic set of lexical entries and a set of lexical redundancy rules most of which express subcategorisation generalisations by generating new entries on the basis of old ones. In other words, a typical redundancy rule says that if a word occurs in such-and-such a context, it also occurs in some other context. To all intents and purposes, the lexical entry/redundancy rule machinery is parallel to the ID rule/metarule machinery of GPSG, with two important exceptions. First, ID rules are part of the syntax not the lexicon (though in head-driven phrase structure grammars the subcategorisation information they express is transferred to the lexicon thereby eliminating this distinction). Secondly, subcategorisation is expressed not by reference to syntactic categories but by reference to grammatical functions, which are taken to be primitives of the theory. The advantage of this is that it permits grammatical processes to be given a uniform description (in terms of the GFs involved) even when the surface syntactic effects are quite different in different types of language (cf 4.3 and 4.4). The entry for each item includes an indication of its argument structure, with the subcategorising functions assigned to the arguments in accordance with the principle of function–argument biuniqueness which prohibits multiple assignments of functions to arguments or arguments to functions. As in GPSG, however, there are cases where thematically relevant functions (subjects of infinitives) have no syntactic realisation and various subcategorising thematic or non-thematic functions have to be interpreted by a rather different kind of redundancy rule (of functional control) as 'filling' the 'empty' subject position. The non-thematic functions involved are simply listed outside the argument frames of the verbs in question.

The functional information derived from lexical entries combined with that derived from the set of C-structure rules constitutes a functional description from which, if the sentence is well-formed, a unique, complete and coherent F-structure can be computed. Like the D-structures of GB theory, these are syntactic representations of the pairings between grammatical functions and predicate arguments, but, as we have seen, the pairings are not direct in cases of functional control. It might, then, be more appropriate to compare F-structures with S-structures. But to the extent that the machinery determining the position and interpretation of syntactic gaps and non-thematic functions/categories is stipulative, this constitutes a deficiency, at least from the point of view of GB theory, though the deficiency is presumably not irremediable in principle (*cf* 5.2).

Grammatical functions provide the link betwen the indirect projections of predicate–argument structure at F-structure and the representations of surface syntactic structure at C-structure; both make reference to a set of GFs which, in the former, are associated with predicate–arguments and, in the latter, with syntactic categories. Since 'relation-changing' grammatical processes are expressed in the form of lexical redundancy rules, the variable encoding of grammatical functions in C-structures is no obstacle to a universal characterisation of the operations involved.

F-structures are input to semantic interpretation rules which either translate them into the formulas of some logical language (such as Intensional Logic) or provide model-theoretic interpretations directly.

As in GPSG, no use is made of transformations. But a major difference between the two theories is the adoption of a formal level of syntactic representation at which the association of GFs with predicate arguments is made explicit. As noted above, F-structures are analogous to the D-structures (or trace/PRO-enriched S-structures) of GB theory, always allowing for the fact that they are not hierarchically organised phrase markers and their relationship with surface (*ie* trace/PRO-less) syntax is determined by reference to primitive GFs. Clearly this second level of syntactic representation requires some defence, given that proponents of GPSG get by with only one. Once again, the best arguments for it would be those which demonstrated that some important process or principle can only be stated in terms of the properties it is supposed to have.

Two pieces of evidence might usefully be introduced here. First, consider the examples in [6].

[6i] *Old Chalky seems likely to resign as head.*
[6ii] *?Old Chalky seems likely to elapse slowly.*
[6iii] *A great deal of headway seems likely to be made this weekend.*

[6iv] ?*A great deal of headway seems likely to be gained this weekend*.

Clearly [6ii] is odd for semantic or pragmatic reasons. Because aged head teachers cannot ordinarily be supposed *to elapse* they cannot be supposed *to be likely*, or *to seem to be likely*, to *elapse* either. The question is whether [6iv] is anomalous in the same way. This would entail arguing that *headway* has a meaning which is only interpretable in conjunction with the meaning of *make* (as in the idiom *make headway*). This is essentially the GPSG solution. It is, however, arguable that there is nothing semantically anomalous about gaining or obtaining headway, and that it is simply a matter of syntactic chance that *make headway* is the English idiom. If this argument is accepted, the oddness of [6iv] is syntactic. GB theory has no difficulty in expressing this, since the D-structure/*move* α (or trace-enriched S-structure) apparatus will always show that *a great deal of headway* in [6iv] occupies an illegitimate initial position in the chain of grammatical functions it bears, namely direct object of *gain*. Similarly, LFG can appeal to F-structure representations at which, thanks to the rule of functional control, *a great deal of headway* will be associated with the thematic subject position of *to be gained*. The assignment of the patient role to this function is, of course, the work of the passive lexical redundancy rule. But this could never have sanctioned such a passive lexical form in the absence of an active *gain headway*. The importance of F-structure here is that, like D-structure, it enables the dependency between the two parts of the idiom *make headway* always to appear adjacent to one another; in D-structure *headway* is always the direct object of *make*, in F-structure it may be either object of *make* or subject of *be made*. The co-occurrence requirement can always be enforced locally, therefore, even if in surface syntactic structure the two elements of the idiom are widely separated, as in [6iv]. Since GPSG has only one level of syntactic representation, the only way to account for the deviance of this sentence, (apart from assuming a syntactic feature [+HEADWAY] shared by the noun *headway* and verb phrases headed by *make*, and requiring these to agree by the CAP (*cf* 3.4.3), a hopelessly *ad hoc* solution), is to adopt the semantic explanation outlined above. This, frankly, seems less than compelling.

A still more persuasive argument for F-structure is provided by the so-called cross-serial dependencies of Dutch (*cf* 4.9, [79]). Consider [7], which might occur as a subordinate clause after *dat* (= *that*).

[7] *Jan Piet Marie zag helpen zwemmen.*
Jan Piet Marie saw help swim
'Jan saw Piet help Marie swim'

Although sentences of this type rapidly become unprocessable as more noun phrases and verbs are added, it seems reasonable to attribute this, in the conventional way, to performance limitations. To account for sentences of this sort we need a set of phrase structure rules such as those in [8].

[8] S → NP VP
VP → NP{VP}
{V'}
V' → V (V')

These would assign a structure to the sentence in [7] like that in [9].

[9]

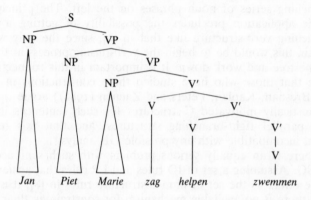

It should be noted, first of all, that a structure such as this, assuming that it represents more or less correctly the essential properties of [7], fails completely to reflect the predicate–argument structure of the proposition that the sentence expresses. It is, furthermore, difficult to see how any well-motivated syntactic deformation of that predicate–argument structure could be devised, and to this extent sentences of the type illustrated in [7] constitute a serious problem for the Projection Principle. It might conceivably be possible to argue that there is a progressive process of head-raising (and adjunction) out of VP into the head position of S, namely INFL, as illustrated in [10].

[10]

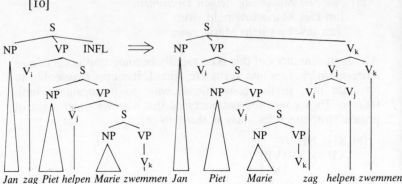

Jan zag Piet helpen Marie zwemmen   Jan   Piet   Marie   zag   helpen zwemmen

This would entail adopting a left-branching series of verbs on the right in order to get the correct sequence, as opposed to a right-branching series of noun phrases on the left. The principle of cyclic application precludes the possibility of getting a right-branching verb-structure like that in [9], since the only way to obtain this would be to begin the verb-raising process at the top of the tree and work down. It is important in this connection to note that those who have studied these constructions in depth (*eg* Bresnan, Kaplan, Peters and Zaenen (1982)) argue that the linguistically motivated C-structures for such sentences involve two parallel right-branching structures, and that this renders them incompatible with any possible GB analysis.

There is an equally serious problem with such sentences for GPSG. Assuming a set of ID rules and LP rules that achieve the same effect as the set of phrase structure rules in [8], it is clear that there is no available mechanism for constraining their operation so as to guarantee that there will be the right number of verbs at the bottom on the right for the set of noun phrases at the top on the left. The only recourse is to adopt a policy of semantic filtering whereby sentences that cannot be given a coherent model-theoretic interpretation are marked as ungrammatical. This in itself would represent something of a retreat from the objective of devising a set of syntactic rules to generate all and only the sentences of a given language, but need not be viewed as a major catastrophe. The real difficulty, however, is the fact that the ID rules required to generate structures such as [9] do not seem to provide much of a basis for predicting the necessary semantic interpretation rules, because the categories denoting the relevant functors and arguments seem hopelessly jumbled from the point of view of predicate–argument structure. The construction of a suitable set of rules and meaning postulates would clearly require considerable ingenuity.

By contrast, the filtering of the output of a set of C-structure rules such as those in [8] can be accomplished effortlessly by F-structure representations. These represent predicate–argument structure, albeit indirectly, and furthermore are compatible with the syntactically motivated right-branching verb complex of [9], because the connection between C-structure and F-structure is effected only by the set of non-configurationally-defined GFs that both make reference to. The F-structure for [7] is given in [11].

$$
[11] \begin{bmatrix}
\text{SUBJ} & [\text{PRED} \quad \text{'JAN'}] \\
\text{PRED} & \text{'SEE} <(\text{SUBJ}) (\text{OBJ}) (\text{VCOMP})>' \\
\text{TENSE} & \text{PAST} \\
\text{OBJ} & [\text{PRED} \quad \text{'PIET'}] \\
\text{VCOMP} & \begin{bmatrix}
\text{SUBJ} & \\
\text{PRED} & \text{'HELP} <(\text{SUBJ}) (\text{OBJ}) (\text{VCOMP})>' \\
\text{OBJ} & [\text{PRED} \quad \text{'MARIE'}] \\
\text{VCOMP} & \begin{bmatrix}
\text{SUBJ} & \\
\text{PRED} & \text{'SWIM} <(\text{SUBJ})>'
\end{bmatrix}
\end{bmatrix}
\end{bmatrix}
$$

The association of the object arguments of SEE and HELP with the syntactically unexpressed subject arguments of HELP and SWIM is a straightforward matter of functional control (*cf* 4.7). The importance of F-structure becomes apparent when it is appreciated that F-structure representations of sentences with too many verbs for the available number of noun phrases will fail to meet the Completeness Condition (*ie* the PREDs of the superfluous verbs will make reference to GFs for which no values can be specified) and F-structure representations of sentences with too many noun phrases for the available number of verbs will fail to meet the Coherence Condition (*ie* in the case of our example sentence, if an extra NP appeared, this would be assigned the OBJ function of the VCOMP containing the SWIM PRED, which is inconsistent with the SWIM semantic form because this is not subcategorised by OBJ). F-structures, therefore, effectively filter the set of C-structures generated by the rules in [8], and do so in a completely straightforward fashion that avoids the problems that arise from having no syntactic representation of predicate–argument structure (GPSG) or a configurational representation of predicate–argument structure (GB theory). This follows directly from the fact that F-structures employ a universal notation for the pairing of GFs and predicate arguments that is independent of constituent structure, and constitutes a powerful argument in favour of this level of representation.

Turning now to the analysis of unbounded dependency constructions, it was noted in Chapter 2 that standard theory transformational grammars employed movement rules that contained an essential variable in their structural descriptions, and that restrictions on such unbounded movements were simply listed as exceptions (*cf* 2.2.4). In more recent work, however, these unbounded dependencies have been reduced to chains of bounded dependencies enforced by the subjacency condition (*cf* 2.3.7). The extent to which the grammars of different languages permit apparently unbounded movement is a function of the choice of bounding nodes (or barriers) in that language. In other words, boundedness of movement is now taken to be the norm, and 'unbounded' dependencies result only when chains of bounded movements are permitted because of a 'liberal' definition of barrierhood. This approach has its analogue in GPSG, where each constituent on the path of nodes between a 'displaced' phrase and its associated gap is characterised by the presence of the SLASH feature (*cf* 3.5). In each case the value of SLASH is determined by the category of the 'displaced' phrase and the information is passed along the projection path by the Foot Feature Principle (*cf* 3.4.3). This analysis allows a simple treatment of 'unbounded' dependencies by means of ID rules, because in no case is there a need for information about a gap to be passed over a greater distance than that between a daughter constituent and its immediately dominating mother, a fact which greatly facilitates the parsing of sentences involving constructions of this type (3.8). In the version of LFG presented in Chapter 4, however, 'unbounded dependencies' are treated as *essentially* unbounded, much as in early transformational work (4.8). But as was pointed out, in the latest versions of LFG (*eg* Kaplan and Zaenen (1985)) this analysis has been modified to bring it into line with the GB position, so that 'displaced' phrases and their associated gaps are linked by a sequence of grammatical functions terminating in the thematic grammatical function assigned to the gap position.

In all three theories, however, (including pre-modification LFG), the presence of a gap is dependent upon lexical government (or, in GB theory, some other form of proper government such as co-indexing from COMP). This requirement is enforced in GB theory by the Empty Category Principle (2.3.9), and in GPSG by the Lexical Head Constraint (3.4.2 and 3.5); only lexical ID rules can be input to metarules, so if SLASH termination is handled by metarule, it follows that the gaps in question will always be in the subcategorisation frame of a lexical head (*ie* governed by that lexical head in GB terms). In LFG gaps are similarly permitted only in positions that are associated with subcategorising (hence governed) grammatical functions. In short, there seems here to be a process of theoretical convergence. Just as the development of 'head-driven' phrase structure grammars might be interpreted as an attempt to incorporate into GPSG the idea of syntax as a theory of the permissible relations between (projections of) lexical semantics and surface syntactic structure, so the reanalysis of 'unbounded' dependencies as chains of grammatical functions in LFG might be seen as an attempt to bring the theory into line with the prevailing view that such dependencies are only apparent. Similarly, the proposal that gaps are dependent on governing lexical heads, however formulated, has been a leading idea in all three frameworks for some time, but once again the influence of GB theory is apparent. This is particularly clear in the case of GPSG, since in early work the 'bare VP' analysis of subject dependencies was effected by a condition prohibiting SLASH features on left branches (such as that terminating in a subject NP), and the introduction of the LHC looks very like an attempt to incorporate the import of the ECP while retaining the well-motivated analysis of subject dependency constructions (recall in particular the co-ordination facts discussed in 3.5, example [58]).

5.2 *Move* α

Perhaps the most important difference between GPSG and LFG on the one hand and GB theory on the other concerns the putative generalisation expressed by the rule schema *move* α. In GB theory passive and subject-to-subject raising are treated as instances of NP-movement, and this process is deemed to be sufficiently like other cases of movement, particularly *wh*-movement, for these to be conflated in the form of a general schema, with essential differences falling out from the effect of various principles of universal grammar. Furthermore, equi constructions fall under the theory of control and are quite distinct from raising phenomena.

In the other two theories completely different mechanisms are employed to handle 'unbounded' dependency constructions (such as those involving 'displaced' *wh*-phrases) from those employed to tackle passivisation, raising and equi constructions. But, as was noted in the previous section and elsewhere, the 'raising' of subjects both to subject and to object positions in a higher clause is treated in a parallel way in these theories, an analysis which is incompatible with the principles of GB theory (raising to object would violate the θ-criterion amongst other problems); and furthermore, raising is closely associated with what in GB theory would be cases of control. Thus in LFG we have lexical redundancy rules of passivisation and (for raising and equi constructions) functional control. In GPSG we have a passive metarule complemented by a special semantic interpretation rule which makes the translations of the constituents admitted by the output ID rules arguments of the function f_P to produce a formula that is interpreted by a meaning postulate in such a way as to guarantee that active and corresponding passive sentences receive the same denotations. In the case of raising and equi constructions the 'missing' subjects are allowed for directly by permitting bare VP complements to lexical heads in ID rules (much as they are allowed for in the C-structure rules of LFG), and once again the translations of the constituents admitted are made the arguments of the functions f_R or f_E to produce formulas whose interpretations are given by meaning postulate. Crucially no null NPs are envisaged in either theory (whether corresponding to trace or to PRO), and NPs are allowed to appear in θ-positions in surface structures without being associated with corresponding null θ-positions (traces). This constitutes a denial of the Projection Principle and is motivated by a commitment to 'concrete' syntax and a conviction that matters of semantics, in particular representations of predicate–argument structure, should not be allowed to determine the form of syntactic representations of surface structure when there are strong, albeit often theory-bound, syntactic arguments to the contrary.

This position would be more persuasive, of course, at least from the point of view of GB theorists, if the places where syntactic gaps are sanctioned, even if the latter do not turn up in syntactic representations, were the consequence of some general theory of redundancy rules, metarules or rules of semantic interpretation, rather than having to be stipulated instance by instance as is presently the case. On the other hand, the boundedness of the relationships involved in these constructions is an automatic consequence of the machinery used to characterise them in LFG and GPSG (lexical entries and lexical redundancy rules on the one hand and lexical ID rules and metarules on the other), while GB theory has to impose the subjacency condition on that subset of the phenomena that fall under NP-movement. It might also be argued that some of the alleged differences between PRO and NP-trace that are used to justify the separation of control and raising constructions are really rather suspect. For example, it is supposed to be the case that the relationship between a displaced NP and its trace is subject to subjacency while that between the controller of PRO and the null pronominal is not. In fact this distinction is only true if both 'anaphoric' and 'functional' control (to use the LFG terms, see 4.7) are lumped together. Given that there are clear differences between the two cases, and given that functional control is always bounded, it is at least arguable that functional control and raising should be brought together in the way that LFG and GPSG require.

This is made even more plausible when one considers that the argument that 'displaced' NPs always occupy θ-positions, which is the basis for linking raising with passivisation, is also suspect. If it is one of the criteria for determining the set of S-internal θ-positions that they can be filled by 'dummy' elements such as (non-referential) *it* and *there*, as in the examples in [12],

[12i]   *It seems that Chomsky got it wrong.*
[12ii] *There seems to be a flaw in the analysis.*
[12iii] *It was believed that Chomsky was infallible.*
[12iv] *There was believed to be some advantage in postulating transformations.*

then the non-occurrence of these elements in the subject position in the examples in [13],

[13i] *It* (non-referential) *was run over by a bus.*
[13ii] *There was knocked down by a taxi.*

might be used as an argument that the subject position of a passive sentence is ordinarily a θ-position except in cases such as [12iii] and [12iv], where the verb in question happens to take a postposed sentential complement that functions as 'logical' subject, thus rendering the examples parallel to [12i] and [12ii] in the relevant respects. If this argument is accepted, the basis for treating the majority of examples of passivisation as essentially parallel to subject-to-subject raising would be seriously undermined. Though the subject NP is in a sense 'displaced' from the point of view of lexical semantics, it must now be generated 'in place' without being associated with a trace in post-verbal position. Any analysis involving movement from D-structure object position to S-structure subject position would obviously violate the θ-criterion at both levels of representation. It is also worth stressing the point that the new analysis would render the Projection Principle as currently conceived untenable; *ie* it would not now be possible to identify arguments/thematic roles in a one-to-one way with certain configurationally defined grammatical functions.

It should also be borne in mind that the distinction between NP-trace and locally controlled PRO based on the view that the former must be (properly) governed while the latter is ungoverned can only be upheld if one is prepared to believe that S̄, a barrier to government, is 'pruned' in the examples in [14], allowing government across S,

[14i]   *GB theory seems* [s t *to be in trouble*]

[14ii] *GB theory is believed* [s t *to be a real breakthrough*]

but is not pruned in the examples in [15], thereby blocking government.

[15i]   *Chomsky tries* [s̄ [s PRO *to attain explanatory adequacy*]]

[15ii] *Chomsky persuades Bresnan* [s̄ [s PRO *to call it a day*]]

The presence of S̄ in [15] cannot be justified on the grounds that there is the possibility of an optional complementiser, (contrast *I want very much* (*for you*) *to leave*), since the combination of a lexical subject with *for* is absolutely excluded with both these verbs, exactly as it is excluded in the cases of *seem* and *be believed* in [14]. If the impossibility of an overt complementiser is sufficient grounds for supposing that S̄ has been pruned in one set of examples why not in the other? And if S̄ is pruned (or not) in both sets of examples, it follows that PRO must be governed (or not) in exactly the same way as NP-trace.

It should be clear from this discussion so far that a determined *advocatus diaboli* can pick holes in almost any theoretical position by judicious selection of weakspots and suppression of perceived strengths. So here each of the supposed differences between NP-trace and PRO has been called into question, on not altogether implausible grounds, in order to redress the balance which thus far had been tipping in favour of GB theory. If the NP-trace/PRO distinction as standardly formulated cannot be satisfactorily defended, there is, of course, no obstacle to the unified treatment of raising and equi phenomena advocated by both LFG and GPSG.

To complete the assessment of the generalisation supposedly expressed by *move* α, however, we must now turn to the question of whether NP-movement and *wh*-movement can be collapsed into a single grammatical rule, as in GB theory, or whether two (or more) different kinds of mechanism are called for, according to the type of relationship involved. There are, of course, certain essential differences between NP-movement and *wh*-movement which *move* α must abstract away from. This is legitimate in so far as the differences follow from independently motivated principles of universal grammar. Consider the table in [16].

[16]

	NP-trace	*wh*-trace
Parallels 1 2 3	subjacent to antecedent antecedent in $\bar{\theta}$-position properly governed	subjacent to antecedent antecedent in $\bar{\theta}$-position properly governed
Differences 4 5	A-bound in governing category Caseless	free (*ie* $\bar{A}$- bound) Case-marked

The differences given in 4 and 5 follow from the principles of binding theory and Case theory respectively, and so do not have to be 'built in' to the rule itself. If a D-structure position is one that would not be Case-marked at S-structure, an NP with lexical content in that position *must* move to some position in S that *is* Case-marked if the associated S-structure is not to be excluded by the Case Filter. If, on the other hand, a D-structure position may be Case-marked at S-structure, a phrase in that position *may* move, but only to a position where Case is not assigned. This need not be stipulated in the Case theory, since movement to any position in S (including the subject of infinitive slot where no Case is assigned) would fall foul of the binding theory which requires Case-marked traces to be free (*ie* not bound within S). Because the only other suitable position is COMP, and because the only items which can stand in COMP at LF are quantifiers of quantifier-like expressions, it also follows that the items which get moved to this position in the syntax will be *wh*-phrases. In the case of NP-traces, of course, the binding theory requires that the moved NP not only be in S (guaranteed in any case by Case theory) but within the minimal S that contains the item that governs its trace.

Similarly, the parallels given in 2 and 3 of [16] follow from government theory and θ-theory respectively. The ECP requires all traces to be properly governed, and the θ-criterion prevents any argument from being assigned more than one θ-role (*eg* by being moved from one θ-position to another). The second condition, of course, is a general condition of well-formedness (presumably at LF), and is in no way specific to movement phenomena. The ECP, however, is a condition specific to cases of movement. But it should be recalled that it holds true only by stipulation of many NP-traces. Thus, as we have seen, the subject trace in the sentences in [17],

[17i] *Gerald seems* [s t *to be on the right track*]
[17ii] *Joan is believed* [s t *to have a good theory*]

is properly governed by the higher verb only on the assumption that S-pruning has taken place (and that government is not blocked by S). These requirements are necessary, of course, in order to distinguish NP-trace from PRO, which has to be protected from external government by S̄. But we have already seen that the supposed presence or absence of S̄ in cases where the complementiser *for* is excluded lacks convincing independent support (*cf* the discussion of [14] and [15]). In these circumstances, it is reasonable to argue, in support of LFG and GPSG, that equi and raising phenomena are essentially alike and that sentences of *both* types lack complement subjects precisely because external government (*ie* across a clause or sentence boundary of any kind) is prohibited, contrary to GB assumptions. This would effectively make both types of construction cases of control (which is how they are analysed in LFG and GPSG), with the controller in a θ-position in equi constructions but not in raising constructions (or passive sentences such as that in [17ii]). The structural position of raising controllers would follow from the requirement that NPs must be finite clause subjects or governed by a sister lexical head to receive Case.

Such an analysis entails a theory in which the only permissible NP 'traces' are gaps that *can* be properly governed (*ie* by a sister lexical head). A post-verbal trace in the majority of passive sentences is excluded if, as was argued above, the subject position is ordinarily a θ-position (*cf* [12] and [13]), so we are in fact left with only *wh*-traces. This is exactly in line with the LFG and GPSG demarcation of formal machinery. These distiguish 'unbounded dependency' constructions from the rest, and unify raising and equi to the exclusion of passive.

Since the proper government requirement for NP-traces (as opposed to *wh*-traces) can be made to look rather suspect, the last remaining parallel between the two types of movement, observance of subjacency, is clearly of great importance in any attempt to demonstrate their essential unity. The role of subjacency in the characterisation of *wh*-movement is clear. In 2.3.7, for example, the Complex Noun Phrase, Sentential Subject and

Wh-island Constraints were all shown to follow from the sub-jacency condition, on the assumption that S̄, NP and, in certain circumstances, S, are the relevant barriers for English, and that movement may not cross more than one barrier.

Unfortunately the role of subjacency in characterising NP-movement is not at all clear. It is, of course, possible to point to ungrammatical sentences such as [18],

[18] *Gerald seems [s̄ that [s it is certain [s t to win the day]]]

where subjacency has been violated on the assumption that the first S becomes a barrier for movement after S̄-pruning following a raising predicate (see 2.3.7, especially the discussion of [223i]). But here there is also a violation of the binding condition for anaphors, since the trace of the moved NP is not bound in its governing category (*viz* the S *it is certain* t *to win the day*). It seems in fact that there is no sentence type in which subjacency alone is demonstrably crucial in constraining NP-movement.

We must, then, conclude that the generalisation which *move* α purports to express is not altogether compellingly supported by the available evidence and that theories which employ different mechanisms for 'unbounded' dependencies from those used to handle the more obviously bounded processes like passivisation, raising and equi are not demonstrably deficient because of this. Furthermore, there seems to be no compelling reason why raising and 'local' equi phenomena should not be analysed in essentially the same way, always allowing for the different thematic status of the controller in the two cases. Given certain reasonable assumptions about government, and more restrictive ones than those commonly made by GB theorists, a theory which adopted this approach would seem to be expressing a significant gener-alisation. Bouchard (1983) and Koster (1984) both in fact consider revisions of GB theory in which verbs such as *try*, as well as verbs of the *seem* and *believe* types, permit S̄-pruning. This makes locally controlled PRO a bound anaphor governed by the verb of the higher clause across S, and so pulls together one subset of 'control' phenomena with cases of bound anaphora so as to unify equi and raising in much the same way as in GPSG or LFG. PRO is distinguished from trace in these cases by whether or not the antecedent has an independent θ-role, as expected.

5.3 Conclusions

In general, work in GB theory is characterised by two faults which I hope have been illustrated in the course of this, and preceding chapters. The greatest weakness is the tendency to construct complicated and sophisticated theories of the workings of universal grammar that are scarcely ever as well-supported as one would like by the available evidence or even by the currently employed representational apparatus. It is, of course, true that explanations for the data can only be constructed if linguists are prepared to speculate, but it is to be hoped that future versions of the theory will require less dubious tinkering with descriptive analyses. The second weakness is directly connected with the first. Because the emphasis of research has moved away from descriptive precision, it is possible to overlook much of the tinkering that has to be done in order to get the data to fall out from current theoretical assumptions, and it is all too easy to minimise the problems that any given stage of the theory's evolution faces. Sloppiness and imprecision of formulation at the descriptive level can only, in the long run, undermine serious attempts to achieve explanatory adequacy. The consequences of adopting this or that theoretical proposal at the level of universal grammar must be properly worked out at the level of language-specific grammar, and the interpretation of the data that the general theory imposes should not fly in the face of low-level, but often quite compelling, argumentation. This in turn requires a very careful statement of the principles of the general theory.

That said, it would be impossible to overemphasise the fact that a great many, some would say most, of the really exciting ideas in grammatical analysis in the last ten years have come out of work in GB theory and its predecessors. The assault on *move* α mounted in the preceding section did not, of course, constitute a knockdown argument. In its defence one could, for example, point to the way in which research within the framework that proposes this generalisation has paved the way for a potentially restrictive and explanatory theory (given some tightening-up of presentation) of how far surface syntax can deviate from configurational projections of predicate–argument structure by showing that the thematically relevant but superficially null positions created by *move* α have properties that follow from the properties of analogous overt elements. That there are problems in the execution of this idea, and that many of these follow from assumptions made about the nature of grammatical representation, is undeniable; and in some cases GPSG and LFG offer empirically better-supported analyses that conflict with it. But the great weakness of both of these approaches, at least from the point of view of Chomsky's conception of the goals of the enterprise, is that in many areas of investigation their proponents have so far failed to develop the associated general theories of grammar to the point where they can interpret particular analyses on offer as consequences of general principles of grammatical organisation rather than matters of chance. And the fact that Chomsky is felt, in some general way, to have the right kind of objectives, even though he may be thought to make inappropriate representational assumptions, is demonstrated by the fact that both GPSG and LFG have in recent years sought to incorporate, as part of the process of developing a theory of grammar compatible with their representational assumptions, analogues of theoretical proposals first advanced in the context of GB theory (cf 5.1). The value of GPSG and LFG, even though these theories have shown that perfectly good, and sometimes superior, analyses of familiar data can be achieved in the context of quite different assumptions about the form of grammars, can only be fully appreciated when those assumptions have been properly articulated as a coherent theory of grammar.

Nevertheless, they have successfully re-emphasised the importance of precise formulation and attention to detail if linguistic theory is not only to achieve its own objectives but also to have fruitful relations with work in neighbouring disciplines. However successful in its own terms, linguistic theory cannot operate indefinitely in isolation from potentially important alternative sources of data, and the success of these approaches in engaging the interest of psychologists and computer scientists and in promoting the development of a theory of performance that recognises the possibility that grammars may have properties determined by the uses to which they are put has in the last year or so begun to have its effect on GB theorists, some of whom, notably Berwick and Weinberg (1982 and 1984), have tried (in part successfully) to show that grammars of the type they advocate, despite standard arguments to the contrary, are in fact compatible with processing considerations.

It should be clear from the discussion so far that there are disagreements of substance between the three theories discussed in this book. Advocates of LFG have some very strong arguments to support the idea, rejected in GB theory and irrelevant in GPSG (see below), that the relationship between predicate–argument structure and surface syntax is best stated in terms of representations that make reference to a universal set of primitive grammatical functions rather than to constituent structure configurations. Both GPSG and LFG, while differing in terms of the status they assign to grammatical functions, reject the Projection Principle and the generalisation expressed by *move* α in favour of a unified treatment of equi and raising phenomena. The realism of GB and LFG theorists contrasts with the agnosticism of GPSG proponents, who tend to regard their theory of syntax as defining devices for generating sentences and assigning structural descriptions rather than for expressing the nature of the relationship between syntactic projections of predicate–argument structure (like D-structure and, less directly, F-structure) and surface syntax, and who, accordingly, advocate a single level of syntactic representation. The significance of mathematically defined notions of generative power is emphasised by proponents of GPSG, and to a lesser extent by advocates of LFG, but denied by GB theorists. Many more such differences could easily be added to the list. These should not, however, be allowed to obscure some important parallels. For example, the emergence of 'head-driven' phrase structure grammars, as developed by Pollard (1984 and 1985), allows for statements of subcategorisation and lexical predicate–argument structure to be closely linked, paving the way for the development of GPSG as a theory of how lexical semantics and surface syntax are related. This development brings GPSG much closer to LFG (in fact to earlier versions of that theory which lacked independent F-structure representations), and we might well expect both of these frameworks in the future to try to develop explicit theories of the extent to which (surface) syntactic structure may deviate from what is predictable from the semantic properties of lexical heads, and so begin to evolve in the same general direction as GB theory. At an appropriate level of abstraction from the details of analysis, it is likely that such theories will incorporate many proposals that are analogous to proposals in GB theory, while always allowing for different executions of the ideas they embody in line with the representational assumptions of the frameworks involved. We might, then, conclude that syntacticians seem to be converging on the notion that many aspects of surface syntactic structure follow from the semantic properties of the predicates denoted by the heads of phrases at that level, and that one of the most important tasks of syntactic theory is to come up with a concise account of those aspects which are not predictable in this way.

In line with this focusing on the semantic/syntactic properties of lexical items that appear as heads of phrases is the shared emphasis on the locality of syntactic processes and relations. 'Unbounded' dependencies in the literal sense have disappeared in favour of chains of bounded dependencies whose domains are determined by the 'governing' properties, or spheres of influence, of lexical heads (and, in GB theory, certain other categories). These domains can very largely be equated with those required for the statement of subcategorisation requirements in GPSG and LFG, but have to be rather more liberally defined in GB theory to allow for government across S and so-called antecedent government from COMP. Thus in GB theory all S-structure gaps (with the exception of PRO and pro) have to be properly governed in conformity with the ECP (though we might legitimately ask whether the rather unsatisfactory definition of proper government is not a function of the representational consequences of the Projection Principle); and in GPSG and LFG (at least in the modified form mentioned above, in which 'unbounded' dependencies are analysed in terms of chains of grammatical functions connecting one clause to the next), even though the *move* α generalisation is rejected, both the actually postulated *wh*-gaps (more correctly in LFG, the functions borne by these) and the NP positions (again, in LFG, the functions associated with these) involved in the statement of processes such as passivisation are all necessarily in the domain of lexical heads because the mechanisms employed to characterise the relevant construction types (metarules and lexical redundancy rules) operate by definition on lexical ID rules and lexical forms. Furthermore, the boundedness of such processes is also an automatic consequence of the fact that they are stated in LFG and GPSG as processes on subcategorisation frames. In GB theory, by contrast, the boundedness of *wh*-movement follows from the imposition of the subjacency condition, and that of NP-movement from the requirement that anaphors be bound within the minimal S that contains the item that governs them. In this area at least, it might plausibly be argued that (modified) LFG and GPSG are superior to GB theory in that what is an unmotivated constraint on movement that has to be 'explained' by principles of universal grammar in the latter turns out to be the inevitable consequence of the tools of grammatical description if either of the former theories is adopted. On the other hand, it must not be forgotten that the subjacency condition represents a very neat generalisation about displacement possibilities that has no obvious analogue in terms of the available apparatus of LFG and GPSG.

We might, then, conclude that there are a number of 'leading ideas' which are determining the direction of contemporary syntactic research but that these may be 'executed' in a variety of different ways with different consequences. Paradoxically, however, it seems that the theory which has been most productive in the framing of these leading ideas, GB theory, is often characterised by less than compelling executions of them; and the theories which have concentrated on explicit and carefully formulated descriptive analyses (GPSG and LFG) have so far failed to contribute as effectively as they might to the framing and development of explanatory grammatical principles. What this shows is that issues of descriptive and explanatory adequacy cannot be effectively tackled in isolation from each other, and it is to be hoped that in the years to come researchers, whatever their theoretical allegiances, will refrain from partisan polemics and seek to promote the development of their subject in a liberal spirit and with a general awareness of the consequences of descriptive proposals for issues of theory and of the implications of theoretical principles for descriptive analysis.

5.4 Relevant reading

Sells (1985) (including a postscript by Wasow) presents an outline of the three theories discussed in this book and concludes with a discussion of their place in the development of generative grammar and of some points of convergence.

Many of the books, articles and papers in the GPSG and LFG literature seek to stress the advantages of these approaches over the treatment adopted in transformational theories (*cf* 3.9 and 4.10). There is some informal discussion of GPSG and LFG in Chomsky, Huybregts and van Riemsdijk (1982), and Koster and May (1982) is an extended defence of the theory of clausal complements to raising and equi verbs against the VP analysis advocated by Brame (1976, 1978 and 1979) and adopted in GPSG and LFG. Williams (1981) reviews the GPSG treatment of unbounded dependencies and Williams (1984) includes a critical evaluation of LFG from the point of view of GB theory. In general this discussion of alternatives is cheerfully partisan, and the verdict is a foregone conclusion once one knows the allegiance of the author in question.

In 5.1 the discussion of the GPSG approach to NP-movement dependencies involving idiom chunks is based on Sag (1982), and the Dutch cross-serial dependency example comes from Bresnan, Kaplan, Peters and Zaenen (1982). (The problem with data of this kind was first noted by Huybregts (1976)). Pullum and Gazdar (1982) argue that data of this kind do not show that Dutch is not a strongly context-free language and provide a set of context-free rules to make the point. Though their proposals guarantee that the number of NPs matches the number and valency of the verbs involved, this result is only achieved by enforcing 'linked' choices between the options allowed in different rules. It is far from clear, however, whether there are mechanisms within the framework of GPSG that could enforce these restrictions, and the problem of developing adequate semantic interpretation rules on the basis of the structures proposed remains unsolved.

The problems discussed in 5.2 (examples [14] and [15] that arise in connection with S̄-pruning have not gone without comment in the GB literature. As noted, both Koster (1984) and Bouchard (1983) in fact assume that verbs such as *try* permit S̄-pruning, so that PRO in these cases becomes a bound anaphor. The only distinction now between this kind of PRO and NP-trace, therefore, is that the antecedent of the former has a distinct θ-role. This position, at an appropriate level of abstraction, is not very different from that adopted in LFG and GPSG, since (subject-to-subject) raising and this kind of 'local' equi both now involve the same binding relationship between 'controller' and 'controllee' (*viz* 'anaphor' binding alias functional control). This revision of the standard GB position is clearly an improvement in that it eliminates the need for an unmotivated distinction in pruning requirements between raising and equi verbs. It does, however, involve some reassessment of the basis for the trace/PRO distinction, as noted.

The reinterpretation of S and S̄ presented in [2] is advocated in Chomsky (1986b). The parallelism between clauses and NPs (with some languages relating S, others S̄, to the root node of NPs) together with the reanalysis of N as DET is discussed in Horrocks and Stavrou (1987). The standard view that N is the head of NP is challenged in Lyons (1977: *p* 392) and the view that determiners are heads is supported by Hudson (1984: *p* 90). Szabolcsi (1985) deals with NP/S̄ parallelism in Hungarian.

Bibliography

AKMAJIAN, A., and F. HENY (1975) *An Introduction to the Principles of Transformational Syntax*, Cambridge, Mass. and London: MIT Press.

AOUN, J. (1981) *The Formal Nature of Anaphoric Relations*, Doctoral dissertation, MIT.

AOUN, J., and D. SPORTICHE (1983) 'On the formal theory of government', *The Linguistic Review* 2, 211–236.

BACH, E. (1974) *Syntactic Theory*, New York: Holt Rinehart Winston.

BACH, E. (1979) 'Control in Montague grammar', *Linguistic Inquiry* 10, 515–31.

BELLETTI, A., L. BRANDI and L. RIZZI (eds) (1981) *Theory of Markedness in Generative Grammar*, Pisa: Scuola Normale Superiore.

BERWICK, R., and A. WEINBERG (1982) 'Parsing efficiency, computational complexity and the evaluation of grammatical theories', *Linguistic Inquiry* 13, 165–91.

BERWICK, R., and A. WEINBERG (1984) *The Grammatical Basis of Linguistic Performance: language use and acquisition*, Cambridge, Mass. and London: MIT Press.

BOOK, R. V. (1973) 'Topics in formal language theory'. In A. V. Aho, (ed), *Currents in the Theory of Computing*, Englewood Cliffs, New Jersey: Prentice Hall, *pp* 1–34.

BOUCHARD, D. (1983) *On the Content of Empty Categories*, Dordrecht: Foris.

BRAME, M. (1976) *Conjectures and Refutations in Syntax and Semantics*, New York and Amsterdam: Elsevier North Holland.

BRAME, M. (1978) *Base-generated Syntax*, Seattle: Noit Amrofer.

BRAME, M. (1979) *Essays Toward Realistic Syntax*, Seattle: Noit Amrofer.

BRESNAN, J. (1978) 'A realistic transformational grammar'. In M. Halle, J. Bresnan and G. A. Miller (eds), *Linguistic Theory and Psychological Reality*, Cambridge, Mass. and London: MIT Press, *pp* 1–59.

BRESNAN, J. (ed.) (1982) *The Mental Representation of Grammatical Relations*, Cambridge, Mass. and London: MIT Press. (Papers by Bresnan in this volume referred to in 4.10: 'The passive in lexical theory', *pp* 3–86; 'Polyadicity', *pp* 149–72; 'Control and complementation', *pp* 282–390).

BRESNAN, J., R. M. KAPLAN, S. PETERS and A. ZAENEN (1982) 'Cross-serial dependencies in Dutch', *Linguistic Inquiry* 13, 613–35.

BRODY, M. (1984) 'On contextual definitions and the role of chains', *Linguistic Inquiry* 15, 355–80.

BUTTERWORTH, B., B. COMRIE and Ö. DAHL (eds) (1984) *Explanations For Language Universals*, Berlin: Mouton.

CHOMSKY, N. (1957) *Syntactic Structures*, The Hague: Mouton.

CHOMSKY, N. (1963) 'Formal properties of grammars'. In R. D. Luce, R. R. Bush and E. Galanter (eds), *Handbook of Mathematical Psychology II*, New York: Wiley, *pp* 323–418.

CHOMSKY, N. (1964) *Current Issues in Linguistic Theory*, The Hague: Mouton.

CHOMSKY, N. (1965) *Aspects of the Theory of Syntax*, Cambridge, Mass.: MIT Press.

CHOMSKY, N. (1970) 'Remarks on nominalization'. In R. Jacobs and P. S. Rosenbaum (eds) *Readings in English Transformational Grammar*, Waltham, Mass.: Ginn and Co. (Reprinted in Chomsky (1972b).

CHOMSKY, N. (1972a) *Language and Mind* (extended edition), New York: Harcourt Brace Jovanovich. (First edition 1968).

CHOMSKY, N. (1972b) *Studies on Semantics in Generative Grammar*, The Hague: Mouton.

CHOMSKY, N. (1973) 'Conditions on transformations'. In S. R. Anderson and P. Kiparsky (eds), *A Festschrift for Morris Halle*, New York: Holt Rinehart Winston; (Reprinted in Chomsky (1977a)).

CHOMSKY, N. (1975) *Reflections on Language*, London: Temple Smith.

CHOMSKY, N. (1976) 'Conditions on rules of grammar', *Linguistic Analysis* 2, 303–351. (Reprinted in Chomsky (1977a)).

CHOMSKY, N. (1977a) *Essays on Form and Interpretation*, New York and Amsterdam: Elsevier North Holland.

CHOMSKY, N. (1977b) 'On *wh*-movement'. In P. Culicover, T. Wasow and A. Akmajian (eds), *Formal Syntax*, New York: Academic Press, *pp* 71–132.

CHOMSKY, N. (1980a) *Rules and Representations*, Oxford: Basil Blackwell.

CHOMSKY, N. (1980b) 'On binding', *Linguistic Inquiry* 11, 1–46.

CHOMSKY, N. (1981a) *Lectures on Government and Binding*, Dordrecht: Foris.

CHOMSKY, N. (1981b) 'Markedness and core grammar'. In Belletti, Brandi and Rizzi (eds), (1981).

CHOMSKY, N. (1981c) 'Principles and parameters in syntactic theory'. In N. Hornstein and D. Lightfoot (eds), *Explanation in Linguistics: the logical problem of language acquisition*, London: Longman, *pp* 32–75.

CHOMSKY, N. (1982) Some Concepts and Consequences of the Theory of Government and Binding, Cambridge, Mass. and London: MIT Press.

CHOMSKY, N. (1986a) *Knowledge of Language: its nature, origin and use*, New York: Praeger.

CHOMSKY, N. (1986b) *Barriers*, Cambridge, Mass. and London: MIT Press.

CHOMSKY, N., R. HUYBREGTS and H. VAN RIEMSDIJK (1982), *The Generative Enterprise*, Dordrecht: Foris.

CHOMSKY, N., and H. LASNIK (1977) 'Filters and control', *Linguistic Inquiry* 8, 425–504.

CLEAVELAND, J., and R. UZGALIS (1975) *Grammars for Programming Languages: what every programmer should know about grammar*, New York: American Elsevier.

CULICOVER, P. W. (1976) *Syntax*, New York: Academic Press.

DOUGHERTY, R. (1969) 'An interpretive theory of pronominal reference', *Foundations of Language* 5, 488–508.

DOUGHERTY, R. (1970) 'A grammar of coordinate conjoined structures', *Language* 46, 850–98.

DOWTY, D. (1982) 'Grammatical relations and Montague grammar'. In P. Jacobson and G. K. Pullum (eds), *The Nature of Syntactic Representation*, Dordrecht: Reidel, *pp* 79–130.

DOWTY, D., R. E. WALL and S. PETERS (1981) *Introduction to Montague Semantics*, Dordrecht: Reidel.

EARLEY, J. (1970) 'An efficient context-free parsing algorithm', *Communications of the ACM* 13, 94–102.

EMONDS, J. (1976) *A Transformational Approach to English Syntax: root structure-preserving and local transformations*, New York: Academic Press.

FARMER, A. (1984) *Modularity in Syntax*, Cambridge, Mass.: MIT Press.

FIENGO, R. W. (1974) *Semantic Conditions on Surface Structure*, Doctoral dissertation, MIT.

FIENGO, R. W. (1977) 'On trace theory', *Linguistic Inquiry* 8, 35–61.

FINER, D. (1985) 'The syntax of switch-reference', *Linguistic Inquiry* 16, 35–55.

FLICKINGER, D. (1983) 'Lexical heads and phrasal gaps'. In M. Barlow, D. Flickinger and M. Wescoat (eds), *Proceedings of WCCFL* 2, *Stanford Linguistics Association*, *pp* 89–101.

FODOR, J. A. (1983) *The Modularity of Mind*, Cambridge, Mass.: and London: MIT Press.

FODOR, J. A., T. G. BEVER and M. F. GARRETT (1974) *The Psychology of Language: an introduction to psycholinguistics and generative grammar*, New York: McGraw-Hill.

FODOR, J. D. (1978) 'Parsing strategies and constraints on transformations', *Linguistic Inquiry* 9, 427–473.

FODOR, J. D. (1980) 'Parsing, constraints and the freedom of expression', Mimeo, University of Connecticut.

FODOR, J. D. (1983) 'Phrase structure parsing and the island constraints', *Linguistics and Philosophy* 6, 163–233.

FORD, M. (1982) 'Sentence planning units: implications for the speaker's representation of meaningful relations underlying sentences'. In Bresnan (1982), *pp* 797–827.

FORD, M., J. BRESNAN and R. M. KAPLAN (1982) 'A competence-based theory of syntactic closure'. In Bresnan (1982), *pp* 727–96.

FREIDIN, R. (1978) 'Cyclicity and the theory of grammar', *Linguistic Inquiry* 9, 519–49.

GAZDAR, G. (1981a) 'Unbounded dependencies and coordinate structure', *Linguistic Inquiry* 12, 155–84.

GAZDAR, G. (1981b) 'On syntactic categories', in *Philosophical Transactions (Series B) of the Royal Society* 295, 267–83.

GAZDAR, G. (1982) 'Phrase structure grammar'. In P. Jacobson and G. K. Pullum (eds), *The Nature of Syntactic Representation*, Dordrecht: Reidel, *pp* 131–86.

GAZDAR, G., E. KLEIN, G. K. PULLUM and I. SAG (1982) 'Coordinate structure and unbounded dependencies'. In M. Barlow, D. Flickinger and I. Sag (eds), *Developments in Generalized Phrase Structure Grammar: Stanford working papers in grammatical theory* 2, Bloomington: Indiana University Linguistics Club, *pp* 38–68.

GAZDAR, G., E. KLEIN, G. K. PULLUM and I. SAG (1985) *Generalized Phrase Structure Grammar*, Oxford: Basil Blackwell.

GAZDAR, G., and G. K. PULLUM (1981) 'Subcategorization, constituent order and the notion "head"'. In T. Hoekstra, H. van der Hulst and M. Moortgat (eds), *The Scope of Lexical Rules*, Dordrecht: Foris, *pp* 107–123.

GAZDAR, G. and G. K. PULLUM (1982) *Generalized Phrase Structure Grammar: a theoretical synopsis*, Mimeo, Indiana University Linguistics Club.

GOLD, E. M. (1967) 'Language identification in the limit', *Information and Control* 10, 447–74.

GOLDBERG, J. (1985) 'Lexical operations and unbounded dependencies'. In W. Eilfort, P. Kroeber and K. Peterson (eds), *Papers from the 21st Regional Meeting*, Chicago: Chicago Linguistics Society, *pp* 122–32.

GRAHAM, S. L. (1976) 'On-line context-free language recognition in less than cubic time', in *Proceedings of the eighth annual ACM symposium on the theory of computing*, 112–120.

GRUBER, J. (1965/76) *Lexical Structures in Syntax and Semantics*, Amsterdam: North Holland. (Published version of MIT doctoral dissertation, 1965).

HALE, K. (1979) *On the Position of Walbiri in a Typology of the Base*, Bloomington: Indiana University Linguistics Club.

HALE, K. (1983) 'Warlpiri and the grammar of non-configurational languages', *Natural Language and Linguistic Theory* 1, 1–43.

HARMAN, G. (ed) (1974) *On Noam Chomsky: critical essays*, New York: Anchor Books.

HARRIS, Z. S. (1962) *String Analysis of Language Structure*, The Hague: Mouton.

HELKE, M. (1971) *The Grammar of English Reflexives*, Doctoral dissertation, MIT.

HIGGINBOTHAM, J. (1983) 'Logical form, binding and nominals', *Linguistic Inquiry* 14, 395–420.

HOEKSTRA, T., H. VAN DER HULST and M. MOORTGAT (eds) (1980) *Lexical Grammar*, Dordrecht: Foris.

HORROCKS, G. C. (1983) 'The order of constituents in Modern Greek'. In

G. Gazdar, E. Klein and G. K. Pullum, (eds) *Order, Concord and Constituency*, Dordrecht: Foris, *pp* 95–112.

HORROCKS, G. C. (1984) 'The lexical head constraint, $\overline{X}$-theory and the "pro-drop" parameter'. In W. de Geest and Y. Putseys (eds), *Sentential Complementation*, Dordrecht: Foris *pp* 117–126.

HORROCKS, G. C. and M. STAVROU (1987) 'Bounding theory and Greek syntax: evidence for *wh-* movement in NP', *Journal of Linguistics* **23**, 1

HUANG, J. C.-T. (1982) *Logical Relations in Chinese and the Theory of Grammar*, Doctoral dissertation, MIT.

HUDDLESTON, R. (1976), *An Introduction to English Transformational Syntax*, London: Longman.

HUDSON, R. (1984) *Word Grammar*, Oxford: Basil Blackwell.

HUYBREGTS, R. (1976) 'Overlapping dependencies in Dutch', *Utrecht Working Papers in Linguistics*. **1**, 24–65.

JACKENDOFF, R. S. (1972) *Semantic Interpretation in Generative Grammar*, Cambridge, Mass. and London: MIT Press.

JACKENDOFF, R. S. (1977) *$\overline{X}$-Syntax: a study of phrase structure*, Cambridge, Mass. and London: MIT Press.

JACOBSEN, B. (1986) *Modern Transformational Grammar (with particular reference to the theory of government and binding)*, Amsterdam: North Holland.

JAEGGLI, O. (1982) *Topics in Romance Syntax*, Dordrecht: Foris.

JOHNSON, D. E. (1979) *Toward a Relationally-based theory of Grammar*, New York: Garland.

KAMEYAMA, M. (1984) 'Subjective/logophoric bound anaphor *zibun*'. In J. Drogo, V. Mishra and D. Testen (eds), *Papers from the 20th Regional Meeting*, Chicago: Chicago Linguistics Society, *pp* 228–38.

KAMEYAMA, M. (1985) *Zero Anaphora: the case of Japanese*, Doctoral dissertation, Stanford University.

KAPLAN, R. M. (1978) 'ATNs and what to do about them', Mimeo, Cambridge, Mass.

KAPLAN, R. M. (1980) 'Computational resources and linguistic theory', paper presented at the Second Theoretical Issues in Natural Language Processing Conference, Urbana, Illinois, 1978, published in G. Lavandel (ed) *A Decade of Research*, New York: Bowker.

KAPLAN, R. M. and J. BRESNAN (1982) 'Lexical-functional grammar: a formal system for grammatical representation'. In Bresnan (1982), *pp* 282–390.

KAPLAN, R. M. and A. ZAENEN (1985) 'Grammatical functions and long-distance dependencies', Mimeo, Xerox-PARC.

KARTTUNEN, L. (1977) 'Syntax and semantics of questions', *Linguistics and Philosophy* **1**, 3–44.

KATZ, J. J. and J. A. FODOR (1963) 'The structure of a semantic theory', *Language* **39**, 170–210.

KATZ, J. J. and P. M. POSTAL (1964) *An Integrated Theory of Linguistic Descriptions*, Cambridge, Mass.: MIT Press.

KAYNE, R. S. (1981a) 'Two notes on the NIC', in Belletti, Brandi and Rizzi (1981), reprinted in Kayne (1984).

KAYNE, R. S. (1981b) 'ECP extensions', *Linguistic Inquiry* 12, 93–133, reprinted in Kayne (1984).

KAYNE, R. S (1984) *Connectedness and binary branching*, Dordrecht, Foris.

KEMPSON, R. M. (1977) *Semantic Theory*, Cambridge: CUP .

KEYSER, S. J. and P. M. POSTAL (1976) *Beginning English Grammar*, New York: Harper and Row.

KLEIN, E. and I. SAG (1982/3) 'Semantic type and control'. In M. Barlow, D. Flickinger and I. Sag (eds), *Developments in Generalized Phrase Structure Grammar: Stanford working papers in grammatical theory* 2, Bloomington: Indiana University Linguistics Club, *pp* 1–25, (Reprinted in *Linguistics and Philosophy* 6 (1983)).

KOSTER, J. (1984) 'On binding and control' *Linguistic Inquiry* 15, 417–459.

KOSTER, J. and R. MAY (1982) 'On the constituency of infinitives', *Language* 58, 1, 116–143.

LASNIK, H. (1976) 'Some thoughts on coreference', *Linguistic Analysis* 2, 1–22.

LASNIK, H. (1980) *Learnability, restrictiveness and the evaluation metric'*, Mimeo, University of Connecticut.

LASNIK, H. (1981) 'Restricting the theory of transformations'. In N. Hornstein and D. Lightfoot (eds) *Explanation in Linguistics: the logical problem of language acquisition*, London: Longman, *pp* 152–73.

LASNIK, H. and M. SAITO (1984) 'On the nature of proper government', *Linguistic Inquiry* 15, 235–89.

LASS, R. (1976) *English Phonology and Phonological Theory: synchronic and diachronic studies*, Cambridge: CUP.

LASS, R. (1980) *On Explaining Language Change*, Cambridge: CUP.

LEVELT, W. J. M. (1974) *Formal Grammars in Linguistics and Psycholinguistics Vol. 2*, The Hague: Mouton.

LEVELT, W. J. M. (1979) 'On learnability: a reply to Lasnik and Chomsky', Mimeo, Nijmegen.

LEVIN, L., M. RAPPAPORT and A. ZAENEN (eds) (1983) *Papers in Lexical-Functional Grammar*, Bloomington: Indiana University Linguistics Club.

LYONS, J. (1977) *Semantics* (2 Vols.), Cambridge: CUP.

LYONS, J. (1981) *Language, Meaning and Context*, London: Fontana.

MALING. J. and A. ZAENEN (1982) 'A Phrase structure account of Scandinavian extraction phenomena'. In P. Jacobson and G. K. Pullum (eds), *The Nature of Syntactic Representation*, Dordrecht: Reidel, *pp* 229–282.

MANZINI, M. R. (1983) 'On control and control theory', *Linguistic Inquiry* 14, 421–46.

MATTHEWS, P. H. (1979) *Generative Grammar and Linguistic Competence*, London: Allen and Unwin.

MATTHEWS, P. H. (1981) *Syntax*, Cambridge: CUP.

MOHANAN, K. P. (1981) 'Move NP or lexical rules: evidence from Malayalam causativisation', Mimeo, Department of Linguistics and Philosophy, MIT.

MOHANAN, K. P. (1983) 'Functional and anaphoric control', *Linguistic Inquiry* **14**, 421-46.

MONTAGUE, R. (1970a) 'English as a formal language'. In B. Visentini *et al.* (eds), *Linguaggi: nella società e nella tecnica*, Milan: Edizioni di Communità.

MONTAGUE, R. (1970b) 'Universal grammar', *Theoria* **36**, 373-98.

MONTAGUE, R. (1973) 'The proper treatment of quantification in ordinary English'. In J. Hintikka, J. M. Moravcsik and P. Suppes (eds), *Approaches to Natural Language*, Dordrecht: Reidel.

MUYSKEN, P. C. and H. C. VAN RIEMSDIJK, (eds) (1985) *Features and Projections*, Dordrecht: Foris.

PAPI, M. and J. VERSCHUEREN, (eds) (1986) *Proceedings of the 1985 International Pragmatics Conference at Viareggio*, Amsterdam: Benjamins.

PERLMUTTER, D. M. (1980) 'Relational Grammar'. In E. Moravcsik and J. Wirth (eds), *Syntax and Semantics 13: current approaches to syntax*, New York: Academic Press.

PERLMUTTER, D. M. (ed), (1983) *Studies in Relational Grammar 1*, Chicago: University of Chicago Press.

PETERS, S. and R. RITCHIE (1973) 'On the generative power of transformational grammars', *Information Sciences* **6**, 49-83.

PINKER, S. (1982) 'A theory of the acquisition of lexical interpretive grammars'. In Bresnan (1982), *pp* 655-726.

POLLARD, C. (1984) *Generalized Phrase Structure Grammars, Head Grammars and Natural Language*, Doctoral dissertation, Stanford University.

POLLARD, C. (1985) 'Phrase Structure Grammar without metarules'. In M. Cobler, J. Goldberg, S. Mackaye and M. Wescoat (eds), *Proceedings of WCCFL4*, Stanford: Stanford Linguistics Association, *pp* 246-61.

POPPER, K. R. (1972) *Conjectures and Refutations*, London: Routledge and Kegan Paul.

POPPER, K. R. (1973) *Objective Knowledge*, Oxford: OUP.

POSTAL, P. M. (1969) Review of A. McIntosh and M. A. K. Halliday, *Papers in General, Descriptive and Applied Linguistics*. In *Foundations of Language* **5**, 409-439.

POSTAL, P. M. (1972) 'On some rules that are not successive cyclic', *Linguistic Inquiry* **3**, 211-222.

POSTAL, P. M. (1974) *On Raising*, Cambridge, Mass.: MIT Press.

PULLUM, G. K. (1976/79) *Rule Cyclicity and the Organisation of a grammar*, New York: Garland. (Published version of University of London doctoral dissertation (1976).)

PULLUM, G. K. (1982) 'Free word order and phrase structure rules'. In J. Pustejovsky and P. Sells (eds), *Proceedings of the Twelfth Annual Meeting of the North-eastern Linguistic Society*, Amherst: Graduate

Linguistics Student Association, University of Massachusetts, Amherst.

PULLUM, G. K. and G. GAZDAR (1982) 'Natural languages and context-free languages', *Linguistics and Philosophy* **4**, 471–504.

RADFORD, A. (1981) *Transformational Syntax: a student's guide to Chomsky's extended standard theory*, Cambridge: CUP.

REINHART, T. (1976) *The Syntactic Domain of Anaphora*, Doctoral dissertation, MIT.

RIEMSDIJK, H. C. VAN (1983) 'The case of German adjectives'. In F. Heny and B. Richards (eds) *Linguistic Categories: auxiliaries and related puzzles 1*, Dordrecht: Reidel.

RIEMSDIJK, H. C. VAN and E. WILLIAMS (1986) *Introduction to the Theory of Grammar*, Cambridge, Mass.: and London: MIT Press.

RIZZI, L. (1982) *Issues in Italian Syntax*, Dordrecht: Foris.

ROSENBAUM, P. S. (1967) *The Grammar of English Predicate Complement Constructions*, Cambridge, Mass.: MIT Press.

ROSS, J. R. (1967) *Constraints on Variables in Syntax*, Doctoral dissertation, MIT. (Distributed by the Indiana University Linguistics Club. Extracts are printed in Harman (1974), *pp* 165–200).

ROUVERET, A. and J.-R. VERGNAUD (1980) 'Specifying reference to the subject: French causatives and conditions on representations', *Linguistic Inquiry* **11**, 97–202.

SAG, I. (1982) 'A semantic theory of "NP-movement" dependencies', in P Jacobson and G. K. Pullum (eds), *The Nature of Syntactic Representation*, Dordrecht: Reidel, *pp* 427–66.

SAG, I. (1985) 'Grammatical hierarchy and linear precedence', Ms., CSLI, Stanford University.

SAG, I., G. GAZDAR, T. WASOW and S. WEISLER (1985) 'Coordination and how to distinguish categories', *Natural Language and Linguistic Theory* **3**, 117–171.

SELLS, P. (1985) *Lectures on Contemporary Syntactic Theories: an introduction to Government-Binding theory, Generalized Phrase Structure Grammar and Lexical-Functional Grammar*, Center for the Study of Language and Information, Stanford University: University of Chicago Press.

SEUREN, P. A. M. (ed), (1974) *Semantic Syntax*, Oxford: OUP.

SHEIL, B. (1976) 'Observations on context-free parsing', *Statistical Methods in Linguistics* **7**, 71–109.

SIMPSON, J. and J. BRESNAN (1983) 'Control and obviation in Warlpiri', *Natural Language and Linguistic Theory* **1**, 49–64.

SOAMES, S. and D. M. PERLMUTTER (1979) *Syntactic Argumentation and the Structure of English*, Berkeley and Los Angeles: University of California Press.

STUCKY, S. (1983) 'Verb phrase constituency and linear order in Makua'. In G. Gazdar, E. Klein and G. K. Pullum (eds), *Order, Concord and Constituency*, Dordrecht: Foris, *pp* 75–94.

SZABOLCSI, A. (1985) 'The possessor that ran away from home', *The Linguistic Review* **3**, 89–102.

THOMASON, R. H. (ed) (1974) *Formal Philosophy: selected papers by Richard Montague*, New Haven: Yale University Press.

VALIANT, L. G. (1975) 'General context-free recognition in less than cubic time', *Journal of Computer and System Sciences* 10, 308–315.

VERGNAUD, J.-R. (1982) *Dépendances et niveaux de représentation*, Thèse de doctorat d'état, University of Paris. (To be published by John Benjamins, Amsterdam).

WASOW, T. (1972/79) *Anaphora in Generative Grammar*, Ghent: E. Story-Scientia. (Published version of MIT doctoral dissertation, *Anaphoric Relations in English*, (1972).)

WIJNGAARDEN, A. VAN (1969) 'Report on the algorithmic language ALGOL 68', *Numerische Mathematik* 14, 79–218.

WILLIAMS, E. (1981) 'Transformationless grammar', review of Gazdar (1981a), *Linguistic Inquiry* 12, 645–53.

WILLIAMS, E. (1984) 'Grammatical relations', *Linguistic Inquiry* 15, 639–73.

YANG, D.-W. (1983) 'The extended binding theory of anaphors', *Language Research* 19, 169–92.

Index